Well-being Past and Present

Well-being Past and Present

The History and Contemporary Practice of a Cultural Phenomenon in Britain

Edited by
Siobhán Hyland, Paul Jackson and Mark Rothery

BLOOMSBURY ACADEMIC
LONDON • NEW YORK • OXFORD • NEW DELHI • SYDNEY

BLOOMSBURY ACADEMIC
Bloomsbury Publishing Plc, 50 Bedford Square, London, WC1B 3DP, UK
Bloomsbury Publishing Inc, 1359 Broadway, New York, NY 10018, USA
Bloomsbury Publishing Ireland, 29 Earlsfort Terrace, Dublin 2, D02 AY28, Ireland

BLOOMSBURY, BLOOMSBURY ACADEMIC and the Diana logo are trademarks of Bloomsbury Publishing Plc

First published in Great Britain 2025

A catalogue record for this book is available from the British Library.

A catalog record for this book is available from the Library of Congress.

ISBN: HB: 978-1-3504-9984-3
ePDF: 978-1-3504-9985-0
eBook: 978-1-3504-9986-7

Typeset by Newgen KnowledgeWorks Pvt. Ltd., Chennai, India

For product safety related questions contact productsafety@bloomsbury.com.

To find out more about our authors and books visit www.bloomsbury.com and sign up for our newsletters.

Contents

Contributors

Emily Bavellas is an art historian and museum professional having recently completed an internship with Northampton Museum and Art Gallery (in collaboration with the National Portrait Gallery), where she was responsible for reviewing and reinterpreting the art collection with a particular focus on mental health, well-being and identity. Emily is currently studying for an MA in Museum Studies at Leicester University, specializing in arts-based community engagement and mental health activism.

Susan Botterill retired at sixty in November 2009 and enjoyed not having to go to work but, after a very busy life, soon got bored and started looking for something to occupy herself. One day she went to a local library and agreed to volunteer at the Christmas Fête. It's now fourteen years on and she is still there. In 2019 library volunteers and her local community campaigned to keep the library open; it is now a community-managed library. The building, once a church, is now 101 years old. Having a lifelong interest in history, Sue has been collecting items and stories together to create an archive that will tell the story of the local community.

Claire Chatterton trained as a general nurse at The London Hospital and as a mental health nurse at the Warneford and Littlemore Hospitals in Oxford and has a long-standing interest in the history of health care. She is a visiting professor at the University of Chester and a member of their Faculty of Health and Society's historical society. She is a fellow of the Royal College of Nursing and is a member and former chair of their History of Nursing Forum. Claire is also a fellow of the Royal Historical Society and a visiting professor at the University of Chichester. This chapter is based on her PhD research conducted at the University of Salford under the supervision of Professor Duncan Mitchell.

Marcella Daye is Senior Lecturer in Tourism Management at the University of Northampton with academic research interests in place branding, participatory methodologies and race health inequalities. She currently sits on the editorial boards of the peer-reviewed journals *Annals of Tourism Research* and *Tourism Planning and Development*. With her experience as a tourism marketing practitioner, Marcella serves as a trustee at the Delapré Preservation Trust, the Sheffield Environment Movement and as a member of the Northamptonshire Heritage and Culture Committee. A scholar activist for equality, diversity and inclusion (EDI), Marcella is a member of the EDI Committee of the Chartered Institute of Business Schools (CABS). She serves on the advisory board as the EDI lead for Healthwatch Northamptonshire and is a current member of the county's Integrated Care Board's Race Health Inequalities Working Group.

Tamsin Greaves runs the Art Power social care project at Mansfield Museum, which was nominated for a Museums Change Lives Award by the Museums Association in 2023. Following a career as a secondary art teacher in state schools, she completed an MA in Museum and Heritage Development at Nottingham Trent University (NTU) in 2021, winning the outstanding contribution award. The researcher is currently a final-year PhD candidate in the Arts and Humanities School at NTU. Her study is concerned with creativity, well-being and post-traumatic recovery for women who are surviving domestic and sexual abuse. She combines the research with a community project coordinator role at Mansfield Museum in the East Midlands and dedicates her chapter to the participants.

Jemima Hubberstey completed her PhD in 2021, which was an AHRC-funded collaborative doctoral award with English Heritage and the University of Oxford, examining the connection between literary coteries and garden design in the mid-eighteenth century, with a focus on the Wrest Circle. She subsequently worked as a postdoctoral researcher on a knowledge exchange fellowship between the University of Oxford, English Heritage and the National Trust, which aimed to reunite the literary legacies of Wrest Park in Bedfordshire and Wimpole Hall in Cambridgeshire. Between 2022 and 2023, she held a postdoctoral research fellowship in the humanities at the University of Oxford, exploring elite women and the intellectual culture of the country house in the eighteenth century. She is now part of the research team at Historic Royal Palaces.

Siobhán Hyland is Associate Lecturer at the Open University and a postdoctoral research assistant at the Centre for Historical Studies, University of Northampton. Siobhán received her PhD in 2023, thesis entitled 'Searchlight Magazine's Investigative Antifascist War Crimes Campaign to Uncover Second World War Era Nazi War Criminals Living in Britain, 1980–1990s'. Most recently, she has an article in *Family and Community History* (2024) entitled 'British Antifascist Communities of Activism since 1945'.

Paul Jackson is Professor of the History of Radicalism and Extremism at the University of Northampton. He specializes in the history and contemporary dynamics of fascism and the extreme right, and his most recent book is *Pride in Prejudice: Understanding Britain's Extreme Right* (2022). He is the curator of the Searchlight Archive at the university, which is one of the UK's largest collections of material related to the recent history of extreme right groups. He has engaged widely with the media, including national and international press, as well as for BBC radio and television, and he has written articles for the *Guardian* and the *Huffington Post*. He has engaged with policymakers, professionals and activists, including creating bespoke training packages related to risks posed by the extreme right.

Daniel Jones is a researcher in Far-Right Studies (post-1945), Associate Lecturer in History and a Searchlight archivist at the University of Northampton. Daniel has run the Searchlight Archive since its creation at the university, opening in the summer of

2013 to users. He completed his PhD in 2021 under Professor Paul Jackson, exploring identity within post-war far-right and anti-fascist print cultures, and publishes around these issues as well as exploring the ethics around archival practice with extreme material. He is an associate fellow of the Royal History Society and the Higher Education Academy, section editor for 'Modern Faiths and Ideologies' in the journal *Religion Compass* and is on the advisory board for Gale Cengage's Political Extremism and Radicalism product.

Amy Luck is a PhD student and a public historian from the University of Birmingham who specializes in understanding, quantifying and sharing the value and impact of cultural heritage, particularly on well-being and mental health. Amy has collaborated with a wide variety of cultural and heritage groups, organizations and projects to support them to evaluate their impact, including National Museum Wales, the Federation of Museums and Art Galleries of Wales, Lyme Park (National Trust), Elizabeth Gaskell's House, Audley End House and Gardens (English Heritage), IWM Duxford, The Holburne Museum, Wessex Archaeology, The Salisbury Museum, Art Care, Anxiety UK, Dulwich Picture Gallery, Wiltshire Creative, Merchant Adventurers' Hall and Northern Heartlands. Amy has also supported international research projects investigating the impact of cultural heritage in the United States, India and Palestine and is a regular attendee and contributor to international networks and conferences, including the International Federation for Public Historians, the National Council on Public History and the European Archaeological Association.

Emma Marshall received her PhD, funded by the Wolfson Foundation, from the Department of History at the University of York in 2024. Her thesis examined experiences and representations of illness and caregiving within seventeenth- and eighteenth-century English gentry families. Her broader research interests include domestic life, medical practice, bodily and emotional experience, and letter writing and reading, and she regularly presents her work at local, national and international conferences. Following her PhD, Emma held research fellowships at the University of York's Humanities Research Centre and the Folger Shakespeare Library in Washington, DC. She is also an experienced university tutor and has worked on a public engagement project at the University of Birmingham. She is currently a research associate of York's Centre for Renaissance and Early Modern Studies and executive committee member of the Social History Society.

Rachel E. Moss is Senior Lecturer in History at the University of Northampton. Prior to this she was a Leverhulme Early Career Fellow in the Faculty of History at the University of Oxford. She has published widely on late medieval family, gender and literary culture and is the author of *Fatherhood and Its Representations in Middle English Texts* (2013), which was the first published monograph on medieval fatherhood. Her current research is on medievalism within far-right political movements.

Sue Niebrzydowski is Professor of Medieval Literature at Bangor University, UK. Her research interests lie in medieval women's engagement with literary culture and practice, topics on which she has published widely. Her most recent publication is *Women's Literary Cultures in the Global Middle Ages: Speaking Internationally* (2023), co-edited with L. Herbert McAvoy, Vicki Kay-Price and Kathryn Loveridge.

Kathrina Perry is a part-time PhD student researching the motivations and social significance of philanthropy in the boot and shoe industry in Northamptonshire in the nineteenth and early twentieth centuries. Her research interests include local and social history, particularly during the late nineteenth and early twentieth centuries. She has an MA in History from the Open University, where her thesis was on the developments of the bus industry in Northampton, 1920–50. Kathrina's previous works include 'Women's Philanthropy and Religion: The Ladies of the Northampton Shoe Trade, 1870–1950' in *Religion Compass.*

Michael Reeve is a social and cultural historian of modern Britain. His research addresses issues of military and civilian endurance, resilience, well-being and welfare in nineteenth- and twentieth-century conflicts. This includes articles in *Cultural and Social History*, *Coastal Studies & Society* and *Critical Military Studies*. His first book, *Bombardment, Public Safety and Resilience in English Coastal Communities during the First World War*, was published by Palgrave Macmillan in 2021.

Mark Rothery is Professor of History at the University of Northampton. He is the author of many studies examining the social and cultural histories of emotions, gender, consumption, material culture and the economic history of landed elites from the early eighteenth to the early twentieth century. Most recently he has an article in *Social History* (2024) entitled 'Emotional Economies of Pleasure among the Gentry of Eighteenth Century England'. He is currently writing a monograph on the history of elite anxieties in eighteenth- and nineteenth-century England, which will be published in 2026.

Ruby Rutter is a historian of emotion, lived experience, domestic spaces and gender, with a specific interest in reconstructing how people in the past understood and navigated their daily lives. Her PhD, titled 'Elite Women, Emotion, and the Lived Experience in the Eighteenth-Century Country House', examined the lived experiences of women in the eighteenth-century country house by knitting together diaries, letters, wills, recipe books, objects and other material culture to reveal how women felt about their lives and homes. She interrogated themes such as mental and physical health, comfort and mortality to build a picture that fleshed out the women's lives, experiences and stories. She is particularly interested in how the history of emotion and well-being can be harnessed in heritage sites to engage visitors and create shared spaces of feeling. Her PhD was supervised by Professors Sasha Handley and Hannah Barker at the University of Manchester and awarded in 2022. Prior to her PhD, she studied BA (Hons) in History of Art at Courtauld Institute of Art (2010–13) and MSt in Literature and Arts at the University of Oxford (2014–16).

Faye Sayer is Associate Professor in Heritage and History and Director of the International Centre for Heritage at the University of Birmingham, UK. Her research specialism is in the value and impact of heritage to the public and community, specifically the social values of participation in heritage and its impact on well-being. Dr Sayer has worked for some of the UK's most significant heritage organizations, including English Heritage, The Portable Antiquities Scheme, and Museum of London. She has developed and evaluated public heritage and history projects, including museum programmes around the world.

Introduction: Well-being past and present

Siobhán Hyland, Paul Jackson and Mark Rothery

In contemporary Western society 'well-being' has become a collective synonym for health and happiness. It has also become a cultural phenomenon shaping a range of social activities flowing and shaping discourses about our physical and psychological conditions. Well-being is an apparently ubiquitous term found in a very wide range of popular and academic discourses and uttered frequently in everyday conversations. When compared with two other such terms, 'immigration' and 'artificial intelligence' in Google Ngram, well-being is found to be more commonly cited than artificial intelligence and only marginally less common than immigration. The term is accepted and used by the World Health Organization, the National Health Service, MIND, the Office for National Statistics and the OECD. 'Good Health and Well-Being' is the third Sustainable Development Goal of the United Nations, and both the OECD and the UN regularly measure well-being, along with a range of other agencies.[1] But well-being is a complex concept that defies simple definitions.

Defining well-being

We would be mistaken if we merely define well-being according to our own personal, familial or professional definitions. The meaning of the term is contingent on social, political, cultural and economic contexts and is, therefore, subject to cultural variance in the contemporary world and across time. We need only consider the very unusual conditions imposed by the Covid-19 virus in the recent past and the way lockdowns tended to compact well-being into the simple but distant pleasures of time spent with family or being free from the fear of mortality. It should be of interest to a range of different academic disciplines, and understanding well-being is also the concern of a wide range of practitioners in health and social services. It is, therefore, worth considering the term itself and its various meanings both now and in the past, which have been far from constant. This is the purpose of this introduction. We will not be providing a comprehensive review of the existing literature, not least because the multidisciplinary nature of the book makes this task too weighty.

The *OED* notes the etymology of the word as deriving from the Italian word *Benessere*. It is a compound of the adverb 'well' and the noun 'being'.[2] It notes three main usages. Firstly, in reference to a state of being health, happy or prosperous, or morally centred in reference to a person or a community. Secondly, the term can refer to a thing or an object, in terms of it being in a safe or good condition. Finally, it can be used in plural form, in reference to large numbers of people. In the *South Wales Echo* in 2012, for instance, a contributor noted, 'The twirling, twinkling displays in shop windows acting as some sort of hypnotic lighthouse for spendaholics does make me fear for all our fiscal wellbeings.'[3] Historically well-being has been used for all of these reasons, although the precise contexts and meanings of that usage have been profoundly different. As Katie Barclay and Francois Soyer note, health and well-being was an important topic for family letters in the eighteenth century because demonstrating care for yourself and your well-being evidenced a desire and a promise to return to family and friends, which was all the more significant in periods of higher mortality.[4] So in 1734 Phillip Doddridge, the non-conformist minister, wrote to his wife, Elizabeth, promising her that he 'will be so just to you as to take all possible Care of myself'. This moderated the inevitable anxieties of family separation and of communication at distance and was a way to be seen to be fulfilling the responsibilities of, in this case, fatherhood and manhood.

Well-being in history

Laura Stroll has provided a useful summary of the history of the concept of well-being. Understandings of the concept of well-being, if not the use of the term, began in ancient Greece and the idea of 'the good life', of a life lived well for the production of happiness and contentment.[5] Many of the ideas generated in this society survived long into the period of modernity. Socrates believed that happiness was not to be found in hedonistic pleasures or the pursuit of wealth. Rather a life lived well was one in which a person pursued truth through learning. Later for Aristotle, 'well-living' or 'well-acting', as he termed it, was to be found through the excellent performance of those qualities that make us human – rational thought, justice, courage, temperance. 'Happiness is the meaning and the purpose of life' he said and, as in the case of Socrates, well-being was not found in wealth and riches, although these might be the preconditions for it. Rather it came through an inner sense of worth.

Later incarnations of well-being in the classical world, in Rome for instance, placed a greater emphasis on public health, the supply of water and systems of sewerage and public baths. Still the balance between pleasure and virtue was central to debates about well-being. Thinkers during the medieval period and the renaissance continued to focus on inner virtue, with more emphasis on religious faith as a means to achieve this. It would be incorrect to assume that medieval well-being was all about spiritual salvation. Psychology was the realm of theologians, and religious thought shaped views of health and well-being. But we can also find quite modern concepts shaping medieval thought here. In a pre-Cartesian context, in which mind and body were considered one rather than separate, as claimed by Descartes, medieval psychology appears to be quite twenty-first century. The concept of the four humours, founded by Hippocrates and developed later by Galen, suggested a mind–body continuum, and well-being rested on the balance between these four humours. St Augustine saw emotions as having cognitive and physical contours, linked both to body and mind and deriving 'moods' from both. Again, we find very so-called modern ideas here and there was clearly an ongoing concern with well-being, expressed as a holistic model of soul, mind, intellect, thought, emotion, affect, senses and the body.

But it was into the early modern period that things changed more abruptly, certainly in the sense that things got more materialistic. As the historians Paul Slack and Phil Withington showed, the religious controversies of the seventeenth century tended to chip away at the spiritual sources of well-being, locating happiness in material circumstances rather than the soul through new theories of political economy that sought economic progress as an objective to be consciously pursued, but also raising questions about the reach and longevity of 'progress'.[6] Daniel Roche had earlier noted that this was a part of a wider transition of European experience from an 'economy of salvation, scarcity and morality to an economy aiming at happiness on earth, relative plenty and utility'.[7] He similarly noted the anxieties this process produced.

The scientific revolutions of the seventeenth century and the enlightenment(s) of the eighteenth changed the way well-being was understood. It could be measured and quantified in the same way that the physical laws of the universe could, through moments and sources of pleasure as good experiences. Amidst an explosion in new writings on happiness as a human condition, writers such as Voltaire and Diderot argued that happiness was not to be found in spiritual devotion but could be found in a secular life and could include sensory as well as intellectual pleasures. Similarly, Adam Smith argued that the pursuit of pleasure, activated through consumer desire, could lend power and force to national economies and the well-being of the nation. This new focus on pleasure and happiness, found in the French and Scottish enlightenments, was enacted through key developments in the eighteenth century such as the urban renaissance and the new consumerism, but also through an enduring emphasis on the family and family life.[8] And it was contextualized in new models of historical change that challenged traditional ideas centred on the Fall of Man or cycles of decay and resurgence, favouring instead progress and purposeful forward development towards a better world.[9]

Modern understandings of well-being began among this new wave of liberal thinking, with the first history of well-being composed by the French military officer and writer Francois Jean Marquis de Chastellux with his 'Essay on Public Happiness' of 1772.[10] His ambition had been to measure taxation, incomes, working hours and leisure time in a broad-ranging study of human behaviour. Like many research projects though, no doubt for the sake of the well-being of the researcher, de Chastellux cut his cloth and simply measured levels of slavery and war, the two things he considered to be the main blocks to well-being. The original project and its ambitions match quite neatly onto some, at least, of the parameters we would probably agree on today in the sense that Chastellux was looking for a holistic overview of the health, physical, psychological and social – of individual people within systems that may or may not tend towards their well-being – ways that those systems might be designed in a way that would guarantee well-being. More exotic ideas, among German enlightenment thinkers such as Karl Marx, similarly sought a world more suited to the human spirit rather than the search for profit and domination.

Attempts to measure happiness and well-being flourished into the nineteenth century, pursued by groups such as the Utilitarians who promoted the 'greatest happiness of the greatest number' as a social good to be pursued.[11] A host of other thinkers addressed themselves to the problem of well-being into the nineteenth century, often referencing conditions in the growing towns, cities and factories of industrial Europe, as well as the squalor and backwardness of the rural poor. But paradigms shifted most meaningfully from the late nineteenth century onwards with the birth of modern psychology. Here thinkers returned to the inner self as a source of well-being. For Freud, a search for the good life was both replenishing and problematic, positive in the sense that strong feelings of pleasure could be achieved but problematic in the search for an absence of pain. Freud suggested the best pleasures were those to be found through constructive work and erotic love, both of which could involve a good degree of pain, not through religious experiences or the sensory pleasures of aesthetics. After Freud psychologists turned their attention to measuring well-being, which has become a preoccupation for all those interested in the topic today.

Later in the twentieth century, amid a wider resurgence of interest in well-being and happiness following the Second World War, in the context of Cold War existential anxieties and concerns over affluence and living standards, economists and psychologists vied for the lead in recording and measuring well-being and thereby deriving firm data for public policy. There was a particular focus on the relationship between economic growth and well-being or happiness. Richard Easterlin, in 1974, found this to be complicated.[12] As GDP rose throughout post-war America, well-being fluctuated. So 'average happiness' rose through the 1950s then declined for the following twenty years. This Easterlin paradox confirmed wider suspicions, dating from classical Greece, that economic growth, wealth and prosperity alone could not lift the human spirit. Such thinking informed the brilliant work of Avner Offer. His 2007 book, *The Challenge of Affluence: Self Control and Wellbeing in Britain and the US since 1950*, explored the age-old tension between limitless potential pleasures and self-management, between economic growth, social responsibility and individual self-management.[13] His notion of well-being engages individuals, communities and nation states. He explores the impact of advertising on public trust, the effects of an abundance of cheap food on health and health-care systems, the challenge of restraint in a consumer economy, and the impact of affluence on marriage and divorce rates and trends. Offer concluded, much as Easterlin had in 1974, that affluence has a complex and often inverse relationship with well-being. Economic growth can put pressure on interpersonal relationships and the structure of the family. The marketing of the motorcar has led to disastrous impacts on the environment and health. Inequality inevitably increases in line with growth.

Well-being today

Since the 1990s we have been living through a golden age of well-being research in terms of both the volume and range of different studies and approaches to the topic, and these go well beyond history of course. The flowering of this area of research is indicated by the monumental six-volume Wiley series.[14] This, along with a broader cultural engagement with the theory and practice of well-being, helps explain the very sharp rise in usage of the term shown in Google Ngram from around 2000 onwards. In fact, it is clear that history is behind other fields of research. There have been notable exceptions. Estes and Sirgy have produced a very useful volume exploring the history of well-being both as a concept and as a measurable quantity in a range of different global regions.[15] There has been a focus on particular groups, such as children, and on specific periods and societies.[16] We have already mentioned Avner Offer's research. Some have made stronger links between indicators such as GDP and well-being and put these in historical perspective.[17] We might also think of Mark Jackson's excellent *The Age of Stress*, which traced an epidemic of stress and anxiety across the twentieth century. Similarly, the engaging work of Braddick and Innes on happiness has been very useful as have other perspectives on happiness as a 'pursuit'.[18]

Historians of emotions have work to offer this field too. Since the mid-1980s this area of study has gradually developed into a global effort to examine the feelings of people in the past, both positive and negative. Anger, shame, guilt, anxiety, fear, love, compassion and nostalgia are just a few of the emotions that now have a history. Emotions have been exposed as catalysts for historical change and human relations. Much of this work might best be described as adjacent to the field of well-being, but there are some important intersections to note. Fay Bound Alberti emphasizes the profound concerns and unease that have accompanied the rise of loneliness as a modern concept and cluster of feelings.[19] According to governments and medical practitioners, loneliness has become an epidemic in recent years, 'devastating for public health'. Particular concerns have been raised in Britain, the 'loneliness capital of Europe'. There has been a focus on the elderly, but research has shown that 'children are lonely, teenagers are lonely; so are young mums, divorced people, old people, and bereaved people'.[20] Alberti argues that loneliness is a construction of modern life. The term as we understand it emerged in the late eighteenth century. In the sixteenth and seventeenth centuries, the closest term was 'oneliness', which simply referred to being alone, sometimes for devotional purposes, without the negative emotional connotations of 'loneliness'.[21] Loneliness as an emotional cluster emerged, it is argued, as a result of the combined forces of secularism, urbanization, the industrial revolution, the development of the individual as a concept and a rising emphasis placed on sociability as a moral necessity and duty. Problems have escalated from the late twentieth century onwards as neo-liberalism (Margaret Thatcher's version of this is emphasized) eroded the value of 'society' and 'community' amidst rising living costs, inflation and changing family structures.[22]

Historians have generally, though, not faced well-being head-on as 'well-being' but rather selected aspects of the overall idea of well-being as their target such as happiness or stress, and they have, as a result, been left in the wake of other disciplines. The cluster of historians working on the 'History of the Body, Health and Well-being', part of the Centre for Health and Humanities at the University of Groningen, is an exception to this rule.[23] The emergence of 'positive psychology', that is, the psychology of positive human functioning, has made remarkable progress in understanding well-being. Psychologists have shown how well-being intersects with a range of internal and external factors, such as the perceptions of friends and family and the clinical relation of the heart rate, to moments of stress. Neuroscientists have found correlations between physical exercise, meditation mindfulness and well-being, but they also stress the importance of underlying personality traits and social relationships in terms of what they can contribute to well-being, or indeed how alterations in these characteristics can lead to anxiety, depression and stress.[24] The economics of well-being and public policy research on the topic has similarly grown into the early twenty-first century with a series of high-profile and well-funded research projects informing policy around a range of things such as social welfare, health care, education and housing. The uses this research has been put to, of course, have shifted with the political prerogatives of the parties in power.

One significant challenge for historians is that the lexicography of 'well-being' as a term is very uneven. In the eighteenth century, for instance, the term appears in the titles of just 129 publications, according to Eighteenth Century Collections Online, even if the term was found in much higher numbers deeper into these texts.[25] Most commonly these references were to the 'well-being of the nation' rather than the individual. So while lamenting the decline of wool manufacturing in the 1730s, for instance, Simon Smith noted that 'many gentlemen of learning … very rarely meet with anything that relates to manufactures … therefore can have no idea of the advantage of them, or that they are necessary to the Wellbeing of the Nation'.[26] It is in fact a post-war preoccupation in the way we have inherited it, and we must account for that when we locate it in diverse historical contexts. It is also, of course, a largely white middle-class preoccupation in our society, a signal of elite status in a hierarchical world of inequalities and prejudice. The way we use 'well-being' today is very different from the uses to which it was put in the past, and it is being used among a small and elite group of people. We must be careful, therefore, to avoid projecting our current understandings of the term into the past, to look for ourselves in the very different worlds of our ancestors and also to search for and encourage diversity in the way we use the term. But we should also recognize that our difficulties in reconciling the lives we lead and the world we live in with the problematic impact this often has on our well-being are not new. We are preoccupied with similar threats to well-being as people were in the past, of war, disease and penury. The search for the 'good life', for the life 'lived well', continues.

Well-being past and present

With this volume our intention is to both develop a more direct historical approach to well-being and to connect these histories with other subject areas and practitioners drawing wider conclusions from this multidisciplinary approach. The volume developed from a conference, 'Wellbeing Past and Present', organized by the Centre for Historical Studies at the University of Northampton in 2023. The conference was attended by historians, social scientists, heritage practitioners and social workers from the local area and beyond. The chapters in this book reflect both the great diversity of perspectives and the high levels of intellectual energy the event inspired. The wider inclusiveness of the conference, beyond the academy and higher education, reflects the founding principles of the Centre for Historical Studies: to engage in conversations and discourses about history with as wide and varied a community as possible.[27] History as a subject of enquiry is suited to these types of conversations, and it *should* be the role of academic historians to facilitate that work. The principle also aligns with the strategic outlook of the University of Northampton, to be embedded and to help co-create relationships within the local community and region.

As this suggests and as many of the chapters in this volume make clear, Northamptonshire lies at the centre of the activities reflected in this volume, although, of course, many of the chapters refer to other and wider geographical spaces. Northamptonshire is a rich county with a diverse range of landscapes and peoples, from urban conurbations such as Northampton Town to the market towns and rural areas beyond. It also has a rich tradition in heritage and the arts and crafts.[28] Many of these themes are reflected in the chapters that follow. Northamptonshire, in some ways, reflects other county communities in the sense of well-being. It has its challenges and it is posing answers to these challenges in the form of services to provide and nurture well-being in its population, whether that be mental health support, speaking therapies, support for ending addiction and so on.[29] The county is specific in its approach to these issues in some ways. There has been a particular focus on rural loneliness and well-being.[30] Also in the absence of national heritage agencies, such as National Trust and English Heritage, who manage very few heritage sites in the county, the heritage sector tends to be led by independent organizations managing individual properties, and these are often very sensitive and proactive in leading activities around the well-being of the public. Delapré Abbey, for instance, near the centre of Northampton, provides a range of these types of services.[31] While some of what follows is very much about our local area, we claim a wider spatial range for the findings of the volume.

Across fourteen chapters the authors in this volume approach the issue across a longitudinal period, in the realms of the country house, in wider heritage and museum settings, in local communities and with reference to health, mindfulness and leisure. In this way, *Well-Being Past and Present* interrogates this commonly used term and asks searching questions about what well-being as a cultural phenomenon reflects about the societies that have so readily subscribed to it. This collection provides novel perspectives on well-being by including and, to some extent, comparing the approaches, theories and methodologies of historians, those working in other academic disciplines and practitioners in archives, libraries and community groups. The volume shows the progress that can be made by transgressing disciplinary boundaries and sharing knowledge across areas of research. Given the diversity of the contributions to this volume both in theme and method, we do not claim one single organizing principle at play here; rather a number of themes emerge from the research materials covering a wide array of relevant approaches in well-being studies. These include heritage sites and country houses; the use of spaces as 'retreats' for promoting well-being; letters and literature as vessels for well-being; the issue of bodily health and well-being; as well as race, ethnicity and differential access to sources of well-being.

Well-Being Past and Present includes chapters that focus on how well-being has been found in places and specific locations, and the country house is a particularly important type of space in which well-being is investigated. Jemima Hubberstey explores concerns about well-being at a country house in Wrest Park, Bedfordshire, now an English Heritage destination. Hubberstey focuses on its eighteenth-century history and the emotional attachment of a circle of friends which she examines through their letters, drawing out how Wrest Park was a place to stimulate the senses, to engage in cerebral reflection and to be enjoyed as a contrast to the pressures of life in the city. Such letters show that the group, centred around Jemima Grey and Phillip Yorke, found Vacuna – their loving name for the mansion and its gardens – to be a place for creativity and intellectual pursuit and a site for friendship to blossom.

Emma Marshall's chapter on comments on well-being found in letters between gentry families of the seventeenth century continues this theme. Such privileged families often lived separated lives, and Marshall highlights how news of illness received through correspondence had the potential to support and ease such suffering as well as create negative impacts. She demonstrates that such correspondence had the potential to both encourage and challenge feelings of well-being. Her exploration of a culture deeply concerned with health draws attention to the communal experience of illness of this period and its relationship to understandings of well-being. Ruby Rutter's contribution focuses on another country house, Nostell Priory, which is near Wakefield. Rutter explains this was a place of emotional labour for elite women and as such placed particular pressures on their sense of well-being. She examines the situation of Sabine Winn and considers how her experiences have been developed into a display at what is now a heritage site. Rutter explains that engaging empathetically with such past lives can lead to deeper reflections on emotions, past and present.

Places forming a retreat and, therefore, a location for distinct forms of bonding to occur is a theme found in Rachel Moss's chapter that considers medieval orchards as a space for homosocial encounters among men. These could be places for men to feel freedom from the constraints of domesticity and the home, according to Moss. She focuses on fifteenth-century letters from two families, the Celys and the Stonors, and examines how orchards, which are relatively understudied locations, provided a site for familial encounters among busy mercantile men. Exploration of such encounters reveals fathers to be concerned with their sons, a contrasting interpretation to older perspectives of fatherhood of this period as disinterested and aloof. Well-being and place are examined in other chapters, as are themes around literature and texts. Books as tools for Christian devotion is explored by Sue Niebrzydowski, who reflects on well-being among mediaeval women through examination of a selection of women-associated Books of Hours. Her chapter considers how these texts were read and re-read by women and were passed between female relatives. They offered a form of bibliotherapy, according to Niebrzydowski, and may have provided such mediaeval women with a language, or taxonomy, of consolation.

Connections between historical and contemporary discussions of well-being are present in a number of chapters. A heritage location forms the focus of Emily Bavellas's chapter on Abington Abbey Retreat. This was a progressive private asylum and is now Abington Park Museum in Northampton. Bavellas examines how the rehabilitative approach to the asylum's patients offers a case study in Victorian psychiatry and the asylum's nature-based therapies that encouraged walks, gardening and flower arranging. Bavellas argues that heritage sites can play an important role in the appropriate representation of mental health and have the potential to destigmatize issues, which should be an important aspect of their future development. Kathrina Perry also focuses on Northampton and considers issues of welfare and philanthropy related to Northampton's shoe industry in Victorian and Edwardian Britain. She draws attention to the often-neglected roles of women involved with organized philanthropy and reveals their significance in providing health and welfare benefits to the community. Sue Botterill, meanwhile, discusses another Northampton location, Abington Community Library, in an oral history conducted by Siobhán Hyland. Botterill explains how it has provided both a sense of community from the 1930s to the present day, and how it has become a place of personal importance. Botterill first encountering a library member, who was an evacuee on 1 September 1939, what was then Lindsay Avenue Library and is now a volunteer-run library. Her account reveals the challenges as well as the rewards of her work, and how the library has become a place of deep personal significance as well as an important aspect of the town's culture, providing a safe, non-judgmental place for reading, community building and solace.

Well-being and attitudes to health are topics explored in several chapters, including Michael Reeve's analysis of tobacco use among First World War soldiers. Locating debates over smoking among soldiers in the legacy of the Crimean War, Reeve draws out tensions between smoking as a unique form of relief from the stress of war, its place in military welfare and its negative impacts. Using varied sources, from popular press and medical reports to personal correspondence between soldiers, this chapter examines the conflicts between ideas of smoking as a seemingly beneficial activity, mass industrialization and tobacco's now-well-established health problems. He shows how the war became, among other things, a testing ground for a wide range of attitudes to smoking and its relationship to soldierly well-being. Claire Chatterton's chapter meanwhile explores issues of mental health and considers the often-neglected history of mental health nurses in post-war Britain. Drawing on archival sources and oral histories, her analysis reflects on the development of the profession from the formation of the National Health Service (NHS) to recent times. Chatterton argues that current debates over the low levels of well-being experienced in mental health nursing, both within the NHS and in the private sector, relate to a longer history of concern over the welfare of those who have worked in the profession. For Chatterton, low morale and poor well-being often experienced today are not new issues and should be contextualized in a history of people being both drawn to the profession and also leaving it due to its impact on well-being.

Heritage locations specifically as places that can promote well-being is another theme that cuts across several chapters. Faye Sayer and Amy Luck's contribution focuses on the role of heritage sites as places where visitors can improve their subjective senses of well-being. Using a range of datasets, their study considers a variety of heritage sites, such as English Heritage's Audley End House, and comments on how such locations can positively and negatively impact on perceptions of well-being. They conclude that heritage locations should be considered as important contexts for policy and practices related to improving well-being. As an example of beneficial practices, Tamsin Greaves reflects on her work at Mansfield Museum, which is a community centre as well as possessing a collection of material. In particular, she discusses the development of creative workshops that have benefitted vulnerable women. Her chapter shows how working with women who have lived experiences of trauma can lead to positive experiences and outcomes. She explains how this work has been influenced by Hiu Yan Lee's concept of the well-being hexagon as well as ideas from positive psychology to develop spaces in a museum context that tangibly facilitate improved well-being.

Finally, issues of race, and especially the barriers to participation found in the heritage and tourism sectors, are examined by Marcella Daye in her exploration of attitudes towards those who are not white. While accessing the countryside and leisure are central to improved well-being, Daye's analysis reveals a common sentiment among racially minoritized communities that their participation in outdoor tourism and leisure is met not only by structurally unwelcoming approaches but also by more overtly racist attitudes, leading to well-founded fears of encountering racism in places that in principle should be beneficial to all. In a different context, issues of race and its impact on researchers are examined by Daniel Jones and Siobhán Hyland, who have both worked for the Searchlight Archive. This is a major collection of profoundly racist material developed by the British extreme right that was collated by the anti-fascist magazine *Searchlight* from the 1960s and is now a research collection based at the University of Northampton. Their chapter explores significant issues of appropriate treatment of such an archive of political extremism and racism and the development of practices to enable this resource to be used for academic research. As they highlight, the well-being of archivists is often poorly discussed, especially when the material they collate is potentially traumatic and disturbing.

Across all the fourteen chapters in *Well-Being Past and Present*, contributors reveal the variegated ways historians and practitioners can engage with issues of well-being, both in historical contexts and in contemporary practices. The aim of this book is certainly not to develop a comprehensive history of well-being, which even if desirable is not likely to be an achievable proposition. Rather it provides a point of departure for future discussions on the broad topic of well-being for historians, for archivists, for heritage sector professionals and for many others. It seeks to contribute to recent calls, including an important intervention by David Stack,[32] for historians to engage with the 'eudaemonic turn'. The issue of well-being is not one to be ignored by those who study and engage with the past but rather should become central to research questions as well as reflection on approaches within the discipline.

Notes

1. 'United Nations Sustainable Development Goals, Goal Three: Ensure Healthy Lives and Promote Well-Being for All Ages', www.un.org/sustainabledevelopment/health/.
2. *Oxford English Dictionary*, www.oed.com/dictionary/wellbeing_n?tl=true&tab=meaning_and_use.
3. *Oxford English Dictionary*, www.oed.com/dictionary/wellbeing_n?tl=true.
4. Katie Barclay and Francois Soyer, *Emotions in Europe 1517–1914: Vol. III Revolutions, 1715–1789* (Routledge, 2021), 85.

5. Sections of what follows are taken from the excellent survey in Laura Stroll, 'A Short History of Wellbeing Research', in David McDaid and Cary Cooper (eds), *Wellbeing: A Complete Reference Guide – Vol. V: The Economics of Wellbeing* (Wiley Blackwell, 2014), 13–31.
6. Paul Slack, 'Material Progress and the Challenge of Affluence in Seventeenth Century England', *Economic History Review* 62.3 (2009), 576–603; Phil Withington, 'The Invention of Happiness', in Michael Braddick and Joanne Innes (eds), *Suffering and Happiness in England 1550–1850: Narratives and Representations* (Oxford University Press, 2017).
7. Daniel Roche, *A History of Everyday Things: The Birth of Consumption in France, 1600–1800* (Cambridge University Press, 2008), 8.
8. Roy Porter and Marie Mulvey Roberts, *Pleasure in the Eighteenth Century* (Bloomsbury, 1996); John Brewer, *The Pleasures of the Imagination: English Culture in the Eighteenth Century* (Routledge, 1997); Maxine Berg, *Luxury and Pleasure in Eighteenth Century Britain* (Oxford University Press, 2007); Mark Rothery, 'Emotional Economies of Pleasure among the Gentry of Eighteenth Century England', *Social History* 49.3 (2024), 294–315.
9. Slack, 'Material Progress'. For an overview of historical models of progress see David Spadafora, *The Idea of Progress in Eighteenth Century Britain* (Yale University Press, 1990).
10. Stroll, 'Short History'.
11. Bart Schultz, *The Happiness Philosophers: The Lives and Works of the Great Utilitarians* (Princeton University Press, 2017).
12. Stroll, 'Short History'.
13. Avner Offer, *The Challenge of Affluence: Self Control and Wellbeing in Britain and the US since 1950* (Oxford University Press, 2006).
14. Felicia A. Huppert and Cary Cooper (eds), *Wellbeing: A Complete Reference Guide, Volumes 1–VI* (Wiley Blackwell, 2014).
15. Richard Estes and M. Joseph Sirgy, *The Pursuit of Human Wellbeing: The Untold Global History* (Springer, 2017).
16. Laura H. Lipman, 'Indicators and Indices of Child Wellbeing: A Brief American History', *Social Indicators Research* 83 (2006), 39–53; Kim Bowes, 'When Kuznets Went to Rome: Roman Economic Wellbeing and the Reframing of Roman History', *Capitalism* 2.1 (2021), 7–40.
17. Robert Costanza, Maureen Hart, Ida Kubiszewski and John Talberth, 'A Short History of GDP: Moving towards Better Measures of Human Wellbeing', *Solutions in History* 5.1 (2014), 91–7.
18. Michael Braddick and Joanne Innes, *Suffering and Happiness in England 1550–1850* (Oxford University Press, 2017); Darrin M. McMahon, 'The Pursuit of Happiness in History', in Michael Eid and Randy J. Larsen (eds), *The Science of Subjective Wellbeing* (Routledge, 2008), 80–97.
19. Fay Bound Alberti, *A Biography of Loneliness: The History of an Emotion* (Oxford University Press, 2019), 2.
20. Ibid.
21. Ibid., 18–19.
22. Ibid., 3–4.
23. University of Groningen Centre for Health and Humanities, 'History of the Body, Health and Well-Being', www.rug.nl/research/research-let/expertisecentra/groningen-centre-for-health-and-humanities/research/?lang=en.

24. Sanda Dolcos, Matthew Moore and Yuta Katsumi, 'Neuroscience and Wellbeing', in E. Diener, S. Oishi and L. Tay (eds), *Handbook of Wellbeing* (DEF, 2018), x.
25. Eighteenth Century Collections Online, www.gale.com/intl/primary-sources/eighteenth-century-collections-online.
26. Simon Smith, *The Golden Fleece: Or the Trade, Interest, and Wellbeing of Great Britain* (London, 1731), 4.
27. See the centre website here: www.northampton.ac.uk/research/research-institutes-and-centres/the-centre-for-historical-studies-chs.
28. Visit Northamptonshire, https://visitnorthamptonshire.co.uk/out-and-about/craft-creative-arts/; https://visitnorthamptonshire.co.uk/discover/history-and-heritage.
29. West Northamptonshire Council, www.westnorthants.gov.uk/health-and-wellbeing; North Northamptonshire Council, www.northnorthants.gov.uk/health-and-wellbeing.
30. Northamptonshire Acre Rural Wellbeing Service, www.northantsacre.org.uk/rural-wellbeing-service.
31. Delapré Abbey, Northampton, https://delaprewellbeing.co.uk.
32. David Stack, 'Promoting Wellbeing through History Teaching', *Transactions of the Royal Historical Society* (2024), 1–19.

1

'Mindfulness and the mise-en-page': Women, well-being and the medieval book of hours

Sue Niebrzydowski

In 2019 when beset by a global pandemic, people turned to books and the comfort they brought. In a time of uncertainty that was – for so many – also a period of grief and loss, Abigail Boucher, Chloe Harrison and Marcello Giovanelli suggest that people sought out subject matter that was predictable if not necessarily comforting, finding solace in the security of formulaic genres and previously read books.[1] Books bolstered well-being during that traumatic time, raising the question if similar was experienced in earlier periods of sudden contagion that took many lives and caused emotional distress and economic disruption.

Throughout the Middle Ages one way of dealing with the emotions brought about by pandemic, war, illness, bereavement, the lottery of childbirth and their negative impact upon well-being was to turn to one's prayer book or book of hours. The book of hours, at whose heart lies devotion to the Virgin Mary, contains subject matter that is largely predictable and formulaic.[2] Over four decades ago Susan Groag Bell demonstrated the special relationship between medieval women and their prayer books.[3] The material condition of many books of hours confirms that they were repeatedly read and treasured by the women who owned and, in many cases, bequeathed what became family heirlooms to their female relatives. Drawing on the discourses of literary studies, manuscript studies and bibliotherapy, this essay examines ways in which the act of 'rereading' and interacting with the materiality of their books of hours might foster mental well-being and offer medieval women a taxonomy of consolation beyond that provided by the spiritual content of their prayer books.

Books of hours: Scripts for well-being

The popularity of books of hours, *horae* or 'primers', is evinced by the number of survivals of this kind of book. Eamon Duffy calculates that 'almost 800 manuscript books of hours made for use in England are scattered in libraries all over the world, and surviving printed versions produced for the English market in the two generations before the Reformation are even more abundant'.[4] Virginia Reinburg suggests that 'the book of hours was the single most commonly produced book of the late middle ages. This is why it is often called the medieval best-seller'.[5] That so many copies have survived daily use and the vagary of time leaves us in no doubt of the significant number of books of hours produced in the premodern period. Books of hours range in size from the small to the large, from high-status, bespoke products for the nobility to more modest shop-bought (and in many cases second-hand) copies for those of lesser means. The smallest could be held in the palm, slipped into a wide sleeve or attached to a belt (hence the title 'girdle book') for reading while sitting or standing, while larger books could still be carried to church or used within the home, perhaps at a reading desk or a prie-dieu for those who could afford such furniture.[6] The book of hours comprises a set of defining features, summarized by Christopher de Hamel as 'distinctive cycles of prayers and psalms to be recited at each of the eight "hours" which divided up the medieval religious day – the hours of Matins, Lauds, Prime, Terce, Sext, none, Vespers and Compline ... These short cycles were dedicated to specific religious themes or saints, principally the Virgin Mary'.[7]

In addition to the Hours of the Virgin, a book of hours commonly included a calendar identifying feasts of the Church year; a set of gospel lessons (known as the Pericopes that address key moments in Christ's life: Jn 1.1-14 (outlining Christ's humanity), Lk. 1.26-37 (the Annunciation), Mt. 2.1-12 (the Visit of the Magi), Mk. 16.14-19 (Christ's appearance to the disciples after the Resurrection); the account of Christ's Passion from St John's Gospel; two key prayers to the Virgin (the *Obsecro te* and the *O intemerata*); the Hours of the Cross; the seven Penitential Psalms the focus of which is repentance for sin (Pss. 6, 31, 37, 50, 101, 129 and 142); the Office of the Dead; and suffrages or prayers to the saints. Most books of hours produced in England or abroad for English commissioners followed the 'use' or rites of Sarum (Salisbury). There was opportunity also for including prayers of particular importance to an individual.

Designed to structure the day, the book of hours provided opportunity for prayer and reflection at regular intervals. Insight into how one noblewoman used her book of hours is found in a sermon composed (but never given) by John Sheppey – then prior of the monastery at Rochester, Kent, before he became bishop of Rochester – for the funeral in 1344 of Joan, Lady Cobham, wife of John de Cobham. In his encomium John Sheppey commends the late departed Lady Cobham for whom 'every day was a feast day with her. For unless there was some greater necessity, on no day would she willingly come down from her chamber or speak with any stranger, until she had said matins and the hours of Our Lady, the seven psalms and the litany, almost every day'.[8] Sheppey's praise indicates that Lady Cobham owned and made daily use of a book of hours in a very particular way. When other household duties allowed commencing each day by saying the seven psalms in penitence for her sin, prayers requesting the intercession of the Virgin Mary and that of a panoply of saints provided Lady Cobham with what we might recognize as a mindful daily routine and moments of mindfulness that served as 'either a useful supplement to religious or spiritual practices or an existing feature'.[9]

Eamon Duffy suggests that books of hours served as 'a script for the drama of personal religion, to be the text of the prayers that people prayed'.[10] As the example of Lady Cobham illustrates, how frequently an owner used her prayer book was dictated by personal devotional needs, the events that occurred during her daily life and the time that household and business tasks might occupy. To maintain her well-being a woman needed to balance these competing elements of her life, and her prayer book was one means of building mindfulness into her life.

The power of the written word in fostering well-being was recognized in the Middle Ages. Geoffrey Chaucer understood how literature might aid sleep and restfulness. In *The Book of the Duchess* Chaucer's dreamer-narrator, rendered insomniac by unrequited love, requests 'a romaunce … to rede and drive the night away'.[11] The potential for the texts within books of hours to foster mental well-being and resilience should not be underestimated as Albrecht Classen confirms, 'religion, mental health and spirituality are intimately interlocking entities … and they find some of their most powerful expressions in the arts, in literature … especially in the Middle Ages'.[12] Prayers enable an individual to employ what Harold G. Koenig characterizes as 'religious coping resources' since 'strongly held beliefs':

> Give meaning to difficult life circumstances and provide a sense of purpose … These cognitions also give a subjective sense of control over events (i.e., if God is in control, can influence circumstances, and be influenced by prayer, then prayer by the individual may positively influence the situation) … These beliefs also help to normalize loss and change and provide role models of persons suffering with the same or similar problems (often illustrated in religious scriptures).[13]

With prayers to Christ, the Virgin and saints, the book of hours is scaffolded upon the conviction that life's events, positive and negative, are within God's control and purpose. The book of hours' many texts offer its owner a consolatory script: the lines to be said, silently or aloud, individually or collectively, hourly or daily, to accompany the cradle to grave events that mark human life and that can trigger anxiety.

An Anglo-Norman prayer for safe delivery in childbirth, composed by Matilda Becket (d. *c.*1141), mother of Thomas of London, archbishop of Canterbury (b. *c.*1120), illustrates the power of prayer for the individual. The prayer is preserved in a fourteenth-century book of hours, owned and most probably commissioned by Hawisia du Bois (fl. 1328).[14] The prayer is also found in the Percy Hours (first quarter of the fifteenth century), now British Library MS Harley 1260, made for the Percy family of Alnwick and Warkworth in Northumberland.[15] Only in the Percy Hours is Matilda identified as the prayer's composer: 'cest oroison la mere seint Thomas de canterbirs fiste. Et el la dist deuaunt son enfauntement, et fem qe la dirra ja de son enfaunt ne perra' (this prayer was composed by the mother of saint Thomas of Canterbury. And she spoke it before her childbirth/and the woman who says it will not perish during her own child/birth).[16]

Matilda's prayer is voiced by a pregnant woman. The speaker addresses God, encouraging him to aid the speaker by recalling that he too was once a vulnerable baby born to term and who was breastfed by his mother. The speaker requests that God, for the love that he has for his mother, the Virgin, relieve the speaker's labour pains and, as importantly, ensure that her child is born well and whole. The quid pro quo is that if she survives childbirth the speaker will attend her purification – a very early mention of the ceremony of the 'Churching of Women' – and be as willing a servant of God as was Mary at her Annunciation. The speaker addresses the Virgin directly. Matilda's Mary is the young mother who has suckled her child, and Matilda frames her relationship to Mary as one of mistress and handmaiden, a term used by Mary of herself in the *Magnificat* where Mary anticipates the glory that she will receive as the mother of God. Matilda acknowledges Mary as a compassionate intercessor, giver of succour and Queen of all virgins from whom the speaker invokes aid, along with the apostles, glorious confessors and precious martyrs.

The prayer never loses its focus on the pregnant woman's body. The emotions – evoked as the prayer is 'embodied' or lifted from the page in being voiced – range from anxiety aroused by the recollected or imagined pain of childbirth moving to hope for a successful delivery, the latter triggered and reinforced by chains of association forged by recalled images of Mary's successful motherhood displayed as the Virgin holds her child on her knee or breastfeeds him. The prayer's supplication, bargaining and recalling Mary's own successful motherhood are designed to support the mental well-being of a woman approaching her confinement and that of any woman who was to aid another during labour. That it is included in Hawisia's book of hours suggests that Hawisia, married to Ralph Giliot sometime between May 1328 and 1332, fully expected to become a mother. This prospect may well have been a source of anxiety, but if so this fear was unfounded since, as Kathryn Smith notes, there is no record of the couple having children.[17] Hawisia's decision to include a prayer – 'For menstrual ills and the bloody flux: say this prayer over bread and butter and give it to the sick person to eat and she will be cured' – may offer an alternative to miscarriage and infant mortality as the reason for the couple's apparent childlessness.[18] It is possible that Hawisia suffered menorrhoeal problems that, in turn, impacted her fertility. For this woman, whose pride in her family is conveyed by the many examples of their heraldic designs that litter her prayer book and serve, in Joni M. Hand's words, as a 'vehicle of identity', infertility could have brought with it negative feelings of anxiety, shame and guilt.[19] The inclusion of a prayer for menstrual regulation in her book of hours might have offered Hawisia comfort and supported her well-being when facing the emotional toll of the inability to conceive.

It was to their book of hours that owners turned at moments of crisis – the stresses and strains of quotidian life such as birth (or lack thereof) and death, business and personal interactions, war and pestilence – and on days less dramatic.

Membrane and mindfulness

The prayers and texts within a book of hours had the potential to render negative life events less distressing. In contrast to Freud who defined the psychopathology of religion, following later studies that acknowledge the interconnectedness of religion, spirituality and mental health, Hester E. Oberman contends that 'it is spirituality and the religious experience that restores a sense of sanity as it provides a new and redeeming purpose'.[20]

In focusing on the prayers, gospel readings and related texts within a book of hours, it is possible to overlook the potential of a codex of this kind to foster well-being in ways associated with the book as material object. As Tom Mole advises, focusing on the written word within books can elide the significance of the material codex itself: 'Learning to read means to stop looking at the book in front of us and to start looking through it ... The book itself starts to vanish, to seem as though it's hardly a thing at all. As we gain the ability to lose ourselves in a book, the book as an object begins to get lost.'[21] Mole is not alone in drawing our attention to the significance of the book as object and the many ways in which its owner/reader interacts with it. Theresa Schilhab and Sue Walker also argue for reading as a multisensory practice that 'is about the interaction of a person and an object where the person uses different senses to know and understand the object'.[22]

The connection between material objects and fostering mental well-being is the subject of a study by Inger Beate Larsen, Tore Dag Bøe and Alain Topor, who conclude that interaction with objects that are meaningful to a subject can influence physical, social and emotional movement into the recovery of mental well-being.[23] This emotional movement towards recovery is achieved through the agency for positive change that an object might encourage. Tom Mole acknowledges the power of the book to foster change, observing that books are not just passive tools but capable of exerting forces of their own on their owners.[24] A frequently reread and treasured book of hours, possibly an item once owned by a woman's mother or other female relative or a matrimonial gift and so imbued with memory, is a prime candidate to encourage in its owner's recovery into mental well-being.

Rajlaxmi Jain, a multidisciplinary designer, notes the benefits to well-being that features of the printed book can bring in comparison with on-screen access since with the latter 'you cannot feel textures, tear a page, smell freshly printed paper, paste stickers, scribble with crayons'.[25] Jain focuses here on children's printed books, but the aspects of physicality that, she suggests, improve mental health are all overtly foregrounded in the manufacturing and consumption of medieval books of hours and books in this period more generally.

Roger S. Wieck describes the book of hours as 'a veritable jewel box of devotion', perfectly capturing the beauty, colour and precious gold-leaf illumination of the book of hours that are visible once the book, itself a valued and valuable item of treasure, is opened.[26] The materials from which a jewel box is fabricated are hard, cold and inert, creating a receptacle of fixed form. The leaves of a manuscript book, in contrast, are pliable and made of skin that possesses both a hair and flesh side, the quality of which changes over time through repeated handling. They are also susceptible to the manipulations that Jain associates with fostering mental well-being.

Kathryn M. Rudy has explored the implication of the transfer of grease and dirt from users' fingers to their books of hours, gauging that the dirtiest pages were those most frequently turned to, and turned over, by their owners, and further that the incidence of dirt suggests that users were in the habit of holding their books in a particular way each time they returned to their book.[27] In the act of reading medieval membrane codices, skin touches skin. The final section of this essay considers the potential impact of this contact on the prayer book owner's well-being.

Like all medieval manuscript volumes, personal books of hours contain marks of their use and reuse, as itemized by Christopher de Hamel, 'signs of manufacture, erasures, scratches, overpainting, offsets, patches, sewing-holes, bindings, and nuances of colour and texture'.[28] The owner of a book of hours touched, caressed and on occasion wept over their prayer book in haptic response to what Helen Smith terms 'the sensuousness of books as the products of human hands'.[29] An owner's repeated use of her book of hours was a corporeal quid pro quo: as the membrane leaves gave up their spiritual content, so in turn her body left its trace on her book in a variety of ways, including, as Kathryn M. Rudy's research demonstrates, 'applying grease or dirt through bodily contact, abrading material by repeatedly touching it, poking holes by sewing on objects, and degrading the fibers [*sic*] of parchment, paper, leather, and thread by repeatedly bending and unbending them'.[30] Tom Mole notes the connection between the book and the body, 'the book (like the body) is subject to various infirmities and imperfections'.[31] An owner's personal well-being came at a cost to the very codex that supported her emotional resilience.

Touch was not the only way in which women engaged with their books of hours. Some owners of *horae* ingested their prayer book by kissing the images contained therein. The impetus for this gesture may well have been inspired by clerical practice, as Kathryn M. Rudy notes how 'believers also kissed images in their prayer books, just as the priest would have kissed the missal during Mass'.[32]

British Library MS Harley 2966 – a book of hours made in Bruges in 1410 and owned early in its history by 'Mistres Trigg' – offers one example of kissing one's book of hours.[33] The image on folio 30v of MS Harley 2966 depicts the flagellation of the stripped Christ and offers Katherine M. Rudy evidence 'of the owner's fiery enthusiasm for the body of Christ, as he (or she) touched the image repeatedly with her hands and possibly her lips … She has rubbed the nearly naked body of Christ right off the page, leaving his smeared silhouette against the gold-tooled background'.[34] Such stroking and kissing are purposeful, emotion-driven actions that might aid movement into mental good health. Here the caressing and kissing of Christ's naked and vulnerable body is a vehicle for a range of positive emotions: love (erotic and spiritual), devotion, gratitude for and hope in the salvation brought about by Christ's torment and sacrifice for humanity.

As a woman leafed through her prayer book, she left traces of herself – grease, grime and tears – that abraded her book. It is these markers of human interaction that give a book of hours a personal connection to its users. The transfer of a reader's own corporeality to her book might extend beyond the grease and dirt of her fingers to her saliva and tears, since books of hours retain evidence of images that the owner kissed for osculatory consolation. It is on the kinds of images routinely contained in the books of hours and their impact on well-being that this essay now focuses.

Mindfulness and the mise-en-page

In many ways predictable and formulaic, books of hours were readily customized to meet the devotional needs and personal interests of their commissioners. As Erik Kwakkel notes, 'While the scribe produced a manuscript, the choices leading to its ultimate design were not solely his own. They were also influenced by the individual for whom the book was made.'[35] Depending on the wealth of the commissioner, books of hours might contain elaborate decorative schema: full- or half-page illustrations or illuminations of scriptural figures, biblical events or saints; historiated initials containing human figures; decorated illuminated initials; line fillers of foliage, and borders around text from which animals or comic grotesques emerge, often carrying out tasks familiar from the human world; and frequently these can be in parodic form to elicit a smile from the book user.[36]

As with the texts, certain illustrations were common to books of hours as observed by Virginia Reinburg, 'the hours of the Virgin introduced by a miniature of the Annunciation, the office of the dead opening with a miniature depicting a funeral mass or churchyard burial … Occasionally customers paid for a special image, usually one representing the patron kneeling before God, the Madonna, or a saint.'[37]

Having oneself portrayed in her book of hours – usually at prayer and often in relation to the Virgin or a favoured saint – brought the owner into a close and personal relationship with those whom she believed could support her well-being at difficult and challenging times. A bereaved mother who mourned a lost child might draw comfort from being depicted at prayer before an image of the grieving Virgin as, for example, Mater Dolorosa or the Pietà in which the mother of God sheds tears for her dead child.

The combination of illustration and text is no innocent relationship in a book of hours but one designed to manipulate the book's user. As Stephen G. Nichols observes, 'The dynamics of the parchment page – which I like to think of as the "manuscript matrix" – conjure not an inert place of inscription, but an interactive space inviting continual representational and interpretive activity.'[38] The prayer book's owner has work to do for her book of hours to promote her well-being. Kathryn Smith observes how 'a consistent goal of the images and texts and their relationships to one another is to effect the book owner's emotional, imaginative entry into the world of the sacred narrative as told on the page, and to permit the book owner to share the experience of the sacred figures.'[39] As such, images in books of hours enabled the practice of affective piety, a popular mode of spirituality in the Middle Ages that emphasized the importance of empathy in religious devotion, particularly to Christ's Nativity, his Passion and the suffering of his mother, the Virgin Mary. The images of Christ and his mother found in the books of hours encouraged the owner's 'imaginative entry' into scenes that in turn served as 'intimate scripts' for a meditative and emotional response to the narratives and their spiritual import these images depicted.[40]

One element of the mise-en-page – the term used for the general layout and organization of the manuscript page – that offers further opportunity for interactivity is the images that illustrated prayer books.[41] Eamon Duffy observes how 'the pictures in Books of hours both enhanced the texts that they accompanied and worked independently of them. Many images were designed specifically to arouse intense devotional feeling in those who gazed at them.'[42]

The images in her book of hours encouraged an affective or emotional response in the viewer: identification with Mary's successful motherhood as presaged in images of the Annunciation, her suffering at the Crucifixion as she sees her son put to death, and Christ's suffering for humanity. This identification might be enhanced for those who could afford it by the inclusion of donor portraits that were in direct line of sight – and dialogue – with the Virgin. The composition of the images within a book of hours was designed to inform and reinforce the spiritual messages of Christian salvation and to offer spiritual support and comfort.

The many elements that define images that mark the aesthetic of prayer book illustration could play a role in fostering well-being above and beyond the spiritual support associated with these illustrations. The artist's use of colour might have an uplifting and positive enhancement of the book owner's mood, with illustrations created from a range of vibrant coloured pigments: red, bright blue, dark blue, pink, orange and purple.[43] Both haptic and visual pleasure was to be experienced in touching the cool smoothness of burnished gold leaf with its light-catching, lustral quality used frequently for the almond-shaped mandorlas that surround Christ and his mother, the halo or nimbus used to demark saints to enhance decorative borders and the capital letters within texts.[44]

Recollection of music might also have a positive effect on a woman while she engaged with her book of hours. Lisa Colton observes how 'the experience of musical sound was a highly personal affair, related not to the formal requirements of the Christian liturgy but to individual spiritual identity'.[45] Images in prayer books might include banderols or scrolls containing snatches of chant and music issuing from the mouths of the picture's subjects. One common illustration in the books of hours that employed banderols was the Annunciation of Christ's birth to the shepherds in which a choir of angels reveal the news of Christ's birth. Another illustration ubiquitous to the book of hours is the Annunciation to the Virgin Mary of Christ's conception. In many portrayals of this moment, a banderol issuing from Mary's mouth will contain the first words of the 'Magnificat' that Mary sings on receiving the news from Gabriel. The music associated with these festivals and triggered by the snatches of it in banderols might be sung aloud or conjured up mentally, recalling memories of positive times among family and friends.

One final element of mood-enhancing illustration can be found in the margins of the pages of a book of hours. Recognizable flora and fauna frequently populate the borders of books of hours, evoking the sounds, smells and weather of spring and summer. While this aspect of border illustration has the potential to conjure up positive memory, other features of border illustration foster the well-being in different ways. The addition of comic hybrids – a person whose lower body is that of a dragon, hybrid creature combining several animals – and satirical portraits of contemporary life (a fox wearing a bishop's mitre, rabbits hunting people, women beating their husbands with distaffs) all possessed the potential to improve the reader's mood through laughter in what Martha Driver and Michael Orr term the 'enhanced enjoyment of the written page'.[46]

Conclusions

A woman's book of hours might offer consolation and support in developing resilience against the stresses and anxieties that life can bring in what might be termed a taxonomy of consolation. The texts contained within her book of hours encourage its owner to seek the consolatory God's love and his son's sacrifice, and in the Virgin Mary's power to intercede, above and beyond the spiritual support offered by its texts. On another yet intrinsically related level, the repeated act of returning to her prayer book, of feeling its skin touching hers and encountering the images that offer multisensory stimulation, might not only console but also move its owner forward into better mental health. This is the impression given by Margery Kempe, a medieval mystic from King Lynn, in Norfolk, who at the turn of the fourteenth century records how she finds a moment of peace away from the stresses of juggling being a wife and a mother of fourteen, with her book of hours in her parish church contemplating her own spirituality, 'knelyd upon her kneys, heldyng down hir hed, and hir boke in hir hand' (kneeling, her head lowered and her [prayer] book in her hand).[47] Although from different social backgrounds, Margery Kempe, Hawisia de Bois, Joan, Lady Cobham and Mistress Trigg all experienced moments of mindfulness with their books of hours. In the mayhem caused by a pandemic that was both poorly understood and ill-prepared for, the solace found by contemporary readers in rereading familiar books is something that we share with our medieval counterparts.

Notes

1. Abigail Boucher, Chloe Harrison and Marcello Giovanelli, 'How Reading Habits Have Changed during the Covid-19 Lockdown', *The Conversation*, 5 October 2020, https://theconversation.com/how-reading-habits-have-changed-during-the-covid-19-lockdown-146894 (accessed 16 April 2023).
2. Eamon Duffy, *Marking the Hours: English People and Their Prayers* (Yale University Press, 2011), 67.
3. Susan Groag Bell, 'Medieval Women Book Owners: Arbiters of Lay Piety and Ambassadors of Culture', *Signs* 7.4 (1982), 742–68. See also Mary C. Erler, *Women, Reading, and Piety in Late Medieval England* (Cambridge University Press, 2002); Charity Scott-Stokes, *Women's Books of Hours in Medieval England* (D. S. Brewer, 2006).
4. Duffy, *Marking the Hours*, 3.
5. Virginia Reinburg, *French Books of Hours: Making an Archive of Prayer, c. 1400–1600* (Cambridge University Press, 2014), 20.
6. For details of girdle books of hours see Raymond Clemens and Timothy Graham, *An Introduction to Manuscript Studies* (Cornell University Press, 2007), 55.
7. Christopher de Hamel, *Meetings with Remarkable Manuscripts: Twelve Journeys into the Medieval World* (Allen Lane, 2016), 387.
8. W. A. Pantin, *The English Church in the Fourteenth Century* (Cambridge University Press, 1955), 255–6; also quoted in Nigel Saul, *Lordship and Faith: The English Gentry and the Parish Church in the Middle Ages* (Oxford University Press, 2017), 120.
9. Omar Yousaf, Steven Love, Peter Hampson, James Hedderly and Monica Rogers, 'Conceptualising and Measuring Mindfulness during Worship and Prayer: Scale Development and Initial Validation of the Mindfulness during Worship Scale (MWS)', *Personality and Individual Differences* 196 (2022), 111683.
10. Duffy, *Marking the Hours*, 67.

11. Geoffrey Chaucer, *The Book of the Duchess in The Riverside Chaucer*, ed. Larry D. Benson (Oxford University Press, 2008), 331, lines 48–9.
12. Albrecht Classen, ed., *Mental Health, Spirituality, and Religion in the Middle Ages and Early Modern Age* (De Gruyter, 2014), 40–1.
13. Harold G. Koenig, 'Religion, Spirituality, and Health: The Research and Clinical Implications', *ISRN Psychiatry* (2012), https://doi.org/10.5402/2012/278730.
14. See entry 871 in *Anglo-Norman Literature: A Guide to Texts and Manuscripts*, ed. Ruth J. Dean and Maureen B. M. Bolton (Anglo-Norman Text Society, 1999), 452; Kathryn A. Smith, *Art, Identity and Devotion in Fourteenth-Century England: Three Women and Their Books of Hours* (British Library, 2003), 302–10, appendix 2; Charity Scott-Stokes, *Women's Books of Hours in Medieval England* (D. S. Brewer, 2006), 129–30. Lucy Freeman Sandler identifies Hawisia DuBois [*sic*] as the original owner or donor as her Christian name occurs in prayers on folios 30, 146^{v}, 147 and 147^{v} and she is represented in a heraldic mantle together with a male member of her family in the full-page miniatures at the beginning of the manuscript in *Gothic Manuscripts 1285–1385, A Survey of Manuscripts Illuminated in the British Isles*, vol. 2 (Harvey Miller, 1986), 97.
15. For a detailed description of the manuscript see the British Library Catalogue, www.bl.uk/catalogues/illuminatedmanuscripts/record.asp?MSID=3479&CollID=8&NStart=1260 (accessed 25 February 2016).
16. Dean and Bolton, *Anglo-Norman Literature*, 452.
17. Kathryn A. Smith, 'A Viewing Community in Fourteenth-Century England', in Joyce Coleman, Mark Cruse and Kathryn A. Smith (eds), *The Social Life of Illumination: Manuscripts, Images, and Communities in the Late Middle Ages*, Medieval Texts and Cultures of Northern Europe 21 (Brepols, 2013), 121–76 (p. 125).
18. Smith, *Art, Identity and Devotion*, 254. The prayer is Anglo-Norman and reads 'Pur le curs de ventre et flux de sanc. Dites cest oreisun sur pain e bure, e donez a malade a manger: e il garira'.
19. Joni M. Hand, *Women, Manuscripts and Identity in Northern Europe, 1350–1550* (Ashgate, 2013), 1. Hawisia's heraldic devices can be found listed in Smith, *Art, Identity and Devotion*, 311–14, appendix 3.
20. Hester E. Oberman, 'A Postmodern Perspective on Mental Health, Spirituality, and Religion', in Albrecht Classen (ed.), *Mental Health* (De Gruyter Brill, 2014), 609–711 (p. 701).
21. Tom Mole, *The Secret Life of Books: Why They Mean More Than Words* (Elliott and Thompson, 2019), 7.
22. Theresa Schilhab and Sue Walker (eds), *The Materiality of Reading* (Aarhus University Press, 2020), 1.
23. 'Things Matter: About Materiality and Recovery from Mental Health Difficulties', *International Journal of Qualitative Studies on Health and Wellbeing* 15.1 (December 2020), 1802909, https://doi.org/10.1080/17482631.2020.1802909.
24. Mole, *The Secret Life of Books*, 4.
25. 'Promoting Mental Wellbeing Through Design: An Interview with Rajlaxmi Jain', *Design Inspiration*, www.printmag.com/categories/design-inspiration (accessed 10 May 2023).
26. Roger S. Wieck, *The Book of Hours in Medieval Art and Life* (Sotheby's, 1988), 40.
27. Kathryn M. Rudy, 'Dirty Books: Quantifying Patterns of Use in Medieval Manuscripts Using a Densitometer', *Journal of Historians of Netherlandish Art* 2.1–2 (Summer 2010), https://doi.org/10.5092/jhna.2010.2.1.1.

28. De Hamel, *Meetings with Remarkable Manuscripts*, 3.
29. Helen Smith, *Grossly Material Things: Women and Book Production in Early Modern England* (Oxford University Press, 2012), 9. Smith's comment is made in relation to early printed books but is equally applicable to the handmade books of hours of the later Middle Ages.
30. Kathryn M. Rudy, *Touching Parchment: How Medieval Users Rubbed, Handled, and Kissed Their Manuscripts: Vol. 1: Officials and Their Books* (Open Book, 2023), 1.
31. Mole, *The Secret Life of Books*, 8.
32. Kathryn M. Rudy, 'Kissing Images, Unfurling Rolls, Measuring Wounds, Sewing Badges and Carrying Talismans: Considering Some Harley Manuscripts through the Physical Rituals They Reveal', *Electronic British Library Journal* (2011), 1–56 (p. 2).
33. Rudy, 'Kissing Images', 4, note 5.
34. Rudy, 'Kissing Images', 21.
35. Erik Kwakkel, 'Decoding the Material Book: Cultural Residue in Medieval Manuscripts', in Michael Johnston and Michael Van Dussen (eds), *The Medieval Manuscript Book: Cultural Approaches* (Cambridge University Press, 2015), 60–76 (p. 65).
36. For a study of comic grotesques designed to keep the reader turning over the leaves see Anne Rudloff Stanton, 'Turning the Pages: Marginal Narratives and Devotional Practice in Gothic Prayerbooks', in Sarah Blick and Laura D. Gelfand (eds), *Push Me, Pull You: Imaginative and Emotional Interaction in Late Medieval and Renaissance Art, Volume One* (Brill, 2011), 75–122.
37. Reinburg, *French Books of Hours*, 23, 26.
38. Stephen G. Nichols, 'What Is a Manuscript Culture? Technologies of the Manuscript Matrix', in Michael Johnston and Van Dussen (eds), *The Medieval Manuscript Book* (Cambridge University Press, 2015), 34–59 (p. 39).
39. Smith, *Art, Identity and Devotion*, 184.
40. For a detailed study of affective piety see Sarah McNamer, *Affective Meditation and the Invention of Medieval Compassion* (University of Pennsylvania Press, 2010).
41. See Matti Peikola, 'Aspects of Mise-en-Page in Manuscripts of the Wycliffite Bible', in Denis Renevey and Graham D. Caie (eds), *Medieval Texts in Context* (Routledge, 2008), 28–67.
42. Duffy, *Marking the Hours*, 14, note 2.
43. The illustrations in books of hours were created using paints derived from minium (lead oxide – orangey-red, from which the term 'miniature' derives), lapis lazuli (ultramarine – blue), cinnabar (vermilion – red), lead white (white), woad (producing dark blue) and madder (pink), sea molluscs (purple) and squid (dark brown/black). While research into the psychological functioning of colour is at a nascent stage, the potential for these aspects of the physicality of the book of hours is uplifting, even to the modern reader. See Andrew J. Elliot, 'Color and Psychological Functioning: A Review of Theoretical and Empirical Work', *Frontiers in Psychology* 5 (April 2015), 1–8; Zena O'Connor, 'Color Psychology and Colour Therapy: Caveat Emptor', *Color Forum* 36.3 (June 2011), 229–34.
44. For further details about gilding and its effects see Kathleen P. Whitley, *The Gilded Page: The History and Technique of Manuscript Gilding* (British Library, 2000).
45. Lisa Colton, *Cultural Histories of Noise, Sound and Listening in Europe, 1300–1918* (Routledge, 2016), 45.
46. Martha Driver and David Orr, 'Decorating and Illuminating the Page', in Alexander Gillespie and Daniel Wakelin (eds), *The Production of Books in England 1350–1500*

(Cambridge University Press, 2012), 104–28 (p. 128). For an examination of the social significance of hybrids and manuscript margins see Michael Camille, *Image on the Edge: The Margins of Medieval Art* (Reaktion Books, 2012), and Alixe Bovey, *Monsters and Grotesques in Medieval Manuscripts* (University of Toronto Press, 2002).

47. Barry Windeatt, *The Book of Margery Kempe* (Longman, 2000), chap. 9, lines 658–9, p. 83.

2

'In this orchard, when you would be comforted': Using garden spaces for familial intimacy and well-being in late medieval England

Rachel Moss

In the early summer of 1481, the young wool merchant Richard Cely wrote to his brother George about a conversation he had recently had with their father:

> Sir, our father and I came together in the new orchard last Friday, and he asked me many questions of you, and I told him all as it was, and he was right sorry for the death of the child, and I told him of the good will that the Whigstons and Daltons have to you, and how I liked the young gentlewoman, and he commanded me to write to you that he would gladly that it were brought about and that you laboured it betimes.[1]

Like all the Cely correspondence it gives the impression of being written in haste, personal details tightly packed alongside matters of business. Yet the letter records a potential moment of peace in the lives of these busy merchants: an opportunity for father and son to catch up in the open air in a location commonly understood by medieval people to be productive in both literal and figurative senses. Cultivated outdoor spaces were essential to medieval well-being.

Scholars have long been aware that gardens occupied an important place in the medieval spiritual imagination.[2] A garden not only offered an actual physical space to experience the health-giving, spiritually enriching benefits of the natural world but also formed a vital part of the medieval mental landscape. There has been relatively limited work on orchards as a subset of medieval gardens, although they were a common feature of monastic, elite, rural and urban landscapes – that is, everywhere – but what work there has been indicates that orchards were considered to be particularly healthful, generative spaces beyond the literal fact of their fruit production.[3] Recent research also suggests that as literary landscapes, orchards were imbued with queer potential, as spaces that offered the possibility of transgressing normative gender roles and sexual behaviour.[4] These two views of orchards – as spiritual heartlands and as queer landscapes – point not to contradictions but to the multivalence of this type of garden and to their as-yet-untapped generative potential for historians.

Unsurprisingly, the multiple possibilities offered by medieval gardens mean there has also been a rich recent scholarship on their gendered connotations, in both literary and literal landscape terms. This builds on wider work about the gendering of medieval space in medieval society more broadly, where research has tended to focus on the specifically gendered attributes of particular locales.[5] For instance, many scholars have written on the association of the medieval enclosed garden with women and how its walls could be both a signifier of patriarchal control and a tempting invitation to (sexual) breach.[6] There is also interesting work on the masculine associations with forest landscapes, from the hearty woodland brotherhood of Robin Hood legend to the wilder mysteries of Merlin and Lancelot's respective madnesses in the wilderness.[7] Outside of these secular milieus, that most of the work on medieval gardens has been on monastic spaces is a reminder that much academic discussion of medieval gardens is implicitly gendered, since it deals with single-sex communities.[8] But of course most people in the Middle Ages did not live in monasteries, and few spaces – public or private – could exclusively belong to either men or women. While medieval texts made the domestic sphere a female one, in truth much male enterprise took place in the medieval household, while the supposedly masculine public sphere was occupied by women for practical economic reasons as well as social ones.[9] Understanding this shifts the intellectual framing of medieval space from simple questions about why some spaces might be considered masculine or feminine into more complex discussions of how space might be used homosocially and familially by medieval men and women and what ways we might read these landscapes as a consequence.

In this chapter, these questions are applied to a specific subset of elite men: the socio-economic cluster of gentry and mercantile families that in the late fifteenth century formed a broadly bourgeois society with overlapping – though not identical – priorities and concerns. The chapter sets the Celys' urban orchard excursion alongside another outdoor meeting between father and son recorded in the contemporaneous Stonor family letter collection to explore the ways in which outdoor spaces may have allowed for the temporary relaxation of rigid familial hierarchies. It argues that gardens, understood to be sites that allowed for personal and collective well-being, could be generative spaces for developing affective relationships. Through the privacy and release from domestic responsibilities offered by garden spaces, elite medieval men were able to exercise a kind of affective homosocial intimacy freed from some of the constraints of operating within the medieval home.

What was a medieval garden?

Throughout the twentieth century, medieval gardens were the subject of periodic academic attention; but it was from the 1980s onward that critical interest in them particularly began to bloom. The year 1981 saw the foundation of the *Journal of Garden History*, the same year that Teresa McLean and John Harvey both wrote monographs on medieval gardens which remain influential to this day.[10] Since then, although gardens have remained a relatively marginal area for academic study – at least partly because they often require an interdisciplinary approach – there have been regular publications, the most influential contribution recently being Patricia Skinner and Teresa Tyers's 2018 collection *The Medieval and Early Modern Garden in Britain.*

Defining the medieval garden has proved problematic; as Skinner and Tyers observe, 'gardens were and still are diverse, complicated spaces rich with interpretative possibilities'.[11] Nor is it useful to draw clear distinctions between the productive garden and the pleasure garden; for medieval people, gardens 'could serve an aesthetic as well as a material purpose … The various motives involved were not mutually exclusive, but complementary'.[12] We find medieval horticultural writing as early as the ninth century, and it became an important genre, where information on how to garden sat alongside discussion of which plants had what health-giving properties – both spiritual and physical – and a clear recognition that gardens were a source of pleasure for gardener and visitor alike.[13] Walahfrid Strabo, abbot of Reichenau (*c.*808–849), described the orchard garden of his mentor in terms that connected the productivity of the trees with the happy productivity of the boys in the abbot's care:

> The peach-tree turns its leaves this way and that
> In and out of the sun, and the boys at play,
> Your happy band of pupils, gather for you
> Fruits white with tender down.[14]

While most of what we know about the layout, design and functions of real gardens in the Middle Ages comes from monasteries, the important role gardens played in medieval literature and the regular inclusion of horticultural and botanical texts within medieval household books makes it clear that gardens were a central feature of medieval life.

In spiritual terms, the *hortus conclusus* occupied a pre-eminent role. The image of the enclosed garden came from the Song of Solomon, where medieval theologians wrestled with the overtly sexual content of this biblical text and came to the conclusion that the enclosed but productive garden was a metaphor for the Virgin Mary and her chaste but bountiful womb.[15] These enclosed gardens were a ubiquitous part of monastic cloister gardens, intended to capture a vision of Eden.[16] Meanwhile, more secular images of the enclosed garden show beautiful walled spaces affording privacy for medieval elites, offering them space to make music, read, walk and play.[17]

There is plentiful evidence of gardens built primarily for pleasure in the Middle Ages, where obvious enjoyment is taken from the natural environment.[18] Yet it is also clear that the productive garden was also a place that brought pleasure, and that this was seen as an essential part of their nature: that the enjoyment of being in the cultivated natural environment of a garden, be it a kitchen garden, an orchard or a pleasure park, offered health benefits that medieval people could and should take up. Medieval gardens were planted with many kinds of plants, flowers and herbs, most of which had culinary and medicinal uses, but their functions did not end there. Claire Noble speculates that the flowers of the garden, rich with symbolic meanings, may have been used as objects of spiritual contemplation.[19] Meanwhile, the very scents of the garden and the breezes that blew through it protected garden-users from poisonous miasmas – healthy air was a cornerstone of medieval medicine – while the layout of the garden, encouraging alternation between movement and rest, could play a key part in keeping the user's humoral balance in check.[20] Medieval medicine, based firmly on humoral theory, took a holistic approach to the body and mind, and so a healthy person was one whose spiritual, physical and what we would now term psychological states were all harmoniously aligned – an understanding that has interesting parallels with modern definitions of 'well-being'.[21] Garden spaces, broadly defined, thus played an important role in medieval well-being, and we will see how this played a role in two medieval families discussed hereafter.

The sources and their context

This chapter looks at late fifteenth-century letters from the Celys and the Stonors, who were, respectively, merchant and gentry families from London and Oxfordshire. The two interconnected demographic groups of mercantile and gentry society were subject to social, political and economic changes in the turbulent Wars of the Roses period, although many of the letters in these collections show no sign of being composed in a period of civil conflict, instead reflecting the more everyday preoccupations of busy gentle and merchant households.[22]

What do I mean by 'gentry' and 'mercantile' elites? Historians of this period are broadly agreed that the English gentry as a distinct category emerged out of increased stratification within the late medieval aristocracy. The status of 'gentleman' was recognized by act of parliament in 1413, by which point a gentry elite composed of knights, esquires and gentlemen was well established.[23] The men who made up the late medieval gentry – particularly its lower ranks – did not always have aristocratic origins; the growth of the legal and administrative professions meant that ambitious men with talent might rise from relatively humble beginnings to the rank of gentleman and beyond. Meanwhile, while the fifteenth century was a period hampered by economic depression, urban elites still flourished, with guilds playing an increasingly significant role in the structures of urban governance, and towns developing robust corporate identities through civic building programmes and citizenship.[24]

The use of the word 'gentleman' increasingly blurred the boundary between gentlemen and merchants, since what made someone of 'gentle' status lacked fixed definition in this period. Wealthy merchants were keen to establish their respectable credentials by investing in land and thus quite regularly have lived side by side with the county gentry.[25] Meanwhile, gentry families increasingly diversified their economic portfolios in ways that would have brought them into contact with merchant families for business reasons, which may also have extended to more social connections. We know that the Celys, for instance, were acquaintances of the gentry Plumpton family; it seems likely to me that they also knew (or at least knew of) William Stonor, who speculated in the Calais wool trade – and who took as his first wife the widow of a rich merchant.[26]

Few records of the Cely family survive before the late fifteenth century, but by the time the surviving collection of correspondence begins in 1474 they were well established in the wool trade and owned property in London, Essex and Calais. Richard

Cely senior (d. 1482) was a prominent enough figure in London society that he stood for election as sheriff in 1481.[27] He had three sons, Robert, Richard and George. Robert was the eldest son but after the 1470s was not involved in the family trade; it has been speculated that he may have had difficulties with his mental health or have had a disability of some kind.[28] Richard junior (d. 1493) was treated as his father's heir. He was close to his younger brother George (d. 1489), but fell into a dispute with George's widow over the payment of their joint debts – through which sad circumstance the letter collection survives, because 247 letters from the period 1472–88 were gathered together en masse as evidence and was preserved by the Court of Chancery.[29]

The Stonor correspondence covers a much more extensive period of time – 1290–1483 – but the richest part of the correspondence dates to the later fifteenth century and is composed of letters to and from Thomas Stonor (1424–1474) and his son William (?1449–1494). The family lived in Oxfordshire and, unlike their more famous counterparts the Pastons, seem to have mostly stayed out of national politics, although William briefly forfeited his estates after backing the failed rebellion against Richard III in 1483; they were restored to him on Henry VII's accession in 1485. Thomas had a steady and successful local career, serving on the commission of the peace continuously from 1466 to his death in 1474. William's first wife Elizabeth Ryche (d. 1479) brought family connections to the wool trade, which William developed to his profit. During this period he was also knighted and eventually made a very socially successful match to Anne Neville (d. 1486), the eldest daughter of John, Marquis of Montagu, neatly demonstrating that an interest in trade did not preclude social advancement.[30]

That we have so many records from these families is sign that letter-writing was an essential skill for gentry and mercantile people in this period. The careers of gentlemen and merchants alike meant they were often peripatetic, travelling around the country and abroad on their own business and in the service of patrons, and they wrote frequently to their wives, brothers, adult sons and business associates. Letters of this period are often brief to the point of terseness; they are structured using conventional templates and lack the rhetorical flourishes of later missives. This makes them sound dull, and certainly many historians have, in the words of Virginia Woolf, dismissed them as containing 'no writing for writing's sake'. But their very mundanity is part of what makes them fascinating, because it is a mark that letter-writing in English had become commonplace for the first time in history.[31]

Middle English letters, through their form as much as their content, give us insights into both ideological expectations about father–son relationships as well as evidence for real interactions between these men.[32] The structure of medieval English letters, based on the Latin *ars dictaminis*, reified pre-existing social hierarchies by emphasizing the relative statuses of sender and recipient, but also provided scope for emotional connection.[33] In linguistic terms, the composition of Middle English letters relied on both social deixis (language that emphasizes social difference) alongside empathetic deixis, that is language which reflects and reinforces an emotional bond between writer and recipient.[34] Late medieval English letters between fathers and their adult sons thus strongly reflected the hierarchical nature of the family, where the *paterfamilias* was expected to be treated with deference and respect, but they were also repositories of surprisingly candid moments of emotion, including expressions of mutual affection.

In this chapter, we will see how these letters – brief and formulaic though they are – can act as snapshots of moments in family history that few other medieval sources can provide, and that in those moments fathers and sons use outdoor spaces to speak freely about sensitive matters in ways that may have consolidated their emotional connections with one another.

In the new orchard last Friday: Making space for sharing secrets

In the early summer of 1481, George and Richard Cely junior were both in their early twenties and were employed in the family wool business. As usual, Richard was in London with their parents, and George was in Calais. George seems to have lived year round in Calais, with his elder brother Richard crossing over only occasionally, and his father not at all. This physical distance required much back-and-forth communication by letter, which accounts for the high volume of letters the family exchanged in this period.

To make sense of their locations, a brief explanation of the wool trade is required. The Cely family serves as a good example of how the business of the wool trade operated. One member of a partnership in the wool trade – in this case Richard Cely senior, or sometimes his son Richard junior – would be responsible for visiting their middleman in the wool producing regions of England to examine the samples, agree to a sale and have the wool transported to London. He would oversee the loading of the wool at the port for transport to Calais, where another member of the partnership (in this case, George Cely) would receive it. This partner would usually be responsible for arranging the practicalities of selling the wool onward from Calais. Why Calais? Because medieval English government required that all overseas trade in certain goods be transacted at specific designated market towns or ports, referred to as the 'staple ports'. At these specified places, merchants were required to submit their goods to inspection and to pay a levy to the Crown on goods for export to the Continent. Calais was still an English possession in this period, and so it was here in this English outpost on the Continent that the wool trade's complex imports and exports were processed. High export taxes and tight regulations made fewer and fewer merchants of means interested in joining the Merchants of the Company of the Staple, especially since the growing English cloth trade pushed down the demand in Europe for English wool. By the mid-1470s the Calais fellowship was mostly composed of men of reasonably modest means, such as the Cely brothers whose interest in the wool trade generated them each an income of around £100 a year: a respectable sum, and one that could allow a man to be included in the category of 'gentleman', but not enough to be considered *wealthy*.[35]

Accordingly, these young men hoped to make their fortunes not just from their profession but also through successful marriages. In the quotation that opened this chapter, Richard junior reported that he had met with the sister of a family friend and, having judged that she was a potential match for George, had discussed the matter with their father. Richard and George were both actively on the marriage market at this point, and both discussed likely opportunities with an air of brotherly camaraderie: but it is likely that, since the young woman was the sister of George's friend John Dalton, this was a match that had to be taken seriously and so was worthy of discussion with their father. Richard brought the matter up with Richard senior as they walked together in their new orchard, and Richard senior instructed his son to encourage George to pursue the opportunity: 'He commanded me to write to you that he would gladly that it were brought about and that you laboured it betimes.'

So far, so wholesome. However, these men were not just talking about respectable marriage prospects, but also discussed the death of a child. The child in question was George's illegitimate baby. In this period George had an ongoing relationship with Margery, a lower status woman who worked in a pudding shop frequented by George and his friends; from these letters it is clear is that not only was Richard senior aware of the relationship, he was sympathetic to his son's loss: 'I told him all as it was, and he was right sorry for the death of the child.'[36]

In this letter, Richard junior and George appear to have been both in friendly confidence with their father and under his paternal authority. For elite men in this period, 'adolescence' was a life stage that extended well into the twenties, a period that allowed young men the licence for social and sexual conduct that would not befit mature men of means. At this point in their lives, the Cely sons were in a transitional life phase as they began to move from adolescence into manhood, their sexual behaviour (that is, having premarital sex with lower status women) and obedience to their father reflecting their place in the adolescent life stage, while their attempts to find wives indicate a shift toward attaining manhood.[37] According to medieval law, they were still under their father's authority, and paternal *auctoritas* was taken enormously seriously by both legal and moral authorities, with one medieval poem sombrely warning that filial disobedience will lead to the utter destruction of a youth's character.[38] However, the father–son relationship was also coded in terms of responsibility and obligation on both sides, for their mutual benefit. Fathers had a range of responsibilities toward their adult sons. If they expected their sons to help the family profit, they in turn were expected to help their sons establish their careers. Sometimes this could be in very practical ways, usually related to money. Less tangible but even more important was the ability of a father to extend his influence, making use of his connections to aid his son.

Assessing what best served the family as well as the son himself could be complicated. Marital negotiations at this level of society, for instance, involved weighing up the relative values of dowries and jointures and trying to ensure the best financial settlement for the family in the long term.[39] Fathers played a key role in running marital negotiations and could make or break a son's chances, as we will see later in this chapter. It was a serious family obligation – but it often was tempered with an understanding that sons had feelings that needed to be considered.[40] Richard senior was told about George's marriage prospects because his approval was required to make a match; but perhaps just as necessary for his son's future well-being were his father's affection and advice.

This initial analysis has given us some insights into the emotional landscape between the Cely brothers and their father, which is in this case was intimately bound up with the literal physical landscape of the family orchard. There is unfortunately no further surviving information about the Cely orchard, but it is very likely to have been not a rural space but a firmly urban or urban-adjacent location. Medieval London (and the surrounding towns that would one day be swallowed by London) was crisscrossed with gardens and orchards.[41] According to Christopher Dyer, the largest concentration of gardens in England was in the two miles southwest of London, from Holborn to Westminster. When Richards senior and junior went to inspect their new orchard, they likely visited somewhere within walking distance of their busy mercantile household in London. For medieval city-dwellers, gardens were not just a privilege but also a necessity, providing space for the growth of food. Rich officials and merchants had substantial pleasure gardens, but many ordinary townsfolk produced crops at, Dyer estimates, a far higher output than their rural counterparts. Restricted for space, city farmers were creative and used limited plots to intensively produce crops as varied as onions and flax – crops that could be grown and harvested around other employment and so did not require full time care.[42]

Already, then, we have an interesting image of the two Richards. Perhaps taking time out of a busy Friday, they met at their new orchard. Did they go there to inspect it, or did they plan to meet specifically to talk about George Cely's marital prospects and the sad loss of his baby? In literary and religious sources from this period, orchards were a ripe spot for both recreation and relaxation. The Cely family would undoubtedly have known Syon Abbey, which stood on the banks of the Thames in what is now Hounslow. The richest convent in England in the fifteenth century, Syon exerted significant cultural and economic influence, one example of which is the English translation of St Catherine of Siena's *Dialogue of Divine Revelation*, produced specifically for the convent – and entitled *The Orchard of Syon*.

This text included a new prologue specifically for the nuns of Syon. These nuns were imagined to be educated, high status women, and in the text they are depicted at prayer, study and recreation.[43] The orchard was considered to be an ideal place for this and is incorporated into the new prologue: 'In this orchard, when you would be comforted, you must walk and see both fruit and herbs.'

Annette Grise argues that *The Orchard of Syon* depicts the text itself as an orchard, where the nun-reader can go to 'disport … and walk about' in order to both relax and to exercise her mind.[44] The orchard space, both literal and figurative, is refreshing to body and mind, offering comfort to the spirit, and there seems to me to be a pleasing emphasis on the value of recreation to the well-being of the sisters of Syon, either through the imaginative play offered by reading or by actual walking outdoors.

Of course, there is no evidence that the Cely men would have known about an intellectual text intended for the spiritual edification of a female religious audience. However, the perceived benefits of an orchard must have been well known for the metaphor of the text to work for readers, and the casual way the metaphor is used suggests perhaps a broader social understanding that orchards were healthy garden environments. Other late medieval English texts similarly depict orchards as a place of recreation, contemplation and relaxation, which seems very likely to me to have been a literary reflection of real contemporary usage of orchard space and perhaps made such a place an ideal location for a busy father and son to catch up on each other's news.

Why not do this at home, since, after all, they were under the same roof? For the privileged modern reader, *home* may be associated with privacy, but in the hectic merchant households of the later fifteenth century a walk outdoors may well have offered a safer space for confidential conversation than inside the house. As Jeremy Goldberg has noted, it was very easy for conversations to be overheard in busy mercantile households, and court records are full of evidence presented by witnesses who had overheard supposedly secret conversations.[45] In homes where people shared beds, where many servants lived and where business was transacted in rooms adjacent to or shared with domestic spaces, it might be difficult to find a place to talk where a discussion would not be overheard. Given the sensitive nature of the Cely conversation – in particular, the news about the death of George's illegitimate child – it might have seemed prudent for father and son to go out for a walk to a place where they would not be overheard. Orchards, whether decorative or practical in purpose, were outside, but they were certainly not public – one of their defining features was that their space was usually delineated with a wall, or at least a ditch. It would seem like a good place to have what was undoubtedly a lengthy conversation.

It was also a conversation that dealt with a morally grey area that the Celys may have not wished to be overheard by anyone outside their intimate circle. While premarital affairs were common and indeed expected for men of George's age and status, siring bastards was still potentially socially shameful and seems to have required delicacy in discussion.[46] Meanwhile, although orchards were associated in the medieval imagination with spiritual reflection and replenishment, there was also a liminal element to orchards that suggests they were associated with potential breaches of the social and moral order, which perhaps made an orchard location particularly apt for discussing George's indiscretions.

The late medieval romance *Sir Gowther* survives in two late fifteenth-century manuscripts and details a very significant sexual encounter that takes place in an orchard. While we unfortunately have no idea what, if any, recreational reading the Celys did, Middle English romances were commonly read by families of their social rank, often being included in the household miscellanies that brought together all the texts a busy merchant or gentry home might need: primers for children, medical recipes, religious tracts, practical and political texts and stirring stories of knightly adventures. In *Sir Gowther*, the duke and duchess of Estryke are childless and the duchess prays for a child by any means necessary, which any reader of fairytales could tell you is a bad idea. Subsequently, a demon disguised as her husband waylays her in their orchard and she conceives a baby that will grow up to be a man of prodigious appetites of all kinds.

> In her orchard upon a day
> She met a man, the truth to say,
> That her love besought,
> And looked as much like her lord as could be;
> He laid her down under a tree,
> And with her his will he wrought.[47]

The orchard belongs to the castle but lies outside it, thus apparently offering an ideal space to be occupied by both demonic and prosaic presences. Perhaps this straddling of the barrier of the respectable and illicit was what made an orchard an ideal place for the Richards, senior and junior, to discuss George Cely's sexual escapades and their consequences. The orchard was probably at a little distance from their home but was a formalized and likely walled area of cultivation. In practical terms, it offered privacy from eavesdropping, perhaps specifically from the ear of Mrs. Cely, but it seems to do medieval people a disservice to imagine that all their decisions would be made purely pragmatically. Perhaps when Richard Cely thought 'I want to have a private conversation with my father', choosing an orchard as a location came as much out of imaginary spaces that had grown from his reading as from a practical desire to be out of his mother's earshot.

Let him walk with you: Making space for difficult conversations

Returning to the *Orchard of Syon* – from the profane to the sacred – it is striking that the text explicitly says that 'when you would be comforted', the reader should turn to the orchard. That text is talking about spiritual solace offered by the tranquillity of nature, but perhaps this garden space could also a place for a more human, familial tenderness. This certainly seems to have been the case for the Celys, where the intimacy shared by Richards senior and junior in their orchard was also extended to include George, who may have been at a spatial distance but through the medium of letters was incorporated into this moment of masculine solidarity.

An example from the Stonor letters suggests that a walk outdoors might have promised a more intimate connection between another father and son than could be afforded within the late medieval gentry house. In mid-1472 Thomas Mull, a retainer of the Stonor family, wrote to his master Thomas Stonor regarding Stonor's son and heir, William. While Mull was in service to Stonor, the relationship between them was not so separated by status as later servile relationships; Mull was a son-in-law to Thomas Stonor's stepfather and here serves as a reminder that within the late medieval household the lines between servants and family were frequently blurred.[48] A higher-status servant like Thomas Mull was expected to offer his master honest counsel and for that advice to be treated with respect and consideration. Mull had this to say about William Stonor:

> Call him forth [to go] with you when he is at home with you, and let him walk with you, and give [him] words of good comfort, and be a good father to him, as I certainly know you are … For, sir, he is disposed to be a muser and a studier.[49]

Like Richard and George Cely, William Stonor was a son in his early twenties who was beginning to make forays into the competitive medieval marriage market. At the point of this letter's composition, he was in advanced negotiations with a lady named Margery Blount. Not long before Mull's letter, William had written hopefully to his father, saying: 'I trust verily to almighty Jesus and to your good fatherhood that I shall speed well of my matter, for I have had comfortable treatment from my mistress.'[50] However, soon thereafter Mull in the role of intermediary wrote to William reminding him of how much his father had promised as a jointure and warned him that the amount was fair. But Margery was a young, rich widow – the jackpot in medieval marriage mart terms – and her family pressed for a much more generous settlement for her jointure. Thomas Stonor was unwilling to be moved to offer a higher sum, which was perhaps the sensible financial decision given Blount's family advised her to request an enormous three hundred marks.[51]

It was then that Thomas Mull suggested that father and son have a man-to-man chat, much as Richard Cely senior and junior did a few years later. We are given little indication of what kind of space in which Mull imagined William and Thomas Stonor would take their walk, although he was certainly thinking of a walk outside rather than the polite turn about the drawing room of a later age. The most obvious answer is that they would have walked in the garden, where they could discuss the finer points of William's marriage suit in the shadow of the house where he would one day bring a wife home. Cleaving close to the house would be particularly appropriate given the topic of conversation; while Mull suggested that William might need a private space to unburden his heart, the matters the Stonor men were discussing were as much questions of family economy as of human feeling and were necessarily closely bound up with the household.

Thomas Stonor was expected to comfort his son and be a 'good father', which in this context seems to mean that he should be sympathetic to his son's plight – perhaps more sympathetic than he had hitherto been – but this needed to be balanced alongside his wider responsibilities as head of the family. Mull described William as a 'muser and studier', perhaps indicating that the young man was prone to introspective moods, and the implication of the letter is that this setback had depressed his spirits. Mull's letter, then, might be read as a tacit criticism of Thomas's behaviour toward William; while it was the *paterfamilias*'s duty to safeguard the family finances, perhaps he has done so at the expense of taking care of his son's feelings. However, there is no suggestion in Mull's letter that he thought Stonor senior should reconsider his position on the finances available for the Blount match. While the head of the household might receive good counsel from his friends and retainers and was clearly expected to offer his son a sympathetic fatherly ear, in the end his role as head of the household and final arbiter in matters moral and financial was sacrosanct. We do not know if Thomas took Mull's advice and went on a walk with William, but in one way or another he put an end to the matter: William never mentioned Margery Blount again.[52]

Conclusion: Beyond the family hierarchy

While work on medieval fatherhood has moved beyond the traditional readings of medieval fathers as disinterested and distant, and noted that direct demonstrations of affection were not just possible but also desirable and expected, what has not been considered is the specific role of outdoor spaces in negotiating these relationships.

These two sets of letters demonstrate that the idea of carving out time for father–son bonding through intimate and sensitive conversation was known to late medieval men and may have been part of a wider discourse of the psychological as well as physical benefits of making use of outdoor spaces for reflection and communication: for inward thought and for outward connection. Thomas Mull's letter to Thomas Stonor suggests that the walk as a mechanism for facilitating father–son bonding was a known and indeed necessary method, and that if a father was not availing himself of the resources available to make himself act as a good father, a trusted friend could politely remind him of his duties. Richard Cely senior may not have needed such a reminder when he met with Richard junior; he was clearly both a fussier but also perhaps more openly affectionate father than Thomas Stonor, and it seems credible that he had suggested the walk to his son precisely for the purposes of grilling him about his brother's romantic prospects and social life. Despite these differences in family dynamics, it seems clear from both examples that fathers and sons walking together may have been a deliberately planned activity allowing for familial bonding and paternal advice-giving. These men understood that walking and spending time outdoors facilitated familial well-being.

The Stonors and Celys were discussing quite sensitive matters – but if they were using the outdoors for privacy, it seems likely that it was less to keep secrets and more because it permitted them a certain openness in their communication that was less possible within the busy gentry and mercantile household, where the father had to more clearly occupy the authoritative role of *paterfamilias*. Within households of this social rank, while affectionate relationships were common and indeed encouraged, the hierarchy of the household was also strictly enforced. While the two case studies used herein provide suggestive rather than definitive evidence, it seems likely that in outdoor spaces related to, but distinct from, the interior domestic space, elite medieval men were able to exercise a homosocial intimacy freed from some of the constraints of the regulated household. These garden spaces offered the possibility for emotional vulnerability, a blurring of hierarchical lines and an easing of social control. What medieval gardens may have offered, then, is indeed what the *Orchard of Syon* promised: a comfort not just of the body, but also of the heart.

Notes

1. Richard Cely junior to George Cely, 4 June 1481, *The Cely Letters*, ed. Alison Hanham (Early English Text Society, Original Series 273, 1975), no. 117, p. 107. All references from the Cely letters are from this edition, hereafter *CL*. Translations from Middle English are my own.
2. For a thorough overview of the scholarship on gardens, see Patricia Skinner and Theresa Tyers, 'Introduction: The Garden at the Intersection of Pleasure, Contemplation, and Cure,' in their edited collection *The Medieval and Early Modern Garden in Britain* (Routledge, 2018), 3–15.
3. See, for example, Laura L. Howes, 'Use and Reception', in Michael Leslie (ed.), *A Cultural History of Gardens in the Medieval Age* (Bloomsbury Academic, 2013), 75–100 (pp. 76–7, 83–4).

4. Amy Morgan, '"To play bi an orchardside": Orchards as Enclosures of Queer Space in Lanval and Sir Orfeo', in Skinner and Tyres, *The Medieval and Early Modern Garden*, 91–101.
5. See the excellent edited collection *Gender in Medieval Places, Spaces and Thresholds*, ed. Victoria Blud, Diane Heath and Einat Klafter (University of London Press, 2019).
6. See L. L. Howes, *Chaucer's Gardens and the Language of Convention* (University Press of Florida, 1997); Liz Herbert McAvoy, 'The Medieval Hortus Conclusus: Revisiting the Pleasure Garden', *Medieval Feminist Forum* 50.1 (2014), 51–74; Z. Çetiner-öktem, 'Medieval Gardens: Body, Space, and the Allure of the Locus amoenus', *Hacettepe Üniversitesi Edebiyat Fakültesi Dergisi* 36.2 (2019), 272–81.
7. A sample of many interesting articles: Amanda Richardson, '"Riding Like Alexander, Hunting Like Diana": Gendered Aspects of the Medieval Hunt and Its Landscape Settings in England and France', *Gender & History* 24.2 (2012), 253–70; S. Harlan-Haughey, *The Ecology of the English Outlaw in Medieval Literature: From Fen to Greenwood* (Routledge, 2016); I. B. Akçeşme, 'Ecocritical Insights into Medieval Epic Romances: A Comparative Study of Le Morte D'Arthur and Dede Korkut Stories', in Erdem Erinç, Ali Küçükler and Seniye Vural (eds), *Understanding Culture through Language and Literature* (Cambridge Scholars, 2018), 3–34.
8. There are many articles on monastic gardens; one I found useful in writing this chapter is Claire Noble's 'Spiritual Practice and the Designed Landscape: Monastic Precinct Gardens', *Studies in the History of Gardens & Designed Landscapes* 20.3 (2000), 197–205.
9. On domesticity, gender and the medieval household, a good starting point is 'Introduction. Medieval Domesticity: Home, Housing and Household', in Maryanne Kowaleski and P. J. P. Goldberg (eds), *Medieval Domesticity: Home, Housing and Household in Medieval England* (Cambridge University Press, 2011).
10. Teresa McLean, *Medieval English Gardens* (Dover, 1981); John Harvey, *Mediaeval Gardens* (Timber Press, 1981).
11. Skinner and Tyers, 'Introduction', 5.
12. Harvey, *Mediaeval Gardens*, 2.
13. Howes, 'Use and Reception', 75–83.
14. Walahfrid Strabo, *Hortulus*, trans. Raef Payne (Hunt Botanical Library, 1966), ll. 435–8. The volume is available online via The Hunt Institute for Botanical Documentation, whose website is worth looking at for a number of images from the manuscript itself. 'Hortulus', www.huntbotanical.org/admin/uploads/hibd-hortulus-facsimile.pdf (accessed 1 August 2024).
15. Johanna Bauman, 'Verbal Representations', in *A Cultural History of Gardens*, 117–35 (p. 119).
16. McAvoy, 'Gendered Spaces of Flourishing', 19.
17. Howes, 'Uses and Reception', 92.
18. Howes, 'Uses and Reception', 85–92.
19. Noble discusses how real pressed flowers, as well as images of flowers, are found in personal devotional texts, which may be indicative of their role in religious contemplation. Noble, 'Spiritual Practice and the Designed Landscape', 203.
20. Baumann, 'Verbal Representations', 122, and Noble, 'Spiritual Practice and the Designed Landscape', 202.
21. See, for instance, Felicity Huppert and Timothy So's discussion of 'flourishing' as an essential means of defining well-being, characterized by ten hedonic and eudaimonic aspects: F. A. Huppert and T. T. C. So, 'Flourishing across Europe: Application of a

New Conceptual Framework for Defining Well-Being', *Social Indicators Research* 110 (2013), 837–61, https://doi.org/10.1007/s11205-011-9966-7.
22. For a more detailed overview of these social categories and of the families discussed herein, see Rachel E. Moss, *Fatherhood and Its Representations in Middle English Texts* (D.S. Brewer, 2013), 16–24.
23. Chris Given-Wilson, *The English Nobility in the Late Middle Ages: The Fourteenth-Century Political Community* (Routledge and Kegan Paul, 1987), 1–2, 57; Peter Coss, *The Origins of the English Gentry* (Cambridge University Press, 2003), 239–54; K. B. McFarlane, *The Nobility of Later Medieval England* (Clarendon Press, 1973), 122–5.
24. Rosemary Horrox, 'Introduction', in Rosemary Horrox (ed.), *Fifteenth-Century Attitudes: Perceptions of Society in Late Medieval England* (Cambridge University Press, 1994), 1–2; Jennifer Kermode, *Medieval Merchants: York, Beverley and Hull in the Later Middle Ages* (Cambridge University Press, 2002), 25–7.
25. Michael Bennett, 'Careerism in Late Medieval England', in Joel Rosenthal and Colin Richmond (eds), *People, Politics and Community in the Later Middle Ages* (St Martin's Press, 1987), 19–39 (p. 34).
26. A postscript in a letter from Richard junior to his brother George reads: 'Plomtton p[r]ays you to delyuer thys byll to hys brother Nowell', *CL*, no. 99, p. 87. On William Stonor's wool trade connections, see 'Introduction' to *Kingsford Stonor Letters 1290–1483*, ed. Christine Carpenter (Cambridge University Press, 1996), 55 (this collection hereafter referred to as *SL*). The Celys may have at any rate known Elizabeth and her first husband Thomas Ryche, a mercer. Alison Hanham, *The Celys and Their World: An English Merchant Family of the Fifteenth Century* (Cambridge University Press, 1995), 196–7. The Calais wool trade was a relatively small world and it seems unlikely to me that anyone could have worked in it without at least some passing acquaintance with its other merchants.
27. *CL*, 'Introduction', xii.
28. Hanham, *The Celys and Their World*, 82–91.
29. *CL*, 'Introduction', viii–ix.
30. *SL*, 'Introduction', 50–63; Moss, *Fatherhood*, 20, 194.
31. Virginia Woolf, *The Common Reader* (Hogarth Press, 1925), 37; Moss, *Fatherhood*, 26–8.
32. Moss, *Fatherhood*, 73–81.
33. George A. Kennedy, *Classical Rhetoric and Its Christian and Secular Tradition* (University of North Carolina Press, 1999), 213–14, and Linda Ehrsam Voigts, 'A Letter from a Middle English Dictaminal Formulary in Harvard Law Library MS 43', *Speculum* 56 (1981), 575–81 (p. 577).
34. Susan Fitzmaurice, *The Familiar Letter in Early Modern English* (John Benjamins, 2002), 35, and Moss, *Fatherhood*, 75–6.
35. Pamela Nightingale, *A Medieval Mercantile Community: The Grocers' Company and the Politics and Trade of London, 1000–1485* (Yale University Press, 1995), 216, 527–8; Hanham, *The Celys and Their World*, 224–5; Jenny Kermode, *Medieval Merchants: York, Beverley and Hull in the Later Middle Ages* (Cambridge University Press, 1998), 168. I summarize this complex history in more depth in my article: Rachel E. Moss, 'Ready to Disport with You: Homosocial Culture amongst the Wool Merchants of Fifteenth-Century Calais', *History Workshop Journal* 86 (2018), 1–21.
36. I discuss this relationship in depth in my chapter Rachel E. Moss, 'An Orchard, a Love Letter, and Three Bastards: The Formation of Adult Male Identity in a

Fifteenth-Century Family, in John H. Arnold and Sean Brady (eds), *What Is Masculinity? Historical Dynamics from Antiquity to the Contemporary World* (Palgrave Macmillan, 2011), 226–44, and also Moss, *Fatherhood*, 175–6.

37. Moss, *Fatherhood*, 40–72.
38. 'Duodecim abusiones', l. 12, in Kathleen Forni (ed.), *The Chaucerian Apocrypha: A Selection* (Medieval Institute, 2005). For more on obedience, see Nicholas Orme, *Medieval Children* (Yale University Press, 1996), 82–3; Shulamith Shahar, *Childhood in the Middle Ages*, trans. Chaya Galai (Routledge, 1990), 169, and Moss, *Fatherhood*, 72–5, 87–93.
39. Moss, *Fatherhood*, 93–4, Keith Dockray, 'Why Did Fifteenth-Century English Gentry Marry?', in Michael C. E. Jones (ed.), *Gentry and Lesser Nobility in Late Medieval England* (Sutton, 1986), 61–80 (pp. 61–4, 73–6).
40. Moss, *Fatherhood*, 94–7.
41. Teresa McLean, *Medieval English Gardens* (Dover, 1981), 77–8.
42. Christopher Dyer, *Everyday Life in Medieval England* (Continuum, 2001), 21–127.
43. P. Hodgson and G. M. Liegey (eds), *The Orcherd of Syon* (Early English Text Society, Original Series 258) (Oxford University Press, 1966).
44. C. Annette Grisé, '"In the Blessid Vineȝerd of Oure Holy Saueour": Female Religious Readers and Textual Reception in the Myroure of Oure Ladye and the Orcherd of Syon', in Marion Glasscoe (ed.), *The Medieval Mystical Tradition: England, Ireland and Wales: Exeter Symposium VI* (D. S. Brewer, 1999), 193–213.
45. P. J. P. Goldberg, *Communal Discord, Child Abduction, and Rape in the Later Middle Ages* (Palgrave Macmillan, 2008), 106. For more on privacy, see Diana Webb, *Privacy and Solitude in the Middle Ages* (Hambledon Continuum, 2007), and Diane Shaw, 'The Construction of the Private in Medieval London', *Journal of Medieval and Early Modern Studies* 26.3 (1996), 447–66.
46. Moss, *Fatherhood*, 170–6.
47. *Sir Gowther*, in Anne Laskaya and Eve Salisbury (eds), *The Middle English Breton Lays* (Medieval Institute, 1995), ll. 68–72. The translation is mine. I have discussed this episode in the romance in *Fatherhood*, 64–5, and Rachel E. Moss, '"Let Him Walk with You": Telling Stories about Fifteenth-Century Men, and the Women They Left Behind', *Medieval Feminist Forum* 58.1 (2022), 128–45.
48. Mull was married to Richard Drayton's daughter. See Elizabeth Noble, *The World of the Stonors: A Gentry Family* (Boydell, 2009), 173. On late medieval service, see Michael Hicks, *English Political Culture in the Fifteenth Century* (Routledge, 2002), and Horrox, 'Service', in *Fifteenth Century Attitudes.*
49. This letter is undated but in the context of other letters in the collection, it is likely to have been composed in May or June 1472.
50. *SL*, no. 122, p. 213.
51. A mark is two-thirds of a pound, so this is nearly 200 pounds, which would have been an extremely generous settlement for a family of Stonor's rank. On jointures, see Barbara J. Harris, *English Aristocratic Women 1450–1550: Marriage and Family, Property and Careers* (Oxford University Press, 2002), 49–51.
52. Before we get too caught-up in sympathy for William, it is worth noting that he went on to marry three times, each match more elevated than the last, and can by medieval standards be thought to have succeeded admirably in the marriage market.

3

'In your well-being is cheife felicity': Physical, social and emotional health in seventeenth-century family letters

Emma Marshall

In the summer of 1653, the young gentlewoman Anne Pole (née Newdigate) was visiting her parents at Arbury Hall in Warwickshire. It seems that her husband German, to whom she had been married for three years, had been with her before returning alone to the couple's home of Radbourne Hall in Derbyshire. On 3 August, Anne wrote to German, 'deare Love … I am & have bin ever since you went, very restlesse for feare you should not bee well after your journey … I must beg of you to lett me heare from you how you doe by the post for in your wellbeing is cheife felicity'.[1] German's reply is lost to us, but Anne's anxious pleadings raise an intriguing question: what did 'well-being' mean to seventeenth-century letter-writers?

Senses of 'well-being' in this period have received little critical attention from historians. It is usually mentioned only cursorily and as a synonym for bodily health. While Ilana Krausman Ben-Amos, for example, draws parallels between gifts of medicine or caregiving and epistolary enquiries about 'well-being', she does not interrogate contemporary understandings of this term.[2] Linda Pollock, meanwhile, implicitly equates 'well-being' to physical health in her studies of early modern parent–child relations.[3] 'Welfare', on the other hand, is a more popular topic of historiographical enquiry. Yet it has been explored primarily in the context of poor relief, support for maimed soldiers and war widows and other forms of provision, often localized, for society's needy.[4] Keith Snell has written about the eighteenth- and nineteenth-century parish as 'the locus for welfare', while Steve Hindle similarly terms its early modern predecessor a 'welfare republic'.[5] A parallel branch of scholarship identifies welfare provision as a form of governance. Stemming from notions of paternalism or patronage, elite masters, landlords and employers cared for the bodies of their subordinates to increase productivity and bolster their own reputation and hegemony as heads of the hierarchy. Social, cultural and political power went hand in hand and had welfare at their heart.[6] Work in the 1980s and 1990s also discussed various kinds of informal domestic carework, performed by families and neighbours, as 'welfare'. However, it largely focused on poor families and their tactics against economic hardship.[7] Elite families' concern about their own welfare has been overlooked by comparison.

This chapter argues that 'well-being' and 'welfare', as invoked in personal letters, referred to the complex entanglement of individuals' physical and emotional health and its relationship to the social cohesion of the gentry family. As such, these terms highlight seventeenth-century understandings and expressions of, and challenges to, notions of connectedness and meanings of family membership in this period. This study is based on an extensive analysis of elite familial correspondence held in archives across England. The aforementioned Pole family, who were especially fond of writing about 'well-being', figures prominently.

Letters were vitally important to the gentry, who sat just below the aristocracy in the social hierarchy and whose lifestyles changed significantly during the seventeenth century. Gentlemen and women regularly travelled between London and the countryside to fulfil political or financial obligations, or to seek medical aid or sociable company, developing a mental world of 'national or regional dimensions'.[8] Sociability, often contemporarily called 'company', was a facet of gentry identity which grew in importance in this period, closely linked to urbanization.[9] By the turn of the eighteenth century, London was the peak of England's 'top-heavy urban hierarchy' and the place to see and be seen.[10] Yet even among those who did not own or rent townhouses in the metropolis, the social practice of staying with friends and family across the country structured daily life.[11]

As both a catalyst for and a product of people's broadening horizons, the period under study here also witnessed a boom in communications infrastructure and services. Between 1637 and 1715, regular carrying services in and out of London doubled in capacity. Following the Glorious Revolution in 1688, there was an increase in the number of letters carried by the Penny Post, and Paul Slack estimates that within 10 miles of the General Post Office, the Post was transporting nearly 1 million letters per year by 1700.[12] As gentry lives became ever-more peripatetic, epistolary correspondence took on a new meaning as the lifeblood of dispersed families. Prolonged separation across wide distances could strain social bonds. Frequent letter-writing was an attempt to bridge these gulfs. During illness, its importance increased still further. When one could not be physically present with a sick loved one and witness their changing condition, letters were necessary substitutes. Did correspondence offer comfort for sufferer and/or family members at these times? How were senses of individual and group well-being fostered or challenged by this medium of communication?

This chapter will probe these questions by considering the intersections of physical and emotional health, letter-writing and receiving and family cohesion and prosperity in the seventeenth century. It begins by examining how epistolary news of physical welfare or good health, or concern for it, produced emotional well-being and satisfaction. It also highlights hitherto undiscussed meanings of 'welfare' and its link to 'care' within letters and letters' status as expressions of care in and of themselves. The second section explores how, by contrast, 'fellow-feeling' meant that letters could produce emotional or even bodily distress rather than comfort. Examining the shared language used to convey and respond to news of bad health, it argues that receiving news of illness, but also no news at all, could threaten the sense of individual well-being and that of the family as a social unit. Finally, I suggest a particular class element at play in such feelings and discussions of 'well-being', which had special meanings for the seventeenth-century gentry.

Welfare, care and fellow feeling

In the past, as today, news of a family member's good health or recovery from sickness was met with great happiness and relief. This was part of the socio-emotional bond between loved ones, often known as 'fellow-feeling'.[13] In the context of letters, Sarah Pearsall sees 'fellow-feeling' or 'sympathy' as a shared 'fantasy' between writer and reader 'in which time and distance are obliterated' and an impression of intimacy is created.[14] Gary Schneider likewise emphasizes the imagination and emotion inherent in letter exchange, interpreting early modern correspondence not solely as communication, but as 'communion'.[15] This idea has recently been developed by Karen Harvey, who argues that letters played a central role in the creation and sustenance of familiarity, intimacy and compassion in the eighteenth century. She states that 'forging sympathy', or recognizing another person's physical or emotional feelings, 'was arguably the overriding purpose of many familial epistolary relationships'.[16] Yet the special role of letters and letter-writing in this form of social, physical and emotional communication requires further attention. I wish to develop Harvey's argument that letters could be the vehicle of and the catalyst for sympathy, which was 'constructed and affirmed through discussions of the body' in particular, through an examination of 'welfare'. The complex meanings of this term have been overlooked but help us to unpick the tangled relationship of sympathy, family and health in letters.

Correspondents often stated that their emotional satisfaction was conditional upon the physical well-being of a family member. In February 1626, Thomas Knyvett was away from home on political business when his newborn son Nathaniel tragically died. Thomas's wife Katherine had apparently also been unwell following the birth. He wrote to her lamenting their infant and told her that 'thy welfare (which I hear is in a good forwardness againe) is the only happiness I vallewe in this world'.[17] Here, 'welfare' seemed to denote primarily physical health, referring to Katherine's recovery from childbirth and her lying-in period. However, it may also have carried connotations of mental and emotional stability, as Katherine grieved for the loss of her baby. Thomas, moreover, drew a positive correlation between his wife's welfare and his own happiness, demonstrating his love and concern and emphasizing the couple's strong emotional connection *in absentia*. Sir Ralph Verney's adult son Edmund similarly recognized the connection between health and satisfaction in a letter to his father in February 1678/9, when Ralph was suffering from an ague, or serious and recurring fever, in London. Edmund wrote 'truly for yr welfare & myne are so complicated together, that should you Miscarry (wch God forbid) I could Take no >more< joy in this world without you'.[18] 'Miscarry', in this context, was a synonym for 'die'.[19]

To what extent were such expressions simply polite epistolary conventions, or did they represent 'genuine', felt emotions? From a distance of over three hundred years, it is problematic to speculate and impossible to know for certain. However, 'fellow-feeling' was thought to have very real effects; happiness was shared between individuals, but so was emotional and even physical pain and suffering.[20] There was no clear distinction between body and mind in seventeenth-century medical or lay understandings. Disturbances of the 'passions', sometimes defined as emotions in modern scholarship but also closely linked to fluxes, flows and imbalances of the four humours, could affect a person's body, mind and soul simultaneously.[21] In addition, the act of writing about a feeling could engender it. In this way, letters could be catalysts for 'real' sensations by functioning as 'emotives', identified by William Reddy as an emotional expression with the ability to change both speaker (or indeed, writer) and addressee.[22]

However, the above statements, particularly that of Edmund Verney, were also calls to action with a distinct social function. Edmund specified that his own 'joy' was dependent on receiving positive news of his father's health, as he added, 'I Live in Hopes of Better Tydings of you by the next Returne.'[23] With this comment, Edmund subtly reminded Ralph of his letter-writing obligations. During sickness, when a person's condition could change in the blink of an eye, it was vital to maintain regular communication and ensure satisfaction on both sides. Serious illness threatened to disrupt social, economic and emotional dependences within families and to transform identities. Sir Ralph Verney was Baronet of Middle Claydon, an engaged and active landlord, a respected master of many servants and a justice of the peace and deputy lieutenant, among other political roles.[24] Edmund, as his father's heir, was keenly aware of the responsibilities which would fall to him upon Ralph's demise. When the prospect of death loomed, correspondence informed recipients of their own changing position within the family and wider world, as well as the writer's current state of health. Letters thereby imposed a sense of order and mitigated instability and uncertainty.

Historians of early modern England have primarily focused on the social, political and economic meanings of 'welfare' within discourses of state and community. In his analysis of central authority and its relationship with the localities, Steve Hindle discussed the notion of the 'commonweal' or 'commonwealth'.[25] Across all levels of society, individuals and groups were bound to one another by bonds of mutuality and obligation. Individual lives were woven into a web of relationships, both giving to and receiving from others. For example, a gentleman landlord provided homes, work and other necessities for his tenants, whose social deference and political loyalty in turn upheld his elite status. The 'commonwealth', in the macro sense of the term, therefore 'created cohesion by evoking a sense of identification with and obligation to others' and helped to shape personal and social identities.[26] But as an entity comprising shared burdens and benefits, its ideals also applied to the family unit.[27] Interestingly, both the state and family were depicted as a 'body politic' in political and literary discourse, particularly in the earlier part of the century. In text and image, the king or father was represented as the 'head' of an organism which constituted distinct yet interdependent parts, relying upon one another to function effectively.[28] 'Body politics' were significant in more ways than one for families; individual welfare, including physical health, shaped relationships and roles. The family was a network or 'commonwealth' of individuals whose bodily and emotional well-being depended upon and contributed to that of one another. When good health prevailed, or care and communication facilitated the shared experience of sickness, it produced a sense of group cohesion.

Family members often linked welfare and well-being to 'care' in correspondence and specifically equated being 'careful' with the maintenance of physical health. Alan Macfarlane sees phrases such as 'be carefull of your self' in letters as straightforward expressions of 'tenderness', affection and concern.[29] However, the Pole family letters hint at a more complex, cyclical relationship between physical health, emotional well-being and familial communication, which is difficult but important to unpick. In September 1660, when Anne and German Pole were again staying at her parents' home of Arbury, German was 'troubled' with one of his recurring colds. This subsequently developed into measles, a potentially life-threatening condition. Anne described German's gradual recovery to his mother, Millicent, reassuring her that '[German] is much better now, I shall not faile to give you an account next post how hee is & if hee were not in a very hopeful condition I could not write my selfe, I am & shall bee more carefull of him, then of my owne life, preferring his wellbeing before all this world can afford'.[30] As used by Anne Pole, 'careful' implied a kind of sustained attention to and nurture of the body when health was threatened. This encouraged physical well-being, which in turn promoted mental and emotional health. Moreover, Anne seemed to associate the term with epistolary practice, as she discussed letter-writing, being 'careful' and well-being in the same sentence. Her comment might suggest that care was manifested not only in emotional concern and physical assistance, but in writing about the sick individual and communicating their condition to other family members. Well-being was a collective concern; an individual's personal state of health was shared with others as an important form of social and emotional intimacy.

Individuals were also entreated to be 'careful' of themselves. Three years prior to German's measles, again with awareness of the potential danger of colds in mind, Anne Pole told her husband, 'I shall heartily pray for the continuance of your wellbeing, and must intreat you to bee carefull of your selfe … I am very much afraid you should take cold.' She added, 'I pray you send me truely word how you doe', hinting, liked Edmund Verney, at the centrality of letter-writing and honest communication to personal peace of mind during illness.[31] The threat posed by one person's ill health to the emotional well-being of their relatives is also evident in a letter sent by the aforementioned Sir Ralph Verney to his 'cozen' Mall Eure in 1658. Mall's mother, an aunt or cousin of Ralph's, was unwell with an unspecific illness. Ralph explicitly invoked the notion of care in his note: 'I know you will bee very carefull of her, but I feare she still is, as she ever was, too carelesse of her selfe.' He asked Mall to urge her mother to prioritize her own health, 'at least for our sakes, whose happinesse >& contentment< depends soe much uppon her welfare'.[32] The idea of welfare engendering happiness recurred here and was achieved through being 'carefull', as opposed to 'careless'. Care seemed to be measured in degrees and could be shown to another or to oneself; it was the act of preserving health through sensible, cautious activity. Ralph seemed to imply that to be careless was a form of selfishness, a quiet rejection of the communal obligations and goals which shaped family life. If Mall's mother did not maintain her health for her own benefit, she should do it 'for our sakes'. Her family's emotional welfare 'depended' upon her bodily welfare. Furthermore, Mall herself had a familial duty to perform which overrode existing tensions with her cousin. Ralph pointedly added in his letter, 'I know too well by my late experience, that you are noe ways [inclinate?] to hearken to some of my desiers, & propositions, yect in this concerning your deare Mothers health, I doubt not but you will most readily conceive with.'[33] The cause of this ill feeling is unclear, but Ralph set health apart as a matter on which consensus and cooperation was vital.

Letters about health were contemporarily viewed as artefacts of care, or tangible expressions of attention and concern, and should be approached as such by historians. In 1652, Anne Pole's brother, Richard Newdigate, expressed thanks for her 'extraordinary love towards mee & my brother expressed in your frequent inquiries concerning our health & welfare'.[34] He clearly viewed discourse about 'health & welfare' as a badge of familial belonging and confirmation of affection. Moreover, these emotional benefits meant that when a person was unwell, letters became a kind of social, or even medical, sustenance. In 1701, the elderly father of Irish politician Alan Brodrick was suffering from a great 'weakness', 'numnesse' and 'swelling'. Alan told his brother St John, who had a fractious relationship with their father, that 'a line from you would more comfort him then any other cordial'.[35] Like Ralph Verney's letter to his cousin, this note reminded a relative of their responsibilities to both care and communicate during a third party's sickness. The idea of letter-as-medicine was echoed by the sick themselves. In September 1684, Charles Coke, a distant relative of the Poles, was slowly recovering from an unspecified complaint. He wrote to his nephew, 'no Cordiall at present refreshes me so much as the acceptable newes of all your well-being wch yours of ye 10th instant afforded me yesterday'.[36] Here, epistolary news of well-being encouraged similar feelings in letter recipients; in line with fellow-feeling, good health bred good health, and correspondence was the channel through which it was achieved. Such language may be viewed simply as epistolary custom. But given our understanding of the mind–body connection in early modern theory and fellow-feeling's ability to cause perceptible emotional and even bodily changes, we should not underestimate the power of letters in this context. If family members could not be present to physically tend to their sick, their letters were nonetheless therapeutic texts with the ability to offer relief and comfort.[37]

Bad news, silence and the threat to well-being

Of course, there was a flip side to this coin. As noted above, 'sympathy' or 'fellow-feeling' was not an abstract phenomenon, but recognized in early modern medicine and quotidian life as manifesting in both bodily and affective symptoms. Crucially, it had negative as well as positive effects. People could become physically ill in response to their loved ones' sicknesses, often experiencing similar symptoms.[38] For instance, the eighteenth-century philosopher David Hume defined sympathy as the sharing of pleasure *or* pain and understood fellow-feeling as bodily responses to another person's suffering.[39] Because letters were the frequent carriers of unfortunate news, the connectedness fostered by correspondence could sometimes threaten, rather than encourage, well-being.

Consequently, the same language was used to both communicate and respond to illness. Sufferers of various ailments frequently described their symptoms as making them 'uneasy'. In the late seventeenth century, perennial invalid Anne Pelham told her cousin Sir Edward Harley that she was 'so troubled wth my cough & hoarsnes yt I am very uneasie'.[40] Shortly before her death in 1708, Anne Chaytor similarly wrote from Yorkshire that her persistent cough 'gives me such a soreness in my right side makes me very uneasy' in a letter to her father William, jailed in London's Fleet Prison.[41] Additionally, in one of the many letters about health which traversed his family's Irish and English estates, Alan Brodrick told his brother that 'I may have taken cold and that may contribute much to my uneasiness'.[42] Such terminology was echoed by correspondents to describe their own emotional reactions. From her home in London, Katherine Mordaunt told her brother John, based in Warwickshire, that she 'cannot be easey to be from you when you are not well'.[43] Some decades later, in 1739, Susannah Thorp was 'very unease ever since' hearing her cousin was ill, even though they lived relatively close to one another, in East and North Yorkshire respectively.[44] 'Trouble' had a similar double meaning, as illustrated by the Harley family. In a late seventeenth-century letter to his wife, Sir Edward Harley wrote that 'ye Gout began in my Left Ankle next day twas more troublesome', while his cousin Anne Pelham was 'troubled wth swellings … & of late I am troubled wth my throat' in 1691.[45] They also used the term in response to news of sickness. In 1664, Edward was 'much troubled at my brothers faynting fitts', while thirty years later Edward's daughter told him that 'it is a great trouble to hear of ye continuance of your painfull distemper'.[46] This linguistic mirroring is evidence of sympathy or fellow-feeling and perhaps a particular epistolary technique to communicate this. However, it also highlights the blurred boundary between individual and familial well-being. Through its textualization in letters, suffering was not confined to the body. It could spread, sometimes across many miles, to cause emotional and possibly also physical distress to distant correspondents.

Receiving bad health news was deeply worrying, and this worry manifested in the overlap between emotional, mental and physical senses of 'trouble' and 'unease'. However, the absence of correspondence, or of news of health within it, also compromised personal and familial senses of well-being. Delays and silences were a common feature of seventeenth-century correspondence. They had both social and structural causes; the demands of family life and carework, along with an unreliable postal system, could disrupt epistolary communication. Moreover, as a skilled physical activity which required a clear head, steady hand, sharp eyesight and the ability to sit up, letter-writing was difficult when unwell.[47] In 1631, Joan St. John told her grandmother that she had been 'in so much pain for almost a weeke' with toothache, which had been cured by having the offending tooth drawn. Even so, she ended her letter with an apology: 'I dare not be too bold in righting for fear I should bringe the ruine into my teeth againe, therefor I beseech you pardon my brevity'.[48] Writing's ability to intensify pain, either directly or by drawing the writer's attention to it, often prompted sick individuals to employ a family member or literate servant as an amanuensis.[49] This, in turn, meant that letters written in a sufferer's own hand held a special significance. In her study of love letters, Fay Bound argues that by 'representing the self as a suffering being, emotion became a commodity to be purchased or exchanged'.[50] She also states that 'the physical act of letter writing was suggestive of the giving of the self' and 'could be exploited for rhetorical effect'.[51] The same can be said for letters about sickness, in which bodily distress was imbued with social meaning. For instance, when Anne Pelham wrote that 'my stomach hath bine so swelled yt writing is a greatter disturbance then any person no present can imagine … I never writ with greater difficulty' to her cousin Sir Edward Harley, she stressed that she was sacrificing her own comfort to maintain communication.[52] She valued her relationship with Edward, and her familial obligations to him, over her personal well-being; in some situations, physical and social welfare were incompatible, rather than complementary.

Susan Whyman speaks of a 'psychological dependence upon letters' in the eighteenth century, even describing it as an 'addiction'.[53] This term implicitly emphasizes the physical and emotional impact of letter-writing and reading, as discussed above. For the upper classes, this dependence took root in the seventeenth century. The Verney family archive, for example, holds thirty thousand personal letters dating from the 1630s to the mid-eighteenth century.[54] Long before 1700, the Verneys were sending and receiving several letters a day. Sarah Pearsall notes that not receiving an expected letter could prompt 'enormous, stomach-churning anxiety', again hinting, perhaps unconsciously, at the letter's power to cause perceptible physiological sensations.[55] We may return here to Anne and German Pole. On 13 October 1653, Anne wrote to her husband: 'I cannot but feare that you are not well because I heard not from you this post [… this] doth extreamely trouble mee, therefore I must beg of you to lett mee heare how you doe assoone as you can, for I am & shall bee, in a restlesse condition till I heare from you, I pray thee be carefull of your selfe for my sake.'[56] Anne's pleading note reiterates the oft-repeated connections between illness, communication (or lack of it) and emotional distress and exemplifies the intense anxiety which met epistolary silences. In particular, Anne's mentions of 'fear', 'trouble', 'restlessness' and self-care as a familial obligation echo themes already discussed in this chapter and neatly illustrate the cyclical nature of well-being within families.

Moreover, recipients were aware that letters were carefully constructed, 'performative' texts and not unmediated reflections of real life.[57] As such, they were unsatisfactory substitutes for in-person witnessing and interaction when illness struck. Clare Brant notes that correspondents used strategies of both 'expressiveness and concealment' in their letters, and yet little has been said about sick writers deliberately withholding or bending the truth about their condition.[58] This was, however, a common tactic, or at least it was suspected to be so by others. Writers may have intended to protect their family members from worry, but their silences paradoxically caused more anxiety, suspicion and frustration.[59]

In January 1701, the Tory politician Sir John Mordaunt and his younger wife, Lady Penelope, were temporarily absent from each other. During a stay in London, Penelope had been afflicted by gout across her body. Although she noted in a letter to her husband that her hand was 'a litle beter' than it had been, her 'stomack and teeth are worse, for I have it in all these places; and can't sleepe anights'.[60] At their country estate of Walton Hall in Warwickshire, John received his wife's news badly, replying 'some expressions in your last [letter] trouble me exceedingly'.[61] His fears were magnified by the death of the couple's infant daughter that same month, which had devastated Penelope. In another letter from the same period, John told his wife that 'I am under great cares & apprehencions for you, doubting you give me ye best Acco[un]t of yor selfe, & that you may be worse then you represent to me'.[62] However, this suspicion, prompted by sparse accounts of health, was mutual. In 1698, following John's insistence that 'I am extreamly well & find not ye least cold or disorder upon me', Penelope replied: 'I have been very uneasie My Dearest ever since I rec[eive]d yors of ye 27th … I feare it is worse then you represent it to me … I shall not sleep quiccly until I heare from you again & that you are better'.[63] In the Mordaunts' correspondence, we see the familiar language of 'trouble' and 'unease' as emotional reactions to news of bad health. But again, such sensations were not purely affective; Penelope was unable to sleep for fear that her husband was concealing his poor state of health. Sleep was one of the six 'non-naturals', widely understood as the foundation of physical health in the seventeenth century, and lack of sleep and changes in night-time routines were often cited as causes of illness.[64] Penelope's poor-quality slumber thereby threatened her own health. As she lay awake, dwelling on her husband's latest letter and imagining his sufferings, her emotional and bodily well-being likewise declined.

Well-being, class and gender

This chapter has focused on the seventeenth-century gentry, a privileged social stratum who had the education, skills and money needed to regularly write and send letters. But did perceptions and discourses of well-being have a unique significance for this group? What was the precise connection between class and health in this context? Some tentative suggestions can be drawn from the evidence discussed above.

In their work on early modern Italy, Sandra Cavallo and Tessa Storey state that 'the focus on physical characteristics of the gentleman brought with it renewed attention on the care the body required in order to appear to be perfect and glowing with health'. Consequently, they argue, 'wellbeing was a precondition of gentility'.[65] However, this statement requires further explanation and nuance. Cavallo and Storey seem to interpret well-being as bodily health, which was key to establishing and expressing identity within the social hierarchy. But as the present study has argued, well-being was not simply a personal state, limited to one individual. Rather, it encompassed physical, emotional *and* social health and prosperity. Crucially, well-being was deeply enmeshed in family relations; it was contingent not only upon adherence to regimens and the maintenance of a healthy domestic environment, but upon the fulfilment of obligations of 'care'.[66] Gentility, then, was partly maintained through the social cohesion of the family as achieved through mutual mental and physical welfare. One had to personally care for one's own body through such practices as washing, resting and eating well, but also had to pay attention to and be 'careful' of the bodies of loved ones.

Moreover, information about the body should be regularly and honestly shared through correspondence, and assurance of other people's good health helped to maintain one's own well-being. Historians of the letter have frequently grappled with its situation on the boundary of 'public' and 'private', with Brant arguing for its occupation of a third, overlapping zone which she terms 'personal'.[67] While letters may have been intended for a particular recipient, they were often read aloud or circulated among others. Letters could also be written by more than one person, as in the frequent use of amanuenses during sickness.[68] This chapter has highlighted another, less obvious way in which letters about the body, which may seem to modern readers an intensely personal subject, had very public significance. News about one person's health affected that of their loved ones, and this health in turn shaped the ways in which gentlemen and women were viewed by wider society. Well-being influenced the gentry's reputation as socially and politically active figures of authority.

Finally, we might ask whether understandings and discourses of well-being and welfare were gendered among the seventeenth-century gentry. Lisa Smith argues that while women performed much of the quotidian medical and carework in homes, theories of household management and social order also obliged husbands and fathers to oversee the physical welfare of their families. This could include calling for physicians and deciding on treatments.[69] Similarly, Hannah Newton finds that many fathers and mothers were equally involved in tending to their sick children. Such scholarship shows that men and women alike performed 'carework', broadly defined as physical and emotional support for the sick.[70] My sources support these conclusions; correspondence demonstrates men and women's shared concern with bodily, and indeed emotional and social, well-being. In a kind of epistolary carework, wives and husbands, mothers and fathers, daughters and sons and sisters and brothers alike exchanged health news, emotional expressions and reminders of obligations to be both 'careful' and communicative.

Conclusion

In recent years, we have seen for ourselves the importance of communication to feelings of well-being, especially during illness. During the Covid-19 pandemic and resulting lockdowns, the threat to mental health, usually nourished by social interaction, was an important secondary concern to the virus itself. Separation, isolation and distant communication, now as then, can influence the ways we experience, interpret and share our bodily and emotional sensations within families.[71] Yet telephone calls and instant digital and video messaging mitigate some of the problems faced by our ancestors. Letter-writers' inscriptions of sick and caregiving bodies were not unmediated snapshots of 'authentic' experience, but constructed textual depictions. This shaped the expression of emotion, trust, intimacy and familiarity and the ways in which it was received, within correspondence.

Well-being and welfare were collective concerns navigated across distance through letters in the seventeenth century. This paper has argued that historians must continue to deconstruct boundaries between the medical, emotional and social to better understand seventeenth-century communal experiences of illness, especially as experienced through letter-writing and reading. The gentry's preoccupation with health, and epistolary discourse about 'well-being' in particular, demonstrates that 'body politics' were central to familial interests in this period. In a recent volume on writing and embodiment in the long eighteenth century, Goldsmith, Haggerty and Harvey argue that epistolary discussions about illness and well-being created and sustained 'intimacy and sympathy'. However, they add that such discourses also 'anchored and legitimised the writers' place in society, and particularly in relation to the recipient of the letter'.[72] Correspondence about health and welfare was not simply an epistolary convention, nor solely a token of love and concern used to overcome physical distance between writer and recipient. Rather, it confirmed shared membership of a family, usually the primary unit through which social status and economic prosperity were achieved and maintained. In this way, the body was the fulcrum around which anxieties about personal, familial and social identity revolved.

At least as it was used explicitly in correspondence, the term 'well-being' had a wider resonance than simply physical health. One person's emotional state fluctuated in relation to another's bodily state. In an age in which the body was thought to have a porous boundary with and be highly responsive to its physical and social environment, and corporeal metaphors symbolized the commonwealth, a person's body did not belong to them alone. It was public property, a common currency, a shared familial asset. One person's illness, incapacity and death could threaten group stability, throwing finances into disarray and destabilizing lines of inheritance. Of course, it also caused intense emotional suffering which could be manifested in physical symptoms through fellow-feeling. Interest and emotion, the twin drivers of family life, were inextricably entwined here.[73] Individuals could nurture their own or one another's well-being through care and carefulness. And during separations, letter-writers had a duty to keep one another informed of their well-being, or lack of. Good news about health enhanced the recipient's own sense of well-being; of relief, contentment, or 'felicity', to use Anne Pole's term. By contrast, news of ill health or an absence of news endangered well-being in recipients. It sparked fear, anxiety and restlessness, as the 'trouble' or 'uneasiness' of the sick body was mirrored in family members' emotions. Consequently, well-being had communal as well as personal significance and cannot be separated from understandings of the family. Edmund Verney's remark to his sick father succinctly expresses this complex relationship: 'Truly yr welfare and myne are so complicated together.'[74]

Notes

1. Matlock, Derbyshire Record Office (RO), D5557/2/18/34.
2. Ilana Krausman Ben-Amos, *The Culture of Giving: Informal Support and Gift-Exchange in Early Modern England* (Cambridge University Press, 2008), 147–50.
3. Linda A. Pollock, *Forgotten Children: Parent–Child Relations 1500–1700* (Cambridge University Press, 1983), 124; Linda Pollock, 'Parent–Child Relations', in David I. Kertzer and Marzio Barbagli (eds), *The History of the European Family, Vol. I: Family Life in Early Modern Times, 1500–1789* (Yale University Press, 2001), 191–221 (pp. 194–6).
4. The literature on these subjects is extensive and cannot be cited in full here. However, see, for examples, Steve Hindle, 'A Sense of Place? Becoming and Belonging in the Rural Parish, 1550–1650', in Alexandra Shepard and Phil Withington (eds), *Communities in Early Modern England* (Manchester University Press, 2000), 96–114; Steve Hindle, *The State and Social Change in Early Modern England, c.1550–1640* (Palgrave Macmillan, 2002), 171; Stewart Beale, 'Military Welfare in the Midland

Counties during and after the British Civil Wars, 1642–c.1700', *Midland History* 45.1 (2020), 18–35, https://doi.org/10.1080/0047729X.2020.1712080.

5. Keith Snell, *Parish and Belonging: Community, Identity and Welfare in England and Wales, 1700–1950* (Cambridge University Press, 2006), 18; Hindle, 'A Sense of Place?' 99.
6. Nicholas Abercrombie and Stephen Hill, 'Paternalism and Patronage', *British Journal of Sociology* 27.4 (1976), 413–29, https://doi.org/10.2307/590182; G. E. Mingay, *The Gentry: The Rise and Fall of a Ruling Class* (Longman, 1976), 190; J. V. Beckett, *The Aristocracy in England, 1660–1914* (Basil Blackwell, 1986), 353–4; Keith Wrightson, 'The Politics of the Parish in Early Modern England', in Paul Griffiths, Adam Fox and Steve Hindle (eds), *The Experience of Authority in Early Modern England* (Macmillan, 1996), 10–46, (p. 21); Douglas Hay, 'Patronage, Paternalism, and Welfare: Masters, Workers, and Magistrates in Eighteenth-Century England', *International Labour and Working-Class History* 53 (1998), 27–48 (p. 27), https://doi.org/10.1017/S014754790001365X; Hindle, *The State and Social Change*, 171; Brodie Waddell, *God, Duty and Community in English Economic Life, 1660–1720* (Boydell Press, 2012), 117; Andy Wood, 'Deference, Paternalism and Popular Memory in Early Modern England', in Steve Hindle, Alexandra Shepard and John Walter (eds), *Remaking English Society: Social Relations and Social Change in Early Modern England* (Boydell Press, 2013), 233–54 (p. 240).
7. Peter Laslett, 'Family, Kinship and Collectivity as Systems of Support in Pre-industrial Europe: Consideration of the "Nuclear-Hardship" Hypothesis', *Continuity and Change* 3.2 (1988), 153–75, https://doi.org/10.1017/S026841600000093X; Peregrine Horden, 'Household Care and Informal Networks: Comparisons and Continuities from Antiquity to the Present', in Peregrine Horden and Richard Smith (eds), *The Locus of Care: Families, Communities, Institutions and the Provision of Welfare Since Antiquity* (Routledge, 1998), 21–67.
8. Felicity Heal, *Hospitality in Early Modern England* (Clarendon, 1990), 152; Felicity Heal and Clive Holmes, *The Gentry in England and Wales* (Macmillan, 1994), 188, 288–9, 311–15; Keith Wrightson, *English Society, 1580–1680* (Oxford University Press, 2002), 41.
9. Phil Withington, 'Company and Sociability in Early Modern England', *Social History* 32.3 (2007), 291–307 (p. 297), https://doi.org/10.1080/03071020701425338.
10. Beckett, *The Aristocracy in England*, 364; James M. Rosenheim, *The Emergence of a Ruling Order: English Landed Society, 1650–1750* (Longman, 1998), 69; Amanda Vickery, *Behind Closed Doors: At Home in Georgian England* (Yale University Press, 2009), 14; Peter Borsay, 'Introduction', in Peter Borsay (ed.), *The Eighteenth-Century Town, 1688–1820* (Routledge, 1990), 1–38 (p. 5).
11. Ralph A. Houlbrooke, *The English Family 1450–1700* (Longman, 1984), 48; Heal, *Hospitality in Early Modern England*, 152.
12. Paul Slack, *The Invention of Improvement: Information and Material Progress in Seventeenth-Century England* (Oxford University Press, 2015), 25.
13. Hannah Newton, *Misery to Mirth: Recovery from Illness in Early Modern England* (Oxford University Press, 2018), 113; Katherine Ibbett, 'Fellow-Feeling', in Susan Broomhall (ed.), *Early Modern Emotions: An Introduction* (Routledge, 2017), 108–11 (pp. 108–9).
14. Sarah Pearsall, *Atlantic Families: Lives and Letters in the Later Eighteenth Century* (Oxford University Press, 2008), 84.

15. Gary Schneider, 'Affecting Correspondences: Body, Behaviour, and the Textualization of Emotion in Early Modern English Letters', *Prose Studies* 23.3 (2000), 31–62 (p. 56), https://doi.org/10.1080/01440350008586715.
16. Karen Harvey, 'Sympathy in Practice: Eighteenth-Century Letters and the Material Body', in Sarah Goldsmith, Sheryllynne Haggerty and Karen Harvey (eds), *Letters and the Body, 1700–1830: Writing and Embodiment* (Routledge, 2023), 85–102 (86, 88).
17. Thomas Knyvett, letter to Katherine Knyvett, 20[?] February 1626, in Bertram Schofield (ed.), *The Knyvett Letters (1620–1644)* (Constable, 1949), 71–2.
18. London, British Library (BL), M6363/32.
19. 'miscarry, v., sense 1.b', *Oxford English Dictionary*, www.oed.com (accessed 26 February 2024).
20. Harvey, 'Sympathy in Practice', 98; Olivia Weisser, 'Grieved and Disordered: Gender and Emotion in Early Modern Patient Narratives', *Journal of Medieval and Early Modern Studies* 43.2 (2013), 247–73 (p. 247), https://doi.org/10.1215/10829636-2081969; Olivia Weisser, *Ill Composed: Sickness, Gender and Belief in Early Modern England* (Yale University Press, 2015), 81; Newton, *Misery to Mirth*, 12.
21. Severine Pilloud and Micheline Louis-Courvoisier, 'The Intimate Experience of the Body in the Eighteenth Century: Between Interiority and Exteriority', *Medical History* 47 (2003), 451–72 (p. 471), https://doi.org/10.1017/S0025727300057343; Hannah Newton, *The Sick Child in Early Modern England, 1580–1720* (Oxford University Press, 2012), 6, 123.
22. William M. Reddy, *The Navigation of Feeling: A Framework for the History of Emotions* (Cambridge University Press, 2001), xii, 105; Barbara H. Rosenwein and Riccardo Cristiani, *What Is the History of Emotions?* (Polity Press, 2018), 34.
23. BL, M6363/32.
24. M. W. Helms, Leonard Naylor and Geoffrey Jagger, 'Verney, Sir Ralph, 1st Bt. (1613-96), of Middle Claydon, Bucks', in Basil D. Henning (ed.), *The History of Parliament: The House of Commons, 1660–90* (Boydell and Brewer, 1983), www.historyofparliamentonline.org/volume/1660-1690/member/verney-sir-ralph-1613-96 (accessed 26 October 2023).
25. Hindle, *The State and Social Change*, 17.
26. Keith Wrightson, 'Mutualities and Obligations: Changing Social Relationships in Early Modern England (Raleigh Lecture on History)', *Proceedings of the British Academy* 139 (2005), 157–94 (p. 167), https://doi.org/10.5871/bacad/9780197263945.003.0007.
27. Patricia Crawford, *Blood, Bodies and Families in Early Modern England* (Routledge, 2004), 3.
28. Margaret Healy, *Fictions of Disease in Early Modern England: Bodies, Plagues and Politics* (Palgrave, 2001), 12, 47, 66, 214–27; Margaret Healy, 'Medicine, Metaphor, and "Crisis" in the Early Modern Social Body', *Journal of Medieval and Early Modern Studies* 46.1 (2016), 117–39, https://doi.org/10.1215/10829636-3343147; Kevin Sharpe, *Reading Authority and Representing Rule in Early Modern England* (Bloomsbury, 2013), 123, 213; Don Herzog, *Household Politics: Conflict in Early Modern England* (Yale University Press, 2013), 30–1.
29. Alan MacFarlane, *The Family Life of Ralph Josselin, A Seventeenth-Century Clergyman: An Essay in Historical Anthropology* (Cambridge University Press, 1970), 107.
30. Derbyshire RO, D5557/2/61.
31. Derbyshire RO, D5557/2/35.

32. BL, M636/16.
33. Ibid.
34. Derbyshire RO, D5557/2/20.
35. Alan Brodrick, letter to St John Brodrick, 18 December 1701, in 'Texts & Studies Series 15: Anglo-Irish Politics, 1680–1728: The Correspondence of the Brodrick Family of Surrey and County Corke, Vol. I, 1680–1714', ed. David Hayton and Michael Page, *Parliamentary History* 38.S1 (2019), 38–326 (pp. 103–4), https://doi.org/10.1111/1750-0206.12436.
36. Derbyshire RO, D5557/3/4/3.
37. Newton, *Misery to Mirth*, 85.
38. Harvey, 'Sympathy in Practice', 98; Weisser, 'Grieved and Disordered', 247; Weisser, *Ill Composed*, 81; Newton, *Misery to Mirth*, 12.
39. Javier Moscoso, *Pain: A Cultural History* (Palgrave Macmillan, 2012), 55–6.
40. BL, Add MS 70121.
41. Northallerton, North Yorkshire County Record Office, ZQH 9/17/78.
42. Alan Brodrick, letter to Thomas Brodrick, 16 March 1709/10, in 'The Correspondence of the Brodrick Family, Vol. I, 1680–1714', ed. Hayton and Page, 235–6.
43. Warwick, Warwickshire County Record Office (CRO), CR1368/59.
44. Leeds, West Yorkshire Archive Service, WYL1015/1/Box 13/1.
45. BL, Add MS 70128; BL, Add MS 70121.
46. BL, Add MS 70128; BL, Add MS 70116.
47. Gary Schneider, *The Culture of Epistolarity: Vernacular Letters and Letter-Writing in Early Modern England, 1500–1700* (University of Delaware Press, 2005), 113.
48. Joan St. John, letter to Lady Joan Barrington, 9 August 1631, in *Barrington Family Letters, 1628–32, Camden Fourth Series, Vol. XXVIII*, ed. Arthur Seale (Royal Historical Society, 1983), 200.
49. James Daybell, *The Material Letter in Early Modern England: Manuscript Letters and the Culture and Practices of Letter Writing, 1512–1635* (Palgrave Macmillan, 2012), 74–5.
50. Fay Bound, 'Writing the Self? Love and the Letter in England c. 1660–c. 1760', *Literature & History* 11.1 (2002), 1–19 (pp. 5, 7), https://doi.org/10.7227/LH.11.1.1.
51. Bound, 'Writing the Self?' 9–10.
52. BL, Add MS 70121.
53. Susan Whyman, *The Pen and the People: English Letter-Writers, 1660–1800* (Oxford University Press, 2009), 60.
54. Susan Whyman, '"Paper Visits": The Post-Restoration Letter as Seen through the Verney Family Archive', in Rebecca Earle (ed.), *Epistolary Selves: Letters and Letter-Writers, 1600–1945* (Ashgate, 1999), 15–36 (p. 15).
55. Pearsall, *Atlantic Families*, 37.
56. Derbyshire RO, D5557/2/18/1.
57. Willemijn Ruberg, 'The Letter as Medicine: Studying Health and Illness in Dutch Daily Correspondence, 1770–1850', *Social History of Medicine* 23.3 (2010), 492–508 (p. 505), https://doi.org/10.1093/shm/hkq012; Carolyn James, 'Letters', in Susan Broomhall (ed.), *Early Modern Emotions: An Introduction* (Routledge, 2017), 176–9 (p. 176).
58. Clare Brant, *Eighteenth-Century Letters and British Culture* (Palgrave Macmillan, 2006), 332. An important exception is Rachel Feldberg's recent work on the late eighteenth-century letters of William Constable, who 'omitted all mentions of physical limitations' to 'refashion his identity' according to ideals of masculinity. Rachel

Feldberg, 'Absent Bodies: Gouty Brethren and Sensitive Hearts in William Constable's Letters from the Grand Tour 1769–1771', in Goldsmith, Haggerty and Harvey (eds), *Letters and the Body*, 17–39, (pp. 18–23, 34).

59. Ruberg, 'The Letter as Medicine', 505.
60. Warwickshire CRO, CR1368/26.
61. Warwickshire CRO, CR1368/8.
62. Warwickshire CRO, CR1368/7.
63. Warwickshire CRO, CR1368/2; Warwickshire CRO, CR1368/3.
64. Sandra Cavallo, 'Conserving Health: The Non-Naturals in Early Modern Culture and Society', in Sandra Cavallo and Tessa Storey (eds), *Conserving Health in Early Modern Culture: Bodies and Environments in Italy and England* (Manchester University Press, 2017), 1–20.
65. Sandra Cavallo and Tessa Storey, *Healthy Living in Late Renaissance Italy* (Oxford University Press, 2013), 44.
66. Cavallo and Storey focus primarily on domestic routines and environments aimed at preserving health in *Healthy Living in Late Renaissance Italy*.
67. See, for example, Daybell, *The Material Letter*, 12; Gabriella Del Lungo Camiciotti, 'The Construction of Epistolary Identity in a Gentlewoman's Communication Network of the Seventeenth Century: The Case of Jane Lady Cornwallis Bacon', *Journal of Early Modern Studies* 3 (Letter Writing in Early Modern Culture, 1500–1750) (2014), 133–49 (p. 135), https://doi.org/10.13128/JEMS-2279-7149-14168; Susan Whyman, 'The Correspondence of Esther Masham and John Locke: A Study in Epistolary Silences', *Huntingdon Library Quarterly* 66.3/4 (2003), 275–305 (p. 291), ww.jstor.org/stable/3818084 (accessed 3 March 2024); Brant, *Eighteenth-Century Letters and British Culture*, 5.
68. James Daybell, 'Social Negotiations in Correspondence between Mothers and Daughters in Tudor and Early Stuart England', *Women's History Review* 24.4 (2015), 502–27 (pp. 508–9), https://doi.org/10.1080/09612025.2015.1015325.
69. Lisa Smith, 'The Relative Duties of a Man: Domestic Medicine in England and France, ca. 1685–1740', *Journal of Family History* 31.3 (2006), 237–56 (pp. 237–8), https://doi.org/10.1177/0363199006287784.
70. Newton, *The Sick Child in Early Modern England*, 4–5, 93, 112, 224.
71. Deborah Lupton and Karen Willis, 'Covid Society', in Deborah Lupton and Karen Willis (eds), *The Covid-19 Crisis: Social Perspectives* (Routledge, 2021), 3–13 (pp. 5–6).
72. Sarah Goldsmith, Sheryllynne Haggerty and Karen Harvey, 'Introduction', in *Letters and the Body*, 1–14 (p. 10).
73. Hans Medick and David Warren Sabean, 'Introduction', in Hans Medick and David Warren Sabean (eds), *Interest and Emotion: Essays on the Study of Family and Kinship* (Cambridge University Press, 1984), 1–8 (p. 3); Hans Medick and David Warren Sabean, 'Interest and Emotion in Family and Kinship Studies: A Critique of Social History and Anthropology', in *Interest and Emotion*, 9–27 (p. 13).
74. BL, M636/32.

4

'The only place that can heighten my enjoyment of my friends': Well-being at Wrest Park in the mid-eighteenth century

Jemima Hubberstey

Introduction

On 8 June 1741, Philip Yorke (1720–1790), later second earl of Hardwicke, wrote a sonnet to his younger brother Charles (1722–1770), urging him to set aside his studies at Cambridge and join him at his wife's ancestral home at Wrest Park, Bedfordshire.[1] In many respects, the poem, with its invitation to 'breathe a purer air' in Wrest's 'wide garden' and promise to 'thy mind renew' from 'this short respite', draws on a well-established literary tradition of the country house as a place of retirement and resonates with the proto-romantic sentiment of nature as a source of creative inspiration and physical restoration.[2] Yet the poem does not simply rehearse tired literary tropes. Drawing too on more personal references, the suggestion of passing 'the fleeting hours in converse sweet' alludes to discussions with their friends, hinting too at the key role the gardens would play in facilitating sociability and restoring their mental and physical health. Nor is time spent at Wrest Park merely a frivolous escape; at the end of the sonnet, the final line promises that such a respite will, in time, 'crown thy well spent early days'. In the mid-eighteenth century, Yorke and his wife, Jemima Marchioness Grey (1722–1797), regularly hosted a circle of select friends – the Wrest Circle – where they would write verses, debate and converse and, importantly, share in the enjoyment of Wrest Park. Using the Wrest Circle as a case study, this chapter explores the way in which the country house provided a distinct space for shared literary endeavour and intellectual fulfilment that ultimately contributed to the coterie's sense of well-being.

The Georgian country house has prompted a plethora of scholarship examining it in its social, intellectual and political context, and since the emotional 'turn' and the increased interest in the home in the past decade, there is growing work on the country house as a lived space.[3] In literary studies, there is a much longer tradition of considering how spaces shaped literary practices and sociability, stemming from Habermas's influential model of the democratic public sphere epitomized by coffeehouses, lending libraries and reading societies,[4] though more recent studies have returned to the domestic sphere by considering intellectual and literary pursuits within the home.[5] Despite these developments, work remains to be done connecting the literary culture of the country house with the history of emotions and sociability that also greatly influenced the compositions written there. This is all the more pressing as the aristocratic, country-house coterie remains an overlooked topic, and despite increasing acknowledgement of the way in which aristocratic writers engaged with print culture in the eighteenth century, such studies still hinge on the question of public influence rather than the more personal dynamics that brought groups together.[6] This chapter proposes to redress this by exploring the Wrest Circle not in terms of its literary merit or fame but rather by considering the way in which Wrest Park fostered creativity and well-being for its inhabitants.

Though approaches to it vary across history, most scholars accept that in all times and places, humans have enquired into questions of well-being.[7] The concept of well-being – though used to encapsulate a range of ideas and experiences – can be broadly defined as the state of being healthy, happy or prosperous, as well as physical, psychological or moral welfare, or, as one sociological study puts it, the ways in which humans can be, do and live well.[8] Most studies divide subjective well-being into two categories, *hedonia* and *eudaimonia*, both of which can be traced back to the ideas of Aristotle and ancient Greek philosophy. Hedonic happiness is associated with the idea of maximizing pleasure and the absence of pain, as well as the cultivation of knowledge and the freedom to pursue activities; while eudaimonic happiness refers to self-development and social or intellectual fulfilment and flourishing.[9] Though other definitions of happiness and well-being have been posited by scholars, these two terms remain the principal categories.[10] For the purposes of this chapter, these distinctions add nuance to our understanding of the different ways in which Wrest Park facilitated well-being – though they are inextricably linked. In hedonic terms, Wrest Park maximized pleasure for inhabitants by providing a comfortable, sociable and stimulating environment that offered the space and freedom for the coterie's creative pursuits. Yet, in eudaimonic terms, the ability to share in these pursuits allowed them to fulfil their creative and intellectual potential, particularly when societal pressures meant that many coterie members could not pursue their literary activities elsewhere.

Surveying the country house and the literary circles that met there through the lens of well-being has two implications. The first is that it provides a deeper understanding of the motivations for writing beyond the desire for fame or public influence. Borrowing from studies in psychology and sociology, there is a helpful distinction between the often privileged 'Big-C' creativity, which refers to the works of famous writers or artists, and 'little-c' creativity, which refers to the informal, everyday potential for creativity that is vital to a healthy and happy life.[11] Though some members of the Wrest Circle did aspire to publish and receive literary recognition, this chapter proposes that most members preferred to write for their own enjoyment and to share in those creative pursuits with friends. Secondly, it offers a new opportunity to explore how far the country house facilitated well-being through providing inhabitants with a sense of social, intellectual and creative fulfilment. This is not to say that all country houses operated in this way. Indeed, while the estates of the elite were often spaces of leisure and luxury designed to provide pleasure and comfort, and Wrest Park was no exception in this respect, this alone did not guarantee well-being or happiness.[12] Surviving letters show that Wrest

Park was unusual, giving members a reprieve from the pressures they faced in their public lives or even, as in the case of Margaret Heathcote, a temporary escape from her own domestic unhappiness. This chapter therefore proposes that Wrest Park provided a unique environment that, through its comparative freedoms, allowed creativity and friendships to blossom and flourish.

The literary circle at Wrest Park

As Yorke's sonnet shows, Wrest Park played an important role in facilitating sociability and well-being, providing a space for visitors to enjoy respite in the gardens and converse with their friends. But for its mistress, Jemima Marchioness Grey (née Campbell, 1723–1797), granddaughter of Henry Grey, Duke of Kent, Wrest had especial personal significance as a place where she had spent many fond childhood summers and where, in her married life, she would play a key role as literary hostess. Returning to Wrest in 1743, she wrote to her aunt: 'It is not only returning to the Country & a Country Life (which I love everywhere) but it is the only Place I am fond enough of to make those Words peculiarly charming, to the only Place that can heighten my Enjoyment of my Friends.'[13]

The charms of Wrest Park clearly lay not just in the rural charms of the Bedfordshire countryside – though as this chapter will explore, the escape from London had significant value to its inhabitants. The real importance for Grey lay in the happiness of sharing Wrest Park with her friends. The early letters between Grey and her childhood friends, the Bluestocking Catherine Talbot (1721–1770), and her young aunt, Mary Gregory (née Grey, 1719–1761), show that Wrest had always played an important role in providing a space for their shared reading and creativity. After watching a performance of *Henry V* in 1747, Grey wrote to Talbot recollecting 'the Remembrance of our reading it with much Pleasure at Wrest the third or second Time you were there (ay! In our Old Friend 39 I believe!)'.[14] Talbot too had fond childhood memories of Wrest. When she was visiting in the summer of 1751, she explored the house while reminiscing about these early years, describing in her diary her 'Pilgrimage to the Apartment that was once L: [Mary] & A:s [Jemima's] where in our young years we were so giddily merry'.[15]

Talbot might not have felt as 'giddily merry' as in her childhood years, but the surviving correspondence and literary compositions from the 1740s and 1750s indicate that this spirit lived on through the next generation at Wrest Park under the influence of Grey and her husband. Though their marriage in 1740 had been arranged as an alliance between two powerful political families, the young couple shared a love of books and history, and early into their married life they invited their friends together at Wrest Park, effectively forming a coterie which they termed their 'Society at Wrest'.[16] The circle consisted of both Grey's childhood friends, Mary Gregory and Catherine Talbot, as well as Yorke's siblings, Charles, Elizabeth (later Lady Anson, 1725–1760) and Margaret (later Lady Heathcote, 1733–1768), in addition to his friends from the University of Cambridge, John Lawry (1714–1779), Daniel Wray (1701–1783) and Thomas Birch (1705–1766). Later, the poets Thomas Edwards (1699–1757) and

Richard Owen Cambridge (1717–1802) became visitors at Wrest, albeit as more peripheral members. Yorke and his Cambridge friends had already collaborated on at least two literary works, the *Athenian Letters* (1741–3), a fictional series of letters set during the Peloponnesian Wars, and *The Philosopher* (1738–41), which was modelled on Addison and Steele's *The Spectator*. These compositions marry the authors' serious academic, historical and literary interests with a playful, even puerile humour. Despite its serious themes, *The Philosopher* also satirizes university life; one composition makes fun of the college fops ('Dick Trifle', 'Tom Jolly' and 'Lord Sparkish') who care more about dazzling the dons with their waistcoats than their wit.[17] The Wrest Circle's private *Wrestiana* manuscript, composed at Wrest between 1742 and 1783, is similarly infused with a precocious, youthful spirit that is both scholarly and playful in equal measure as the authors frequently depict their friends as characters within it, each given their own coterie sobriquet. It was the main work produced by the Wrest Circle and, as the name suggests, was inextricably connected to the physical space at Wrest Park. Wrest Park, 'that ancient honourable seat', as Philip described it in his sonnet to Charles, was already steeped in generations of history, which appealed to the friends and readily inspired their verses.[18]

There had actually been an earlier seventeenth-century coterie at Wrest Park that centred on Grey's ancestor, Elizabeth Talbot (1582–1651), which included the poets, Thomas Carew (1595–1640) and Samuel Butler (1613–1680), the scholars Robert Cotton (*c.*1570–1631) and John Selden (1584–1654) and the miniaturist Samuel Cooper (1609–1672). The eighteenth-century circle was certainly aware of this longstanding literary legacy: Grey once remarked to Talbot that she had read some of Thomas Carew's poems that he had written from Wrest and was amused at descriptions of 'the hospitable life of the Lord & Lady there, the ample Board groaning with the weight of Sirloins, the double Moat round the House & much more'.[19] Wrest's long aristocratic history also inspired the eighteenth-century coterie and they both romanticize and playfully parody it in the pages of *Wrestiana*. One composition, 'Letter to the Honble [*sic*] Mr Y', invents a fictional history about the 'delightful mansion of the noble Family of Grey', pretending that Grey's ancestor copied a mistranslation onto the 'great window at the North End of the high dining Room'.[20] The 'mistranslation' playfully challenges the 'honour' of Grey's family by pretending that her ancestor was not as 'well-skill'd in all Public Learning' as stated in history books, perhaps a joke on the fact that Grey and her family had always valued education and learning. Elsewhere in *Wrestiana*, a fictional meeting is imagined between Daniel Wray and John Selden, as the latter remarks on Wray having 'succeeded in my Apartment at Wrest or trod the ground; or Sat under the Oak which I used to frequent a Century agoe [*sic*]'.[21] Selden's connection to Wrest Park must have been a particular delight to Philip Yorke, who had already written a defence of Selden in *The Philosopher* while still a student in 1738.[22] Wrest Park and its history is therefore interwoven into the fabric of the *Wrestiana* manuscript, exemplifying the significance of the country house to the group's identity. Yet the manuscript also offers playful, imaginary possibilities in bringing past and present together, offering a further degree of escapism from the world outside.

Indeed, the sociable verses and comical compositions written by the group indicate how far they wrote largely for their own amusement, rather than for literary recognition. Scholarly work on sociable verses has shown that although this literary form was often denigrated, the fact that some such verses were published shows that they had professional value, especially for women writers.[23] Yet in this instance, the compositions in *Wrestiana* remained in manuscript form and are rather indicative of the close personal bonds and teasing humour within the circle as the authors wrote primarily for their own and their friends' entertainment. In 'Fragment of Le Libraire a la Mode Comedie Italienne en trois Actes' ('The Fashionable Bookseller: Italian Comedy in Three Acts'), a play fragment written by Philip Yorke and Daniel Wray, they make fun of the length and obscure themes within the *Athenian Letters* – an extensive work they had composed with their friends at Cambridge – imagining it as unsuited to the popular tastes in the literary marketplace. The scene depicts a fictional conversation between Charles Yorke and Robert Dodsley, the fashionable publisher and bookseller, imagining Dodsley's reaction if he had been tasked with printing the work. (It had, in fact, been James Bettenham who was responsible, only printing a copy for each of the twelve contributors to preserve its confidentiality.) The comedy lies in the contrast between Charles Yorke's veneration of the *Athenian Letters* as a sincere work between friends, in contrast to Dodsley's disdain as he throws the manuscript down in frustration at the prospect of editing and selling it:

> *Scenes changes to the Inner Room. Mr Dodsley Solus, at Table with the 4th Vol. of* Athenian Letters *before him.*
>
> D. [Dodsley]: Sixteen and Eighteen is 34, and 17 is 51 Sheets – and the damned 4th Vol. as big as any of them … (*Scratches his head.*) This will never do; I shall make a sad hand of it … Zounds – 4 Volumes about Hormus and Ahriman, Fire, and the Devil Knows what!
>
> (*Throws down the Book.*)
>
> Enter C.Y. [Charles Yorke] introduced by Young D [James Dodsley].
>
> C. [Charles Yorke]: Mr Dodsley, you seem not to consider that is my large Paper Copy, Turkey binding, and corrected by the brow quill of a very ingenious Friend.
>
> D. [Dodsley]: (*Picking up the Book.*) Sir – really – upon my word Sir – I was so engaged – I was so engaged – it was a very interesting Part – the Book slipt.[24]

It is likely that the play fragment was acted or read out loud at Wrest Park; other plays written by the family were certainly performed, so it is not difficult to imagine the entertainment the coterie might have had acting the scene out themselves.[25] The composition is self-conscious in its allusion to the contrast between the tastes of the commercial print trade and their own country house entertainment, having Charles Yorke insist that the *Athenian Letters* should be printed straight away so 'we may have it for our Country amusement against the long Vacation'.[26] The fragment shows that though the writers had a serious understanding of the literary world, they preferred instead to write for one another so they could share in the enjoyment of their compositions in the summer months at Wrest.

Many years later in 1774, at the age of seventy-two, Daniel Wray looked back fondly on the sociable verses written in these earlier years, remarking to Philip Yorke that 'those days of Sobriquets and Higgmigriggs were good days, let the Wise say what they can to the contrary'.[27] For Wray, though the verses did not possess particular literary merit, the memories of writing them with friends, for whom they invented their 'Sobriquets', far from being a source of embarrassment, was one of comfort and enjoyment in his later years.

'I can form no Idea how it is possible to *live* anywhere else': Experiencing Wrest Park

Importantly, Wrest Park provided an ideal place in the summer months for members to escape their usual routines and, free of their usual concerns, immerse themselves in the environment and enjoy one another's company. As early as 1741, Charles wrote to Philip that 'I hope Wray will continue with you, that we may all have a meeting in your Elysium'.[28] Yet the idealized, even fantastical tone in some letters make it difficult to determine the real experience of staying at Wrest. For instance, alluding to James Thomson's *Castle of Indolence* (1748), which satirizes the idle country house lifestyle,[29] Catherine Talbot wrote to the Bluestocking Elizabeth Carter that 'I am here in an enchanted Castle, with no one earthly thing to do, no one interruption of business, real or pretended', with 'the most delightful groves to wander in all day, and a library that will carry one as far as ever one chuses to travel in an evening'.[30] In any case, it is safe to say that members of the coterie did at least view Wrest Park as a welcome change from their daily lives – temporarily freeing them from their usual obligations and responsibilities and allowing them to enjoy the environment at Wrest Park, alongside the company and literary activities. Talbot's diary from 14 September 1751 gives far more insight than her letters to Carter, providing a glimpse into how guests spent their time at Wrest and the key role that conversation and sociability played:

> Our days past pretty uniformly in a delightful Place, the Weather was vastly fine, & I lived in a state of studious idleness quite new to me, for I had no earthly thing to do. For a morning & night [I read a] Book I had taken out of their Library Dr Scotts *Christian Life*, which I own I like enormously … Our Breakfast Chatty & Cheerful. From 11 to 3 I was generally with my dear Ang [Angelina; Talbot's nickname for Grey]: Walking in those Fine Gardens whch [which] were in high beauty & resting between whiles. Post days with Letters from our best Friends made an agreeable break in our Walks. We read together the Essay on Man at 3 ½ we dined, & Conversed till 5 ½. Then an hour Musick … then to Tea in the Library, where we sat over our Several Books till supper was brought in at Ten, & Cheerful Char [Charles Yorke] kept us till 11 ½. We laughed over the Follies of Courts many Centuries since buried, or debated the Politics of a hundred years ago. Sometimes on matters of Literature, the Style or Merit of Authors.[31]

In this account, there is a combination of lively intellectual stimulation as they debate history, literature and politics, as well as space for reading quietly and companionably in the library.

Many members of the circle resided mostly in London, and the gardens at Wrest – with their shades and fragrances – offered a welcome respite from the hustle and bustle of London. Elizabeth Anson once remarked upon leaving Wrest that 'My Hearing grieves that … the Music of the Birds, or Lady Grey's Harpsichord' should be disturbed by 'the unintelligible cries of London' and that her sense of smell 'suffers extremely by the loss of the Perfumes of Hay & Honeysuckles'.[32] The sensory observations highlight how far the garden at Wrest was not merely decorative, but contributed too to inhabitants' well-being as they experienced, sensed and enjoyed it.[33] Yet it was not only the topographical differences that stood out, but the differences in setting and sociability. Following one of his habitual summers at Wrest, Daniel Wray despaired that upon returning to London,

> I am fallen into a situation so intensely different, kennels for canals, Dusty East-winds instead of Honeysuckled Zephyrs, Rawthmells for the Hill-house, and Birch alone to supply the place of all the Borlacian Poets & Charles the Critic. – But it is not only a London in August; Let me go where I will every Situation & amusement will be long unpleasant & lackless to me, after having grown into an Inhabitant of Wrest.[34]

Wray's play on 'kennels' and 'canals' emphasizes the contrast between the dirt and waste in the city and the simple beauties of the countryside. But he places emphasis on the difference in company too, highlighting the contrast between Rawthmells and the culture of the London coffee house and the intimate, playful sociability at Wrest Park; the 'Borlacian Poets' refer to the authors of 'The Borlaciad' in *Wrestiana* (Philip Yorke, Daniel Wray and perhaps Mary Gregory), while 'Charles the Critic' is Charles Yorke.[35] It is interesting too that coterie sociability is inextricably bound up in both the manuscript and the space itself, as the friends are synonymous with their compositions and even their identities as 'Inhabitants of Wrest'.[36] Wray's nostalgia for summer at Wrest Park represents a longing both for the physical space as well as for the friends and literary activities that made it such a cause for happiness and enjoyment.

In 1744, the Yorkes' father, the first earl of Hardwicke, appears to have stayed at Wrest Park for some respite from the sounds of construction at their nearby estate at Wimpole Hall in Cambridgeshire. Hardwicke wrote his thanks for 'the great Refreshment & Pleasure at Wrest', remarking that:

> I never in my life spent a Vacation with greater pleasure, or found more benefit from this last. The Satisfaction of mind, which I received there, must have contributed very much to it, & the hardening, which the air & exercise of Rest gave one, enabled me so well to stand the Cold air we met with at Derham's, that I did not in the least feel it otherwise than in a mere blood-shot Eye & that is now in a manner gone.[37]

As Hardwicke's letter suggests, Wrest Park provided mental stimulation from the libraries and discussions and physical benefits as a result of the air and exercise afforded. But it wasn't simply the extensive and beautiful grounds that guests enjoyed: an agreeable visit also owed much to good company and conversation. Following a later visit in 1747, Elizabeth Anson wrote to Grey that her father had spoken much of Wrest: 'The improvements made in the house, of the beauty of the Garden, the excellence of the Pine-apples, Cherries, Strawberries, Venison … and above all the Company', adding her own reflection, 'I can form no Idea how it is possible to live anywhere else, nay, indeed we do not live here at present, we meerly exist.'[38] Anson's emphatic differentiation between living and existing offers important insight into her understanding of well-being: acknowledging that living is not simply attending to basic needs, but having a life enriched. For Anson, the fact that this enrichment is provided by 'above all the Company', highlights the key role that sociability played in cultivating the experience of Wrest Park. For members of the Wrest Circle, their heightened enjoyment of the place and emotional attachment to it is inextricably linked to their friends and sharing in that space together.

Of course, as most of these accounts are written by close friends and family, they are nonetheless from the perspectives of privileged guests, rather than owners. Although Yorke and Grey evidently thoroughly enjoyed entertaining their friends and created opportunities for them to share in that space together, one does wonder how far they could always partake in the studious idleness that Talbot describes.[39] Daniel Wray joked that the young couple were such attentive hosts, they should not be surprised if they made more work for themselves and their guests never wanted to leave, writing to Yorke:

> I dined lately with [Isaac Hawkins] Browne & his Wife: They talk of the Day spent at Wrest, as it deserves, and will by all means have me contrive some thing like it in town. You & Lady Grey must blame your own Behaviour for bringing you into such Scrapes: For my own part you Both have made it impossible for me not to take all opportunity of being with you.[40]

In fact, for much of the year, the couple were not entertaining their friends at Wrest and experienced the place very differently without them. In the summer of 1750, when their friends had dispersed and Yorke was in Cambridge on political business, Grey found herself alone at Wrest and took refuge in the gardens, choosing to pass her time in the newly built root house in the Mithraic Glade, a secluded part of the woodland at Wrest that was created in homage to the *Athenian Letters*. She writes to Catherine Talbot:

> Mr Y: is gone to Cambridge – to the Assizes – a Club Meeting – & I know not what foolish Business, & has left me to inhabit the Root-Hermitage & recommend myself to the Protection of Mithras (you must know I have been deeply engaged in the *Athenian Letters* of late).[41]

The vogue for hermitages in the eighteenth century was deliberately intended to evoke a romanticized solitude and create a sense of proximity to the natural world. Yet even then, paradoxically, though places of retreat were experienced in solitude, they invited thoughts of friends and the desire for companionship. In a letter to Grey, Elizabeth

Anson draws attention to her own hermitage at Carshalton, a 'thatched-roofed cottage', where she imagines that 'the Trees and Birds of Carshalton … whisper and warble forth their compliments to an Inhabitant at Wrest'.[42] It is significant that in her own solitude, Grey chose a place in the gardens that reminded her of their friends and their literary compositions, after all, some of the *Athenian Letters* were composed in the woodland. In 1741, Lawry wrote that he was 'glad to hear of the [Athenian] Letters … indited in the Groves at Rest'.[43] Not only did Grey want to experience the space in the gardens that reminded her of friends, but the experience of revisiting those spaces was powerful enough to prompt Grey to describe it in her letters to those friends, knowing they would understand the significance. Evidently, then, the gardens came to represent more than a sensory delight – though they must have been enjoyed regardless – but acted as a reminder of friendships and their shared literary endeavours, providing a source of comfort and companionship in an otherwise isolated space.

'There being no forms at Wrest to constrain anybody from doing what they like': The permissive environment at Wrest Park

It would be easy to assume that any country house might provide the benefits of retirement and retreat. This final part of the chapter will consider how far, to close associates of the family at least, Wrest Park was an exceptional environment that offered freedoms members of the circle could not recreate anywhere else. In this respect, although the environment at Wrest Park often maximized pleasures for guests – allowing them to enjoy the garden views and country air, the company of friends and the pursuit of their shared literary activities, it also, importantly, provided a sense of purpose and intellectual fulfilment. Many members of the coterie were careful in how far they could display their learning and literary interests: and their compositions in *Wrestiana* remained a private shared endeavour between friends.[44] The group was fairly unusual in that the women were afforded equal respect as intellectuals – akin to the later Bluestocking salon. John Lawry considered the 'Ladies of Rest' to be 'distinguished in an uncommon degree', while Daniel Wray decided that he so much preferred the 'Variety', 'Elegance & Delicacy' that the ladies introduced to conversation, that he would 'despise those Male-Companys' back at Cambridge University.[45] The hetero-sociability was met with some surprise by Thomas Edwards, who observed that 'the Library is the general rendezvous for both the Ladies and the Gentlemen at their leisure hours; hither the Ladies bring their work, and here if there is no company, they drink Tea'.[46] In this respect, while the group still respected the boundaries of polite sociability, in which men and women were seen to complement and improve the other through conversation, socializing in this way in the country house was still unusual. But Wrest Park was, after all, Grey's inheritance, and as hostess (and a Marchioness in her own right) she exercised considerable authority.

It might seem remarkable, therefore, that Grey is often at pains to hide her intellectual interests and, unlike the later Bluestocking Circle, never sought publication. Though she certainly impressed her male peers within the group, anxiety about coming across as a female intellectual was particularly heightened when socializing with fashionable company outside the coterie and Wrest Park. On one occasion, she was mortified that while drinking tea with 'fine gem'men' in her London home, she had been forced to admit she was reading Horace and fled the room in horror, remarking to Catherine Talbot that 'an Old Latin Poet … by no means belongs to a Fine London Lady'.[47] Wray, who was with her on the occasion, was oblivious to Grey's embarrassment, and while she was trying to make her excuses he 'found nothing better to talk of but Electrical Experiments, & appointing a Day for me to go … to see them'.[48] Although the men in the circle actively encouraged female learning, as Grey's comment suggests, they did not necessarily understand the anxiety elite women experienced about exposing themselves to ridicule for showing their intellectual interests. After confessing that she read Horace, Grey was convinced that she would be ridiculed as a 'femme scavante [*sic*]'.[49] Evidently, place was an important factor, and when leading the life of a 'Fine London Lady' far beyond the library and gardens at Wrest Park, Grey was acutely aware of not risking society's judgement, though Wray would consider it a 'loss to us all' that she did 'not oftener exert her Good sense & excellent Taste'.[50]

Even for the men in the group, many of them had their own reasons for not seeking publication – though later in life, Yorke did take some public role as a member of the Society of Antiquaries, the Royal Society and as a founding member of the British Museum. The Yorke brothers in particular, ever endeavouring to follow in their father's formidable footsteps, suppressed their private literary ambitions to pursue careers in politics and the law. In *Wrestiana*, one composition written by Catherine Talbot teases that the brothers' careers were inimical to true wit and literary genius, stating that 'Philips Brow – / With Publick Cares is wrinkled Now: / Ingenious Mirth forgot', while Charles, having 'aspired to Wits Fantastick Prize', has neglected his studies and 'Laws dim Lamp unheeded burns'.[51] Yet Philip Yorke's letters in the early years of his marriage indicate the immense pressure and even fear of public life, writing to his friend, the historian Conyers Middleton, that

> the Great Fortunes [his marriage] wch so suddenly & so early have brought me into the Scene of public life, before I had time even to take a view of it, as they claim all they duty & gratitude I can shew to those who have advanced me far beyond my expectations as well as merits, so they really give me no small degree of uneasiness to acquit myself in such a manner, as not to make my Friends ashamed of me.[52]

Though Middleton warned Yorke not to be lured by the 'charms of a studious & indolent life',[53] Wrest Park nonetheless became a space where he could escape the pressures of the public eye and replicate the same camaraderie he had enjoyed at Cambridge, which resonates particularly in the sonnet inviting his brother to enjoy 'converse sweet' in the gardens. Even in Yorke's political poems in *Wrestiana*, he depicts Wrest Park as an escape from public duties. It is worth noting that the Yorkes' family property, Wimpole Hall, situated more conveniently for the Cambridgeshire elections, was their main seat for politicking, whereas Wrest, more removed geographically, became more readily a space for retreat and respite.[54] Interestingly, in 1747, around the time that Philip Yorke and Soame Jenyns were standing as MPs for Cambridgeshire, they wrote odes to one another on the occasion. While Jenyns writes that 'the Candidate for Quiet prays/ Sick of the Bumpers, and Huzza's/ Of blest Electioneering', Yorke responds to his 'Worthy Brother Knight', noting that while others might seek escapism through the frivolities of the racecourse or even through drink, he invites Jenyns 'Amidst Wrest Groves to moralize' with 'Old Books' and 'Old Friends'.[55] For Yorke, his sense of well-being at Wrest Park is derived, not from hedonistic pursuit, but rather inviting old friends to share in the gardens and library at Wrest where they might 'moralize', which provides a deeper sense of fulfilment and self-improvement. Through contributing to *Wrestiana* and inviting friends to Wrest Park, Yorke is able to find a creative outlet that allows him to bridge contradictory cultural positions between his public life in politics and 'the charms of a studious & indolent life' at Wrest Park, finding a sense of fulfilment beyond the political career that had been obliged to pursue.

Wrest Park and the intellectual camaraderie could also provide a temporary escape from domestic unhappiness, which was certainly the case with Yorke's youngest sister, Margaret. Thirteen years younger than her eldest brother, she did not immediately become a part of the coterie at Wrest Park. However, no less precocious than her siblings, she readily joined in the coterie activities: as early as 1743, when she was ten years old, Daniel Wray praised 'Miss Peg's Extempores' at Wrest Park, and by the age of fourteen, she was joining in the literary games.[56] One of Talbot's compositions in *Wrestiana* remarks on 'Peggy fam'd for tuneful Skill' and teases that she might too quickly latch onto the sociable verses in vogue in the group, fearing that 'sober Peggy's Prudent Head' would 'Grow fertile in Conceits: In Tricks, and Forgeries, and Bams, in Quips, and Cranks and Jokes, and Flams, And all her Sister Cheats'.[57] While this composition is in jest, it does show how far the teenager had thrown herself enthusiastically into the creative and spirited environment at Wrest Park. Her 'Epistle addressed to Lady Grey at Wrest Park', written in 1747, asks Grey to spare a few moments 'to a young Bard' and inspire her verses as she recites 'Vacuna [Wrest]'s much-lov'd elegant delights'.[58] Though her ode was not included in *Wrestiana*, it was eventually published posthumously in *The Gentleman's Magazine* in November 1781 and in the sixth volume of *Bell's Classical Arrangement of Fugitive Poetry* (1786), and Lady Mary Capell (later Forbes, 1722–1782) transcribed it into her personal anthology of eighteenth-century verses alongside notable authors.[59]

Margaret would look back nostalgically on these early experiences of Wrest Park, writing to Grey, 'I remember the time, in days of yore, when I used to spend whole weeks together at Wrest (happy days indeed)'.[60] Her marriage at the age of sixteen to Gilbert Heathcote in 1749 proved to be an unhappy one. It was a politically and financially motivated arrangement; Heathcote's grandfather was a colonial merchant who, as London's leading importer from Jamaica, was reputed to be the wealthiest commoner in England.[61] Margaret's relations with her husband's family were strained, and Heathcote himself did not leave a favourable impression with the Yorkes. Their brother, Colonel Joseph Yorke (1724–1792), was particularly critical and believed their father should take Heathcote to task, for 'I do not see why we are to be browbeat so continually by such a brute, or where the harm can happen from his being forced into a little better manners'.[62] The main bone of contention, however, what Margaret referred to as the 'grating subject', was that her husband often prevented her from visiting Wrest Park. In August 1753, Margaret wrote to Grey, longing for the comparative freedoms at Wrest:

> I ... assure you that it is not for want of my most earnest persuasion that Mr. Heathcote ... decline[s] your Ladyship's & Mr Yorke's most obliging invitation [to Wrest]. He returns his best compliments & thanks, but does not seem to care to think of leaving this place so soon again ...; as to there being no forms at Wrest to constrain any body from doing what they like, he must be sensible of that, & how agreeable the way of life is though he experienced it but for two days some time ago; as to myself, the happiness I have so often enjoyed there is yet so fresh in my memory that were it in my power I would not stay to finish my Letter. The new room & root house I doubt not are excessive pretty, & I should certainly be extremely glad to see them but at the same time I must add that they are no temptations comparative to what the company I should find there affords me.[63]

For Margaret, it is interesting that despite the new improvements at Wrest – the root house, designed by Thomas Edwards, and the new room in the house, completed by Henry Flitcroft – it is the company and friendships at Wrest Park that she particularly values and to which she attributes her past happiness. Her reference to 'there being no forms at Wrest to constrain any body from doing what they like' also resonates with Talbot's letter to Carter, when she notes that there is 'no one interruption of business', suggesting the comparative freedom at Wrest Park.

At her own country house at Stocken, Margaret's life was no doubt materially comfortable. Though few of her possessions have survived, nearly all of her letters are written on expensive gilt-edged paper, which, as scholars have shown, was a particular indicator of wealth and status.[64] However, despite possessing these luxury goods, the one thing Margaret truly valued – her time for private reading and study, was subject to the movements of her in-laws. An avid reader, on 25 November 1753, she wrote to Grey of her impatience to read Samuel Richardson's *Sir Charles Grandison*, but remarked that 'as ... I expect the family from Normanton to pass a week here I have so far prevailed upon myself as to lock up Sir Charles Grandison with a determined resolution not to look in it till they are gone'.[65] Her letters to friends became her only means of maintaining the camaraderie and intellectual stimulation she had enjoyed at Wrest, sending poems to Talbot, Grey and her sister for commentary.[66] Even then, her sister was often occupied in political business at the Admiralty, and the absence of letters caused her much anguish.[67] Often, unable to rely entirely on letters, she came to rely on herself for entertainment, writing to Grey, 'I never was so totally without amusements of any kind (but what my own Eyes, Fingers, or Brains can procure me) than I am now.'[68] When Margaret was finally able to visit Wrest again in 1757, Grey seems to have gifted her several books from the Wrest library – she wrote in thanks:

> I should now, if possible, express my Sense of the obligations your Ladyship in particular confered upon me, by robbing yourself (wch I own went sorely against my Conscience, as I am sure the Books were highly valued by you) to contribute to my solitary amusement; & it is certain that I promise myself the highest pleasure in their perusal, & shall regard them as the chief ornament of my Book-case for many reasons, but for none more than for the sake of the amiable Giver.[69]

It is particularly touching that Grey gifted the books to Margaret in the full knowledge that she had little entertainment at home. But Margaret's letter shows the books were valuable not only for their content, but for the fact that they belonged to the Wrest Library and had been given to her by Grey, allowing her to feel connected to both the place and her beloved sister-in-law. In the same way that Grey would retreat to the root-house to be reminded of their friends, the books from the Wrest library clearly had emotional value to Margaret as they brought her closer to Grey and their shared literary interests. For Margaret, despite the material advantages of her lifestyle at Stocken, her only true source of happiness and fulfilment came from the gifts and correspondence that connected her to her friends and the intellectual camaraderie at Wrest Park.

Conclusion

Returning to the sonnet quoted in the introduction, in which Yorke invites his brother to Wrest in order to 'in its wide garden breathe a purer air' and partake in 'converse sweet', Wrest Park evidently played a key role in nurturing well-being and sociability. At the same time, the poem's reference to time at Wrest Park as 'well-spent early days' hints too at the greater satisfaction and personal fulfilment to be derived from a 'short respite'. Studies of literary circles have tended to hinge on the question of publication and influence, but returning to the setting of the country house and the way that members experienced it invites a reconsideration of the reason that aristocratic coteries came together. In the case of the Wrest Circle, members clearly wrote for their own enjoyment, finding at Wrest Park, under the custodianship of Yorke and Grey, a space and escape for creativity and sociability that they were not afforded elsewhere. Indeed, the playful and teasing tone in *Wrestiana* strongly hints at the personal nature of these compositions, showing how far they were written solely for the entertainment of the authors and their friends. Of course, there would need to be further investigation whether other country house coteries operated in this way, but the surviving correspondence suggests that Wrest Park was unique in providing such an escape. As Margaret Heathcote's letters show, the country house, despite its material advantages and luxuries, did not necessarily guarantee creative or intellectual freedom. Wrest Park, then, provided a sense of well-being to members of the coterie not only through the immediate pleasures and entertainments of sharing in literary compositions in a beautiful and comfortable place, but, as this chapter has argued, affording members the space and freedom for pursuits that ultimately gave them social, intellectual and creative fulfilment.

Notes

1. Philip Yorke, 'Sonnet. To Mr. Charles Yorke (his brother)', in *A Catalogue of the Royal and Noble Authors of England, Scotland and Ireland*, 4 vols (John Scott, 1806), IV, 339.
2. Christopher Thacker, *The Wildness Pleases: The Origins of Romanticism* (Routledge, 2018, first printed 1983); David Fairer, *English Poetry of the Eighteenth Century, 1700–1789* (Routledge, 2002), 195.
3. See, for instance, Mark Girouard, *Life in the English Country House: A Social and Architectural History* (Yale University Press, 1993); Dana Arnold, *The Georgian Country House: Architecture, Landscape, and Society* (Sutton, 2003); Matthew Dimmock, Andrew Hadfield and Margaret Healy (eds), *The Intellectual Culture of the English Country House, 1500–1700* (Manchester University Press, 2018); Joan Michèle Coutu, Jon Stobart and Peter Lindfield (eds), *Politics and the English Country House, 1688–1800* (McGill-Queen's University Press, 2023); for emotions and spaces, see Susan Broomhall (ed.), *Spaces for Feeling: Emotions and Sociabilities in Britain, 1650–1850* (Routledge, 2015); and for the country house as a lived space, see Jon Stobart and Mark Rothery, *Consumption and the Country House* (Oxford University Press, 2016), and Jon Stobart, *Comfort in the Eighteenth-Century Country House* (Routledge, 2022).
4. Jürgen Habermas, *The Structural Transformation of the Public Sphere: An Inquiry into a Category of Bourgeois Society* (MIT Press, 1991), 59; Peter Clark, *British Clubs and Societies 1580–1800: The Origins of an Associational World* (Oxford University Press, 2000), 3; Brian Cowan, *The Social Life of Coffee: The Emergence of the British Coffeehouse* (Yale University Press, 2005), 3; Elizabeth Eger, *Bluestockings: Women of Reason from Enlightenment to Romanticism* (Palgrave Macmillan, 2010), 69; Will Bowers, 'The Many Rooms of Holland House', in Will Bowers and Hannah Leah Crummé (eds), *Re-evaluating the Literary Coterie, 1530–1830* (Palgrave Macmillan, 2016), 159–80, https://doi.org/10.1057/978-1-137-54553-4_9.
5. Abigail Williams, *The Social Life of Books: Reading Together in the Eighteenth-Century Home* (Yale University Press, 2019); Leonie Hannan, *A Culture of Curiosity: Science in the Eighteenth-Century Home* (Manchester University Press, 2023), 1–2.
6. Moyra Haslett, *Pope to Burney, 1714–1779: Scriblerians to Bluestockings* (Palgrave Macmillan, 2003); Betty Schellenberg, *Literary Coteries and the Making of Modern Print Culture, 1740–1790* (Cambridge University Press, 2016).
7. Darrin M. McMahon, 'From the Happiness of Virtue to the Virtue of Happiness: 400 B.C.–A.D. 1780', *Daedalus* 133.2 (2004), 5–17, https://doi.org/10.1162/001152604323049343; McMahon, *Happiness: A History* (Grove Press, 2008).
8. 'Well-being, *N.*', *Oxford English Dictionary* (Oxford University Press, 2024), https://doi.org/10.1093/OED/7175092406; T. Lomas, B. W. Case, F. Cratty and T. J. VanderWeele, 'A Global History of Happiness', *International Journal of Wellbeing* 11.4 (2021), 68–87 (p. 69), https://doi.org/10.5502/ijw.v11i4.1457.
9. Lomas et al., 'A Global History of Happiness'; Ian Bache and Karen Scott, *The Politics of Wellbeing: Theory, Policy, and Practice* (Palgrave Macmillan, 2018), 9–12.
10. Bache and Scott, *The Politics of Wellbeing*; Faye Sayer, *Heritage and Wellbeing: The Impact of Heritage Places on Visitors' Wellbeing* (Oxford University Press, 2024), 4–5; Carol D. Ryff, Jennifer Morozink Boylan and Julie A. Kirsch, 'Eudaimonic and Hedonic Well-Being: An Integrative Perspective with Linkages to Sociodemographic Factors and Health', in Matthew T. Lee, Laura D. Kubansky and Tyler J. VanderWeele

(eds), *Measuring Well-Being: Interdisciplinary Perspectives from the Social Sciences and the Humanities* (Oxford University Press, 2021), 92–135.

11. Frederic Kiernan, Jane W. Davidson and Lindsay G. Oades, 'Researching Creativity and Wellbeing: Interdisciplinary Perspectives', *International Journal of Wellbeing* 10.5 (2020), 1–5 (p. 2), https://doi.org/10.5502/ijw.v10i5.1523; A. Montuori and R. E. Purser, 'Deconstructing the Lone Genius Myth: Toward a Contextual View of Creativity', *Journal of Humanistic Psychology* 35.3 (1995), 69–112, https://doi.org/10.1177/00221678950353005. This has further been nuanced to include 'mini-C' and 'pro-C'; see James C. Kaufman and Ronald A. Beghetto, 'Beyond Big and Little: The Four C Model of Creativity', *Review of General Psychology* 13.1 (2009), 1–12, https://doi.org/10.1037/a0013688. For a study of creative well-being in practice, see John Wright, *Research Digest: Everyday Creativity* (Centre for Cultural Value, 2022).
12. See Jon Stobart, *Comfort in the Eighteenth-Century Country House* (Routledge, 2022).
13. Bedford, Bedfordshire and Luton Archives and Records Service (BLARS), L30/9a/1, fol. 4 (Jemima Grey to Mary Gregory, 8 May 1743).
14. BLARS, L30/9a/4, fol. 57 (Jemima Grey to Catherine Talbot, 26 December 1747).
15. London, British Library (BL), Add. MSS 46690, fol. 29 (14 September 1751).
16. BLARS, L30/9/3/5 fol. 157 (Elizabeth Anson to Jemima Grey, 7 July 1748).
17. New Haven, Beinecke Library, Osborn c368, 'No. 12. Letters from Two Fellow Commoners, Giving an Account of How They Spend Their Time the University', *The Philosopher*, fols 76–85.
18. Philip Yorke, 'Sonnet. To Mr. Charles Yorke (His Brother)', 339.
19. BLARS, L30 9a/5 fol. 5 (Jemima Grey to Catherine Talbot, June 1747).
20. Private collection, 'Letter to the Honble Mr Y', *Wrestiana*, fols 65–6 (signed 'P', Philip Yorke).
21. Private collection, 'Nouveaux Dialogues des Morts & des Vivans Dialogues Second A l'Enfer', *Wrestiana*, fol. 85 (signed 'L', John Lawry).
22. Bienecke Library, Osborne c368, 'No. 8. Mr Selden vindicated from some severe aspersions of Dr Drake, in a Letter to the Philosopher', *The Philosopher, Or, Essays on Various Subjects begun at Cambridge*, fols 49–57 (signed 'P', Philip Yorke).
23. Kathleen Keown, 'Sociable Productions: Women's Poetry 1730–1760' (unpublished doctoral thesis, University of Oxford, 2018), https://ora.ox.ac.uk/objects/uuid:5020c78b-5123-4e6f-8db3-f6161b673475 (accessed 3 January 2025).
24. Private collection, 'Fragment of Le Libraire a la Mode comédie Italienne en trois Actes', *Wrestiana*, fol. 15.
25. By the late eighteenth century, family theatricals were certainly a tradition, evidenced by surviving plays, including as 'The Woodcutter', performed by the grandchildren of Philip and Charles Yorke in 1797, in BLARS, L31/340/61.
26. Private collection, 'Fragment of Le Libraire a la Mode comédie Italienne en trois Actes', *Wrestiana*, fol. 16.
27. BL, Add. MS 35402, fol. 140v (Daniel Wray to Philip Yorke, July/August 1774). Though there is no formal dictionary definition of 'higgmigrigg' – it is possibly a word of Wray's own invention – in the context, it is likely to mean a miscellaneous collection of trivial verses, loosely combining 'higgle', defined by Samuel Johnson as 'a confused mass', and 'grig', defined by Johnson as 'anything below the natural size' or 'a merry creature', in Samuel Johnson, *A Dictionary of the English Language* (J. and P. Knapton, and T. Longman; C. Hitch and L. Hawes; A. Millar, and R. and J. Dodsley, 1755).
28. BL, Add MS 35360, fol. 118 (Charles Yorke to Philip Yorke, 30 July 1743).

29. James Thomson, *The Castle of Indolence: An Allegorical Poem. Written in imitation of Spenser* (A. Millar, 1748).
30. Catherine Talbot, letter to Elizabeth Carter, 24 October 1751, in *A Series of Letters between Mrs Elizabeth Carter and Miss Catherine Talbot*, ed. Montagu Pennington (F.C. and J Rivington, 1800), 51.
31. BL, Add. MS 46690, fols 28^{v}-29^{r} (14 September 1751).
32. BLARS, L30/9/3/2, fol. 157 (Elizabeth Anson to Jemima Grey, July 1748).
33. This is a point highlighted in Kate Felus's *Secret Life of the Georgian Garden* (I.B. Tauris, 2016), which reminds us 'how important use and enjoyment of their gardens was to the Georgians' (3).
34. BL, Add. MS. 35401, fol. 22 (Daniel Wray to Philip Yorke, 16th August 1743).
35. 'The Borlaciad' is signed 'G. P. W'. It is likely that 'G' refers to Mary Gregory rather than Jemima Grey, as Mary was, by this point, married to a historian at Oxford, Dr David Gregory, and had insight into Oxford life. The 'High Borlace' was a drinking society in Oxford.
36. In 'Epistle from Wrest to the Ingenious Philemon' in *Wrestiana*, the group refers to themselves as 'the inhabitants of Wrest', fol. 20. (signed 'P', Philip Yorke, 'W', Daniel Wray, and 'L', John Lawry).
37. BL, Add. MS 35351, fol. 42 (Lord Chancellor Hardwicke to Philip Yorke, 18 October 1743).
38. BLARS, L30/9/102/9 (Elizabeth Anson to Jemima Grey, 11 June 1747).
39. Kate Felus, *Secret Life of the Georgian Garden*, 29.
40. BL, Add. MS. 35401, fol. 41^{v} (Daniel Wray to Philip Yorke, 11 November 1744).
41. BLARS, L30/9a/6, fol. 21 (Jemima Grey to Catherine Talbot, 11 August 1750).
42. BLARS, L30/9/3/16, fol. 196 (Elizabeth Anson to Jemima Grey, 6 June 1750).
43. BL, Add. MS 35605, fol. 94^{v} (John Lawry to Philip Yorke, 25 June 1741).
44. For an exploration of the way in which aristocratic writers sought to reconcile 'aristocratic manners' and 'commercial print publication', see Markman Ellis, '"An Author in Form": Women Writers, Print Publication, and Elizabeth Montagu's Dialogues of the Dead', *ELH* 79.2 (2012), 417–45 (p. 418), https://doi.org/10.2307/23256760. While Catherine Talbot's works were published, it was only after her death, and she was never fully reconciled to publication. See Betty Schellenberg, 'Catherine Talbot Translates Samuel Richardson: Bridging Social Networks and Media Cultures in the Mid-Eighteenth Century', *Eighteenth-Century Fiction* 29.2 (2017), 201–20, https://doi.org/10.3138/ecf.29.2.201.
45. BL, Add. MS 35401, fol. 15 (Daniel Wray and Philip Yorke, 11 August 1742).
46. Oxford, Bodleian Library, MS Bodl 1010, fols 157–8 (Thomas Wright to Nathaniel Paice, 17 August 1745).
47. BLARS, L30/9/4, fols 30–2 (Jemima Grey to Catherine Talbot, 18 January 1744/5).
48. BLARS, L30/9/4, fols 30–2 (Jemima Grey to Catherine Talbot, 18 January 1744/5).
49. BLARS, L30/9/4, fols 30–2 (Jemima Grey to Catherine Talbot, 18 January 1744/5).
50. BL, Add. MS 35401, fol.116^{r} (Daniel Wray to Philip Yorke, 19 August 1747).
51. Private collection, 'Stanzas in answer to all the preceding False-Wit', *Wrestiana*, fol. 112 (signed 'T', Catherine Talbot)
52. BL, Add. MS 35605, fol. 54^{v} (Philip Yorke to Conyers Middleton, May 1740).
53. BL, Add. MS 35605, 131^{v} (Conyers Middleton to Philip Yorke, 14 November 1742).
54. Letters from Philip's father, Lord Chancellor, describe how Wimpole was used during elections. He specifies, 'I sent Lloyd to Wimple on Saturday, who … has instructions to make preparations for you & your Friends … also to settle with Mr Serjeant what

Preparations are to be made against the day of Election, for I suppose you must go from Wimple, & that some of your Friends will meet you there'. BL, Add. MS 35351, fol. 104^{v} (Lord Chancellor Hardwicke to Philip Yorke, 16 June 1747).
55. Private collection, 'Horace Ode the 1st Imitated to S. J. Esq', *Wrestiana*, fols 120–1.
56. BL, Add. MS 35401, fol. 38 (Daniel Wray to Philip Yorke, 7 September 1743).
57. Private collection, 'Stanzas in answer to all the preceding False-Wit', *Wrestiana*, fol. 144 (signed 'T', Catherine Talbot).
58. Margaret Yorke, 'Epistle addressed to Lady Grey at Wrest Park', in *Bell's Classical Arrangement of Fugitive Poetry* (John Bell, 1789), 141–2; *Gentleman's Magazine* 51.11 (1781), 532.
59. Brotherton, BC MS Lt 119, fols 178–82.
60. BLARS, L30/9/56/21 (Margaret Heathcote to Jemima Grey, 30 July 1756).
61. Nuala Zahedieh, 'An Open Elite? Colonial Commerce, the Country House and the Case of Sir Gilbert Heathcote and Normanton Hall', in Madge Dresser and Andrew Hann (eds), *Slavery and the British Country House* (English Heritage, 2013), 71–7 (pp. 73–4).
62. Qtd. in Philip Chesney Yorke, *The Life and Correspondence of Philip Yorke Earl of Hardwicke Lord High Chancellor of Great Britain*, 3 vols (Cambridge University Press, 1913), II, 159.
63. BLARS, L30/9/56//7 (Margaret Heathcote to Jemima Grey, August 1753).
64. Ruth Larsen, 'An Archaeology of Letter Writing: The Correspondence of Aristocratic Women in Late Eighteenth and Early Nineteenth Century England', in Caroline Archer-Parré and Malcolm Dick (eds), *Pen, Print and Communication in the Eighteenth Century* (Liverpool University Press, 2020), 75–88.
65. BLARS, L30/9/56/8 (Margaret Heathcote to Jemima Grey, 25 November 1753).
66. BLARS, L30/9/56/38 (Margaret Heathcote to Jemima Grey, 25 June 1758).
67. For instance, one on occasion she writes to Grey that 'for Lady Anson your Ladyship has often heard me complain of her as a bad correspondent, but she is really now worse than ever', in BLARS, L30/9/56/10 (Margaret Heathcote to Jemima Grey, 2 August 1754).
68. BLARS, L30/9/56/13 (Margaret Heathcote to Jemima Grey, 16 August 1755).
69. BLARS, L30/9/56/30 (Margaret Heathcote to Jemima Grey, 11 August 1757).

5

'Showing feelings': Exploring and exhibiting women's well-being and emotion in the English country house

Ruby Rutter

In the late 1760s, Sabine Winn (1734–1798) wrote the following words to her absent husband, Sir Rowland Winn, fifth Baronet Nostell (1739–1785), 'I hope you still have time to remember a poor woman in one of the more desolate and ill-fated corners of the universe.'[1] The 'desolate corner' in question was – somewhat incongruously – Nostell Priory near Wakefield in West Yorkshire, now a National Trust property. This large Palladian mansion house designed by James Paine, decorated by Robert Adam, furnished by Thomas Chippendale and set within 300 acres of gardens and landscaped parkland does not feature high on the list of unpleasant environments, but it was not the material properties of Nostell that shaped Sabine's view of it, rather the experiences that she was enduring within its walls. Sabine was not a typical eighteenth-century elite woman; she was Swiss French, spoke little English and had not been trained for a life as mistress of a large country house. Furthermore, her much-adored husband was often away from Nostell either visiting the family's other estates or desperately pursuing a political career in London. Separated from the man for whom she had abandoned all that was comforting and familiar in Switzerland, unable to understand her servants, shunned by her Winn in-laws (who disapproved of Rowland's choice of wife) and struggling to adapt to the cultural and social expectations placed upon her as the wife of an English baronet, Sabine's sense of well-being all but disappeared as she retreated into herself and sank into a desperate state of melancholy.

Sabine's well-being – or lack thereof – is integral to her story and her experience of Nostell Priory, yet the well-being of women like Sabine had rarely been considered in country house scholarship or heritage interpretation until relatively recently. This is remarkable considering that these environments were considered the 'woman's domain' over which they wielded domestic authority and governance as part of their role as mistresses of the house.[2] Indeed, in a keynote speech given at the National Trust's 'Women and Power: Redressing the Balance' conference in March 2019, Annie Reilly noted how women 'have shaped our houses, our gardens, our landscapes, our objects and the very foundation of our organisation', yet their stories have often been 'pushed to the edges or gone entirely unrecorded'.[3] How then can we fully understand a place until we examine the experiences and feelings of the women who help shape it? For example, by disregarding Sabine's well-being (or lack of it) we ignore how it moulded both the story and materiality of Nostell Priory and omits a key puzzle piece in the house's history. It is imperative, therefore, that we understand how the country house influenced the well-being of its women mistresses and residents so that we can better ascertain how such places functioned as lived environments and re-establish how important women's experiences are in the stories of the heritage sites we visit today.

How can we seek to explore and exhibit the history of women's well-being in the country house, however? As this chapter will show, the answer to this question is – quite simply – the study of emotion. Emotion is an integral component of well-being, as good emotional health directly contributes to one's ability to process and accept feelings, manage stress, develop resilience and respond effectively during difficult periods – all contributing factors to an individual's overall well-being and their ability to function effectively in their daily lives. The rise of the history of emotions as a discipline and the 'emotional turn' in museology means that historians and curators alike now have a methodology for identifying and analysing emotional clues in historical sources that allows them to build wider narratives surrounding the well-being of people from the past. Thus, the stories of women like Sabine can now be interpreted in new and meaningful ways that prioritize feeling and well-being in spaces where their voices and experiences were previously overlooked.

This chapter explores how said 'emotional turn' has opened the door for new approaches in interpreting women's well-being and lived experiences via their emotional testimonies. It will show how the use of digital media and other innovative modes of display provides the freedom and creativity to explore these narratives, facilitating dialogues of feeling between today's visitors and those long gone. To do so, this chapter will first consider what is meant by the 'emotional turn' and how it pertains to museum and heritage interpretation using the example of the National Trust's *Red House: Poem of a House* – a digital media installation – as an indicator for how emotion can be successfully conveyed in these spaces. It will then explore how these approaches were adopted in a 2024 installation at Nostell Priory, *Behind the Walls: Sabine Winn at Nostell Priory*, which used emotion to explore Sabine's well-being during her life at Nostell Priory. This chapter will show how emotion and the study of the history of emotions can be used to access and explore well-being in heritage interpretation and will demonstrate how vital this work is in uncovering women's stories (and those of other marginalized groups) after centuries of neglect. It will also demonstrate how such explorations can be used as a tool to service the well-being of visitors, reframing heritage sites as places of retreat, introspection and therapy and providing a fresh approach to the way we interact with these spaces.

Emotion and the past: Accessing and curating feeling

What is the history of emotions?

Emotion is a nebulous and slippery term that has numerous physiological, neurological, cultural and social applications that colour every aspect of life from unremarkable everyday occurrences to extraordinary, once-in-a-lifetime events. While subjective, emotion punctuates our existence as we constantly examine and respond to our own emotional experiences while also monitoring and second-guessing those of the people around us. Assessing the emotions of people in the past is nothing new per se, as Thomas Dixon notes, 'narrative historians routinely speculate about the motivations of protagonists' and attribute 'key decisions to emotional states from jealousy, enmity, or vengeance to devotion, desire and empathy'.[4] Developing the study of emotion in history as a field in its own right is, however, is a relatively new approach that has gained prominence in the last couple of decades. Emotions history provides a framework for how historians can assess the ways humans have experienced and sought to express feeling; positing emotion as the product of the cultural and social environments in which they occur and accessing it via the language and objects that people have used to give form to feeling. For example, a love letter provides evidence for an individual's externalization of internal feeling and presents it in a manner that we – separate from that feeling – can comprehend.[5] William Reddy has compared emotions to colours, noting that both 'have a strong subjective or experiential character' but that these 'reported experiential qualities display great constancy from one person to another'.[6] Thus, while we can never replicate feeling exactly, we can navigate it using the markers that have been left for us throughout the centuries, situated them within their historical context and draw on a universal cognisance of those particular experiences. Studying emotion and using this methodology to examine the well-being of people in the past enriches our understanding of culture, society and human interaction and illuminates how people *felt* about their lives and not just *how* they lived them. In terms of museum and heritage display, emotion can therefore provide a useful means of engaging audiences and facilitating a dialogue of empathy and understanding in ways that traditional cabinet-and-textboard displays cannot.

Museums and the 'emotional turn'

The shift towards feeling and affect in the display and curation of museum spaces roughly mirrored the advent of the emotional turn in academia. This shift reflected what Gaynor Bagnell termed the 'process of individualization' that began in the early 2000s, noting that the turn of the twenty-first century brought with it a new kind of museum visitor who inhabited a 'new social space, a mediascape' that prioritized the individual.[7] As a result, people were engaging with museum and heritage spaces in a self-referential way and, instead of visiting for intellectual stimulation alone, visitors were also wanting to make sense of their own identities and lived experiences through the exhibits.[8] Recognition of this phenomenon produced a curatorial 'move away from text-centred exhibitions' and towards a 'stronger engagement with non-verbal channels of communication' that facilitated visitors' emotions, imaginations and sensory experiences and centred them as more dynamic components of an exhibition rather than passive consumers of information.[9] Curators and museum professionals responded with modes of affective curatorship that, as Marzia Varutti has argued, comprised three main perspectives: (1) emotion elicited by exhibition design, (2) the engendering of emotional responses via specific visitor activities and (3) emotions as exhibition theme.[10] These perspectives embraced new technologies like lighting, soundscapes and digital elements that aided visual storytelling by inviting the visitor to immerse themselves in the exhibit and validated their emotional responses to the stimuli. In the early 2000s, the Imperial War Museum in London embraced Marzia's first and second perspectives with its Trench Experience where visitors to the museum's First World War galleries walked through a mock trench and were told stories about the experiences of various soldiers via mannequin vignettes that lined the route. The exhibit design was immersive and theatrical; there was the constant sound of shell bombardment and men crying out, low lighting and staging such as duckboard floors and sandbags lining imitation mud-packed walls. There were also carefully curated props like field telephones, facsimile maps and soldiers' letters and photos from home. The exhibition was designed to stimulate a sense of ill-being and unease as visitors were forced to experience the past in a way that prioritized human feeling, sensation and emotion.

Varutti's third perspective – emotions as exhibition theme – reflects how the conceptualization of what *belonged* in museums also changed in line with the prioritization of feeling and affect. For example, the Museum of Broken Relationships in Zagreb, Croatia (established in 2010) is dedicated to housing donated personal items that tell stories of the romantic break-ups of ordinary people. Exhibits include a vast array of objects from keyrings, toys, shoes and books, to dreadlocks, an axe and kitchen appliances – all of which are displayed alongside a note from the original owner detailing the story of their broken relationship and their emotional affinity to the object. For example, a plush Snoopy toy is explained as being a seventeenth-birthday gift given to the owner by their ex-husband who, after thirty years of marriage and three sons, fell in love with another woman.[11] The collection highlights how everyday objects can become saturated with feeling and emotion, capable of conveying often painful human stories. The museum has been described as 'a museum of feelings' in its clever ability to capture and convey the human experience of love through often unremarkable objects, emphasizing the idea that the ordinary things that populate our lives are often markers of emotion and experience that is personal and hidden from the world. The experience of well-being (and illbeing) is, therefore, capable of being transferred onto the objects that surround us as they become saturated with emotional meaning. When presented in a museum setting with an explanatory note from the owner, visitors to the Museum of Broken Relationships are thus invited to examine the private emotions of others and the forms they've assumed, creating an important history of feeling.[12]

Emotion and country house interpretation: The well-being of national identity

Despite delivering similar objectives to museums – the preservation of the past, education, spectacle and accessibility – country houses face a singular set of curatorial challenges and are required to function in ways distinct from purpose-built museum and gallery spaces. For example, the curation of a country house must be done with concern for the building's conservation as well as the objects in the collection. Spaces cannot be physically altered to the extent that the team at the Imperial War Museum were able to construct the Trench Experience, and any grand-scale installation is subject to risk assessments and likely to incur costly conservation measures and protections. On the other hand, as a historic lived environment, a country house already holds the kind of emotional data that the Trench Experience sought to replicate in its interpretation and display. Here, the past is implicit as soon as the visitor steps over the threshold with both the house and its collection representing the debris of the human experiences and emotions that played out there.

There is of course another – often contested – layer of emotion that reflects the status of country houses and other heritage settings as identity-forming national landmarks. In recent years, the National Trust has found itself acting (rather unwillingly) as the battleground for the culture wars in which groups tussle over which reading of British history ought to be dominant in heritage interpretation. For example, programming that has seen the country house acknowledge colonialism, sexism, LGBTQIA+ stories and classism in its history has been met with resistance by groups for whom the inclusion of marginalized people contravenes their (narrow) idea of Britain and Britishness. Despite many members of groups like Restore Trust insisting that their criticism of the National Trust is free from feeling and reliant on historical 'fact' or 'common sense', it is arguably based solely on emotional notions of personal and national identity – notions that are being frequently contested as contemporary research evolves.[13] For example, in an interview with *The Telegraph* in October 2022, former Restore Trust director, Zewditu Gebreyohanes, argued that 'factual information' has been replaced by 'trendy interpretations of history' and described the inclusion of Winston Churchill's home of Chartwell in Kent in a report that examined Trust properties' links to slavery and colonialism as 'anti-British.'[14] Gebreyohanes made this statement despite the Trust's report being factually compiled, evidence-led and deliberately free from specific 'judgements about people or the places'.[15] The relationship between the English country house and ideas of national identity is arguably a phenomenon that was instigated with the Victoria and Albert Museum's 1974 exhibition *The Destruction of the Country House 1875–1975*. This exhibition documented the demise of the country house and the wide-scale destruction of important buildings and included a 'hall of destruction' decorated with tumbling columns superimposed with images of demolished houses.[16] The exhibition sparked outcry and prompted the public to reconceptualize their role in the protection and preservation of heritage sites, inspiring the formation of campaigning groups like Save Britain's Heritage.

In many ways, the action that *The Destruction of the Country House* inspired the public to take to protect the nation's country houses is a story about universal concern for well-being of the nation's history and cultural landscape. Therefore, resistance to changes in country house interpretation is arguably born from this concern. However, the fear that exploring new avenues of interpretation or points of view might disassemble what many hold dear in terms of national identity runs contrary to the history of the country house itself. As Stephanie Barczewski has argued, the English country house has survived precisely because of its ability to adapt to, withstand and embrace change, whether in the guise of religious reformation, civil war, invasion, or political upheaval.[17] In fact, the 'conservative, nostalgic view of English identity' that is seen in popular media such as Downton Abbey and espoused by Gebreyohanes and others is one born in the twentieth century and reinforces the idea of class hierarchy and compassionate conservativism without considering the human stories within these systems. Thus, to truly ensure the well-being and preservation of British history and heritage, said history cannot rely on nostalgia and must instead be subject to constant re-evaluation and re-interpretation. As contemporary interests and fields of study evolve, previously overlooked perspectives will naturally be revealed, and exposing these to an interested public will ensure that these sites survive and thrive in the future.

Poem of a House: An installation at Red House, Bexleyheath

Poem of a House was a 2017 installation at Red House in Bexleyheath, the family home of William Morris (1834–1896), and is an excellent example of how the voices of marginalized and forgotten people can be revived via emotional storytelling that foregrounds well-being. The project was led by filmmaker and director David Bickerstaff and his team at NewAngle Productions and focussed on re-establishing the stories of Red House's female residents who have all but been eclipsed by Morris's status as one of Britain's most important artistic figures.[18] In an interview in March 2024, Bickerstaff explained this decision to focus specifically on the women's stories:

> Visitors know that they're visiting William Morris' house, and his presence is inferred by the house itself and by everyone else – and everyone else tended to be female. Women were working in this space and making the things that we know and associate with Morris, but they were also talking and laughing and sharing experiences. None of this was recorded but is fundamental to the finished [Morris & Co.] products, and we wanted to show that.[19]

Red House was designed by Morris and the architect Peter Webb in 1859 and as well as acting as a family home for Morris and his new wife Jane Burden, it was built to be a 'Palace of Art' and, upon completion in 1860, became a creative hub for prominent artistic figures like pre-Raphaelite painters Edward Burne-Jones and Dante Gabriel Rossetti and acted as the birthplace for Morris's company, Morris, Marshall, Faulkner & Co.[20] Morris's creative endeavours at Red House were, however, largely facilitated by the women in his life – wife Jane, cook Charlotte Cooper, housemaid Jane Chapman and nanny Elizabeth Reynolds – who not only undertook domestic work to maintain the household but also contributed creatively to many Morris & Co. designs. Despite this, little to no records of the women's work or experiences in the house remain, with Jane Morris, a talented embroiderer, bookbinder and calligrapher whose work often inspired her husband, noting in 1904, 'why should there be any special record of me when I have never done any special work?'[21] Jane's dismissive comments about her value and contribution are reflective of Victorian patriarchal attitudes to women and indicate why evidence of both her domestic and creative work is sparse. Much of Jane's life has remained somewhat of a mystery, glimpsed at only occasionally in the biographies of Morris, Rossetti, or her later lover Wilfred Scawen Blunt.[22] In her monograph about Jane's life, Wendy Parkins notes that a paucity of textual sources relating to her have rendered her a woman with no history, with her story instead being 'enhanced by reference to the creative work of William Morris and Dante Gabriel Rossetti, as if their literary and artistic productions could illuminate her life as well as theirs'.[23]

However, while source scarcity is a problem for the historian, it is not an insurmountable one, as demonstrated by Parkins's interdisciplinary approach to her biography of Jane that combined, 'elements of historical method' with 'the construction of character in ways compatible with the novel'.[24] This methodology involved Parkins taking those surviving fragments of historical truth and applying well-founded embellishments that fleshed out the essence of who Jane was. For example, Parkins reads Jane's handiwork as evidence of self-construction that was 'shaped by conventions and practices concerning art and authorship, emotion and relationships, gender and class'.[25] She argues that Jane's 'Daisy' wall-hangings at Red House are a pertinent example of this as they evidence her changing class identity from a working-class woman to a member of the genteel middle following marriage to Morris; The simple repeating pattern of the hangings was typically worked by middle-class women at this time, whereas the blue serge fabric was more commonly used for working-class clothing.[26] Jane returned to this fabric so often in her Morris & Co. designs that it later became synonymous with her husband's socialism – an irony that epitomizes the co-opting of women's self-expression as male ingenuity. Parkins notes that material culture like Jane's wall hangings, coupled with sources that illuminate the more binary facts about Jane's life (birth date, parentage etc) provide access to her emotional construction of self and her social and cultural locus. This, Parkins argues, is created through both 'material and discursive processes and that we can interpret these processes of self-construction through the objects that remain – letters, embroidery, designs'.[27] Thus, despite a lack of documentary evidence, by examining the objects that Jane regularly engaged with Parkins was able to construct a picture of Jane's emotional well-being that revealed the rhythm and nuance of her daily life.

Given that extant sources of Jane Burden are meagre in number despite her prominent status within the Arts and Crafts movement, those relating to the other women at Red House are practically non-existent, particularly those pertaining to their well-being and emotion. As such, when working on the *Poem of a House* David Bickerstaff and his team found that they too needed to adopt an interdisciplinary, intertextual approach that provided visitors with an understanding of the women's emotional, domestic and creative contributions. To do so, the team initially considered projection mapping archive imagery onto furniture in the house to connect Morris & Co.'s creativity with the domestic space. It was felt, however, that this interpretation was more in line with 'traditional museology' and lacked dynamism which meant visitors 'might not feel that emotional connection' that they were seeking to convey.[28] The team instead decided to take advantage of Red House's status as a site of creativity and use those few surviving textual sources as inspiration for a poetic, emotions-led interpretation that restored the women's experiences – in short plugging the archival gaps. This involved working with scriptwriter Jerome Vincent to create a free-flowing monologue that communicated the innermost thoughts of the entire 'sisterhood of vibrant women [who] worked together' by cycling through a variety of topics and feelings relating to what the team interpreted a women's experience of Red House to be.[29] Bickerstaff acknowledged that this approach walked a thin line between interpretation and anachronism, however, and so to avoid making unfounded historical claims he explained that the script had to be performed by someone who was 'free from contemporary baggage or interpretation of the past' and embody the role of a neutral character *à la* Greek theatre, telling the story 'almost dispassionately, but then breaking off to play a different part or assume another voice'. Actress Fiamma Bennett assumed this role and performed what Bickerstaff described as a 'one-woman show' where she 'laughed, cried and talked passionately about an internal emotion but then at other times described the garden, mimed performing a task, or recited a list – weaving the idea of women's emotion and well-being into the fabric of daily life at Red House'.[30] Bennett's performance was then layered with vibrant and evocative imagery such as Morris & Co. wallpaper designs, photographs of fruits and flowers that grew in the garden, paint swatches, embroidered fabric and décor from the house itself.

The use of images of Morris & Co. designs alongside Bennett's spoken word performance successfully re-established the women's contribution to the designs we typically associate with Morris. Furthermore, using the Red House dining room as the location for the projection rather than a location more explicitly evocative of artistic production also helped to centre the women's narratives and creative outputs within the domestic sphere, emphasizing the value and importance of all forms of labour. Staging the installation at the Red House, and including archival imagery, also inferred legitimacy and authenticity to the project despite the words that Bennett performed being a modern interpretation of feeling and emotion. This dynamic allowed visitors to embark on, 'an augmented journey through which they could trigger their imagination beyond what was there already' and enabled them to 'imagine beyond the script and reconstruct experience and emotion within themselves'.[31] In so doing, Bickerstaff and his team created an experience for visitors in which they were required to engage emotionally with the themes and stimuli being presented to them which, in turn, turned the installation into a well-being exercise in and of itself.

In the same way that Parkins felt that an interdisciplinary approach to Jane Burden's biography recovered her voice from the fragments of sources about her life, Bickerstaff noted that digital media allowed the team to sidestep the restrictions of archival integrity with traditional text-and-board displays while still providing a meaningful and engaging experience for visitors. The result was an installation that injected a space long associated with male enterprise and achievement with women's work and emotion and encouraged visitors to recentre these women in their understanding of the Arts and Crafts Movement. The *Poem of a House* won the National Trust Experiences Award in 2017 in the Best Storytelling category, and its ability to pull through emotion and access human feeling in a way that both illuminated the stories of the house, the women who lived there and those visiting a century and a half later is testament to what can be achieved via a minimally invasive, relatively low-cost project.

Behind the walls: Sabine Winn at Nostell Priory

As discussed in this chapter's introduction, the well-being of Sabine Winn during her time as mistress of Nostell Priory in the eighteenth century had a profound effect on the house, its servants and her family, and it is this story that curator Simon McCormack sought to flesh out when he embarked on a re-interpretation of her dressing room in 2022. Appropriately naming the re-interpretation, *Behind the Walls: Sabine Winn at Nostell Priory*, McCormack set out to tell Sabine's story in a way that engaged visitors with themes of mental health and well-being, and that also revealed the very human story that was woven into the very fabric of the house. Much work on Sabine Winn has viewed her pleas for affection and attention from her husband and her disquietude to life at Nostell with irritation rather than as evidence of human feeling and experience. In recent yearsacademics like Kerry Bristol and Serena Dyer have re-examined the nuances of her life and character. I too became interested in Sabine's letters during my doctoral study in which I explored how the pressure to perform elite femininity in the country house, coupled with her 'otherness', deeply affected her well-being.[32] I was therefore thrilled to be involved with and contribute my research to McCormack's creative interpretive installation which re-presented Sabine's story as one that elicited empathy and understanding, rather than condemnation. This section discusses how the approaches to museum and heritage display discussed previously in this chapter were adopted for *Behind the Walls* and how McCormack and his team combined academia, heritage interpretation and community engagement to create an emotions-led installation that encouraged visitors to Nostell Priory to consider the role that well-being plays in their interpretation of the house today and in the past.

Who was Sabine Winn?

Sabine was born in Vevey on the Swiss French border on 25 March 1734 to Jacques Phillipe d'Hervart (1706–1765) Baron de Saint-Légier and Jeanne Esther Dunz d'Hervart (1707–1779). Jacques Phillipe held the position of Governor of Vevey and, as the only surviving d'Hervart child, Sabine was set to inherit a fortune of £70,000 upon her father's death.[33] In Vevey, Sabine enjoyed a lavish lifestyle and a dynamic and fashionable social circle and, when she married the serious, religious and much older Major Gabriel May in 1754, steadfastly refused to leave her friends and family for life as a military wife in her husband's native Bern. The couple's marriage was disconnected and passionless as a result, and when Sabine was introduced to the handsome Rowland Winn in 1756, she soon found herself entangled in a 'little affair' with the Englishman.[34]

Rowland was intoxicated with the beautiful Sabine, who was described as 'a being of angelic order' with 'fine dark eyes sparkling with a radiance exclusively their own'.[35] Rowland's father, the fourth Baronet Nostell, was less than impressed with his son's liaison with Sabine however and urged Rowland to leave Vevey for nearby Lausanne to remove all temptation. Rowland eventually acquiesced, writing to reassure his father that the affair had been, 'only a little amusement', but he kept Sabine in his thoughts and when Gabriel May died in 1759, immediately sought her hand in marriage. Rowland's father, still uncomfortable with his son's choice of bride but unable to object to a daughter-in-law with such a large fortune, attempted to persuade his son to change his mind by warning of the dangers of a non-English wife:

> Picture a foreign wife at the head of the dinner table ... unable to converse ... as an alien [she will be] unacquainted with the language, customs, and manners of the English nation, which you will have observed are very different than those of other countries.[36]

Rowland's three sisters also questioned Sabine's suitability in a letter to their father, writing, 'we are afraid we shall be greatly at a loss to keep up conversation with her, as you say she knows nothing of the English language & we have forgot the greatest part of our French'.[37] Sabine's fitness to manage a large country estate was thus already in question before she had even set foot on English soil. Despite all objections, the couple married on 4 December 1761 and soon departed Switzerland for London, but Rowland's family's words of caution would prove to be prophetic.

Sabine and Rowland spent several dazzlingly happy years in London, where the cosmopolitan diversions and diverse society reminded Sabine of her social life in Vevey. Fashionable elites would converse easily in French – removing the need for her to learn English – and her status as a Swiss French woman intrigued her peers and gilded her with a patina of exoticism. However, Sabine's experience of her new country would change dramatically when the couple were required to move to Yorkshire to be nearer the Winn family estates in 1763. The couple lived first at Badsworth Hall near Pontefract – a house rented to them by the Marquess of Rockingham – before moving to Nostell Priory following the death of Rowland's father in 1765. Seeking to make Nostell feel more like home, Rowland and Sabine embarked on an extensive renovation project, commissioning Robert Adam to remodel the house and buying fashionable Chippendale furniture and expensive décor such as a bird of paradise wallpaper scheme that still hangs in Nostell's staterooms.[38]

Much of the renovation project was fuelled by a desire to create a fashionable hub in which to host lavish parties and exert political and social influence among their peers. Sadly however, the harmony of Nostell's interiors and their promise of sociability was not to be, nor was it reflected in the couple's marriage as Rowland – desperate to fulfil a political ambition and obtain a peerage – regularly left his wife in Yorkshire as he travelled to London.[39] Still unable to speak English, Rowland's absences meant that Sabine was frequently left without anyone to confide in or provide companionship. This language barrier also meant that Sabine struggled to communicate with Nostell's household staff and was unable to assert her authority when Rowland was not there to translate, making her appear disinterested and standoffish to those who served her every day. These boundaries encouraged resentment and mistrust between Sabine and her household staff, and they began to defy her authority.[40] In her many letters to Rowland, Sabine complained of 'gossipy, quarrelsome housekeepers' who allowed the junior staff to help themselves to the sideboard, and scullery maids who refused to milk cows and make bread.[41] Worst of all, however, was the licentious behaviour of some of the servants who regularly snuck into each other's rooms. In October 1775, Sabine wrote to her husband about the escalating discord in the house:

> She [the housekeeper'] is infamous … Clement [the steward] is twenty times a day in the housekeeper's room … she [the housekeeper] makes a scandalous noise in front of everyone and is prone to abominable extravagance. She is the worst quality of person that I ever had the chance to meet, and she is a real plague to the reputation of this house.[42]

The conditions between Sabine and her staff, her increasing loneliness and her deep longing for her husband meant that her well-being began to rapidly disintegrate, affecting her health and her happiness. In a 1765 letter to Rowland, Sabine wrote, 'come comfort me, make me well again with your presence', demonstrating how closely she aligned her happiness with him and how little comfort she derived from Nostell without his company.[43] In another letter from 1769 Sabine sadly lamented, 'I live only for you, and yet I am always without you' and – following a particularly long period of separation – she dramatically conveyed how unsettling and unpleasant Nostell was without Rowland, 'I hope however that you still have time to remember a poor woman in one of the more desolate and ill-fated corners of the universe.'[44] As Fay Bound Alberti has written, loneliness is not simply being alone but is 'a conscious, cognitive feeling of estrangement or social separation from meaningful others; an emotional lack that concerns a person's place in the world'.[45] Those suffering from loneliness and isolation are thus more likely to view their surroundings unfavourably as a lack of 'personal control, socially supportive relationships, and restoration from stress and fatigue are all affected by properties of the built environment'.[46] For Sabine, Nostell Priory is likely to have represented the physical manifestation of her suffering and ill-being, meaning that no amount of fashionable wallpaper could cover the emotional chasm her husband left behind every time he embarked for London. As a result, Sabine's dejection consumed her and she remarked that 'the way I am living right now would be better described as vegetating like a plant, like a creature. I am not at my best; I can't sleep nor eat'.[47] Despite recognizing that the apathy that she felt towards her life was insupportable, Sabine's despondency overpowered her and prevented her from functioning in the manner expected of an elite mistress, writing in another letter that she was 'bored to death; it is not in my power to get used to this life'.[48] Remarking that it was 'cruel to be left alone', Sabine retreated to her dressing room and her 'cher lit' (dear bed) for comfort, locking herself away from a world that ignored, rejected and increasingly refused to modify its boundaries to accommodate her.[49]

The installation

In many ways, Sabine's life is completely alien to any modern visitor to Nostell. Everything from her lifestyle to the pressure placed on her by the Winn family to be the perfect elite mistress, embodying all the ideals of eighteenth-century femininity. There are aspects of her lived experience that are incredibly relatable however, such as her sense of loneliness, isolation, apathy and marital disharmony. It was therefore important for McCormack and the curatorial team to devise programming that not only re-established Sabine's voice for *Behind the Walls* but also enabled access points for visitors to assimilate their own experiences with Sabine's narrative, building a greater connection to and deeper understanding of Nostell Priory.

The reinterpretation of Sabine's life was concentrated in her dressing room, but traditional text panels ran throughout the house's normal visitor route providing context for Sabine's story and building tension ahead of the visitors' engagement with the main exhibition space. All nine rooms of the visitor route communicated aspects of Sabine's life and established the obstacles that she faced as mistress of Nostell, juxtaposing the beautiful interiors with stories of discomfort and unhappiness. For example, the dining room referenced the fourth Baronet's comments about Sabine's inability to converse at the head of the dinner table. These panels conveyed the kind of social and cultural purgatory that she occupied by never being fully accepted by her in-laws, social equals, or staff. To further communicate this, the panels also led with Sabine's testimony and that of those around her instead of a curatorial analysis of the primary sources to ensure that her emotional experiences weren't sanitized by third-party interpretation.

Finally, following the scene setting of the previous rooms, visitors entered Sabine's dressing room and were confronted with an interpretation focused specifically on accessing her inner world via a digital media installation and objects specific to her life. During the eighteenth century, dressing rooms, or closets, were synonymous with female privacy and were one of the few rooms in the house whose boundaries were to be respected.[50] As noted above, Sabine often retreated to her dressing room during difficult times and it was there that she spent most of her time writing, reading and practising crafts. Her dressing room thus provided her with solace and comfort amidst the hostility of the house and was arguably the space in which she allowed herself to feel the most pain and anguish far away from prying eyes. McCormack's decision to use the dressing room as the site through which Sabine's inner world was explored was thus pertinent and meaningful.

McCormack and the team were somewhat limited with what they could physically change about the space; the original blue walls had long been painted over and restoring it to Sabine's taste would be both costly and invasive. Objects relating to Sabine could be displayed in the room however, with a small selection of furniture such as a harpsichord, a Chippendale commode (or dressing table) and a pair of French-style chairs being brought in from elsewhere in the house. A secretaire that had been made for Sabine was also displayed alongside a selection of Sabine's letters and their translations which symbolically returned the missives to their place of creation and centred the secretaire as the location in which Sabine may have committed her feelings to paper. The secretaire was commissioned for Sabine for the Winns' London house, and it is not confirmed whether she would have used it at Nostell before 1785, however, its inclusion is an example of McCormack's 'lateral not literal' presentation that captures the essence of experience over strictly factual interpretation.

Several paintings were also hung in the room, some of these were contemporary to Sabine's time at Nostell such as a series by Antonio Zucchi depicting scenes from classical mythology and a set of forty-four cabinet paintings purchased by

Rowland – both of which had previously been reintroduced by the Trust as part of a more traditional approach to the house's presentation. McCormack and his team also included objects that explicitly drew out the emotional themes of the installation, like a painting of Cleopatra being bitten by an asp which evoked the idea of failed love, tragedy and painful separation from one's romantic partner. This painting also neatly conveyed the idea of beauty muting emotional pain and mirrored Sabine's enduring loneliness in a cosmetically sumptuous house.

The dressing room also hosted some of Sabine's dressed prints. Deriving from *decoupage à la mode* (a process involving the pasting of prints onto furniture and then sealing with varnish), dressed prints were decorated with delicately cut pieces of fabric, cord, ribbon or other prints and papers and then drawn or painted on and embroidered to emphasize certain elements. The prints Sabine decorated were sent to her by Rowland between 1761 and 1765 and featured romantic imagery of couples together in domestic settings. Sabine had also written, 'Monsieur Rowland Winn gave me this picture, Sabine Winn née Herwart' – explicitly denoting the prints as a gift from Rowland to herself and connecting their relationship and affection with the image on the reverse. Indeed, Serena Dyer has speculated that Sabine used swatches of fabric from hers and Rowland's clothes which infers romance and physical togetherness.[51] Not only was this a hobby that brought Rowland and Sabine closer but would have also supported her well-being by providing her with an outlet through which to express herself creatively. As with the example of the Snoopy soft toy from the Museum of Broken Relationships, the presence of these prints in the installation acted as evidence of Sabine's emotions and well-being made flesh. On the back of each print's frame are the room name and location, indicating that they were originally hung in the dressing room.

While the installation was intended to convey Sabine's emotional responses to her experiences, it was also meant to evoke feeling and introspection in its visitors. McCormack noted that the dressing room thus needed to go further than simply displaying her belongings and provide audiences with the tools to elicit emotion and self-reflect on their own experiences. He explained:

> Rather than present the room in its latest iteration or try to create a facsimile restoration of how it might originally have looked, our ambition for Sabine's dressing room is for it to be an immersive experience that shares the emotive complexity of Sabine's story. We aim for visitors to feel/witness what Sabine may have felt, how she felt 'othered' in her own home by the language barrier and lack of agency.[52]

McCormack was clear, however, that the project had to be careful not to directly recreate or dramatize Sabine's words and feelings and present these as fact as this approach risked anachronism and contentious overinterpretation. Instead – and much like the *Poem of a House* – the installation had to encourage visitors to engage with Sabine's story and use the evidence presented to them as a starting point for a journey of self-reflection and interpretation that was personal and sensitive to them. A survey of visitors to Nostell Priory undertaken by placement students Harry Ellerd-Cheers, Louise Edge and Leah Williams-McIntosh during the preliminary research stage of this project showed that people were drawn to Sabine as her story of isolation and loneliness touched on memories of their own well-being during the recent Covid-19 pandemic and lockdown. The prospect of visiting a country house and engaging with an installation in a way that tapped into these emotions was a cathartic one for people who were still processing the trauma caused by the confiscation of social connection and community. These findings also reflected those of the National Trust more widely, whose visitor data shows that human stories appeal most to visitors. As McCormack noted, presenting heritage interpretation in a way that encourages visitors to feel and reflect on their own experiences makes 'country houses relevant and accessible and makes people feel like they belong; [it] brings the past to life, and allows these places to be shown as continually evolving, lived spaces, not mausoleums of stuff and grandeur'.[53]

Using the *Poem of a House* as inspiration to achieve this goal, McCormack sought to commission a digital media installation that would be projected on to the walls of Sabine's dressing room and foster a connection to the past by aiding visitors in viewing 'the materiality of the house primarily through the lens of lived experience'.[54] Manchester-based design team 24 Design were awarded the commission and project lead Charlotte Smithson explained the team's motivation behind the installation in an interview in June 2024:

> It's easy to make assumptions about the lives of women like Sabine. Lots can be read into her habits, interests, wellbeing and lifestyle but we'll never really know what life was like for her or how she felt. This project gave us the opportunity to examine what we know about her and find ways of relating to her in today's context.[55]

24 Design's vision for the installation involved working with local mental health charity, Mindful Movers, to document their interaction with and interpretation of Sabine's story. Mindful Movers are a 'walk and talk' group based in and around Wakefield whose focus is to improve well-being through mental and physical health. The group often meet at Nostell to walk around its vast gardens and parklands, and it was felt that this established relationship with the estate within the context of the group's own mental health and well-being meant that they would be able to reflect on Sabine's story in a perceptive way. 24 Design worked with the group over several sessions in which they discussed Sabine's life, read her letters, held her belongings and talked about their own experiences with well-being, mental health and Nostell Priory. The final session acted as a culmination of these discussions and was filmed so that the final digital media projection would include the rich array of topics, thoughts and feelings that the group had been developing over the previous weeks. Of this process, Smithson explained:

> During the research stages of creating this work, the group held fascinating discussions in response to reading Sabine's letters and looking at her personal belongings [and had] had lots of unanswerable questions about the life she lived. The dynamic amongst Mindful Movers is one of ease – as a group they seem very comfortable to talk and discuss ideas, share their experiences and support one

> another. We wanted to capture that in the film and provide a glimpse into their conversations. Hearing them tell Sabine's story and reflect upon how they think she might have felt, revealed the strong sense of fondness the group has established for her. They make her feel much more accessible than a woman in painted portraits.[56]

The group covered vast ground in their discussions from the idea that Sabine's dressing room was the place where she could just 'be Sabine' in a house where there 'seemed to be no space for her', to the consideration of the role that pets played in her life and how they indicated her desire to improve her well-being as it 'calms the heart to stroke a dog' and that 'animals don't judge you'.[57] Another group member perceptively compared their own use of an anxiety band to regulate emotion with Sabine's engagement with textiles and the dressed prints, noting that grounding oneself with different textures and tactile engagement with your surroundings is something that is often talked about in therapy today.

These discussions were wholly led by the group with 24 Design choosing to avoid regulating the discussion in line with the historical facts of Sabine's life, wanting to instead draw out how her story touched the group's own experiences and in turn allowing the project to become one primarily concerned with introspection. This approach meant that McCormack and 24 Design could sidestep any issues of anachronism or overinterpretation of Sabine's feelings that may have occurred with a more traditional installation and instead encourage Mindful Movers (and National Trust visitors subsequently) to layer this space with their own emotion and create a connection with Nostell that was personal and meaningful. Of their involvement with the installation, the group explained that it had been 'an amazing opportunity' to 'look at Sabine through the lens of lived experience' and made them feel closer to her and to the house. As such, the entire project became one that enriched the well-being of the group as they found comfort in learning about and empathizing with Sabine while thinking about their own experiences. That Nostell Priory is the setting for their walks and meetings also highlighted how a place can be one of both enjoyment and endurance depending on a myriad of complicated and personal components and influences.

The final projection on to the walls of the dressing room included Mindful Movers' discussions alongside images of material culture relating to Sabine such as paintings, drawings, letters, pages of books from her personal library, close-up images of the dressed prints and textiles and images of the house and garden. The result was a creative interpretive installation that showcased the material remnants of Sabine's life in conjunction with digital media that invited visitors to explore their own imaginings of the emotional history of the dressing room and self-reflect on their own experiences, coping mechanisms, well-being activities and what brought them joy and comfort in their own lives.

Conclusions

This chapter has shown how affective developments in museology and heritage interpretation following the 'emotional turn' have facilitated new modes of display that promote greater engagement with visitors by appealing directly to how they feel.

It has demonstrated how these approaches have been used to convey the experiences of historic figures, creating environments that encourage visitors to imagine the past by presenting emotionally suggestive stimuli that triggers their own conception of that feeling. This process allows visitors to museums and heritage sites to navigate these spaces by prioritizing their individual responses. In so doing, such installations also foster stronger relationships between visitors and heritage sites by facilitating a sense of belonging and inclusivity and recognizing them as individuals who move through and interact with spaces emotionally – just like those who came before them. As the testimony of the Mindful Movers group at Nostell Priory has shown, this process can be deeply enriching and contribute to a sense of purpose and meaning in life while also revealing the importance of well-being throughout history. Furthermore, by demonstrating that well-being is something that has always been of primary concern to people, and not something that has found popularity in modern culture, we are also able to dispel criticisms of the pursuit of well-being as 'wishy washy' or antithetical to ideas regarding the British 'stiff upper lip'. In conclusion, the successful engagement with emotion in these exhibitions highlights the significant role that museums and heritage sites can play in promoting individual and collective well-being. By curating spaces that encourage emotional connection to and reflection on the past, heritage institutions can contribute to a more meaningful and fulfilling experience for their visitors and ensures the role of the English country house remains a space for everyone, forever.

Notes

1. WYAS Wakefield, WYW1352/1/4/29/17, Sabine Winn to Sir Rowland Winn, n.d., original text in French: *J'espère néanmoins qu'il te reste des moments pour te rappeler d'une pauvre femme dans un des coins de l'univers de il n'est point en mon pouvoir de m'accoutumer à cette vie.*
2. See Trevor Lummis and Jan Marsh, *The Woman's Domain: Women and the English Country House* (Penguin, 1993).
3. Presenter Anne Reilly (6–7 March 2019), *Women and Power: Redressing the Balance* (Keynote), National Trust, St Hugh's College, Oxford, www.torch.ox.ac.uk/women-and-power-redressing-the-balance-keynote (accessed 2 February 2024).
4. Thomas Dixon, *The History of Emotions: A Very Short Introduction* (Oxford University Press, 2023), 1.
5. For an introduction to the field, see Rob Boddice, *The History of Emotions* (Manchester University Press, 2018); Barbara H. Rosenwein and Cristiani Riccardo, *What Is the History of Emotions?* (Cambridge University Press, 2018); Thomas Dixon, *The History of Emotions* (Oxford University Press, 2023).
6. William Reddy, *The Navigation of Feeling: A Framework for the History of Emotions* (Cambridge University Press, 2001), 3.
7. Gaynor Bagnell, 'Performance and Performativity at Heritage Sites', *Museum and Society* 1.2 (2003), 87–103 (p. 96).
8. Andrea Witcomb, 'Toward a Pedagogy of Feeling: Understanding How Museums Create a Space for Cross-Cultural Encounters', in *The International Handbooks of Museum Studies: Museum Theory* (John Wiley & Sons, 2015), 321.

9. Sheila Watson, 'Emotions in the History Museum', in *The International Handbook of Museum Studies: Museum Theory* (John Wiley & Sons, 2015), 283–301 (p. 287); Marzia Varutti, 'The Affective Turn in Museums and the Rise of Affective Curatorship', *Museum Management and Curatorship* 38.1 (2023), 61–75 (p. 63).
10. Varutti, *The Affective Turn*, 64.
11. '"A Plush Snoopy" Leiden, Netherlands', *Museum of Broken Relationships,* https://brokenships.com/explore/a-plush-snoopy.
12. Sirje Helme, 'Museum of Broken Relationships', in *Revisiting Museums of Influence* (Routledge, 2020), 121–4 (p. 121).
13. Peter York, 'Who Are the Culture Warriors? A Closer Look at the Group Piling Pressure on the National Trust', *Art Newspaper*, 10 November 2023, www.theartnewspaper.com/2023/11/10/who-are-the-culture-warriors-a-closer-look-at-the-group-piling-pressure-on-the-national-trust (accessed 10 February 2024).
14. Simon Heffer, 'The National Trust Has an Agenda: Skewing History so It's Anti-British', *The Telegraph*, 14 October 2022; Celia Richardson, 'Churchill and Chartwell: Telling the Whole Story', *National Trust Blog*, 2020, ww.nationaltrust.org.uk/who-we-are/news/churchill-and-chartwell-telling-the-whole-story (accessed 10 February 2024).
15. Heffer, 'The National Trust Has an Agenda'; Richardson, 'Churchill and Chartwell: Telling the Whole Story'.
16. Roy Strong and John Harris, *The Destruction of the Country House, 1875–1975* (Thames and Hudson, 1974).
17. Stephanie Barczewski, *How the Country House Became English* (Reaktion Books, 2023), 33.
18. David Bickerstaff, 'Poem of a House', *Atomic TV,* www.atomictv.com/redhouse.html (accessed 15 January 2024).
19. David Bickerstaff, interview conducted by Ruby Rutter, 7 March 2024.
20. Jan Marsh, *William Morris and Red House* (National Trust Books, 2005), 18.
21. Quoted in Wendy Parkins, *Jane Morris: The Burden of History* (Edinburgh University Press, 2013), 1.
22. Parkins, *Jane Morris,* 8.
23. Parkins, *Jane Morris,* 1.
24. Parkins, *Jane Morris,* 2.
25. Parkins, *Jane Morris,* 2.
26. Parkins, *Jane Morris,* 150.
27. Parkins, *Jane Morris,* 2.
28. David Bickerstaff, interview conducted by Ruby Rutter, 7 March 2024.
29. David Bickerstaff, interview conducted by Ruby Rutter, 7 March 2024.
30. David Bickerstaff, interview conducted by Ruby Rutter, 7 March 2024.
31. David Bickerstaff, interview conducted by Ruby Rutter, 7 March 2024.
32. See Ruby Rutter, *Elite Women, Emotions and the Lived Experience in the Eighteenth-Century Country House, 1700–1830* (unpublished doctoral thesis, University of Manchester, 2022).
33. Serena Dyer, *Material Lives: Women Makers and Consumer Culture in the 18th Century* (Bloomsbury Academic, 2021), 125; Christopher Todd, 'A Swiss Milady in Yorkshire: Sabine Winn of Nostell Priory', *Yorkshire Archaeological Journal* 77 (2005), 205–24.
34. WYW1352/1/1/4/27, 19 October 1756. Original text in French: *une petite affaire.*

35. Catharine Cappe, *Memoirs of the Life of the Late Mrs. Catharine Cappe* (London: 1823), 75.
36. WYAS Wakefield, WYW1352/1/4/48/10, fourth Baronet Winn to Rowland Winn, 21 March 1761; WYAS Wakefield, WYW1352/1/4/3/7, fourth Baronet Winn to Rowland Winn, 4 June 1761.
37. WYAS Wakefield, WYW1352/1/1/4/15 Catherine, Ann, Mary and Elizabeth Winn to their father the fourth Baronet Nostell, 28 November 1761.
38. Todd, *A Swiss Milady*, 212.
39. Kerry Bristol, 'A Tale of Two Sales: Sir Rowland Winn and No. 11 St James's Square, London, 1766–1787', *History of Retailing and Consumption* 2.1 (2016).
40. Lesley Milroy, *Language and Social Networks* (Blackwell, 1775), 2; Kenneth McRae, *Conflict and Compromise in Multilingual Societies* (Wilfrid Laurier University Press, 1983), 16.
41. WYAS Wakefield, WYW1352/1/4/29/6, Sabine Winn to Sir Rowland Winn, 9 October 1775.
42. WYAS Wakefield, WYW1352/1/4/29/8, Sabine Winn to Sir Rowland Winn, 17 October 1775.
43. WYAS Wakefield, WYW1352/1/4/29/17, Sabine Winn to Sir Rowland Winn, n.d.
44. WYAS Wakefield, WYW1352/1/1/5/9, Sabine Winn to Rowland Winn, 5 September 1769; WYAS Wakefield, WYW1352/1/4/29/17, Sabine Winn to Sir Rowland Winn, n.d.
45. Fay Bound Alberti, *A Biography of Loneliness* (Oxford University Press, 2019), 5.
46. Gary W. Evans, 'The Built Environment and Mental Health', *Journal of Urban Health* 80.4 (2003), 536–55 (p. 356).
47. WYAS Wakefield, WYW1352/1/4/29/15, Sabine Winn to Sir Rowland Winn, n.d.
48. WYAS Wakefield, WYW1352/1/4/29/17, Sabine Winn to Sir Rowland Winn, n.d.
49. WYAS Wakefield, WYW1352/1/4/29/10, Sabine Winn to Sir Rowland Winn, 3 November 1775.
50. See Tita Chico, *Designing Women: The Dressing Room in Eighteenth-Century English Literature and Culture* (Bucknell University Press, 2005); G. J. Barker-Benfield, *The Culture of Sensibility: Sex and Society in Eighteenth-Century Britain* (University of Chicago Press, 1996); Patricia Meyer Spacks, *Privacy: Concealing the Eighteenth-Century Self* (University of Chicago Press, 2003).
51. Dyer, *Material Lives*, 153.
52. Simon McCormack, interview conducted by Ruby Rutter, 1 April 2024.
53. Simon McCormack, interview conducted by Ruby Rutter, 1 April 2024.
54. Simon McCormack, interview conducted by Ruby Rutter, 1 April 2024.
55. Charlotte Smithson, interview conducted by Ruby Rutter, 25 June 2024.
56. Charlotte Smithson, interview conducted by Ruby Rutter, 25 June 2024.
57. *Behind the Walls: Sabine at Nostell Priory*, June 2024–October 2024, National Trust.

6

Ecotherapy at Abington Park Museum: Lessons from the history of well-being

Emily Bavellas

This chapter aims to demonstrate that well-being and the quest for improved well-being has been an integral facet of human life for millennia, and that now, more than ever, we need to learn from past practices to improve our well-being in the present.

In the Western world we often regard ecotherapy as a modern form of treatment, seen perhaps as the latest in an expansive list of alternative well-being fads. However, the therapeutic benefits of nature have been recognized and appreciated by many cultures and civilizations for thousands of years. This chapter will examine the history of nature-based therapy and explore how Victorian asylums were surprisingly progressive in their approach to treating mental illness, relying heavily on a nature-based approach. I will also focus on how we can take inspiration from past well-being practices, such as ecotherapy, and integrate them into present well-being schemes in museums and heritage sites, allowing us to reconnect and learn from the past, and in doing so shine a light on a historical practice that is mistakenly regarded as a contemporary remedy. I will explore the history of Abington Park Museum through the work of medical historian Dr Clare Hickman.[1] This much-loved museum was a former Victorian asylum where elements of ecotherapy were regularly practised as part of patient care. Dr Hickman has been instrumental in unearthing this form of treatment at Abington, as well as within many other Victorian asylums.

To support the discussion of learning from past well-being practices I will focus on an emerging well-being initiative that is being developed at Abington Park Museum. The ecotherapy project at Abington Park Museum aims to support service users as it is imperative that museums and heritage sites do more to support current and potential visitors who live with mental health conditions. Despite mental illness being one of the leading causes of disability in the UK, museums and heritage sites do little to acknowledge or accommodate this. Overall, the sector continues to ignore the mental health community. In the rare instances that focus is given to issues surrounding mental health, there is continuous misrepresentation or tokenism, which further perpetuates stigmatization and disempowerment.

Ecotherapy: Principles and history

It is vital to understand what ecotherapy (also known as nature or green therapy) is and what it entails. Ecotherapy is an umbrella term for a broad variety of formal therapeutic activities that take place in a natural outdoor environment. Ecotherapy can encompass a diverse range of activities including social and therapeutic horticulture, animal assisted interventions, environmental conservation, care farming, nature arts and crafts, green exercise and wilderness therapy.[2] The mental health charity Mind describes ecotherapy as a 'regular, structured activity' that is led by trained professionals, focuses on a specific activity, takes place in a green environment, aims to explore and appreciate the natural world and involves some form of social interaction.[3]

While it is impossible to specify an exact date, evidence of ecotherapy practice can be found throughout many ancient civilizations across the globe, demonstrating that it is not by any means a modern phenomenon. During the sixth century BCE, Cyrus the Great 'intuitively built green gardens in the crowded urban capital of Persia to increase human health and promote a sense of calm in a busy city'.[4] The Ayurvedic system of medicine was developed in ancient India over five thousand years ago. Based on Hindu principles Ayurveda features a range of comprehensive techniques and treatments. As one of the oldest medical systems still in use today Ayurveda practitioners believe that our environment influences our health and well-being. Quality time spent in nature is therefore advised for a healthy mind and body; 'health is defined as a state of equilibrium with oneself which is inextricably linked to the environment'.[5]

In ancient Greece nature was perceived as a powerful tool, used to support the processes of recuperation and restoration. Throughout Greece temples were built to Asclepius, the god of medicine and healing, whose snake-entwined staff is the predominant symbol for healthcare worldwide. Sacred healing temples (Asklepeion) were built in pastoral settings surrounded by lush gardens and groves. Key to Asklepeion treatment was its holistic approach to care, with major emphasis placed on healing through the natural environment. The healing temples were immensely popular throughout ancient Greece, with garden activities and forest walks prescribed to patients as part of their healing regimen; in many ways it was remarkably similar to social prescribing practices today.

The Asklepeion of Kos is believed to have been built in the third century BCE; the site is recognized as one of the oldest surviving archaeological sites in Greece and is regarded as the most significant classical monument on the isle of Kos. The Asklepeions became redundant due to the rise in Christianity throughout the region. The devastating Anatolia earthquake of 554 AD was the final blow for the Asklepeion of Kos which was tragically toppled and buried. The site was eventually rediscovered by local Greek historian Iakovos Zarraftis and German archaeologist Rudolf Herzog in the early twentieth century; it is now the most popular tourist attraction and a great source of pride to the island. On a recent visit to the Kos Asklepeion what struck me instantly was how verdant and tranquil the entire area is. The site was intentionally built on a hillside surrounded by a pine forest; the site is divided over three levels, with each level climbing up higher into the hills, giving those that reach the very top a spectacular panoramic view of the Aegean Sea.

Hippocrates, often regarded as the 'father of modern medicine', was born on the island of Kos and fervently believed in the healing power of nature. He also determined that mental illnesses were not caused by demonic possession or spiritual punishment, which was a common belief during this period. As Ivanovic-Zuvic has shown 'psychological and mental illnesses were viewed as the effect of nature on man and were treated like other diseases. Hippocrates argued that the brain is the organ responsible for mental illnesses, (and) believed that mental illnesses can be treated more effectively if they are handled in a similar manner to physical medical conditions'.[6]

Despite this significant finding, various cultural and religious beliefs continued to stigmatize and demonize those suffering from mental illness. The rise in Christianity throughout Europe meant 'that the existence of demons and the power of religious healing was widely canvassed',[7] with those suffering from mental illness often subjected to gruelling healing rituals over a prolonged period; 'lunatics were placed in the church and chained by the ankle, and for eighteen days efforts were made to exorcize the evil demons who had possessed them'.[8] The history of mental health treatment has therefore been greatly complicated by a continuous cycle of progress and regress, due to prejudice, fear and stigmatization. While other areas of healthcare can be documented with a clear linear path to advancement and progress the same cannot be said for mental healthcare which has suffered from numerous controversies and setbacks throughout the years.

While there were notable setbacks for mental health treatment during this period, examples of ecotherapy were still evident. The rise in Monasticism throughout the world led to monastic gardens, which influenced and 'dictated the garden style of the medieval period'.[9] Not only were monastic gardens used to grow food and medicinal herbs, but they were designed as environments for enhancing contemplation and well-being.

> Indeed, gardens were an integral part of the 'ora et labora' (pray and work) rhythm of monastic life. Monks and nuns spent hours in the garden engaged in quiet manual labour, an embodied form of meditation and devotion to God. Whether pruning vines in the vineyard or contemplating the ephemeral beauty of a rose, they sought to cultivate inner peace and virtue through horticultural practice. In this way, the garden became a bridge between heaven and earth, a place where the sacred and the mundane intertwined.[10]

A brief history of mental health care in Britain

In pre-industrial Britain mental illness was seen as a private domestic issue. It was therefore common for relatives to care for mentally ill family members at home. However, this was often a flawed system as they were either unwilling or unable to cope with complex care needs. As a result, many mentally ill people became homeless or ended up in prison or workhouses.[11] In the late seventeenth-century private asylums grew in number across Britain, with the 'trade in lunacy' firmly established in the eighteenth century. During this period it was widely believed that mental illnesses were caused by moral failing, and sufferers were untreatable. During this period the therapeutic benefits of nature were subsequently sidelined in favour of a custodial approach, which saw asylum patients restrained, with little to no access to the natural environment. The mentally ill were regarded as wild, uncivilized and immoral and would often be subjected to cruel and inhumane practices such as purging and blistering in squalid and unregulated environments.

Changes to mental health treatment came about in the eighteenth century when the field of psychiatry began to grow; with this came the realization that mental illnesses were treatable, and that patients could, and should, be rehabilitated. In the late eighteenth- and early nineteenth-century asylum reforms took shape with the likes of John Connolly, Harriet Martineau and William Tuke spearheading radical changes to mental healthcare treatment. The Moral Treatment approach, developed at the York Retreat by Quaker William Tuke, was humane and focused on non-restraint methods. The Moral Approach was influenced by early Quaker ecotherapy practices and came about in direct response to the suspicious death in 1790 of Hannah Mills, a young Quaker patient at the York Asylum. Moral treatment became popularized after it was unified into a system of care by Tuke's grandson, Samuel Tuke. In 1813 Samuel Tuke published the first full-length account of an asylum, 'Description of the Retreat: An Institution Near York for Insane Persons of the Society of Friends', in which he describes the unified system. Raad and Makari emphasize how influential Tuke's work was; 'many of the psychiatric practices we take for granted today, including the minimal use of coercion, we owe to the influence of this proselytizing book'.[12]

One of the fundamental changes that was applied during the mental health reforms was the importance given to the environment in relation to well-being, with nature now seen as a vital part of the recuperation regimen for asylum patients. This shift towards the healing benefits of nature would fundamentally shape where and how new asylums were built and managed.

Abington Abbey Retreat

Abington Abbey Retreat is an example of a Victorian asylum that was heavily influenced by these reforms, a private asylum opened by Dr Thomas Octavius Prichard in 1845. The asylum was set in a former Tudor manor house in an idyllic rural setting. 'Retreat' was an extremely popular name for asylums in the nineteenth century due primarily to the success of the York Retreat; overall 'retreat' was also seen as a much more pleasant and palatable term for delicate Victorian sensibilities. A former superintendent of the Northampton General Asylum Dr Prichard was an early advocate of the moral treatment system, believing strongly in non-restraint, which he viewed as 'a system of kind and preventative treatment, in which all excitement is as much as possible avoided, and no care omitted'.[13] Dr Prichard died in 1847 and was replaced by his cousin Dr Thomas Prichard, who continued the moral treatment approach to care at Abington.

Clare Hickman has extensively researched the importance of nature in the nineteenth-century asylum, stating that 'the visual experience of landscape and placement of the asylum within a rural setting would have been considered part of the therapeutic regime during the 19th century'.[14] Hickman focuses on Abington Abbey Retreat, believing it to be a prime example of a Victorian asylum that placed nature at the very heart of its treatment plan. She notes:

> In the 1860s Thomas Prichard, the second superintendent of the Abbey Retreat, Northampton, certainly felt that cheerfulness was an emotion to be encouraged within the asylum and seemed to relate it to both the aesthetic role of flowers, 'cheerful parterres', and work with the garden setting, as promoting a 'cheerful tone of thought'.[15]

Hickman goes on to note Dr Prichard's views on the importance of nature in asylum environments:

> In each county, but with few exceptions, will now be found an Asylum, well built, and well appointed, cheerfully situate [*sic*], and surrounded by extensive and well-planned grounds and gardens for the use and recreation of the inmates. the old, dreary, walled in airing courts, in which in former time the patients were accustomed for years to tramp to and fro' like so many felon in a goal, and now transformed into cheerful parteers, the flowers affording pleasing objects of contemplation: and the care of the gardens being, in many instances entrusted to patients, serves as a double purpose – of affording wholesome occupation, and of promoting a tranquil and cheerful tone of thought.[16]

A prospectus for Abington Abbey Retreat (which is on permanent display at Abington Park Museum) clearly demonstrates how important the natural environment was to the asylum and to prospective patients and their families. The front cover proudly shows off a bird's eye view of the lush landscape, while activities such as gardening and flower arranging are mentioned as part of the services offered.[17] By the end of the nineteenth century there was little optimism left for county asylums, regarded as victims of their own success they begun to suffer from overcrowding which meant it was impossible to provide the personalized care required for the moral treatment approach to be therapeutic. To maintain control many asylums resorted to restraining patients once more, a clear example of the progress–regress cycle evident within the history of mental healthcare.

Like many other county asylums Abington Abbey Retreat finally closed its doors in 1892. Hickman notes that prior to closing there was a noticeable decline in the quality of care offered to patients; her research unearthed a letter written by Mrs Capron, a long-term patient at Abington who describes the decline in her quality of care:

> When I came here nearly three years ago, I was told I should find nice gardens and grounds to walk in. I have always been accustomed to these pleasures and amusements and appreciate them. For the first year and a half the Gardens were

> open, and I enjoyed them; but, for the last few months the Gardens have been kept closely locked, giving the surroundings a dismal and prison-like appearance, and very much interfering with the enjoyment of the peace.[18]

After the closure of Abington Abbey Retreat, the manor house and grounds were gifted to the people of Northampton. In 1897 to mark Queen Victoria's Diamond Jubilee the house was reopened as a public museum. Abington Park Museum will celebrate its 127th birthday this year and is considered a much-loved local attraction.

As demonstrated, there are many examples of ecotherapy throughout history, so it is intriguing that we continue to regard it as something new. One of the reasons that we tend to perceive ecotherapy as a modern form of treatment is due to it being an under researched area until the late 1970s. It was during this time that researchers determined that humans (particularly in the west) were becoming increasingly disconnected from nature, causing severe detrimental effects to our physical and mental health as a result. We tend to perceive ecotherapy as a contemporary practice as it only became a structured form of treatment with the emergence of ecopsychology, the term being coined by Theodore Roszak in 1992 in his ground-breaking text 'The Voice of the Earth: An exploration of Ecopsychology'. In this work Roszak noted:

> Just as it has been the goal of previous therapies to recover the repressed contents of the unconscious, so the goal of ecopsychology is to awaken the inherent sense of environmental reciprocity that lies within the ecological unconscious. Other therapies seek to heal the alienation between person and person, person and family, person, and society. Ecopsychology seeks to heal the more fundamental alienation between the recently created urban psyche and the age-old natural environment.[19]

Despite how keenly the Victorians had taken to nature-based treatments, such as 'taking the waters', the British increasingly shied away from connecting with nature during the early twentieth century, with industrialization, modernism and two World Wars severing our connection to nature even further.

Ecotherapy research

Extensive research shows that ecotherapy can improve numerous health issues, as well as having untold social, physical and psychological benefits. For many years Mind has been instrumental in researching and promoting the positive impact of ecotherapy within the UK. Since 2007 the charity has publicly called for a 'new green agenda for mental health highlighting the growing evidence in support of an accessible, cost-effective, and natural addition to existing treatment options, using ecotherapy interventions'.[20] In 2009 Mind was awarded £7.5 million in National Lottery funding to carry out a variety of ecotherapy schemes across the country. 'Ecominds' received funding for five years, which allowed Mind to create 130 ecotherapy projects across the country. The projects were wide-ranging and included activities such as horticulture, walking groups, conservation and park regeneration initiatives. Overall 'Ecominds' helped '12,071 people living with mental health problems to get involved in green activities to improve confidence, self-esteem as well as their physical and mental health'.[21]

The 'Ecominds' project was independently evaluated by researchers at the School of Biological Sciences at the University of Essex. The key findings of the evaluation demonstrated that ecotherapy can be effective in raising mental well-being to 'average' levels; can enhance social inclusion (vital to the recovery of those living with mental health problems); be successful in both increasing contact with and connection to nature, enabling participants to benefit further from the associated health and well-being benefits; improve well-being and social inclusion and equip participants with useful coping skills. It can also help the development of healthier lifestyles and environmentally friendly living.[22]

The concluding comments in the 'Ecominds' report acknowledges the major positive impact the project has had on participants:

> Through the funding of 130 ecotherapy projects and the 12,071 people that directly benefitted from the programme, Ecominds can be considered to have had a major impact, both in terms of supporting people suffering from mental ill-health and in sustaining the provision of ecotherapy services across England. The majority of Ecominds participants will leave the programme with better wellbeing and self-esteem; feel more socially included, will have gained new skills, and developed healthier lifestyles; have enhanced psychological health and wellbeing; and an increased connection to nature. These significant improvements as a result of the Ecominds scheme all have implications for not only the mental wellbeing and resilience of individuals but also for public health and the management of natural environments.[23]

Museums and mental health

Since the Covid pandemic the importance of physical and mental well-being has been brought into sharp focus, with the benefits of spending time in nature recognized and much more keenly appreciated. The pandemic had a massive impact on an already struggling mental healthcare system with a recent report by the Care Quality Commission acknowledging the sharp rise in mental health problems since the first lockdown came into effect:

> The impact of the pandemic on people's mental health is well recognised. The Centre for Mental Health has estimated that up to 10 million people, including 1.5 million children, are likely to need new or additional mental health support as a direct result of the crisis. Over the last year, Mind and Rethink Mental Illness have reported an increase in demand for their services. For example, in the 12 months since the first national lockdown was announced, Rethink reported a 175% increase in demand for advice and information on their website.[24]

Museums and heritage sites have begun to recognize the importance of their visitors' overall well-being, with research clearly demonstrating that 'visiting museums can offer myriad benefits to health and well-being, encompassing both physical and mental health dimensions'.[25] Despite this evidence there is much more that can be done by museums and heritage sites to improve lives, particularly for those living with mental health conditions. While some within the sector are doing an excellent job of implementing therapeutic well-being into their public programming, there is still a sense that many are merely paying lip service to the concept without achieving anything truly meaningful or impactful. Abington Park Museum is guilty of this, despite being a wonderful and much-loved museum at the heart of a thriving and diverse community; it is niche, insular and does not currently create as much social impact as it could.

In 2022 the Baring Foundation published the report 'Creatively Minded at the Museum' which investigates how museums can engage creatively with people with mental health problems. The report found that utilizing the arts in a therapeutic manner is still an extremely undeveloped area within UK museums. Despite case studies demonstrating how therapeutic support can be successfully implemented, there still seems to be fear and trepidation within the sector. While museums are attempting to become accessible for all, they are still failing to support and fully include the mental health community. The Baring Foundation states that 'targeted engagement by museums with people with mental health problems is relatively rare, despite a lot of interest in work around wellbeing and a strong commitment to inclusivity'.[26]

The Baring Foundation is a non-profit organization 'which protects and advances human rights and promotes inclusion'.[27] Director and report author David Cutler certainly believes that museums need to do more to reach people living with mental health problems:

> Museums have displayed a lot of interest in their role in contributing to health and wellbeing. However, when it comes to applying these principles to people living with mental health problems, there has been much less concerted or consistent effort, than for say people living with dementia. This report shows that any museum can undertake this work. We hope that this report will help to inspire more museums to engage in this rewarding area.[28]

The report made a series of recommendations. There needs to be explicated recognition by individual institutions and infrastructure bodies that this is an important area that is currently underdeveloped. Museums should proactively reach out to the local NHS and voluntary sector bodies such as Mind to consider ideas for collaboration. Valuing the lived experience and leadership of people with mental health problems, both staff and community members, is essential to developing work in this area. Finally museum funders should make clear the relevance of their funding for this work or offer dedicated funding pots. Wherever possible, this should be long-term funding.[29]

There are many reasons for the lack of support in the museum sector for therapeutic support and practice. Firstly museums have long been regarded as neutral and as such should steer clear of becoming involved in social or political issues. Robert R. Janes describes this as the 'magical belief of neutrality':

> Neutrality is not a foundational principle of museum practice, but rather a result of the museum's privileged position in society. It is a matter of record that museums enjoy a high level of public trust – This, in turn, has fostered a sense of complacency among museum practitioners, underpinned by the assumption that traditional thinking and practices must account for this privileged status.[30]

Another key reason that museums tend to avoid becoming involved in therapeutic practice is due to what the Baring Foundation report describes as 'projectitis'.[31] Appropriate mental health-related support often depends on extremely specific funding, collaboration and training. Cutler notes this and makes this observation:

> Arguably, there has been a tendency towards 'projectitis' where concentrated work to engage people with mental health problems has not outlasted short term funding or the passion of an individual staff member. All funders struggle with insufficient resources to go round but this is a further argument in favour of longer term or core resourcing in this area.[32]

While ecotherapy practice within museum and heritage sites is still a relatively new concept there are a small number of case studies that demonstrate the ways that nature therapy can be interpreted and implemented within this setting. Before focusing on the ecotherapy initiative currently being devised at Abington Park Museum I want to shine a light on two sites that have paved the way with their own unique approach to interpretation and public programming.

The first example is 'Hippocrates Garden' cultural centre in Mastichari, Kos. The site is a replica of an ancient Greek settlement from the fifth century BCE, located in an area where Hippocrates taught his students. The centre now uses the principles of Hippocrates teachings to support its public programming. The gardens were founded in 2008 by Julie Zafeiratou with funding from the European Union co-financing program Leader+. Between 2009 and 2020 Zafeiratou spearheaded a project to replant two thousand trees around the centre; working in collaboration with local schools, the pupils were able to learn about environmental issues, gained gardening skills and practised mindfulness techniques.

As well as working with schools on ecotherapy events and activities the centre also has a wide range of ecotherapy events and activities for families and adults. The site is extremely popular with tourists and locals alike with many returning to the site regularly.

> This location is truly captivating and moorish, or at least it has been for my family who insist on ensuring we visit on each occasion we are on the island. Set within a stunning natural reservation area, the centre allows you to experience traditional and historical Greece whilst appreciating how nature has assisted with healing and

> everyday life, which is a testament to how Hippocrates has ensured this beautiful island has continued to value its importance.[33]

Zafeiratou's mission is to deepen our connection with nature; her work has taken her around the world with the intention of taking the ecotherapy cultural concept beyond Kos; she has collaborated with the National Botanical Garden of Tsolula city in Mexico and has created a 'Garden of Hippocrates' within the national park of the city. In this way Zafeiratou is interpreting well-being from the past to benefit the present.

Closer to home there are some excellent projects that put nature-based therapy at the heart of its mission. One of the most exciting is the Whitworth art gallery in Manchester, which is leading the way with their Natural and Cultural Health Service (NCHS) scheme. Aimed at all ages the NCHS programme features 'outdoor activities that promote good physical and mental well-being. From Meditating in Nature to Gardening for good health'.[34] The majority of the NCHS programme at The Whitworth takes place in their specially designed Art Garden, an 'urban sanctuary' created by renowned landscape designer/gardener Sarah Price:

> Recent development has not only seen the gallery double in size – it has fully integrated it into the park we call home. An art garden designed by Sarah Price, sculpture terrace and orchard garden, alongside our spaces that embrace the park, such as our landscape gallery, learning studio and the café in the trees, all reflect this beautiful setting. Our relationship to the great outdoors isn't limited to plants and gardens. At the Whitworth, we take the inside out via a programme of free events that explore art and nature, with activities such as Welly Walks, messy play sessions (inspired by the natural world) and self-guided trails around the park. Bringing art, nature, and people together through a programme of year-round, outdoor activities – for adults and families, and for health and wellbeing.[35]

The Whitworth also has a dedicated 'Silent space' area, which is part of the wider Silent Space project. Founded in 2016 by Liz Ware Silent Spaces is a charity-based project that works with public parks and gardens to create biodiverse green spaces where people are invited to reflect in silent contemplation:

> There's nothing complicated about a Silent Space. It's rather like the quiet carriage on a train. A biodiverse area of a garden or a park, already enjoyed by the public, is reserved for silent reflection. Research indicates that noise pollution causes damage to our bodies and to our minds. It's little wonder that spending silent time in nature can bring us comfort and help us to feel restored. Being silent in the natural world is a particularly gentle kind of silence. We're soothed by the birdsong and the sounds of the breeze in the trees. Quietly observing and listening, we grow to know and truly value the world we live in – to better appreciate our place within it and our responsibility to protect it.[36]

Engaging with ecotherapy in a museum or heritage environment, particularly somewhere that has a historical connection to nature and healing, allows us to connect with past health and well-being practices. In turn this gives contemporary audiences a deeper understanding of the links between the past and present and to a variety of concepts such as medical advancements, social inclusion and the rollercoaster of progress and regress within the history of mental healthcare.

Ecotherapy at Abington Park

Inspired by Dr Clare Hickman's research we are currently in the process of planning and implementing a public well-being programme at Abington Park that shines a light on the history of the museum as a former asylum, with the aim of focusing on ecotherapy to acknowledge and honour the asylum's progressive work in this area. The grounds that the former patients enjoyed still exist and are now a much-loved public park, which is a perfect location for ecotherapy practice. The well-being series aims to incorporate a key strand of the museum's current interpretation of Abington Park, portraying it as 'a place to breathe' (to relax, breathe and enjoy the beautiful scenery). The historical link to ecotherapy at Abington Park Museum gives our intended programme a unique selling point, as it links the past to the present.

Despite being progressive for its time, Abington Abbey Retreat was reserved only for those wealthy enough to afford its private treatment. The Retreat's prospectus states: 'This establishment is exclusively devoted to the care and cure of male and female patients in the upper and middle ranks of society who may suffer from mental afflictions.'[37] Historically, access to decent mental healthcare has always been sorely limited for those in lower class and income brackets. Sadly this still rings true today. Northampton is a deprived town, with those suffering from mental illness less likely to be employed. Within the UK there are distinct health inequalities and disparities present with deprived areas suffering with greater rates of physical and mental illness. The Office for Health Improvement and Disparities notes:

> Differences in health outcomes are known as health inequalities – unfair and avoidable differences in health across the population, and between different groups within society. Health inequalities arise because of the conditions in which we are born, grow, live, work and age. These conditions influence our opportunities for good health, and how we think, feel and act, and this shapes our mental health, physical health, and wellbeing. Alongside the individual human costs, disparities, and inequalities impact on society as a whole.[38]

Our ecotherapy programme of activities aims to be free or low charge, to support service users and those on lower incomes, something that is especially vital during the current cost-of-living crisis. We aim to provide a variety of ecotherapy activities to suit all ages and abilities. This will hopefully provide a much-needed social hub for Northampton residents, with a focus on supporting better mental health and well-being in deprived areas. A report by the Wildlife Trusts recognizes the relevance and importance of integrated healthcare initiatives that focus on nature-based therapy:

> In current times where there are real concerns about the burgeoning costs of maintaining good public health and tackling health inequalities, combined with the drive for integration in health and social care services, the multiple outcomes gained from nature-based initiatives present a possible solution.[39]

The planned programme of activities will include well-being walks combined with Mindfulness practice and a 'Growing Kindness Gardening Club'. Being kind to yourself is often difficult for those struggling with their mental health. The gardening club therefore aims to promote self-compassion and kindness. There are two planned sites that will be used for gardening activities: The Museum courtyard and Abington Parks sensory garden. We have also planned an Eco-Art Therapy programme, combining ecotherapy with art therapy to produce works of art in nature or by using natural found materials.

This ecotherapy programme is achievable but will rely on further funding, co-creation and support from mental health professionals, as well as the local mental health community. It is this daunting part of the process that most museums tend to shy away from. But, as discussed, there is clear scope for museums to become more involved in mental health care initiatives. At this juncture it is important to stress that while museums have a valid place in supporting health and well-being, museum staff are not mental health professionals so it is imperative to always ensure that any work in this area is approached with the utmost care and should never be implemented without the direct involvement of trained mental health professionals. Laird states the importance of this from an ethical viewpoint:

> The consensus among clinical professionals who work with museums and objects is that museums incur ethical responsibilities when they enter the psychotherapeutic realm. Those ethical dimensions include confidentiality, emotional and physical safety, responsible caring, professional integrity, and related practices. Real and lasting harm can be the accidental outcome of a well-meaning project of therapeutic interaction. In this light, we (and our colleagues) encourage museums to engage with mental health practitioners, psychologists, counselors, and psychotherapists in developing guidelines and protocols for hiring, training, conducting research, managing object donations, and providing healthful and impactful visitor services. Additionally, we encourage museums to identify and develop relationships with external community resources and agencies, such as health and counseling centers, hospitals, and universities. These networks will enable museums to benefit from the expertise of external professionals within the contexts of their own institutions.[40]

Currently progress is proving to be slow and steady with regard to building up the ecotherapy initiative. This pace is not unusual within the museum sector, as sourcing staff and funding can be extremely time-consuming. It is often at this juncture that the dreaded 'projectitis' may begin to creep in. One of the main challenges we currently face is budget and staffing constraints, Abington Park Museum is managed by West Northants Council and as a local authority museum its budget must be carefully balanced and monitored. During times of austerity, culture is often the first victim and this has been the case for Abington Park Museum, with the current cost of living crisis there have been unfortunate but necessary cuts which have resulted in a reduction to the museums opening hours. The reduced opening hours have proven challenging to the scheme as Mind can only provide trained support staff during weekdays when the museum is closed. Therefore, managing this and keeping costs to a bare minimum has been a balancing act with a heavy reliance on voluntary staff.

Our greatest success so far is the forging of a strong partnership with Northamptonshire Mind, who we have now co-created a series of well-being walks with. It was imperative from the start to involve Northamptonshire Mind in this initiative as they have excellent knowledge and understanding of the actual needs of the people within the local mental health community. I am deeply grateful for their commitment and enthusiasm towards this project. The well-being walk scheme is now in full effect and currently runs monthly; attendance has been excellent, which clearly demonstrates demand. Most attendees are service users; this is incredibly positive as this was the key demographic that we aspired and intended to reach. Previously our well-being series has been extremely successful but has not attracted service users for several reasons, most notably cost and a lack of affiliation with mental health communities. Overall museums can be uncomfortable places to visit for those suffering with a mental health condition as they can seem intimidating and imposing.

We are currently in the process of conducting a thorough evaluation, which will be reported using both qualitative and quantitative data; a combination of both is vital for museum-based healthcare initiatives such as this. As the project is still in its infancy, we do not have any conclusive data about the projects' impact yet. So far the evidence collected is proving promising, with many attendees expressing positive feedback which will be beneficial as future qualitative data. The following testimony from participants underpins this assessment:

> 'I didn't know that there was an asylum here, that's really interesting!'
> 'I like that we stop to chat and enjoy the view. I thought we would be walking non-stop for the whole time.'
> 'Was feeling really switched off today, but the fresh air and talking have made me feel a bit better.'
> 'I don't leave the house very often, especially when it gets colder, the lady at Mind told me about this and said it may help. It's been good.'
> 'I just feel a bit clearer you know. Like, my head feels a bit emptier and quieter.'
> 'Abington is a beautiful park; I've been in it before, but I haven't taken the time to enjoy it.'

Due to great feedback and attendance, there is definite scope for increasing the regularity of the walks, particularly during periods where there is increased vulnerability, during winter months, for example (which can be an extremely challenging time of year, especially for those living with a mental health condition). We have recently completed our Christmas well-being walk, which was extremely popular despite the cold weather. A pleasant addition to the group was a mother and her son who wanted to join us during the school holidays. Frankie, aged nine, brought a joyful energy to the group which was infectious. During the session I asked Frankie if he would like to think about what he was enjoying most about the walk; he readily agreed and proceeded to walk around the park while taking notes. His feedback proved to be a real highlight and was greatly appreciated by the whole group during a well-deserved break – 'Happy, fresh air, green grass, freedom, rain, wind, trees, birds, lakes, squirrels, equality'.

To conclude this chapter has examined how well-being and the quest for improved well-being has always been a human necessity. Societies have become increasingly disconnected from nature, and as mentioned previously, this has led to a myriad of negative consequences. To improve our well-being in the present, it is therefore vital for us to look to the past. Museums and heritage sites are increasingly recognizing their new role as places that enhance and improve well-being[41]; this combined with their role of bringing the past to life means they are well situated to teach us about well-being from the past to foster and support improving our well-being in the present and in the future.

This is what we intend to do at Abington Park Museum, to teach people about well-being from the past, to support their present and future well-being. We are only at the very beginning of this project, and there is still a great deal of work to be done, but based on the progress and feedback so far there is real promise of a meaningful ecotherapy programme at Abington Park Museum. In the words of the great Monty Don, 'When you plant something, you invest in a beautiful future amid a stressful, chaotic and, at times, downright appalling world.'[42]

Notes

1. Clare Hickman, 'Cheerful Prospects and Tranquil Restoration: The Visual Experience of Landscape as Part of the Therapeutic Regime of the British Asylum, 1800–60', *History of Psychiatry* 20.4 (2009), https://journals.sagepub.com/doi/10.1177/0957154X08338335 (accessed 12 June 2023).
2. Rachel Bragg and others, *Ecominds Effects on Mental Wellbeing: An Evaluation for Mind* (Mind, 2013), 13, www.mind.org.uk/media-a/4418/ecominds-effects-on-mental-wellbeing-evaluation-report.pdf (accessed 4 October 2023).
3. *What Is Ecotherapy?* (Mind, 2024), www.mind.org.uk/information-support/drugs-and-treatments/talking-therapy-and-counselling/ecotherapy/ (accessed 10 January 2025).
4. Margaret M. Hansen, Reo Jones and Kirsten Tocchini, '(Forest Bathing) and Nature Therapy: A State-of-the-Art Review', *International Journal of Environmental Research and Public Health* 14.8 (2017), 2, https://doi.org10.3390/ijerph14080851.
5. Unnikrishnan Payyappallimana and Padma Venkatasubramanian, 'Exploring Ayurvedic Knowledge on Food and Health for Providing Innovative Solutions to Contemporary Healthcare', *Front Public Health* 4.57 (2016), 1, https://doi.org/10.3389/fpubh.2016.00057.
6. Fernando Ivanovic-Zuvic, 'Epistemological considerations about medicine and mental health in ancient Greece', *Revista Chilena de Neuro-Psiquiatria* (2004), 163–75 (p. 165).
7. Andrew Scull, *Madness in Civilization: A Cultural History of Insanity from the Bible to Freud, from the Madhouse to Modern Medicine* (Thames & Hudson, 2015), 66.

8. Scull, *Madness in Civilization*, 66.
9. 'Gardens with Medieval Features', *National Trust*, www.nationaltrust.org.uk/visit/gardens-parks/gardens-with-medieval-features (accessed 2 January 2025).
10. Alexander Meddings, 'Monastic Gardens: Cultivating the Soul through the Centuries', www.monasteries.com/en-GB/travel-inspiration/monastic-gardens-cultivating-the-soul-through-the-centuries#:~:text=Monks%20and%20nuns%20spent%20hours,and%20virtue%20through%20horticultural%20practice (accessed 9 January 2024).
11. 'A Victorian Mental Asylum', *Science Museum*, 13 June 2018, www.sciencemuseum.org.uk/objects-and-stories/medicine/victorian-mental-asylum (accessed 29 January 2024).
12. Raymond Raad and George Makari, 'Images in Psychiatry: Samuel Tuke's Description of the Retreat', *American Journal of Psychiatry* 167.8 (2010), 898, https://ajp.psychiatryonline.org/doi/full/10.1176/appi.ajp.2010.10020265 (accessed 15 January 2024).
13. Dr Thomas Octavius Prichard, 'Second Annual Report of the Northampton General Lunatic Asylum' (1840), Northampton Records Office.
14. Clare Hickman, 'Cheerful Prospects and Tranquil Restoration: The Visual Experience of Landscape as Part of the Therapeutic Regime of the British Asylum', *History of Psychiatry* 20.4 (2009), 439, https://doi.org/10.1177/0957154X08338335.
15. Hickman, 'Cheerful Prospects and Tranquil Restoration', 431.
16. Dr Thomas Prichard, Northampton Local Studies Library (1868), 54.
17. Abington Abbey Prospectus, Abington Park Museum, *c.*1880.
18. Claire Hickman, 'Cheerfulness and Tranquility: Gardens in the Victorian Asylum', *Lancet Psychiatry* 1.7 (2014), 506, www.thelancet.com/journals/lanpsy/article/PIIS2215-0366(14)00098-4/fulltext (accessed 20 June 2023).
19. Theodore Roszak, *Voice of the Earth: An Exploration of Ecopsychology* (Phanes Press, 2001), 52–150.
20. 'Go Green to Beat the Blues', *Mind*, www.mind.org.uk/news-campaigns/news/go-green-to-beat-the-blues/ (accessed 28 January 2024).
21. Bragg et al., 'Ecominds Effects on Mental Wellbeing', 6.
22. Bragg et al., 'Ecominds Effects on Mental Wellbeing', 5–8.
23. Bragg et al., 'Ecominds Effects on Mental Wellbeing', 8.
24. 'Rising Demand for Mental Health Care', *Care Quality Commission*, www.cqc.org.uk/publications/major-reports/soc202021_01d_mh-care-demand (accessed 20 January 2024).
25. Karen Alexander, 'How Museums Can Help Enhance Physical and Mental Health', *Psychology Today*, 5 June 2024, www.psychologytoday.com/gb/blog/the-art-effect/202406/how-museums-can-help-enhance-physical-and-mental-health#:~:text=Studies%20have%20shown%20that%20exposure,are%20integral%20to%20mental%20health (accessed 11 January 2025).
26. 'How Can Museums Engage with People with Mental Health Problems?' *Baring Foundation*, 3 November 2022, https://baringfoundation.org.uk/news-story/how-can-museums-engage-with-people-with-mental-health-problems (accessed 30 January 2024).
27. 'Our Purpose & Values', *Baring Foundation*, https://baringfoundation.org.uk/about-us/our-purpose-and-values (accessed 30 January 2024).
28. 'How Can Museums Engage with People with Mental Health Problems?' *Baring Foundation*, https://baringfoundation.org.uk/news-story/how-can-museums-engage-with-people-with-mental-health-problems/#:~:text=Museums%20should%20

proactively%20reach%20out,developing%20work%20in%20this%20area (accessed 30 January 2024).

29. David Cutler, 'Creatively Minded at the Museum: Creative and Mental Health Activities in Museums', *Baring Foundation*, https://cdn.baringfoundation.org.uk/wp-content/uploads/BF_Creatively-minded-at-the-museum_WEB_mr.pdf (accessed 20 June 2023).
30. Robert R Janes, 'The End of Neutrality: A Modest Manifesto', *Informal Learning Review* 135 (2015), 3–8.
31. Jonathan Knott, 'It's Time for Museums to Address Mental Health', *Museums Association*, 29 November 2022, www.museumsassociation.org/museums-journal/analysis/2022/11/its-time-for-museums-to-address-mental-health/#:~:text=As%20a%20minimum%2C%20museums%20should,for%20learning%20and%20engagement%20staff (accessed 23 June 2023).
32. Cutler, 'Creatively Minded at the Museum'.
33. 'PhilHislop', review on Hippocrates Garden, www.tripadvisor.co.uk/Attraction_Review-g1177714-d3443465-Reviews-or40-Hippocrates_Garden_Cultural_Center-Mastichari_Kos_Dodecanese_South_Aegean.html (accessed 19 June 2023).
34. 'Natural Cultural Health Service', *University of Manchester: The Whitworth*, www.whitworth.manchester.ac.uk/getinvolved/nchs (accessed 20 January 2024).
35. 'The Gallery in the Park', *The University of Manchester, The Whitworth*, www.whitworth.manchester.ac.uk/whats-on/creativespaces/thegalleryinthepark (accessed 23 January 2024).
36. 'What We Do', *Silent Spaces*, https://silentspace.org.uk/what-we-do/#:~:text=Being%20silent%20in%20the%20natural,our%20responsibility%20to%20protect%20it (accessed 29 January 2024).
37. Abington Abbey Prospectus, Abington Park Museum, *c.*1880.
38. 'Guidance: Health Disparities and Health Inequalities: Applying All Our Health', *Office for Health Improvement & Disparities*, www.gov.uk/government/publications/health-disparities-and-health-inequalities-applying-all-our-health/health-disparities-and-health-inequalities-applying-all-our-health (accessed 28 January 2024).
39. Rachel Bragg, Carly Wood, Jo Barton and others, 'Wellbeing Benefits from Natural Environments Rich in Wildlife: A Literature Review for the Wildlife Trusts', *Wildlife Trusts*, www.wildlifetrusts.org/sites/default/files/2018-05/r1_literature_review_wellbeing_benefits_of_wild_places_lres_0.pdf (accessed 24 October 2023).
40. Ross Laird, 'Mental Health Considerations for Museums: An Emerging Field of Practice and Discovery', June 23 2021, www.rosslaird.com/articles/mental-health/mental-health-considerations-for-museums/ (accessed 15 January 2024).
41. Jocelyn Dodd and Ceri Jones, *Mind, Body, Spirit: How Museums Impact Health and Wellbeing* (RCMG, 2014), 2–60, https://southeastmuseums.org/wp-content/uploads/PDF/mind_body_spirit_report.pdf (accessed 11 January 2025).
42. Helena Horton, 'Gardening Can Do What Medicine Only "Tries to Mimic" for Mental Health, Monty Don Says', *The Telegraph*, 24 February 2019, www.telegraph.co.uk/news/2019/02/24/gardening-can-do-medicine-tries-mimic-mental-health-monty-don (accessed 16 June 2023).

7

Women, welfare and well-being: Philanthropy in the Northamptonshire boot and shoe industry

Kathrina Perry

Prior to the inception of the National Health Service in June 1948, health and welfare were funded by a variety of sources, and many organizations, charities and schemes were necessary to support welfare needs and promote well-being. Much has been written about this subject, particularly exploring donation and subscription schemes linked to specific hospitals. Historians such as Steven Cherry, George Campbell Gosling and Martin Gorsky all explored voluntary funding in hospitals; however, little has been written about women's role in these causes.[1] This chapter will show examples of women who were married to local boot and shoe manufacturers in Northampton and how their actions provide testimony to the importance of women's philanthropy during the nineteenth and twentieth centuries and how these examples link to welfare and well-being causes within the town.

When considering this subject, it is important to explore not only hospitals but also other welfare organizations. This chapter will use the cases of Northampton General Hospital and Manfield Hospital, as well as organizations such as Bethany Homestead and the Charity Organization Society and the various roles undertaken by women within them, such as annual subscriptions, gift donations, bed endowments and even roles on the hospital board as well as more traditional voluntary roles. This chapter seeks to show the involvement of women, particularly with the links to the boot and shoe industry. The main focus is to identify the women and consider their full contributions to include their voluntary work on the hospital boards as well as monetary and gift donations.

This chapter aims to give a broad overview of the involvement and importance these women had in welfare and well-being in Northampton. However, it is important to reflect on the period of the late nineteenth and early twentieth centuries and the context in which these donations and activities were taking place. There were many changes in welfare provision within England, together with extra challenges such as the First and the Second World Wars, which potentially influenced the activities and changes in philanthropic pursuits. A closer look at company records and hospital minutes will also create a broader picture of whether these women were at the forefront of their pursuits or if they go unremarked upon due to society's view on the domestic sphere. Local newspapers such as the *Northampton Mercury* and *Northampton Daily*

Echo also provide useful evidence not only with local events and public appearances being reported but also in the details offered regarding public meetings within local organizations and fund-raising activities.

Philanthropy in welfare

Philanthropy can be split into two strands of support; the first is monetary support and the second is voluntary involvement. Philanthropy in welfare demonstrates this, with charitable giving and fund-raising still seen in society today, as well as support and services provided by the voluntary sector. Philanthropy in welfare during the nineteenth and early twentieth centuries spans a range of activities from charitable donations and subscriptions for voluntary hospitals, including contributory schemes, events and campaigns and bed endowments, as well as voluntary roles such as home visiting, board roles for organizations and organizing fund-raising events. Female philanthropic activities were increasingly visible during this period and were considered 'acts of citizenship'.[2]

Historiography for the role of women often refers to the industrial revolution as creating opportunities for women; however, this often focuses on jobs for the working classes and neglects the pursuits of those middle-class women who, it can be argued, had a significant role in shaping society. Frank Prochaska discussed how, for women, philanthropy was often a vocation seen as an outlet for self-expression.[3] It has also been argued that female philanthropists are more connected to causes which they support financially than their male counterparts.[4] Prochaska points out that generations of academics accepted women's philanthropic efforts but do not show much interest in the origins or scope of their participation or their impact on social forces.[5]

Francesca Moore argues that women's philanthropy is 'anchored squarely in the politics of life, specifically the relationship between women and the health of the nation'.[6] Kathryn Gleadle argues that feminist historians were able to attribute women's caring and benevolent nature to society and, in turn, their philanthropic pursuits.[7] W. K. Jordan even considered the role of women's philanthropy during the period of 1480–1660, which shows that it was not born out of the Victorian era.[8] As argued by Eve Colpus, it is well understood that the legacy of the twentieth-century policy developments which worked towards the welfare state was developed through women impacting on the public sphere.[9]

Many women donated to charitable causes as an annual subscription and not necessarily as an active participant. However, this does not mean that they were less active than men. In fact, when considering the activities of those women who were involved in district visiting, it could be argued that women were more physically active rather than just beneficiaries. The range of activities women participated in were often seen as a calling and would be considered 'feminine virtues'.[10] This research considers the range of civic and social welfare work which was carried out by the middle-class women during the nineteenth and twentieth centuries and contextualizes this by looking at the actions of the wives and daughters of the boot and shoe manufacturers in Northampton.

Much of the literature on women's philanthropy connected to welfare considers social reformers such as Louisa Twining (Workhouse Visiting Society), Octavia Hill (Charity Organization Society) and Elizabeth Fry (prison reform), who were all respectable philanthropists. Others such as Beatrice Webb found opportunities for investigations into poverty.[11] All of these women considered the welfare and well-being of others. Historians have also considered the charitable pursuits of women as acceptable. But as Frank Prochaska argues, they are often not interested in the scale of women's involvement and barely acknowledge the impact their actions had on a local level.[12] This chapter will set out to show examples of women in Northampton, and their involvement in welfare and well-being was just as impactful and important as those who have national notoriety.

Case study: Welfare and well-being in Northampton

Like many industrial towns, Northampton had seen an increase in shoe manufacturers opening factories within the area. The boot and shoe industry in Northampton was the most prominent with three in ten males represented in the labour force in 1841.[13] The 1850s saw the introduction of industrial changes with large warehouses on what is now Campbell Square in the Mounts area of the town opening by Isaac Campbell & Co. and Manfield and Sons. The large-scale structure saw the manufacturers remove themselves from the workforce replace their presence with factory managers and foremen. It can be argued that this move also saw the boot and shoe manufacturers become more involved in public life with many becoming local councillors and politicians. For example, between 1870 and 1950, fourteen of Northampton's seventy-seven Mayors were boot and shoe manufacturers.[14]

Northampton suffered from an epidemic of Tuberculosis in 1899 and shoe workers were vulnerable to contracting the disease, partly due to the unhealth working conditions form working within these large factories. A hundred and eight people died of the disease in 1899 alone. These bleak conditions also had an impact on the children of the town, and there were regular outbreaks of measles, scarlet fever, whooping cough, diphtheria and typhoid fever all seeing regular outbreaks. In 1899, the *Northampton Mercury* reported that several houses in Kingswell Street and St Andrews Place in Semilong, Northampton were identified as unfit for public habitation. These houses were lived in by forty-five people including eleven children. This gives a picture of some of the conditions in Northampton during the period, however, it must be remembered that this picture was not unique in the town and other industrial areas would have seen areas of vast poverty, despite the prosperous factory owners.

Many of the wives and daughters of prominent manufacturers within the town in the nineteenth and twentieth centuries participated in philanthropic activities linked to welfare causes such as charitable donations, fund-raising activities as well as sitting on hospital boards. By creating profiles of these women it has been possible to gain a contextual view of not only their involvement in these activities but also a sense of their priorities when it comes to welfare within the town. Sabina Branch was married to John Branch, owner of John Branch Ltd on Henry Street, moved to Northampton with her husband in the 1890s with the factory of Henry Street being built in 1900.[15] Unlike the other ladies of the shoe industry, Sabina Branch's involvement in public life was less connected to local governance and charitable pursuits, although she did stand for election to the Board of Guardians in the district of St Giles, receiving eleven votes and therefore failing to gain one of the five seats on the board for that district.[16]

Louisa Manfield (*neé* Barran), the daughter of Sir John Barran, first Baronet of Leeds, was married into the Manfield family in September 1909.[17] Sir John had been the Liberal MP for Leeds between 1876 and 1885 and Gladstonian Liberal MP for Otley from 1886. On losing his seat in 1895, Sir John was awarded a baronetcy.[18] Sir John Barran had risen through society as a businessman, a clothing manufacturer.[19] Louisa Manfield was given the title of 'Lady Bountiful' for her concern for the welfare of the people of Moulton and Pitsford.[20] Louisa was very Liberal and very active in the Liberal and Radical movement in Northampton. In April 1910, she was elected president of the Moulton Women's Liberal and Radical Association, an affiliate of the Women's Liberal Association.[21] Harry Manfield described his wife as coming from 'good Radical stock' and suggested in a meeting of the Mid Northamptonshire Liberals in December 1909 that 'it was fortunate that Mrs Manfield was Liberal in principle, because he would not have the pleasure or the reverse of trying to convert her – or, as had been suggested, of being converted himself'.[22]

Louisa Manfield's involvement with the Young Women's Christian Association (YWCA) in Northampton shows her hard working and tenacious manner in the pursuit for charity. She held the position of presidency for twenty years from 1914, only to step down through ill health. During that time she put the welfare and well-being of the girls first and foremost.[23] Her letter to the *Northampton Mercury* in 1914 brought to the attention of the people of Northampton the need for a suitable premises and the protection, presumably for the war effort, to request charity for the organization.[24] The Mayoress of Northampton in 1922 (Mrs Earl) described the YWCA as 'just the place in Northampton where young women could learn something about Christianity and at the same time enjoy themselves'.[25] The YWCA, a national organization still active today, promotes the empowerment of young women, which was the case from its inception in 1855.[26]

Hospitals

Philanthropy in hospitals during the nineteenth and early twentieth centuries was very common and took many different forms. Prior to the advent of the National Health Service in 1948, hospitals relied on donors and annual subscribers for funding as well as fund-raising events.

It must be noted that much of the research around donations and voluntary contributory schemes to hospitals often discuss the figures raised rather than who was making the donations. Work by Steven Cherry, John Pickstone and George Campbell Gosling all discuss the inception of schemes such as Hospital Saturday and Hospital Sunday, as well as workplace collections, but the details of who was donating is rarely discussed, and particularly lacking reference to women. In his work on hospital charities, Burdett praised Hospital Saturday collections in their attempt to encourage self-help to those from 'the industrial and other classes'.[27] Steven Cherry's research into voluntary hospital funding discusses these collection schemes and particularly their links to working classes and the traditions of Friendly societies and trade unions, specifically the nature of promotion.[28] Contributory schemes represented 6.25 million members by the early 1930s and 10.3 million by 1938.[29] Participation in these schemes were regional and historians such as Finlayson argue that community loyalty played a large part into contributions.

It is possible that, given the socio-economic climate of Northampton during the early twentieth century when these schemes were at their peak this would be the case, with many friendly societies being in existence in the town and an established contributory scheme in place at Northampton General Hospital. A healthy workforce benefited the manufacturers and therefore contributory schemes benefit both the workers and the manufacturers. Cherry points out that Northampton General Hospitals gives a contrast to other arranges such as those in Newcastle, Barnsley, Middlesbrough and Wolverhampton. F. F. Waddy notes that the Hospital Week scheme altered its name to the Northampton Hospital and Convalescent Fund and was acting in the way of a friendly society, with money being granted for spectacles and funding convalescent trips to the seaside.[30] Prior to this the Northants Workers Guild provided 10 per cent of hits regular income to the hospital and sought further representation to the Board of Management. However, this was denied and as Cherry states, 'an expanding and financially successful collecting scheme was thus denied any role in hospital management; the exception rather than the rule'.[31] While it is important to consider the monetary value of the donations, particularly with those who donated specific one-off amounts for infrastructure.

When considering the motivations of welfare philanthropy and particularly that of hospitals, John Pickstone identified medical influence, religious non-conformity, individualism and self-help and industrial paternalism. These will all be considered in this chapter. Pickstone argues that the reworking of employer paternalism could be attributed to hospital expansion in the northwest of England, which along with the concept of self-help saw the importance of workpeople's contributions.[32] Cherry argues that the ideology of self-help created fear that charitable hospitals were becoming overwhelmed and abused, with the COS offering dispensaries as an alternative.[33] This in turn, it could be argued led to contributory schemes and collecting such as Hospital Saturday and Hospital Sunday.

It is important, when considering philanthropy in welfare to reflect on the whole of welfare provision and not just those involving the hospitals. Levene et al. argue that the focus on the historical commentary on this topic covers the 'glory' of voluntary hospitals and the criticisms of the Poor Law.[34] Nick Hayes and Barry Doyle's research into the finances of local voluntary hospitals in Leeds, Leicester, Nottingham and Sheffield considered not only contributory schemes but also the activities of members of the local community.[35] Fund-raising in this sense included items such as bedding, magazines and toys for children and food. This resulted in reduced running costs for the hospital, however, it can be argued that in annual reports, for example those of Northampton General Hospital and Manfield Hospital, activities such as these do not show any monetary value and therefore, as Doyle suggests the account books often mask the income coming from charitable endeavours.[36] This is further supported in the annual reports for Northampton General Hospital in 1930–1 where, when acknowledging 'egg week' a note is made to state that the collection of eggs 'assists in a reduction of expenditure and also enables a variety of additions to be made to the standard diet'.[37] We will also see in the case studies referred to in the chapter that other donations would even include medical supply costs including £3,000 for radium.[38] Stephen Yeo argues that this period saw both an attitude change from both political entities as well as the general public and the attitudes towards the poor were changing as a result.[39] Hospitals in particular, attracted support from a large area which in turn resulted in local landowners and business owners using them to display wealth and social status.[40] Lindsay Granshaw argued that the inclusion of aristocracy and landowners created a 'lure' to the middle classes.[41]

Northampton was no different and the women of the boot and shoe factory played a significant part in this. It is not difficult to find examples of charitable giving by the boot and shoe manufacturers for the general hospital and it is well documented that Alice Barratt, wife of William Barratt of Barratt Shoes, was instrumental in the donation to Northampton General Hospital for the Barratt Maternity Home. Northampton General Hospital first opened in 1744 in George Row and by 1793 had opened on the current site of Billing Road.[42] The hospital was funded by subscribers who dispensed 'tickets' to patients and served the County of Northamptonshire. Many subscribers were given the right to nominated beneficiaries, this would then provide them with access to treatment at the hospitals.[43]

From observing the Annual Reports for Northampton General Hospital for the period 1910–11 there were no less than 177 female entries within the annual subscribers. Of these two entries had links to the boot and shoe manufacturers of Northampton, namely Mrs. Harry Manfield and the Misses Turner, daughters of Richard Turner of Turner Bros & Hyde. Throughout the next thirty years these donations continued and by 1939–40, the last Annual report to include a list of subscribers and donors, although the number of female donors had decreased to 134, there were six who can be clearly identified as linked with the boot and shoe industry. It is important to consider that the women referred to here were subscribers in their own right. Whether more were covered by their husband's subscriptions it is unclear.[44]

A key fund-raising movement for many voluntary hospitals including Northampton was that of Hospital Saturday and Hospital Sunday. Hospital Sunday originated in 1859 and gave an opportunity for churches for their local voluntary health provisions.[45] Hospital Saturday, on the other hand, was more a workplace collection, however it had the same premise of raising money for the Infirmary. In Northampton, these schemes ran alongside each other and were coined 'Hospital Week'. According to Cherry, workplace collections and contributory schemes are likely to have been responsible for between 20 and 30 per cent of voluntary hospitals income in the country as a whole between 1935 and 1935.[46]

Philanthropy in the hospital was not just about money. The year 1927 saw Mrs Sears named as one of the vice presidents of the hospital. Over the following years she would be joined by Mrs. Harry Crockett, Mrs. Harry Manfield and Mrs. H. C. Oakeshott, all of whom had links to the boot and shoe industry. They were also joined by Mrs. William Barratt who was the deputy president of the hospital from the late 1930s until the hospital was taken over by the National Health Service in 1948.

There were also regular donations included linen, magazines, eggs and flowers for events such as Harvest and Christmas and regular donors include names, we have already seen such as Mrs. Harry Manfield and Mrs. Sears. James Manfield donated Weston Favell House to the Northampton County Crippled Children's Fund in 1925.[47] The Northamptonshire Crippled Children's Fund was established in 1893 to provide treatment and support for children of Northampton and the wider county up to the age of seventeen.[48] From the first annual reports for Manfield Hospital there were eighty-eight women listed in the list of governors for the hospital. Out of these eight have connections to the boot and shoe industry, albeit four of these where from the Manfield family. It is also notable that there were three of this particular group who held the position of vice-president of the hospital.[49] This is in contrast to Northampton General Hospital for the same period who had yet to appoint any of these women to the board, although Mrs C Sears would join the board as a vice president the following year.[50] It could be argued that this was in part due to the period of the establishment of the hospital as by 1925, women were finding their way into the public sphere. However, it could also be assumed that the because James Manfield was the main donor of the hospital, he invited his wife and daughters to have a seat on the board.

It is unclear whether his wife, Louisa, daughter of Frederick Bostock of Frederick Bostock Limited in Northampton, was involved in the hospital. She is named as a Governor in the first Annual Report for the hospital, however, it is not clear what role this took or the level involvement she held.[51] There is however evidence of bed endowments from Mrs Charles Lewis to Manfield hospital and Louisa and James's daughter, Ellen Manfield, left £500 to the hospital in her will in 1946, which could suggest that she was continuing the family legacy.

Organizations

Guardians of the Poor Union or other such local authority positions were restricted by legislation and therefore female involvement was restricted. By considering the role of the organizations in Northampton, we can see how the ladies of the shoe factories were able to provide a benevolent purpose within them. The Municipal Franchise Act 1869 allowed women ratepayers to not only have the vote, but also allowed them to be elected as poor law guardians. Following on from this the Education Act 1870 introduced Board schools and enabled women to become members of the Local School Board. Because of this Lady Manfield, was able to stand for election on the Northampton School Board in 1877.[52] As discussed by Patricia Hollis, School Board women were often loyally Liberal relations of prominent Liberal men and Lady Manfield was certainly no exception. Moses Philip Manfield, Alderman and future M. P. for Northampton, speaking on behalf of Lady Manfield at a meeting of Unsectarian candidate supporters on 5 January 1877, described his wife as holding 'very broad, earnest, and deep views on both politics and religion, and indeed had educated him a little on those points'.[53]

Incidentally, Lady Manfield was represented by her husband at both this meeting as well as the election results, however, the newspaper reports do not suggest why. It would be difficult not to surmise that this was because she was an unelected female trying to gain access to a male environment. Lady Manfield sat on the School Board from 1877 to the 1880 election, stepping down at the last meeting in 1879. However, this was not to be the end of her involvement in the School Board, and she was to continue as a visitor after her time on the board. To her own admission she felt that 'she could do quite as well as if she was on the Board, and being there alone perhaps she had not always done her own nature justice, being too timid in saying that which would go before the public'.[54] However, this was not to say that as a women she was unsuccessful as a member of the Board, and although another female did not stand until Marianne Hearn stood for election in 1886, Lady Manfield's election result proved that the voters of Northampton were happy to accept a women could stand for office.[55]

Northampton's religious organizations were linked to many charitable organizations as well as the philanthropic activities that took place within the confines of the church itself. These were often linked to welfare causes an, in that capacity, gave the opportunity to support local community. Some organizations such as the Girls' Friendly Society and the Young Women's Christian Association (YWCA) were supporting organizations that promoted the value of churches along with the well-being of the girls who attended. Those such as Bethany Homestead were created by the churches to help provide homes and support to the town's elderly. The Lewis family endowed several beds to Bethany Homestead in 1932 in a similar vain to those for the hospital. There was also the involvement of the churches in the local hospital week fund-raising, particularly on Hospital Sunday.

Louisa Manfield's (Mrs Harry Manfield) involvement with the Young Women's Christian Association in Northampton shows her hard working and tenacious manner in the pursuit of charity. She held the position of presidency for twenty years from 1914, only to step down through ill health.[56] During that time she put the welfare of the girls first and foremost. Her letter to the *Northampton Mercury* in 1914 brought to the attention of the people of Northampton the need for a suitable premises and the protection, presumably for the war effort, to request charity for the organization.[57] The YWCA did achieve their aims of gaining premises of the Memorial Hall, Castilian Street, Northampton which was used as a hostel for the organization.

Along with her husband Mrs T. D. Lewis donated a holiday home in Shutlanger for the Sunday School Union and continued to be involved in fund-raising events to raise funds for the upkeep. This was to give respite and retreat for the Sunday Schools in the town and further.

By the 1870s, organizations such as the Charity Organization Society (COS) suggests that, to alleviate the burden on voluntary hospitals, provident dispensaries could be used as an alternative.[58] The COS was influence by George Goschen's 1869 minute, which called for a closer connection between the poor law guardians and local charities to ensure a fairer distribution of poor relief and in turn ending the distribution of outdoor relief. If was also involved in many official enquiries including the Royal Commission on the Aged Poor 1894 and the Royal Commission on the Poor Laws between 1905 and 1909.[59] Kidd argues that the COS should be considered both in the context of a voluntary sector organization and, due to their influence in the changes in legislation towards the end of the nineteenth century, the state sector.[60]

Northampton's branch of the COS was not established until 1905 and other than those who were mayor during this period had little connection to the boot and shoe industry. Whether this was because the trade was unionized and therefore had its own support mechanism for those on hard times is yet to be proven. Mentions of Edward Lewis, Albert Marlow, James Manfield and Sir Henry Randall appear in the records, however women associated with these manufacturers do not appear, with the exception of Miss Susan Bostock, daughter of Frederick Bostock who was associated with the organization for over thirty years.[61] However this may be due to the fact that many of the women involved, particularly those who were social workers for the organization, were unmarried. Further involvement included a bequest of £1,000 to the Council of Social Services, a later iteration of the Society, for the purpose of St George Homestead, a home for the elderly in the same manner as that of Bethany Homestead.[62]

Legacies

Another example of women's involvement in religious philanthropy was that of Mrs C. Lewis. Her husband, Charles Lewis, was a preacher at the Primitive Methodist church and she was described as a 'generous subscriber' to the church.[63] She left several bequests totalling £500 (approximately £31,416 today) to various funds linked to the Methodist church including the Methodist Missionary Society, the Methodist Ministers Widows' and Orphans' Society, the Methodists Orphanage and the Methodist Local Preachers Aid Fund.[64] Mrs William Barratt left a number of bequests to St George's Homestead, a home for elderly people run by the Volunteer Service[65]; Wardington Court, a home for blind men; and Northampton General Hospital and examples of legacies from the Manfield Family have already been discussed.

Bed endowments were another form of donation and legacy that hospital relied on. For an endowment of an adult bed a person would pay £1,000 (approximately £46,000 today). These were often paid for as a memorial for a family member who had died. Annual reports listed endowments up to and including the year of the report and were added to each year. In 1939–40 there were eight separate endowments linked to women in the boot and shoe industry. Two of these, namely an endowment from Sir James Crocket of Crockett and Jones and one from Charles Lewis of C& E Lewis, were in memory of women, the Late Lady Crockett and Charles Lewis's daughter, Mary Flavell Lewis. The other six were Mrs. Charles Lewis, who endowed two beds in memory of her husband and in memory of their son James. Mrs. Harry Manfield endowed a bed in memory of her husband. Mrs. Elsie Patten and her brother George Lewis endowed beds in memory of their parents, Edward and Mary Lewis. Mrs. C. Sears endowed five beds. It does not state whether this was in memory of anyone or just a generous donation at £5,000.

Manfield Hospital had similar schemes and a number of endowed beds were paid for between 1925 and 1938. They had a variety of schemes including 'Endowed Beds' for a donation of £500 which endowed a bed in perpetuity, 'Named Beds' for a donation of £250 which entitled donors to name a bed during their lifetime or the lifetime of their nominee, and 'Beds "Named" by Annual Subscription' for an annual subscription of £25 which entitled the bed to be named during the period of the subscription.[66] Many of those who had donated at Northampton General Hospital also donated at Manfield Hospital, including Mrs C Sears who was the first to donate towards a bed endowment in 1925.[67]

Conclusion

This research shows that the ladies connected to the boot and shoe industry in Northampton during the nineteenth and early twentieth centuries demonstrated a variety of philanthropic activities to promote welfare and the well-being of the people of Northampton. Large donations made by the likes of Caroline Sears and Catherine Lewis and influential involvement like that of Alice Barratt show that these women made a large contribution and also were respected by their male counterparts. However, organizations such as the Young Women's Christian Association and the Northamptonshire Crippled Children's Fund give examples of where welfare and well-being were the forefront of their activities. Smaller gestures such as donations to the hospitals of magazines and food also show that the well-being of the patients during their recovery from illness was an important aspect in the philanthropy of the ladies discussed in this chapter. Further research could consider the level of involvement the women of the boot and shoe industry had in these institutions and the impact on the working class within the town. Did their presence on the board of the hospitals influence decisions with health care within the town? Philanthropy still happens within the National Health Service today, as was seen particularly in the recent pandemic and by considering the involvement of these women, it can be seen as a practice that has been taken place for many years and a larger focus on well-being is incorporated into this work. However, it is important not to dismiss the work that these ladies carried out a century ago.

Notes

1. Further exploration of this topic includes Steven Cherry, 'Beyond National Health Insurance. The Voluntary Hospital and Hospital Contributory Schemes – A Regional Study', *Social History of Medicine* (1995), 455–82; 'Accountability, Entitlement, and Control Issues and Voluntary Hospital Funding c. 1860–1939', *Social History of Medicine* (1996), 215–33; M. Gorksy, J. Mohan and T. Willis, 'The Financial Health of Voluntary Hospitals in Interwar Britain', *Economic History Review* 55.3 (2002), 533–57; G. C. Gosling, '"Open the Other Eye": Payment, Civic Duty and Hospital Contributory Schemes in Bristol, c. 1927–1948', *Medical History* 54.4 (2010), 475–94.
2. Francesca Moore, 'A Band of Public-Spirited Women: Middle-Class Female Philanthropy and Citizenship in Bolton, Lancashire before 1918', *Transactions of the Institute of British Geographers* 41.2 (2016), 149–62 (p. 150).
3. Prochaska, *Women and Philanthropy in Nineteenth Century England*, 5.

4. Kathleen D. McCarthy, 'The MS. Foundation: A Case Study in Feminist Fundraising', Working Paper, Centre of the Study of Philanthropy, City University of New York, 1995.
5. F. K. Prochaska, 'Women in English Philanthropy, 1790–1830', *International Review of Social History* 19.3 (1974), 426–45 (p. 426).
6. Moore, 'A Band of Public-Spirited Women', 150.
7. Kathryn Gleadle, *Borderline Citizens: Women, Gender and Political Culture in Britain, 1815–1967* (Oxford University Press, 2009), 5.
8. W. K. Jordan, *Philanthropy in England, 1480–1660: A Study of the Changing Pattern of English Social Aspirations* (George Allen & Unwin, 1959).
9. Eve Colpus, *Female Philanthropy in the Interwar World: Between Self and Other* (Bloomsbury, 2020), 13; see also Seth Koven and Sonya Michel (eds), *Mothers of a New World: Maternalist Politics and the Origins of Welfare States* (Routledge, 1990).
10. Prochaska, 'Women in English Philanthropy, 1790–1830', 427.
11. For more on these women see Samuel Jones (ed.), *The Enduring Relevance of Octavia Hill* (Demos, 2012); Lawrence Goodman, 'Octavia Hill, Beatrice Webb and the Royal Commission on the Poor Laws, 1905–9: A Mid Victorian in an Edwardian world', in Elizabeth Baigent and Be Cowell (eds), *Octavia Hill, Social Activism and the Remaking of the British Society* (University of London Press, 2016), 255–73; R. Whelan, *Octavia Hill and the Social Housing Debate: Essays and Letters by Octavia Hill* (IEA Health and Welfare Unit, 1998); Beatrice Webb, *My Apprenticeship* (Longmans, Green, 1926); *Our Partnership* (Longmans, Green, 1948).
12. Prochaska, 'Women in English Philanthropy', 426.
13. William Griffin, 'The Northampton Boot and Shoe Industry and Its Significance for Social Change in the Borough from 1880 to 1914' (unpublished MA thesis, University of Cardiff, 1968), 50.
14. Northampton Borough Council, The Mayors of Northampton, extract from the booklet 'An Exhibition of Civic Portraits' produced for the Central Art Gallery, 1981.
15. *Northampton Daily Echo*, 22 May 1922.
16. *Northampton Mercury (N.M)*, 11 March 1904.
17. *Northampton Daily Echo*, 8 September 1909.
18. David T. Jenkins, 'Barron Family (per c.1842–1952), Clothing Manufacturers', *Oxford Dictionary of National Biography* (2004).
19. Jenkins, 'Barron Family (per c.1842–1952), Clothing Manufacturers'.
20. *N.M.*, 25 February 1944.
21. *N.M.*, 8 April 1910.
22. *N.M.*, 10 December 1909.
23. *N.M.*, 23 February 1914.
24. *N.M.*, 11 December 1914.
25. *Northampton Daily Echo*, 9 December 1922.
26. www.ywca.uk/ (accessed 1 December 2024).
27. H. C. Burdett, *Hospitals and Charities* (Scientific Press, 1914), 131.
28. Steven Cherry, 'Accountability, Entitlement and Control Issues and Voluntary Hospital Funding c. 1860–1939', *Social History of Medicine* 9.2 (1996), 215–33 (p. 224).
29. Steven Cherry, 'Hospital Saturday, Workplace Collections and Issues in Late Nineteenth-Century Hospital Funding', *Medical History* 44.4 (2000), 461–88 (p. 464n).
30. F. F. Waddy, *A History of Northampton General Hospital, 1743 to 1948* (Guildhall Press, 1974), 124.
31. Cherry, 'Accountability', 125.

32. John v. Pickstone, *Medicine and Industrial Society: A History of Hospital Development in Manchester and Its Region, 1752–1946* (Manchester University Press, 1985), 138–41.
33. Cherry, 'Hospital Saturday', 461.
34. Alysa Levene, Martin Powell and John Stewart, 'Patterns of Municipal Health Expenditure in Interwar England and Wales', *Bulletin of History of Medicine* 78 (2004), 635–69 (p. 635).
35. Nick Hayes and Barry M. Doyle, 'Eggs, Rags and Whist Drives: Popular Munificence and the Development of Provincial Medical Voluntarism between the Wars', *Historical Research* 86.234 (2013), 714.
36. Barry M. Doyle, *The Politics of Hospital Provision in Early Twentieth Century Britain. Studies for the Society for the Social History of Medicine* (Pickering and Chatto, 2014), 136.
37. Northampton General Hospital, *Annual Report, 1930–1.*
38. Northampton General Hospital, *Annual Report, 1928–9.*
39. Stephen Yeo, *Religion and Voluntary Organisations in Crisis* (Croom Helm, 1976), 211.
40. Pickstone, Medicine and Industrial Society, 11.
41. Lindsay Granshaw, 'The Hospital', in W. F. Byrum and Roy Porter (eds), *Companion Encyclopedia of the History of Medicine* (Taylor & Francis, 1993), p. 1185.
42. Cynthia Brown, *Northampton, 1835–1935: Shoe Town, New Town* (Phillimore, 1990), 34.
43. Brian Abel-Smith, *The Hospitals 1800–1948: A Study in Social Administration in England and Wales* (Heinemann, 1964).
44. Northampton General Hospital, *Annual Reports 1910–11, 1939–40.*
45. Roger Ottewill, '"Alleviating the Sum of Human Suffering": The Origins, Attributes and Appeal of Hospital Sunday, 1859–1914', *Studies in Church History* 58 (2002), 353–71 (p. 353).
46. Steven Cherry, 'Accountability', 221; also see 'Before the National Health Service: Financing the Voluntary Hospitals, 1900–1939', *Economic History Review* 50.2 (1997), 305–26 (pp. 324–5).
47. Sue Longworth, *The Gift of Manfield: The Story of an Orthopaedic Hospital, 1925–1992* (Park Lane, 2009), 25.
48. J. Beatty, *Northampton Urban Sanitary Authority Annual Report on the Health of the Count Borough of Northampton for the year ending December 31st 1905* (Stanton and Son, 1906); C. Collins, V. Chenery and D. Sweet, *Office for National Statistic: United Kingdom Health Statistics* (Palgrave Macmillan, 2008), 20; A. N. Williams and C. Chan, '"Now Walks Like Others": A Preliminary Enquiry into the Northampton Crippled Children's Fund', *Family and Community History* 16.2 (2013), 130.
49. Manfield Orthopaedic Hospital, *First Annual Report, 1925*, 19–21.
50. Northampton General Hospital, *Annual Report, 1926–7*
51. Manfield Orthopaedic Hospital, *First Annual Report, 1925.*
52. *N.M.*, 6 January 1877; Patricia Hollis, *Ladies Elect: Women in English Local Government* (Oxford University Press, 1989).
53. *N.M.*, 6 January 1877.
54. *N.M.*, 20 December 1879.
55. Marianne Hearn was a female writer under the pseudonym of Marianne Farningham. According to the 1861 Census she was living in Northampton. Her works include *The Christian's World* and *A Working Woman's Life*. For more see Marianne Hearn, *A Working Woman's Life: An Autobiography* (J. Clarke, 1907).
56. *N.M.*, 23 February 1934.

57. *N.M.*, 11 December 1914.
58. Steve Cherry, 'Hospital Saturday', 461–2; Geoffrey Rivett, *The Development of the London Hospital System, 1823–1982* (Oxford University Press, 1986).
59. Bernard Harris, *The Origins of the British Welfare State: Society, State and Social Welfare in England and Wales, 1800–1945* (Palgrave Macmillan, 2004), 28.
60. Alan J. Kidd, *State, Society and the Poor in Nineteenth-Century England* (Macmillan, 1999), 98.
61. CVS, *Willing Hands: A History of the Council for Voluntary Service in Northampton* (Council for Voluntary Service, 1996), 26.
62. Alice Barratt, 'Last Will and Testament', created on 6 May 1953, executed on 8 April 1959.
63. *N.M.*, 8 May 1925, 3 December 1937.
64. *N.M.*, 11 March 1938.
65. Alice Barratt, 'Last Will and Testament', 1953/9.
66. Manfield Hospital, *Annual Report, 1927*, 47.
67. Manfield Hospital, *Annual Report, 1925*.

A panacea for wounds and panic: Tobacco, alcohol and well-being on the Western front during the First World War

Michael Reeve

The First World War was a war of endurance not only because of the uncomfortable and often dehumanizing conditions of life in the trenches but also because of the nature of 'total' warfare itself and the profound effects this had on wartime populations, be they military personnel or civilians.[1] The experience of mechanized warfare strained both individual and collective strategies of endurance and resilience.[2] Combatants and non-combatants needed strategies, techniques and materials to help them endure the changeable wartime environments of the home and fighting fronts. This included physical infrastructure, personal and social behaviours and modes of consumption.[3] The abundant presence – or painful absence – of tobacco supplies at the front affected short-term endurance *and* contributed to soldiers' readiness to recover (a key facet of resilience) following combat or other forms of adversity.[4] For many on the battlefront and behind the lines, smoking became associated with well-being, as a means to attaining better psychological and physical health amid the stresses and privations of war.

For service personnel – the primary focus of this chapter – the First World War was an all-encompassing experience that could overwhelm the senses, affecting the body and mind in ways that many had not countenanced before their involvement in mass, industrialized warfare.[5] The trenches of the Western front presented an environment where certain senses came to the fore within the auspices of warfare itself, due to the nature of the fighting. As conflict archaeologist Matthew Leonard writes, 'the usual, predominantly visual ways of sensing the landscape were suspended and the sensorium was mired in confusion'.[6] The 'conventional hierarchy of sensing' was upended by the driving of men underground, making the visual less important and elevating the senses of hearing and touch and the consciousness of smell.[7] The 'constrictive environment' of the trench – coupled with the experience of intense artillery bombardment (the origin of the term 'shell shock') and the anxiety of long periods of waiting and anticipation – made it a site especially conducive to psychological disorders.[8] This environment also heightened the appeal of smoking as a practical means to combat stress and *ennui*, enabling soldiers to manage the 'ambient anxiety that is their permanent condition' both through tobacco's physiological effects as a mild narcotic and through its usefulness in marking and mastering time, if only fleetingly, in the amorphous and unpredictable context of the battlefront.[9]

As a number of historians have attested, in the main, British military personnel and civilians displayed a remarkable ability to endure the trials of war, demonstrating resilient attitudes and behaviours.[10] If a commitment to home defence and to one's comrades braced most fighting men as they faced the enemy, the constant presence of tobacco, cigarettes and smoking played an important supporting role.[11] Smoking provided an activity for idle and active hands alike, accompanying a variety of activities, from the boredom of waiting or watching (for the enemy across 'no man's land', or the skies for aircraft) and the gruelling work of trench and dug-out building, to the pre- and post-combat moments of preparation and rest.[12] Living and working conditions in the frontline particularly promoted tobacco use, as one soldier who had been stationed in France, Gallipoli and Egypt wrote to his father in 1916: 'If you know what smell is as I do, and shell fire, you would smoke about 20lb. a day. If any harm is done to the Tommy by smoking cigarettes it probably saved thousands from going stark raving mad.'[13] For another, in the line at the Third Battle of Ypres (Passchendaele), tobacco smoke made nausea more bearable, masking the stench of stagnant water and putrefaction from decaying corpses and dead animals. In his words, only smoking a cigarette or pipe continuously could 'keep it down'.[14]

Historians have particularly appreciated the prominent place of the First World War in the rise of the machine-made cigarette, in terms of consumption and cultural significance, as well as the efforts of government and civil society bodies to provide tobacco to troops during the conflict.[15] Significantly, Matthew Hilton, Fiona Reid and Stephen Snelders have demonstrated the connections made during the war between smoking and the well-being and fortitude of the soldier, though a detailed explication of contemporary debates about, and promotion of, tobacco as a quasi-medicine for the treatment of wartime stress and anxiety is relatively scant in these works.[16] As such, the aim of this chapter is to situate military tobacco use during 1914–18 more firmly within discourses of welfare and health, as well as the interrelated concepts of endurance and resilience. This enhanced perspective contributes to the emerging field of military welfare history, as practised by an interdisciplinary scholarly community situated at the nexus of conventional military history, 'history of war' studies and welfare history.[17] It offers a fresh perspective on the 'impact of service' on military personnel, as well as the broader question of how 'welfare impacted warfare' – a reversal of the approach conventionally taken in studies of modern warfare and the development of the welfare state.[18] Just as previous studies in this vein have examined broadly the 'policies, perceptions, ideologies, provisions, and infrastructures' entailed by military welfare, the focus in this chapter is on a cornerstone of military provisioning during the First World War, seen by many to positively impact the everyday health and well-being of the soldier.[19]

As the wide-ranging, multidisciplinary literature suggests, 'well-being' as a concept has no settled meaning and continues to be defined, redefined and contested by scholars spanning the social sciences and humanities, the only consensus being that the phenomenon is 'multi-dimensional'.[20] The approach in this chapter is grounded in the 'common-sense' understanding of well-being presented by contemporaries during the nineteenth and early twentieth centuries, emphasizing the subjective experience of historical actors. However, implicit in this approach is an understanding of well-being as related closely to health, in its psychological/'mental' and physical iterations; with subjective *feelings* of well-being (which might include cognate states such as happiness or cheerfulness), in the past as in the present day, fundamentally connected with access to, and engagement with, the material world and the life-giving and life-sustaining substances it yields for human beings.[21] In the context of the historical study of smoking, an assumption of the interconnection between the body, its surrounding environment and psychotropic substances drawn from it, is implicit in the analysis. This perspective provides a bridge between medical-scientific approaches and historical research, getting to the heart of historical 'experience'. As historian of emotions Rob Boddice notes, drawing upon insights from neuroscience, 'culture inscribes the brain as the brain creates experience in dynamic relation with the world'.[22] 'Bodily sense and … social situation' clearly intersect in the case of wartime tobacco consumption: embodied and experiential 'vernacular knowledge' suggests that tobacco is effective in relieving anxiety and stress, because it tangibly *works* for the smoker, and this process plays out within changeable and even chaotic wartime environments.[23] This interplay between body/mind and environment – and its resulting cultural products and discourses that are part of both expert and lay medical knowledges – helps explain common-sense notions of tobacco's immense value, for combatants and other historical wartime actors, in attaining states of well-being. In other words, the use of tobacco is situation- and environment-specific. Its psychotropic effects make themselves known in specific contexts, in this case modern warfare, through psychosomatic engagement with the substance, in indissoluble connection with the world external to the individual's body. Well-being cannot ever be a universal concept, given its deep embeddedness in history, culture and context. To understand wartime smoking, we must see well-being states – much like emotional states – as a product of the biocultural interaction of the body, brain and wider material and social contexts.[24]

Drawing upon a range of primary source material related to the British experience – including local and national newspapers, tobacco trade publications, the medical press and pamphlets, military conduct manuals and soldiers' correspondence – this chapter argues that, for many doctors, military leaders and civilian commentators during the First World War, tobacco was accorded a medicinal value that demonstrated affinity with earlier conceptions of tobacco as a panacea. By 1914, tobacco had become a central facet of the soldier's routine consumption patterns and was part of common-sense understandings of military welfare. Going beyond a simplistic assumption of tobacco's utility for combatants under fire and duress, this study compares expert and lay understandings of tobacco and health – including the voices of rank-and-file soldiers – with those related to alcohol use in wartime. This analysis brings to the fore the significance and elevated status accorded to tobacco at the expense of alcohol, due to the former's apparent usefulness in underpinning frontline welfare and attaining discipline, in contrast to the latter's problematic association with disorder and inefficiency.[25] This approach demonstrates the intersection of medical and military ideas about tobacco consumption with concepts of health and well-being.

This chapter first deals with the historical roots of tobacco's panacea status and its subsequent adaptation during the nineteenth and early twentieth centuries, followed by a discussion of the ambivalent perspectives of military welfare and medical experts on the use of tobacco and alcohol by service personnel. This was a wartime debate with an already long historical lineage where tobacco ultimately seems to have won the approval, often open and occasionally tacit, of those with an interest in promoting and safeguarding the health and well-being of combatants.

The 'panacea gospel' and the First World War

As a number of historians, including Jordan Goodman, have concluded, the European perception that the consumption of tobacco was a 'panacea' in all manner of everyday scenarios, arose with the gradual transition to 'modern' ways of living.[26] The pressures of urbanization and industrialization created fertile grounds for the everyday use of stimulants and sedatives. As W. A. Penn stated in his 1901 history of tobacco:

> [The] mental strain and worry produced by the stress and speed of modern life, together with the fierceness of competition and the highly strung nervousness of town life, demand a specific [medicine or remedy], both sedative and stimulating; and in tobacco man has found, as did his ancestors, the best of all Nature's remedies to minister to body and mind distressed.[27]

This perspective chimed with contemporary ideas related to the intense temporality of modernity and, in particular, the anxieties and risks associated with everyday life in industrial-urban settings. The prevalence, and historical longevity, of smoking among early modern and modern working people – both peasants and proletarians – is testament to this intertwining of environment, material and practice.[28]

Tobacco was, for early and later modern Europeans, a 'source of physical and psychological comfort that could ease exhaustion, alleviate hunger, and lift a person's mood'.[29] Indeed, as Goodman notes, the arguments of figures such as the early modern Spanish physician and botanist Nicolás Monardes were commonly repeated and disseminated by writers on tobacco until the turn of the nineteenth century at least. Monardes argued, as early as 1571, that tobacco – as a 'sacred curative herb' – could alleviate hunger and thirst and could cure more than twenty ailments, including conditions as varied as toothache and cancer.[30] However, this conclusion was not novel, only 'Europeanized' when it was adapted and delivered to European audiences from the sixteenth century onwards.[31] Perspectives on the medicinal applications of tobacco, derived from Amerindian cultures – including the view that tobacco was a panacea – were 'indigenized', with the plant taking on new meanings within European settings. As such, 'tobacco was grafted on to European culture' and a 'panacea gospel' was accordingly preached by diverse writers, scholars and physicians.[32]

Such views of tobacco as a panacea were confirmed by soldiers and sailors in nineteenth-century wars. For example, a British veteran of the Crimean War (1853–6), reflecting on his experiences over sixty years after the conflict, described tobacco as the 'best antidote' to the 'malarious [*sic*] climates and filthy smells of the East'. Further, in the harsh Crimean winter of 1854–5, 'when we were often half-starved and had to spend long nights in slush and snow in the trenches, we found that a pipe of tobacco soothed the nerves and kept off the pangs of cold and hunger'.[33] In the same period, lay medical ideas related to the use of tobacco smoke as an 'disinfectant in fevers, cholera, and other epidemics on board ship' abounded in the Royal Navy; at the very least tobacco was seen to help sailors 'resist the influence of disease' by '[soothing] the system' in these situations.[34] As would later be repeated in the early twentieth century, popular perspectives underlined the centrality of tobacco to maintaining soldierly welfare, with strongly medical overtones. As a short piece in the *Inverness Courier* stated in January 1855, three years into the conflict with Russia: 'It is well known that a pipe or a cigar – indeed tobacco is all its forms – is an all-powerful panacea to a soldier in the field; it seems at once to warm, to cheer, and to invigorate him, while it is an acknowledged preservative from infectious disease'.[35] Similar sentiments were repeated by journalists, medics and soldiers during the Second Anglo-Boer War (1899–1902).[36]

Though the cigarette had been gaining in popularity since the late nineteenth century – due in large part to innovations in manufacturing that facilitated a mass market from the 1880s – the First World War was seen by many contemporaries to be accelerating this process.[37] Indeed, records suggest that more than half of all tobacco consumed in Britain by 1919 was in the form of cigarettes, with loose tobacco sales declining year on year; at the turn of the century this had been closer to twenty per cent.[38] The living and working conditions wrought by the conflict were swelling the ranks of smokers, both military and civilian. The continuing prevalence and influence of lay medical ideas on perceptions of tobacco use among the public – often buoyed by the complementary views of physicians and military medics – facilitated yet another modern adaptation of the longstanding panacea trope. One trade journal claimed in November 1914 that the war had provided a 'wonderfully authentic certificate to the character of tobacco as a panacea for wounds, panic, home sickness and "Jack Johnsons"'.[39] For this writer, August 1914 had finally silenced the anti-tobacco arguments of temperance supporters by providing proof of tobacco's positive benefits. Bold claims, as to a restorative function for the physically or psychologically injured serviceman, as well as the soldier sheltering beneath barrages of heavy shells, were made all the easier because of positive accounts in the medical press.[40] According to a writer in *The Lancet* in October 1914, drawing upon the established connection of smoking and the stress of modern industrial society:

> With us at home it is a common experience that the smoking of a pipe, cigarette, or cigar does much to allay the restlessness and muscular irritability engendered by mental and physical fatigue. There can, indeed, be little doubt that tobacco fills an important place in the psycho-physiological affairs of the human race, and that the habit of smoking … does something to temper the intensity of the struggle.[41]

Tobacco was incorporated into the war's pharmacopoeia, providing a medicinal and narcotic value that was so normalized as to be largely unquestioned, particularly by the troops themselves, as well as by the civilians that supported them. Of course, tobacco contains nicotine and is highly addictive, affecting the user's 'behaviour and mood with both its presence and its absence'; though concerns at this time remained focused, as they had been since the late nineteenth century, on nicotine's toxicity and the likelihood of poisoning through *excessive* smoking, rather than addiction in the sense we know it today.[42] This was especially so in wartime, when supplies of tobacco – though generally buoyant for British troops owing to the parallel efforts of state and voluntary agencies – suffered peaks and troughs, even if only for a few weeks, leading to complaints from servicemen and calls for better provisions.[43] But it was more than mere physiological compulsion or 'habit' that promoted tobacco use: the meanings and functions of smoking went beyond 'pure nicotine effects' to inform individual behaviours and social practice and were often underpinned by popular medical ideas and personal, embodied experience.[44] Smoking was a ubiquitous part of everyday life in the line, bound up with the rhythms of work, combat and rest. By the close of 1914, those who had not taken up smoking were in the minority. According to official figures, some 96.5 per cent of British servicemen were regular smokers by the close of 1914.[45] They were helped on their way by the two ounces of tobacco issued daily as a ration to troops and by a Christmas gift box, containing a pipe and tinder lighter, along with a commemorative brass tin holding packets of loose tobacco and cigarettes, provided by the Princess Mary's Gift Fund to the majority of men.[46] In 1917 alone, almost 39 million lbs (17,400 tonnes) of tobacco was supplied to government contracts and to military forces abroad, up from over 21 million lbs the year before.[47] In fact, tobacco supply was deemed so important by government that it established a Tobacco Control Board in May 1917 to directly control stocks and regulate prices, seeking to ensure abundant supplies to the fighting front and prevent profiteering at home.[48]

Tobacco lent itself to living conditions at the front, not only because it was eminently portable and easily maintained, but because it had a specific function within Victorian and then Edwardian conceptions of military discipline, morale and, crucially, soldiers' welfare. As one writer phrased it in early 1917: 'The first national aim is to look after the well-being of the troops. Their well-being, both in health and when wounded, is dependent upon a steady supply of smoking material.'[49] Tobacco acted as a conduit between the well-being and endurance of the individual combatant and the resilience of the military unit. It was seen to restore the man's body and mind and, through the experience of sharing cigarettes and communal smoking, could reinforce bonds between comrades.[50] This was particularly important in an army made up of 'citizen soldiers': smoking as a point of continuity with pre-war normalcy could play a role in encouraging sociability and camaraderie, as could the convenience of the machine-made cigarette.[51] While the briar pipe needed to be prepared and filled with care, the increasingly popular cigarette was 'at once ready to smoke, it only requires lighting, and, as a rule, once alight it burns regularly'.[52] This change in smoking practice signalled the transition from the class exclusivity of the pipe-smoking bourgeois connoisseur to the more homogeneous mass consumption of ready-rolled cigarettes, with the latter becoming closely associated with the working class and initially distrusted for their growing popularity among women.[53] In the first weeks and months of the war, the cigarette proved its worth for those sent abroad to fight, whether ashore or afloat; a potent signifier of fortitude in the face of danger, a source of comfort and a veritable treatment for shattered nerves. As an American writer, clearly motivated by his own fondness for tobacco, stated dramatically in 1916: 'Cigarettes have determined the outcome of battles. By the simple act of lighting cigarettes, the men who compose the rank and file of armies have at crucial moments been nerved to deeds of daring that were destined to decide the fate of a campaign and the fortune of a war.'[54]

The ongoing conflict, an extension perhaps of the 'creeping neurasthenia of urban existence' through its psychosomatic effects on participants, only served to reinforce the medicinal role accorded to tobacco.[55] As *The Lancet* put it, 'To the soldier and the sailor in the present war, with his nervous system in a ceaseless state of tension from the dangers and excitement, tobacco must be a real solace and joy when he can find time for this well-earned indulgence.'[56] While health risks were admitted, including heart and respiratory conditions, moderate smoking was promoted as a 'mental anodyne', a characteristic that accounted for tobacco's 'universality in the present bitter days'.[57] However, not everyone agreed that smoking was to be encouraged. Some medics actively discouraged smoking, particularly by men recovering from illness or injury. This was in stark contrast to the efforts of many charitable 'comforts funds', which actively sought tobacco supplies for convalescent soldiers.[58] The neuropathologist F. W. Mott, during the war a major in the Royal Army Medical Corps (RAMC),[59] discussed the impact of war experience on the nerves, including exposure to the 'minor horrors of war': 'foul stenches', rats and other vermin, in addition to the more serious and deadly effects of bombardment and extended periods living in wet and cold trenches and dug-outs.[60] For Mott, writing in the *British Medical Journal*, this resulted in depression of the 'vital resistance of the nervous system', which became 'utterly exhausted', 'worn out by this stress of trench warfare and want of sleep'.[61] The resulting neurological and functional disorders were only worsened by the consumption of tobacco in hospital, where 'laxity of discipline' was rife, particularly because of the care packages provided to convalescent men by civilians: 'The too liberal gifts of cigarettes have produced a cigarette habit in officers and men which is highly detrimental in these cases of war neurosis, especially in cases of irritable dilated heart.'[62] Similarly, A. Marmaduke Sheild – consulting surgeon to St. George's Hospital in London, temporarily attached to a Voluntary Aid Detachment (VAD) Hospital in Exeter – cited the 'want of occupations of a healthy nature' for military convalescents in urban hospitals, where fresh air and exercise could not be readily taken.[63] This meant that some men smoked excessively, though Sheild still appended a war-specific caveat: 'The use of tobacco in moderation has seemed to me of great comfort to wounded men, and I have no doubt it acts as a nerve sedative of value, especially in persistent pain.'[64] The popular, physiological understanding of 'nerve' allowed contemporaries to articulate psychological injuries as having a 'physical or bodily anchor', a perspective that owed much to ambivalences surrounding psychology in the period.[65] Victorian lay perspectives on the restorative characteristics of intoxicants – often including strong spirits like whisky and rum – also maintained a currency, positing that the body's finite 'nerve force', overtaxed by work and the pace of modern life, could be revitalized by the use of tonics and pharmaceuticals, which could 'nourish' the nervous system.[66] Depending on one's view of tobacco, smoking seemingly had the potential to either renew or deplete this vital force.

While a small number dissented, positing tobacco's negative effects on health, generally military and medical writers did not strongly condemn the smoking habit among members of the armed forces. As Fiona Reid notes, 'Smoking was the one area of self-medication which neither the military nor the medical authorities attempted to police.'[67] In early 1915, as more volunteers joined the colours as part of Kitchener's 'new armies', soldiers were said by one local newspaper appeal to be 'Dying for a Smoke'.[68] The *Worthing Gazette*'s charitable tobacco fund alluded to many of the common, and longstanding, medicinal characteristics attributed to tobacco, particularly underlining its associations with endurance and recovery from injury:

> 'Tommy' smokes most when he fights hardest. A pipe or cigarette seems to make him cool under fire, more determined than ever to 'see it through'. It comforts him as nothing else can when after the battle he finds his head splitting with the din and fumes of the conflict, or perhaps lying wounded in the trench or field.[69]

In a similar appeal published later in the war, smoking was associated with happiness and contentment amid the strains and privations of the frontline, in a manner consistent with contemporary images of the ever-cheerful 'Tommy' that were utilized frequently in tobacco advertising[70]: 'From mile to mile of trench there runs the smile – miles of smiles. What else have they to give them pleasure? The dull monotony of the daily duty – the nerve-racking strain of shell-fire and gas, only enhances many times the amount of pleasure to be derived from fresh tobacco.'[71]

Though such depictions of the smiling Tommy were seen as patently 'fake' by some servicemen, jarring with their lived reality, in this case harsh conditions were centred.[72] Rather than masking overlooked realities, smoking was presented as a symbol and source of strength that enabled men to 'bear up' in the face of anxiety and violence and, ultimately, to maintain control of their emotions by avoiding the 'weakness' inherent in weeping or breakdown.[73] Adopting the common 'Letters from the Front' motif, other tobacco fund appeals provided reports from soldiers where tobacco's effects were equated with recovery from the trauma of bombardment.[74] As an example attributed to an officer stationed in France put it: 'From personal experience I can tell you how a Comforts Fund cigarette soothed me, when we had a 5′9 and 4′2, and a "Whiz Bang" at us, and I only had a megaphone for protection. The cigarette helped more than the megaphone.'[75]

Even before the outbreak of war in 1914, writers on military welfare had praised the benefits of tobacco as a soothing narcotic in camp or at the front, while warning against the dangers of immoderate consumption. This ambivalent position was common in late nineteenth- and early twentieth-century Britain, with the importance placed on moderation growing as smoking became 'easier'. This ease of use followed the invention of the friction match and improvements in the industrial production of much 'milder' cigarettes containing flue-cured 'bright' Virginian tobacco, which produced a less alkaline, more palatable smoke with a slower release of nicotine.[76] In addition, military medics' fears of immoderate smoking among the rank-and-file probably reflected a longstanding class-informed paternalism, particularly common from the late nineteenth century, that viewed working-class men as prone to excess and 'moral negligence' if guidance was not provided by their social betters.[77]

While views related to tobacco's qualities were certainly ambivalent when taken together – seeing it variously as a potentially damaging intoxicant or beneficial therapeutic – it did not figure in discussions of 'national efficiency' in the way alcohol notably did.[78] The following section compares expert and lay discussions of alcohol and tobacco use among servicemen, alongside the testimony of soldiers themselves, to better elucidate why tobacco retained its panacea status during the First World War, while alcohol was increasingly the subject of state regulation, if not outright prohibition.[79]

Military welfare and medical perspectives: Tobacco *vs.* alcohol

Drinking was a long-established cultural practice on the eve of the First World War, so public and specialist debates about its effects on health, individual behaviour and social order, as well as government interventions, were also longstanding.[80] This included the introduction, during the late nineteenth and early twentieth centuries, of prohibitory legislation and, during the First World War, direct state intervention in the drink trade.[81] In the face of increasing state involvement in the 'drink question' and the growing social proscription of drunkenness, smoking was increasingly posited as an 'acceptable alternative to drinking', amid fears that excessive alcohol consumption was linked with degeneracy and national decline.[82] Indeed, for W. A. Penn, writing at the turn of the twentieth century, smoking *itself* discouraged drunkenness: 'After dinner a smoker drinks less between the whiffs of his cigar than does a non-smoker, whose whole time is free for the bottle.'[83] Similarly, J. W. Cundall, in a particularly celebratory 1901 pamphlet on 'smoking and smokers', stated matter-of-factly that 'no drunkard is ever a smoker', arguing that immoderate drinking 'inevitably destroys the taste' for tobacco, while smoking alone would not lead automatically to cravings for alcohol.[84]

Anti-alcohol sentiments found ready advocates during the First World War, including the likes of Victor Horsley, a temporary captain in the RAMC and staunch supporter of the temperance movement.[85] Writing in the *British Medical Journal* in January 1915, the surgeon suggested that the liberal application of the rum ration, recently reintroduced after being discontinued in the 1890s, would lead to widespread drunkenness. This, in turn, would result in errors of judgement, illness and a decline in physical endurance; in short, a 'decadence of *moral*',[86] the bedfellow of 'grousing, friction, and disorder'.[87] By contrast, as one writer phrased it in 1917, tobacco was the 'best support of morale there is'.[88] Such perspectives can be clearly situated within contemporary debates, during the latter decades of the nineteenth century, regarding conduct and character in both civilian and military life.[89] In the military sphere, character embodied 'courage, devotion to duty and unselfishness': it was the 'means by which the soldier acquired the moral strength to withstand the stresses of modern warfare'.[90] Therefore, drinking alcohol to excess was not consistent with the character expected of the soldier bound by codes of military comportment, as it undermined the 'moral forces' of 'discipline, zeal, and willpower'.[91] Conversely, the provision of tobacco and cigarettes, officially or otherwise, could act as a 'positive reinforcement' to discipline and friendly conduct between combatants, including between officers and their men.[92] For example, for one officer stationed in France in 1915, many of the hundreds of cigarettes requested from family at home were for distribution to the men in his charge.[93] Though this may not have necessarily led to lasting bonds between officers and men, it could at least promote fellow-feeling and help build rapport amid the harsh realities of trench life.[94]

Temperance advocates like Horsley were particularly troubled by the conventional view, still prevalent within the British armed forces, that alcohol had medicinal properties when applied in certain contexts.[95] As was by now widespread in a range of military and medical publications, emphasis was generally placed on the effects of *excessive* drinking on efficiency and discipline, both in terms of labour productivity and military organization. Commonly, the moderate consumption of alcohol was seen to relieve stress, raising courage and self-confidence before battle; as well as being employed in medical treatment or as an anaesthetic.[96] For instance, in a soldiers' guide written by Surgeon Captain H. Waite, published in 1901, whisky mixed with warm water, prescribed as a stimulant, was recommended as a treatment for frostbite.[97] In a similar manual of 1908, Lieutenant Colonel R. H. Firth (RAMC) recommended 'light red wine' for its antibacterial properties.[98] Following the outbreak of war in 1914, both politicians and the military establishment endorsed the rum ration, citing its perceived value in alleviating the effects of cold and damp in the trenches, while leading soldiers and physicians testified to its fortifying properties prior to battle or when in the line of fire.[99] For temporary Lieutenant Colonel H. R. Kenwood of the RAMC, writing in a wartime pamphlet on soldiers' health, though immoderate alcohol consumption was an 'enemy to discipline', it could provide a 'sense of comfort when one is much exposed to cold and wet; and there may be occasions when such a comforter or stimulant to a special effort is required for the soldier'.[100] Here the emphasis was on individual self-government, as only soldiers that lacked discipline, demonstrating 'weak self-control', would be anything other than 'strictly moderate' in their drinking.[101] As elsewhere, this view may have been informed by prevalent stereotypes about working-class proclivities for overindulgence, particularly among men from urban, industrial backgrounds.[102] Such 'old mentalities' persisted among the officer class and military hierarchies, even with the advent of mass citizen armies.[103] Similarly, the War Office's *Manual of Elementary Military Hygiene* (1912, reissued 1914), while warning against excessive use of alcohol and strong spirits in particular, suggested that 'taken in moderation … beer is not only an invigorating and refreshing beverage, but also a food'.[104]

As one might expect from such conduct manuals, the living and working conditions of men on active service were a common consideration: 'Though it is admittedly quite possible for troops on field service to do entirely without alcohol, yet there are occasions after severe work in inclement weather when an issue of spirits to those used to them will produce a sense of comfort and lessening of fatigue.'[105] This point, while clearly pertinent to the conditions engendered by trench warfare, contrasted with Kenwood's overarching view that the 'effect of alcohol upon a tired man is comparable to the effect of whipping a jaded horse', and so the provision of any stimulating liquors for temporary relief from fatigue was to be reserved for 'emergencies'.[106] The ambivalence surrounding the issue of drinking among servicemen was perhaps due to the ubiquity of alcohol consumption in British culture – which has considerable continuity over time – making unequivocally pro-abstinence arguments difficult to sustain.[107] Though tobacco had its critics within the military and among medics, no official attempts at proscription were seen with regards smoking in the same period, with forms of state control of tobacco and its accoutrements being related more to a concern for maintaining healthy stocks and income from tax and duties than to questions of morality, discipline or social order.[108]

While the effect of tobacco on health was also a topic of intense discussion among medical and military experts, the uneasy consensus was that tobacco was generally beneficial and, even in views erring toward the negative or critical, it was not deemed intoxicating in the same sense as alcohol.[109] As *The Lancet* put it in 1914, even where men smoked to excess, resulting in a 'pernicious' habit, this was 'as nothing compared with an abuse of alcohol'.[110] Indeed, evidence from soldiers' correspondence suggests that heavy smoking was commonplace in the frontline. For example, Captain Dundas Allen, a Platoon Commander in the fourth King's (Liverpool) Regiment, reported in a letter home to have 'smoked nearly 700 [cigarettes] in the last month'. Conditions in the trenches were to blame: 'I must try and stop a bit as I'm sure it can't be good for one, but in the trenches when one is awake on and off most of the 24hrs. one has little else to do'.[111] Through correspondence home, other servicemen pleaded for more tobacco, and especially cigarettes, to be sent to the front. For some, such as Private Alfred Swettenham of second Battalion King's Royal Rifle Corps, this was a frequent preoccupation.[112] And, in a testament to the value placed on tobacco by combatants, Sergeant John Grahl of the first Highland Light Infantry detailed in his service diary the lengths to which his comrades could go to obtain a smoke when tobacco was in short supply at the front: 'Smokes are terrible hard to get[,] some have got hold of some shag [loose, fine-cut tobacco], and are using pieces of brown and printed paper to wrap their shag in, and making what is supposed to be "fags"'.[113] As a ranker in the eighth Leicestershire Regiment commented in his memoirs, following orders that no spent matches or 'fag ends' should litter the trench floor, he and others picked up the cigarette remains and 'put a pin in them and smoked them til [*sic*] they burnt our mouths!'[114]

While drink could lead a fighting man astray, into indiscipline and mortal danger at the front, tobacco held and strengthened its association with self-medication due to the experience of industrialized war.[115] This is not to suggest that tobacco was without critics and advocates for complete abstinence, but that the war enhanced its status, due to the perceived need for practical narcotic and medicinal applications within a context where relatively little was known about the damaging properties of the plant when smoked, beyond fears of immoderate use, habit formation and association with heart conditions following prolonged use.[116]

Conclusion: Smoking as a route to wartime well-being?

Smoking by servicemen was hotly debated during the First World War, a continuation of nineteenth-century discussions about the effects of tobacco on health and its role in lessening the 'impact of service' on the individual and the unit. However, where earlier discussions among physicians and scientists had remained patently vexed and even contradictory, during the First World War – amid steeply rising levels of smoking, particularly in the armed forces – those that recommended smoking as a wartime panacea appear to have won out. The testimony of fighting men, alongside the views of civilian and military doctors, strengthened lay ideas about the medicinal value of tobacco. Though smoking's critics remained vocal throughout the war, their voices were increasingly drowned out by a torrent of 'evidence' that tobacco was a narcotic par excellence for the combatant, not least because of its positive attributes when compared to the dangers of drinking alcohol in a wartime setting that required physical endurance, mental agility and resilience following combat. Indeed, in the battlefront environment, any negative effects attributed to smoking might be readily overlooked by servicemen, particularly as the threat of injury and death was ever-present.[117]

As this analysis of a range of primary sources has demonstrated, tobacco was prized by military and civilian medics for its properties as a self-administered sedative, useful in steeling soldiers in advance of combat and helping them build resilience in the frontline. In this sense, it was treated like any other form of military welfare, and this was reflected in tobacco's presence in the medical press, military field guides and among the manifold materiel distributed to troops through both official-governmental and voluntary-charitable channels. The combination of war environment and experience with prevalent perceptions of the effects of war on mind and body ensured that the individual and social practice of tobacco-smoking was integrated into contemporary understandings of military welfare. The material impact of this relationship was a Western front awash with tobacco and its ubiquity in everyday life. Despite tobacco use being framed in physiological terms – as a means to 'nourish' frayed nerves to endure war – the practice of smoking was about more than satisfying a compulsion for nicotine. Indeed, as noted, the link between nicotine and addiction was not yet understood. Rather, smoking tobacco, particularly in the form of the cigarette, also facilitated sociability between men in the trenches and helped reinforce bonds with home through the receipt of tobacco in care packages.

In terms of health and well-being, tobacco was often assumed to be a somatic means to psychological relief in the frontline and following battle; a view often fortified by, and promoted in, newspapers and medical journals. Such discourse permeated lay medical understandings of the effects of smoking and built upon a longstanding popular culture of self-medication. Everyday life under fire appeared to provide unparalleled impetus to the use of tobacco, helping to cement the popularity of the machine-made cigarette as its cheapness, portability and practicality meant smoking was easier and more accessible. Smoking was a means not only to endurance through access to a calming sedative. It was a way of dealing with the ever-shifting and potentially overwhelming sensorium of the trenches. It also punctuated periods of boredom and intense labour through the temporal aspects of the smouldering cigarette. The declining social acceptability of excessive alcohol consumption, both at the front and at home, further reinforced the role and function of tobacco in line with codes of military discipline and comportment. Though strong liquor had long been deemed a friend of the soldier and sailor – as it was similarly seen as comforting and, in small amounts, invigorating – tobacco could not be credibly associated with loss of self-control and disorder in the way excessive drinking often was. Ultimately, while health problems and acute illnesses were already associated with smoking by some, these paled in comparison to the self-evident benefits the practice had for the physical and psychological well-being of soldiers in an eminently modern war. Conflict on an industrial scale ensured that the panacea gospel renewed its currency and relevance for a new generation, one that would become thereafter associated with the appalling legacies of war and, for some, the damaging excesses of modernity.

Notes

1. Tammy M. Proctor, *Civilians in a World at War, 1914–1918* (NYU Press, 2010), 3.
2. Alexander Watson, *Enduring the Great War: Combat, Morale and Collapse in the German and British Armies, 1914–1918* (Cambridge University Press, 2009), 23.
3. Michael Reeve, 'Managing Risk in the "Danger Zone": Defensive Infrastructure and Public Safety Discourses on the North-East Coast of England during the First World War', *Coastal Studies & Society* 1.2–4 (2022), 180–208; Alex Mayhew, 'Hoping for a Victorious Peace: Morale and the Future on the Western Front, 1914–1918', in Louis Halewood, Adam Luptak and Hanna Smyth (eds), *War Time: First World War Perspectives on Temporality* (Routledge, 2019), 194–219.
4. Julie Anderson, 'Military Resilience', in Leo van Bergen and Eric Vermetten (eds), *The First World War and Health: Rethinking Resilience* (Brill, 2020), 11–15.
5. Matthew Leonard, 'A Sensorial No Man's Land: Corporeality and the Western Front during the First World War', *Senses and Society* 14.3 (2019), 257–70 (p. 263).
6. Leonard, 'A Sensorial No Man's Land', 258.
7. David Howes, 'Foreword: The Engagement of the Senses', in Nicholas J. Saunders and Paul Cornish (eds), *Modern Conflict and the Senses* (Routledge, 2017), xix–xxiii (p. xx); Santanu Das, *Touch and Intimacy in First World War Literature* (Cambridge University Press, 2014), 6–8.
8. Watson, *Enduring*, 27.
9. Richard Klein, *Cigarettes Are Sublime* (Picador, 1995), 142–3.
10. Daniel Ussishkin, *Morale: A Modern British History* (Oxford University Press, 2017), 75; David Monger, Sarah Murray and Katie Pickles, 'Introduction', in David Monger, Sarah Murray and Katie Pickles (eds), *Endurance and the First World War: Experiences and Legacies in New Zealand and Australia* (Cambridge Scholars, 2014), xii–xiv (p. xii); Watson, *Enduring*, 2–4.
11. Watson, *Enduring*, 62–9.
12. Klein, *Cigarettes*, 142–4.
13. 'Tobacco Rations', *The Times*, 6 October 1916, 9.
14. Quoted in Peter E. Hodgkinson, *'Glum Heroes': Hardship, Fear and Death – Resilience and Coping in the British Army on the Western Front 1914–1918* (Helion, 2018), 97.
15. Michael Reeve, 'Special Needs, Cheerful Habits: Smoking and the Great War in Britain, 1914–18', *Cultural and Social History* 13.4 (2016), 483–501; Henry Daniels, 'When the Smoke Cleared: Tobacco Supply and Consumption by the British Expeditionary Force, 1914–1918', *Revue Française de Civilisation Britannique* 20.1 (2015), https://journals.openedition.org/rfcb/218 (accessed 18 December 2024); Chris Wrigley, 'Smoking for King and Country', *History Today* 64.4 (2014), 24–30.

16. Matthew Hilton, *Smoking in British Popular Culture 1800–2000* (Manchester University Press, 2000), 126; Fiona Reid, *Medicine in First World War Europe: Soldiers, Medics, Pacifists* (Bloomsbury Academic, 2017), 135–7; Stephen Snelders, 'Intoxicants and Intoxication on the Western Front 1914–18', in Leo van Bergen and Eric Vermetten (eds), *The First World War and Health: Rethinking Resilience* (Brill, 2020), 71–91 (pp. 74, 85–6).
17. Paul Huddie and Amy Carney, 'Military Welfare History: What Is It and Why Should It Be Considered?' *War & Society* 42.4 (2023), 305–16 (pp. 306–8).
18. Huddie and Carney, 'Military Welfare History', 307. See, for example, Herbert Obinger, Klaus Petersen and Peter Starke (eds), *Warfare and Welfare: Military Conflict and Welfare State Development in Western Countries* (Oxford University Press, 2018).
19. Huddie and Carney, 'Military Welfare History', 306.
20. Aaron Jarden and Annalise Roache, 'What Is Wellbeing?' *International Journal of Environmental Research and Public Health* 20 (2023), 1–4 (p. 1).
21. Susan Oman, *Understanding Well-Being Data: Improving Social Policy, Practice and Research* (Palgrave Macmillan, 2021), 41–2.
22. Rob Boddice, *The History of Emotions* (Manchester University Press, 2023), 45.
23. Boddice, *The History of Emotions*, 30, 158; Donncha Marron, 'Smoke Gets in Your Eyes: What Is Sociological about Cigarettes?' *Sociological Review* 65.4 (2016), 882–97 (p. 884).
24. Boddice, *Emotions*, 45.
25. Rod Phillips, *Alcohol: A History* (University of North Carolina Press, 2014), 247.
26. Jordan Goodman, *Tobacco in History: The Cultures of Dependence* (Routledge, 1993), 54; Jason Hughes, *Learning to Smoke: Tobacco Use in the West* (University of Chicago Press, 2003), 87–8.
27. W. A. Penn, *The Soverane Herbe. A History of Tobacco* (Grant Richards, 1901), 97.
28. Hughes, *Learning to Smoke*, 90–1; Hilton, *Smoking*, 48.
29. Angela McShane, 'Tobacco-Taking and Identity-Making in Early Modern Britain and North America', *Historical Journal* 65 (2022), 108–29 (p. 112).
30. Hughes, *Learning to Smoke*, 6; Goodman, *Tobacco in History*, 44.
31. Goodman, 'Excitantia: Or, How Enlightenment Europe Took to Soft Drugs', in Jordan Goodman, Andrew Sherratt and Paul E. Lovejoy (eds), *Consuming Habits: Global and Historical Perspectives on How Cultures Define Drugs* (Routledge, 2007), 121–41 (p. 131); Anne Charlton, 'Medicinal Uses of Tobacco in History', *Journal of the Royal Society of Medicine* 97 (2004), 292–6.
32. Goodman, *Tobacco in History*, 37, 41, 49.
33. John Hart Dunne, 'Alcohol and Tobacco', *The Times*, 25 November 1915, 9.
34. John Gallagher, 'Influence of Tobacco on Sailors', *The Lancet*, 28 February 1857, 229–30.
35. 'Tobacco for the Crimea', *Inverness Courier*, 4 January 1855, 6.
36. 'The Use of Tobacco on Active Service', *The Lancet*, 10 November 1900, 1365; 'The R.A.M.C. South Africa Fund', *British Medical Journal*, 9 March 1901, 613.
37. Hilton, *Smoking*, 85.
38. Hilton, *Smoking*, 85; Wrigley, 'Smoking', 26.
39. 'A Panacea for Wounds', *Tobacco*, 1 November 1914, 23. Named after the champion African American boxer, 'Jack Johnson' was a popular slang term for the German high explosive shell. See Alexander Watson, 'Soldiers' Humour', *1914–1918 online. International Encyclopedia of the First World War*, 8 October 2014, https://encyclopedia.1914-1918-online.net/article/soldiers-humour/ (accessed 18 December 2024).

40. 'Quotation from the "Lancet"', *Tobacco*, 1 November 1914, 23–4.
41. 'The Role of Tobacco in the War', *The Lancet*, 3 October 1914, 857–8.
42. Tricia Starks, *Cigarettes and Soviets: Smoking in the USSR* (Cornell University Press, 2022), 6; Goodman, *Tobacco in History*, 122.
43. Michael Reeve, '"Something-to-Smoke, at the Right Time, Is a Godsend": Voluntary Action and the Provision of Cigarettes to Soldiers during the First World War', in Kevin Linch and Matthew Lord (eds), *Redcoats to Tommies: The Experience of the British Soldier from the Eighteenth Century* (Boydell Press, 2021), 120–45 (p. 132).
44. Jon D. Kassel, Carol A. Paronis and Laura R. Stroud, 'Smoking, Stress, and Negative Affect: Correlation, Causation, and Context across Stages of Smoking', *Psychological Bulletin* 129.2 (2003), 270–304 (p. 271).
45. Susanna Roughton, 'Cigarette Smoking and "Nerves"', *Journal of the Royal Army Medical Corps* 160.2 (Suppl. 1) (2014), 238–9.
46. Reid, *Medicine*, 136; Peter Doyle, *'For Every Sailor Afloat, Every Soldier at the Front': Princess Mary's Christmas Gift, 1914* (Unicorn, 2021), 117, 126–7.
47. The National Archives (Kew, UK), BT 72/1/TandMCB1, 'Return of Stocks & Consumption in 1917' (Tobacco Control Board Report, 8 March 1918), 6–7.
48. 'Tea and Tobacco under Control', *The Times*, 31 May 1917, 7; 'Tobacco Supplies', *The Times*, 5 July 1917, 3.
49. 'Importation', *Tobacco*, 1 February 1917, 24.
50. Anderson, 'Military Resilience', 12; Joanna Bourke, *Dismembering the Male: Men's Bodies, Britain and the Great War* (Reaktion, 1996), 136.
51. Bourke, *Dismembering*, 131; Helen McCartney, *Citizen Soldiers: The Liverpool Territorials in the First World War* (Cambridge University Press, 2005).
52. 'The Cigarette Habit', *The Lancet*, 7 September 1907, 718.
53. Marron, 'Smoke', 891; Rosemary Elliot, *Women and Smoking since 1890* (Routledge, 2008), 30.
54. William W. Young, *The Story of the Cigarette* (D. Appleton, 1916), 214.
55. Jerome E. Brooks, *The Mighty Leaf: Tobacco Through the Centuries* (Little, Brown, 1952), 252.
56. 'The Role of Tobacco in the War', *The Lancet*, 3 October 1914, 857–8.
57. 'The Soldier and the Cigarette', *The Lancet*, 18 August 1917, 248–9.
58. 'Our Fighting Men Are Short of "Smokes"', *Berwickshire News and General Advertiser*, 14 August 1917, 7; 'Tobacco Fund for 6,000 Wounded Soldiers in Manchester & Salford Hospitals', *Manchester Evening News*, 24 October 1915, 2.
59. Mott later became renowned for his association with the Maudsley Hospital, a psychiatric institution, opened in South London in 1923. See E. A. Sharpey-Schafer and Rachel E. Davies, 'Mott, Sir Frederick Walker (1853–1926), Neuropathologist', *Oxford Dictionary of National Biography*, 23 September 2004.
60. F. W. Mott, 'The Chadwick Lecture on Mental Hygiene and Shell Shock during and after the War', *British Medical Journal*, 14 July 1917, 40.
61. Mott, 'The Chadwick Lecture', 40.
62. Mott, 'The Chadwick Lecture', 42.
63. A. Marmaduke Sheild, 'Some Practical Observations on the Injuries of War', *The Lancet*, 16 December 1916, 1005.
64. Sheild, 'Some Practical Observations', 1005.
65. Jill Matus, 'Emergent Theories of Victorian Mind Shock: From War and Railway Accident to Nerves, Electricity and Emotion', in Anne Stiles (ed.), *Neurology and Literature, 1860–1920* (Palgrave Macmillan, 2007), 163–83 (p. 170); Mathew

Thomson, 'The Popular, the Practical and the Professional: Psychological Identities in Britain, 1901–1950', in G. C. Bunn, A. D. Lovie and G. D. Richards (eds), *Psychology in Britain: Historical Essays and Personal Reflections* (British Psychological Society, 2001), 115–31 (pp. 116–17).

66. Amelia Bonea, Melissa Dickson, Sally Shuttleworth and Jennifer Wallis, *Anxious Times: Medicine & Modernity in Nineteenth-Century Britain* (University of Pittsburgh Press, 2019), 182–3, 188; Jill Kirby, *Feeling the Strain: A Cultural History of Stress in Twentieth-Century Britain* (Manchester University Press, 2021), 41–3, 49.
67. Reid, *Medicine*, 136.
68. 'Dying for a Smoke', *Worthing Gazette*, 19 May 1915, 6.
69. 'Dying for a Smoke', 6.
70. Hilton, *Smoking*, 96.
71. 'Miles of Smiles', *Berwickshire News*, 20 August 1918, 4.
72. Bourke, *Dismembering*, 166.
73. André Loez, 'Tears in the Trenches: A History of Emotions and the Experience of War', in Jenny Macleod and Pierre Purseigle (eds), *Uncovered Fields: Perspectives in First World War Studies* (Brill, 2003), 211–26 (pp. 211, 214–17).
74. Andrew Roberts, *Letters from the Front: From the First World War to the Present Day* (Osprey, 2014), 12.
75. 'The Cigarette Helped', *Worthing Gazette*, 26 July 1916, 7.
76. Hughes, *Learning to Smoke*, 85.
77. Brad Beaven, *Leisure, Citizenship and Working-Class Men in Britain, 1850–1940* (Manchester University Press, 2005), 33.
78. Luke Flanagan, 'The Temptation of War: How Alcohol Affected the Canadian First World War Experience in Hastings, 1917', *Journal of Imperial and Commonwealth History* 49.4 (2021), 688–711 (p. 689).
79. Flanagan, 'The Temptation of War', 690.
80. James Nicholls, *The Politics of Alcohol: A History of the Drink Question in England* (Manchester University Press, 2009), 2–3.
81. Nicholls, *The Politics of Alcohol*, 130.
82. Penn, *Soverane Herbe*, 97; Sara Haslam, 'A Literary Intervention: Writing Alcohol in British Literature 1915–1930', *First World War Studies* 4.2 (2013), 219–39 (p. 222).
83. Penn, *Soverane Herbe*, 97.
84. J. W. Cundall, *'Pipes and Tobacco': Being a Discourse on Smoking and Smokers* (Greening, 1901), 47.
85. Michael S. Dunnill, 'Victor Horsley (1857–1916) and the Temperance Movement', *Journal of Medical Biography* 20.1 (2012), 25–31.
86. Horsley's rendering of the term is closer to the French *le moral*, related to 'military qualities of spirit and determination' from the late eighteenth century, which was still in use during the First World War. While 'morale' gained an increasing currency during the conflict – though its meaning was never settled or fixed – it was not until the Second World War that the term could be said to be in truly common use. See Ussishkin, *Morale*, 2–15.
87. Cited in Reid, *Medicine*, 122.
88. 'Importation', *Tobacco*, 1 February 1917, 24.
89. Ussishkin, *Morale*, 64–5.
90. David Englander, 'Discipline and Morale in the British Army, 1917–1918', in John Horne (ed.), *State, Society and Mobilization in Europe during the First World War* (Cambridge University Press, 1997), 125–43 (p. 126).

91. Ussishkin, *Morale*, 63–4.
92. Bourke, *Dismembering*, 128.
93. Liddle Collection, Special Collections, Leeds University Library (Leeds, UK) (LC), LIDDLE/WW1/GS/0024, private papers of Captain Dundas Allen: Allen to Mother, 18 March 1915; Allen to Father, 22 September 1915.
94. Bourke, *Dismembering*, 128.
95. Victor Horsley, 'On the Alleged Responsibility of the Medical Profession for the Reintroduction of the Rum Ration into the British Army', *British Medical Journal*, 30 January 1915, 205.
96. Łukasz Kamieński, *Shooting Up: A History of Drugs in Warfare* (Hurst, 2017), 8.
97. H. Waite, *How to Keep 'Fit' or the Soldiers' Guide to Health, in Field, Camp & Quarters* (Gale & Polden, 1901), 18.
98. R. H. Firth, *Military Hygiene: A Manual of Sanitation for Soldiers* (J&H Churchill, 1908), 209.
99. Dunnill, 'Victor Horsley', 30; Reid, *Medicine*, 123.
100. H. R. Kenwood, *Health in the Camp: A Talk to Soldiers* (H.K. Lewis, 1915), 48–50. Kenwood was, in civilian life, Professor of Hygiene and Public Health at the University of London.
101. Kenwood, *Health in the Camp*, 48–9.
102. Beaven, *Leisure*, 33; Thora Hands, *Drinking in Victorian & Edwardian Britain: Beyond the Spectre of the Drunkard* (Palgrave Macmillan, 2018), 27.
103. Enzo Traverso, *Fire and Blood: The European Civil War 1914–1945* (Verso, 2017), 164.
104. War Office, *Manual of Elementary Military Hygiene* (Wyman and Sons, 1914), 39.
105. War Office, *Manual of Elementary Military Hygiene*.
106. Kenwood, *Health in the Camp*, 49.
107. Hands, *Drinking*, 2–3.
108. Reeve, 'Voluntary Action', 132.
109. Reid, *Medicine*, 136–7.
110. 'The Role of Tobacco in the War', *The Lancet*, 3 October 1914, 857–8.
111. LC, LIDDLE/WW1/GS/0024, Allen to Mother, 4 June 1915.
112. Imperial War Museum (London, UK) (IWM), Dept. of Documents, Documents.4200, private papers of A. H. Swettenham, letters to mother, 12 October 1918; n.d. (*c.* August–October 1918).
113. IWM, Dept. of Documents, Documents.6473, private papers of J. A. Grahl, diary entry, 6 October 1915.
114. LC, LIDDLE/WW1/GS/0800, Private J.W. Horner, 'The Memories of a Trench Rat 1914–1918'.
115. Reid, *Medicine*, 136.
116. R. B. Walker, 'Medical Aspects of Tobacco Smoking and the Anti-Tobacco Movement in Britain in the Nineteenth Century', *Medical History* 24.4 (1980), 391–402 (p. 395); Joel D. Howell, '"Soldier's Heart": The Redefinition of Heart Disease and Speciality Formation in Early Twentieth-Century Britain', in Roger Cooter, Mark Harrison and Steve Sturdy (eds), *War, Medicine and Modernity* (Sutton, 1999), 85–105.
117. Andrew Russell, *Anthropology of Tobacco: Ethnographic Adventures in Non-Human Worlds* (Routledge, 2019), 173.

9

Well-being from the perspective of community groups: Notes from Abington Community Library, 1939–2023

Sue Botterill and Siobhán Hyland

At the heart of a community-managed library is its volunteers. They bring with them their many and varied experiences and skills from their professional lives and careers. The volunteers at Abington Community Library use their skills to provide a space which enhances the well-being of the community it serves. This chapter is a reflection by a volunteer, Sue Botterill, in the form of an oral history. Sue is aged seventy-five, her last birthday in November. She started volunteering at the library in the summer of 2010, just six months after retiring from her contracted employment. This oral history is a reflection on the history of the library building and the contribution it has made to the local community interspersed with documentary evidence from the archives of the library which Sue has preserved and curated. It reveals the experiences of a volunteer, the impact this can have on the well-being of an individual and of a community as well as a glimpse into the library's unique past and the ways in which it served its community.

The rationale for an oral history interview was to explore Sue's involvement in the library and, therefore, the wider theme of well-being. Sue's motivations to ensure well-being was a key driver of the ways in which she and the library operate are also explored in this chapter. This interview allowed for the emotional reflections that Sue had to be explored, along with the connection to well-being. This co-created chapter in this volume acknowledged both academic and library services to be developed. In this interview, Sue discussed the archival material that she and her fellow colleagues saved from being disposed of. This is important, as this material tells the story of the library and its purpose in the community. As Sue is the subject matter expert, using an oral history as a vehicle for this analysis means that it can be understood from the lived experience of the librarian rather than the academic. It also allows for questions that arise from the material to be answered, a key benefit of oral histories when used with archival material.[1] The oral history was approached in the same way as archival study, in a critically evaluative way.[2] The emotionality of the different pieces of evidence was explored, along with their emotional attachment put upon them by Sue and the other librarians.[3] The very fact of all the members of staff being long-term volunteers demonstrates a connection to the values of the work being undertaken. In order to understand that, the emotional quality of the interview was analysed to have a framework in which to decode them.[4] However, there always seems to be concern when using oral histories surrounding the ways in which if a story is retold, then it is revised.[5] In this case, although the story of the archival material may have been told before, it is the underlying narrative about well-being and how that supports the library's mission which is of key importance.

This chapter is set into several parts, which include the ways in which volunteering is used as a mechanism to support libraries, but with well-being in mind as its key driver. It then goes on to detail the history of the library along with all the activities that are provided for the local community and the impact on the wider network of users. The chapter is divided into sections which provide a context for a particular theme and then an excerpt from the oral history interview. This allows for a useful structure and context for which the oral history can be embedded into the text. However, the theme of well-being is reflected upon in each section, as this is the rationale for the work of the library and the theme of the chapter itself.

Volunteering

Volunteering is vital for a community-managed library to sustain itself. Volunteering is described as unpaid work, undertaken in a voluntary setting which produces meaningful activity.[6] People decide to volunteer in their communities for many reasons and as volunteers, they make a huge contribution to society, the value of which has been increasingly acknowledged in recent years, in a changing workplace.[7] Sue's journey into volunteering started when she attended a coffee morning at the library:

> So I turned up and I went for all about 12 months, really enjoying the atmosphere and chatting to people and stuff, and then, the librarian said 'we're looking for volunteers ….'
>
> What does that mean in the library? I thought, you know, I'm not a professional. 'No, no, she said, you just make tea meet and greet and run stuff. We raise money. The Friends group raises funds to pay for children's events.' I thought that's just up my street, so I started volunteering and as I gradually got to know more and more people, I became more and more involved. And then I joined the Friends Group committee and then obviously, later on, when all the trouble started with the fighting to keep the library open.[8]

Those who volunteer in a library are largely people who have a lifelong love of books and reading and learning and who recognize that this began in childhood, with early memories of being read to by a parent, listening to stories, maybe listening to the radio, reading books at home, borrowing books from the local library. Volunteering, in itself, has been found to increase life satisfaction, self-esteem and physical health.[9] Mental well-being is also reported to be improved with volunteering activities.[10] Therefore, it is not just the visitors to the library who gain from the volunteering, the volunteers benefit too. Sue speaks of the benefits of volunteering:

> So how I got involved and it's the community aspect as well because when you leave work you miss the camaraderie, you know of your work mates and stuff like that. You know, being at home on your own, you think I don't want to do bingo and knitting for the rest of my life and want to do something interesting? So that's what got me involved, and obviously the more I got involved, it's addictive.[11]

The history of the library

The history of the library and of Sue's recollections of her own experience of libraries as sources of well-being are intertwined, which she explained:

> I remember my library as a child in the 1950s – the whole procedure of protracted choosing, then reaching up to the counter on tiptoes, handing over your library ticket, having your books stamped, then rushing home to read your new books – it stays with you. Those beginnings make you a reader for life and are the key to entering other worlds, other lives, to learning, thinking for yourself, gaining knowledge and understanding of the world. There are many ways to expand a child's world, but fostering a love of books is one of the best.[12]

Abington Library started its life off as a Church. In 1922, it was sold to become the new library. Sue stated that it changed only in terms of the objects, rather than the fabric of the building. She noted, 'The pews were replaced by a library shelves and the altar was replaced by a children's play area, so the building is exactly the same … I've always been interested in in old structures, you know, and the history.'[13] In one document held in the library a local newspaper marked this occasion:

> The beginning of a new epoch in the progressive Church work of Abington parish was marked on Monday night when the Town Council sanctioned the sale to Abington Church Council of a site for a new church on the Weston Road. The price of £514 for .759 of an acre, situated at the junction of Lindsay Avenue and Birchfield Road East a commanding position on the brow of a hill overlooking the new estate on Weston Road.[14]

A new church to support the Abington congregation was called Lindsay Avenue Church, which opened on 5 October 1923. However, on 1 October 1938 the congregation moved to new premises as the building was too small. They moved homes to the new and larger Church of St. Alban in Broadmead Avenue, which was consecrated on 1 October 1938.[15] However, the space which previously housed the church was welcomed as a library. This new library was described in detail in the Annual Report of Libraries and Museums:

> Abington Church a brick building in Lindsay Avenue was officially opened by the Mayor, Alderman A.W. Lyne, O.B.E., J.P., as a Branch Library on 30 September. It is conveniently situated in the centre of a new housing estate and with little structural alteration has made a suitable building for the purpose. To judge from the issues during the first month its establishment is more than justified.[16]

The now deserted Lindsay Avenue Church was not forgotten, and as the Second World War began, it was needed for a particular service as a local historian had noted:

> For a while, the old Lindsay Avenue church lay empty, but as the war crisis loomed, it was pressed into service as a distribution centre for gas masks and for the assembly of evacuees.
>
> The Central Public Library was looking to expand its services into the suburbs and purchased the building for £1200 engaging the firm of Messrs W Lessells and Co of Raglan Street, to renovate and convert it for another £300. Eight large bookcases of solid deal faced with oak were constructed, together with a large oak reading table and chairs, 1600 fiction books for adults and 750 non-fiction were bought in, together with 560 for the children's section. The facility immediately became very popular, 331 borrowers' tickets being issued in the first month, and this does did not take account of evacuees, for whom special arrangements were made.[17]

During the first week of the library opening a photograph was published in the *Chronicle and Echo* of the mayor opening the building; a few days after, another article and photograph was of evacuees entering the building. The irony is the church was built on an estate to provide 'homes for heroes' returning from the First World War and some of the first visitors to the library were evacuees at the beginning of the Second World War. When Abington Library celebrated seventy years of operation, recollections of this time period from the first librarian were published:

> Just four weeks into the Second World War, Abington Library was opened after renovation at the cost of £1500. Edna Luck, the first Librarian at Abington was our special guest for the day and kept us amused with many tales of these early days. One story in particular highlight the community spirit. Edna was doing her evening check outside the building to ensure no chinks of light were showing through the blackout curtains when she fell down the coke hole which had been left open from an earlier delivery. Edna hurt her leg and was noticed limping and bleeding by a neighbour who helped her back into the library and rushed home to get a bowl of water and a bandage. Her leg duly bathed and bandaged Edna carried on with the evening shift.[18]

Therefore, this diligence in duty demonstrates how important the work at the library was to its librarians. Additional recollections on the war were reflected upon during a regular well-being class. At the library, there is a 'Thursday Club' where the volunteers meet each week. Sue recalls telling a story there, encouraging other people to discuss their recollections of the outbreak of the Second World War:

> Because apparently the war, I think was the 3 September 1939, the library opened on the … and some of the first people that actually came into the library were evacuees cause they had a special application form for evacuees. And I've actually got a copy of that evacuation form that they had to fill in the membership application. On the panel I was talking about this to some people in the Thursday club, that which is really the Pensioners Club, but we don't call it any age, you know, all the titles that you did, Darby and Joan and all these types, we just call it the Thursday club because anybody can come. And I was telling this story, and somebody said cause they first stood, I think on the corner on 1 September and one person in the audience said oh the war didn't start till such and such. So then somebody else chirped up and said my dad was a policeman, and it's funny, he got orders to do whatever he needed to do. [Another] said my dad was a railway man and he got some orders that he never told the family on the 1st and then somebody else chirped in what they must have known the war were coming. Obviously, anybody in a reserved occupation was prepared on the 1st for when war was declared, so obviously they were doing that with the evacuees as well.
>
> Actually, before the war was declared and it this only cropped up in a conversation about six weeks ago.[19]

This revealed an undiscovered social history within these family stories and the ways in which they were preparing for war. These social interactions within the library setting are key to the psychological well-being of the participants and visitors.[20] These interactions were amplified in the form of a type of marketing, so much so that Sue started to receive evidence of the participants experiences via letter. Sue goes on in the oral history interview to discuss the situation for the child evacuees which were shared with her in the form of a letter:

> Ohh my dad said this on the 1st and then I said well … the evacuees were distributed.
>
> Shall we say on the 1st, which obviously was before the announcement that the war had started, and but when she said those words and everybody, when I say that WI clubs or anything and when I read [letter writer's] words and she says all the children were standing on the grass which is 10 yards from at the door of our library waiting for the kind people of Northampton to come and choose us. And you think the six-year-old, you imagine a six year old nowadays in that situation it would be against safeguarding. It would be against their mental health. It would be against all these other modern phrases that they use about wellbeing and all that was in them days. All they wanted to do was get the kids out of London in case they were attacked by bombs.[21]

It was this particular letter which Sue reflected on and became part of the reason why well-being is important to her and critical to the library service she is a part of. Reflecting on well-being, Sue said:

> And words are so poignant. That's the thing that really hit me and I think this is a serious subject I need because it's well-being in them days when really wellbeing wasn't a word, it was not used in the context that it's used nowadays and that was the first thing that really got me into thinking about well-being as a thing and looking at it through the years and obviously what we do now within the library that's to do with wellbeing.[22]

When the library become seventy years old, the team held a party, which included a special guest:

> In 2009 on our 70th Anniversary we had a party and who should be our special guest – but the original librarian – Edna Luck who was 96. I also have on record, notes from Edna about her time at Abington. In 2019, on our 80th Anniversary, it was time for another celebration with Friends and Supporters. With Members of St Albans Church; the original occupants of our building manning the history stand. Our entertainment for the day was Cedar Road School Choir and ADRE Dementia Choir, we all had a fabulous time.[23]

Sue's commitment to a well-being ethos was even more important when the library, as a council run endeavour was threatened. This represented a challenge to the volunteers and Sue also recollects the transition from council library to community run library facilities,

> What the thing was, obviously, we had a battle plan and everything and we were going to Council meetings. There were protests … they did a 'mums and tots' protest outside the Grosvenor Centre. I mean, I belong to … the county group where all the libraries joined together and that was a legal challenge and lots and lots of things happened and of that nature. But for us it was funny because when it first came out, we were invited to a meeting at the Central Library and then they all said we're thinking about closing you down.
>
> But in a presentation. You know how they do it on the screen and the sheets go by and by about the 10th page it was like we're gonna close you down and then by about 15th page, we expect you to take it over or you're toast or the thing. But in those sorts of words that they use, and we all looked at each other and actually some of the library representatives that were around the table were like 20 years older than me.[24]

Sue archived the main stories in the local newspaper on this issue, which are evocative of similar problems in so many other local and community libraries:

> Further spending cuts could mean an end to the Northampton mobile library service and closure of many branches … Ending the mobile library service would

> save the County Council £133,000 a year and involves the loss of more than 20 jobs ... Closing all 24 libraries listed would save £400,000 deny access to libraries for a further 150,000 people. It would mean cutting the equivalent of 46 full time staff.[25]

The full impact of the loss of Abington Library was documented in the local newspaper:

> As reported by Chronicle & Echo last week, Northamptonshire County Council plans to close Abington Library in Lindsay Avenue as part of its new budget. Borrowers who make more than 500 visits to the library every week, are opposed to the proposal ... Lindsay Avenue branch lends about 100,000 books a year.[26]

This news upset the local community. It is important to reflect on this, as this demonstrates how key a service the library was to the local community. The negative emotion that can sometimes be displayed when analysing comments is vital to aid understanding of the strength of feeling, however uncomfortable this may be.[27] One library user made their strength of feeling known on the library comments sheet when leaving feedback,

> I first used the Lindsay Avenue Library as a 10-year-old. I am now 70. At that time the Central Library was too far to walk and the bus fare was one penny each way almost a week's pocket money. I spent hours as a child in this lovely library. Now after all those years I once again spend hours here and could not walk to Central Library or even Pensioners bus fare 40p each way. What a sad state of affairs.[28]

Although this does not explicitly discuss well-being, it does show the sacrifice the person made as a young person to get to the library. Therefore, this shows the importance of it in their life. Moving on to how this affected the library team, although Sue and the other library staff and volunteers were concerned about the prospect of taking on such a task as to become library custodians, they proved to be highly resilient and adaptable. The team decided to attempt to form a team to take over the management of the library themselves and for it become a community-managed organization. They started the process of acquiring the library as detailed in Sue's interview:

> It was about the third scheme and every time it was deadlines timed in business plans and everything, and then the Community managed life. I think the third scheme that they did then you have the deadline of 12:00 o'clock ... I remember going to the Council to the meetings when some of us gave speeches and ... we all nearly got thrown out of the Council meeting for interrupting the Council meeting. And they stopped the meeting, and they said if you don't be quiet in the gallery, you'll have to leave the premises. It was absolutely vicious, but, I mean, we carried on and then in the end they realised that for the third scheme, they've gotta do something because there's such public uproar. We did well. I did the business plans as part of the team because I was in finance, and I thought I didn't know how to do it. What a library costs they did give us some costs for like the utilities and all that sort of thing, but we marked up a business plan and then we had a

> meeting with them and there were a few things they questioned which I said Ohh, I understand your meaning on that subject. So, I altered the figures and rethought the reply.[29]

When the council library was threatened with closure, Sue and her colleagues began the task of tidying up and restoring the building back to an empty shell:

> And then as we began to sort of tidy up and in draws and things, you know, in rooms that nobody used anymore and stuff like that out the back kitchen and stuff, I found all sorts of archival material. Yes. So I just started putting it in those big plastic boxes and then when [they] threatened to close the library, there were all sorts of tactics that the Council did to sort of then, well, to scare us, to be perfectly honest, because one day we arrived and now outside was like one of those big cage vans, you know, where they collect rubbish. And the councilmen were emptying the drawers of all the paperwork and stuff. And I thought to myself, my goodness, all that archival stuff. The men won't know.
>
> They'll just chuck it and it'll go to the tip. So I spoke to the librarian and she said, well, I know some stuff that's hidden away, she said it needs to be safe just for the history of the library. If the library doesn't exist anymore, so I took it home so as we found bits, we found the original ledgers and letters and all sorts of archival material.
>
> So I put it in my loft and actually through all the fight of keeping the library open, which was about three and a half years, it all sat in my loft.[30]

Abington Library reopened in April 2021, but as a community-managed endeavour. Simon Armitage, Poet Laureate, officially opened the library with a poetry reading under its new management on 1 May, which had to be a live streamed event due to the Covid-19 pandemic.[31]

The material Sue gathered up and stored in her loft now became an important asset for the community library:

> So, then I began, when it was our 75th anniversary of being a library, and I'd have this little bit of experience in public speaking. I said we'll do a talk on the history of the library, so I got out stuff and people are amazed at what we've got. And they add to the materials all the time. You know all I've got this at home. I've got this recollection or whatever, and I just keep it.[32]

The material that Sue has collected and is currently archiving contained some important historical notes:

> Well, in the old history, found the original daily what we would call in accounting or admin terms of daybook where it's got every day in this leather-bound book, you know, with the marbling on the edges and everything handwritten of how many children, how many types of books, Ooh, 15 categories of books. How many of each book went out the building?

How many people attended the library and actually one of the interesting things I got it out to show one of our new volunteers only yesterday because she was wrapping up some old stuff in brown paper to keep it safe and … it had got VE Day. It had got, you know, end of the Japanese war written, you know, King George … and all the days when the library closed or there was a special celebration in the library. And when you flick through the books, it's like loads of figures and numbers of occupancy and numbers of books. But when we opened it and we saw VE Day and [it was] down in the Ledger, do you know what I mean? And it carried on until I can't remember the date, but until they went computerised, I mean, that's one of the things about computers.[33]

Sue has kept a wide range of archival materials, which she uses to advertise the library and its rich history. The building and the services they offer are central to the themes of well-being:

The building has its own sense of space and place. It is accessible, safe and comfortable, a neutral environment, non-judgmental. It is for all members of the community whatever their age, ability, ethnicity or gender. Community groups within the Voluntary Sector encourage and support wellbeing through friendship and by building relationships to help combat loneliness and isolation. Sue stated that in this century, there needs to be friendly spaces: be it a church, library, community centre or youth club and their contribution to society. Libraries promote literacy with all the traditional library services, they also offer the resources for modern communication WiFi, free use of computers together with tuition if necessary. Many libraries have space for events and social and community activities.[34]

People need Community Spaces and Volunteers to run them. Sue and the other volunteers became 'Friends of Abington Library' (FOAL) and assumed management of the library.[35] This was after becoming a Community Benefit Society with a License to Occupy issued by Northamptonshire County Council and West Northamptonshire Council on 24 July 2020. This enabled the team to keep Abington Library open for the benefit of the local community. Their primary aim was to further promote community engagement. The testimonials from the community discuss the ways in which the work that is carried out in the building and in the wider community is integral to their well-being. As with all community groups they try to have a diverse programme with something to suit everyone.[36]

The library has taken on a new and more expansive purpose; it has become a hub for the community, as well as a link for other services. Sue reflects on this below:

So I mean now we share facilities, we share information, we share events, so it's ended up being absolutely marvellous. Do you know what I mean? We donate to them. They donate to us. We collect baby basics. We collect for the food bank. They collect books for us, so we all do our own specialist thing that as a community.[37]

This shows that the library has become a community hub and uses its facility to gather resources, not just for us for them, but for other community benefit programs. One of the key programs they run at the library is the Summer Reading Challenge. These types of activities, as stated by Howard demonstrate positive impacts on well-being.[38]

> The Summer Reading Challenge has a different focus each year – last year it was science based; this year it was more sport orientated. Next year it will be something different. It's a national initiative, supported by the Reading Agency and at local level by the Northampton Library service. The age range to participate is from preschool, up until 12 years of age. It's not stuffy as it has avatars for children to identify with, a personal challenge of reading six books plus, book reviews and lots of online resources to access at home or in the library. The idea is to promote an enjoyment and enthusiasm for reading and to keep the schools' learning momentum going through the summer holidays, so pupils return in September not having lost valuable skills. Each library is allocated several local primaries and in some cases one or two secondary schools to target Year 7 and some Year 8 pupils. It's perfect for us because all our schools sit in the heart of our community and range from some in challenging, disadvantaged catchments to more middle class.[39]

The library has also reached out internationally and is now twinned with Abington Community Library in Pennsylvania. Although partnerships like this are believed to be few in number, Long states that the benefits of international 'twinning' are important for cultural exchange.[40] 'To celebrate our twinning with Abington Community Library, Clarks Summit, Pennsylvania on 7 June 2021, a totem pole was created (it now stands in the library) Children as young as three together with their parents helped with the making and applying paper-mâché to a carpet tube.'[41]

Sue sums up the important space the library holds within the community and the ways in which she and the team facilitate that:

> I have learned over my years as a library volunteer that it is so much more. It is about helping a shy or diffident teenager to find the book they are seeking, encouraging them to tell you about it, or helping people who need something specific and don't know how to locate it, or chatting to people who are simply there to fill their time, who may be lonely and in need of human contact, or those who just want a quiet space to study or learn. It is about engaging with people and learning from them in turn, understanding that we are both giving and receiving by spending time with people who have come to the library. While reading is central to this, other activities – craft sessions, coffee mornings, regular clubs and activities, talks, all contribute to the feeling of belonging to a community, and importantly, of being a vital part of the wellbeing of that community. Both visitors and volunteers benefit in this respect. They can feel that they have a place in a wider community, connecting with other libraries, other groups, and other organisations.[42]

Libraries are trusted spaces in the community, whereby people can access support and share resources. These empower the individual to self-improvement and advancement of self.[43] Additionally, the library facilitates these cultural engagement practices.[44] After the 'Big Community Conversation' in 2021, one of the key areas for the attendees was the theme of mental health and well-being. Sue stated that ways in which the library and the action group has undertaken the giving of support in this regard:

> We started by thinking about people who were isolated in their own homes, not getting out – even afraid to come out – through fear of Covid, of perceived danger, health reasons, low income and many other reasons. There are numerous organisations and groups who meet regularly in the area for little cost to pursue a hobby or sport or just to meet up and talk to others whatever age and gender, able-bodied or with disability. To signpost these activities, we met with Social Prescribers working within GP surgeries who prescribe social or physical activity alongside more traditional medicine. They are keen to collaborate with us and we hope to further our aim to display the database in various venues locally such as supermarkets, shops, GP surgeries, and libraries – anywhere people meet. The work continues as we seek to build a better and strong community together.[45]

Therefore, Sue's experience of well-being is in the way that she supports the library and the ways in which this radiates out to the community. It demonstrates the contribution of well-being to the community it serves.[46] This library has been a key asset for the Abington area for just over one hundred years. During this time there have been many changes in the services it provides and the ways these are delivered. However, the core mission is the same, that at its core, it is a central hub for those seeking space for well-being, in whatever form that may be. This chapter has demonstrated a small case study into the ways in which a library is a centre for well-being. It has shown the lifespan of the library and that the ways that the community has responded to a changing landscape of financial and political issues. Nevertheless, the community of volunteers continued to be committed to the vision and mission of the library, with well-being firmly rooted at its centre and continue to manage the library as a community-managed venture.

Notes

1. Anthony Ince, 'Anti-fascist Action and the Transversal Territories of Militant Anti-fascism in 1990s Britain', *Antipode: A Radical Journal of Geography* 54.2 (2002), 482–502 (pp. 489–90).
2. Bill Addis and Hermann Schlimme, 'Oral History', *Construction History: Journal of the Construction History Group* 31:1 (2016), i–iii (p. i).
3. Harold Rosen, 'A Necessary Myth: Cable Street revisited', *Changing English* 5.1 (1998), 27–34 (p. 27).
4. William Reddy, *The Navigation of Feeling: A Framework for the History of Emotions* (Cambridge University Press, 2001), xii.
5. Harold, 'A Necessary Myth', 31.
6. Utta Tiittanen and Riitta Turjamaa, 'Social Inclusion and Communality of Volunteering: A Focus Group Study of Older People's Experiences', *International Journal of Environmental Research and Public Health* 19.9 (2022), 1–10 (p. 1).

7. Morawski Leszek, Okulicz-Kozaryn Adam and Strzelecka Marianna, 'Elderly Volunteering in Europe: The Relationship between Volunteering and Quality of Life Depends on Volunteering Rates', *Voluntas* 33.2 (2022), 256–68 (p. 257).
8. Sue Botterill, interviewed by Siobhán Hyland, 15 March 2024.
9. Samuelson Appau and Sefa Awaworyi Churchill, 'Charity, Volunteering Type and Subjective Wellbeing', *Voluntas (Manchester, England)* 30.5 (2019), 1118–32 (p. 1118).
10. Faiza Tabassum, John Mohan and Peter Smith, 'Association of Volunteering with Mental Well-Being: A Lifecourse Analysis of a National Population-Based Longitudinal Study in the UK', *BMJ Open* 6.8 (2016), 1–8 (p. 7).
11. Sue Botterill, interviewed by Siobhán Hyland, 15 March 2024.
12. Sue Botterill, email to Siobhán Hyland, 26 January 2024.
13. Sue Botterill, interviewed by Siobhán Hyland, 15 March 2024.
14. *Northampton Independent*, 7 October 1922.
15. Public Transport Experience, 'Monday's Bits and Pieces' (2024), https://publictransportexperience.blogspot.com/2019/10/mondays-bits-and-pieces-3.html (accessed 22 July 2024).
16. *Annual Report Libraries and Museums 1938/39*, 7.
17. Alan Burnham, 'From Barn to School and Lending Library', *Chronicle and Echo*, 30 January 1999.
18. Barbara Leigh, *News from the Areas*, 30 September 1939–2009, Abington Library Celebrates 70 Years.
19. Sue Botterill, interviewed by Siobhán Hyland, 15 March 2024.
20. Cut Afrina, Fitriah M. Suud, Nurrahma Yanti, S. Safrinal, J. Sardi, A. T. Wati and others, 'Social Interaction in the Library: A Student Psychological Perspective', *SHS Web of Conferences* 202 (2024), 1–11 (p. 2).
21. Sue Botterill, interviewed by Siobhán Hyland, 15 March 2024.
22. Sue Botterill, interviewed by Siobhán Hyland, 15 March 2024.
23. Sue Botterill, email to Siobhán Hyland, 26 January 2024.
24. Sue Botterill, interviewed by Siobhán Hyland, 15 March 2024.
25. 'Cash Cuts Threaten to Close Libraries', *Chronicle and Echo*, 4 January 1980.
26. 'Residents in Protest over Library Closure', *Chronicle and Echo*, 13 January 1999.
27. Michael E. Harkin, 'Feeling and Thinking in Memory and Forgetting', in Monica Greco and Paul Stenner (eds), *Emotions: A Social Science Reader* (Routledge, 2008), 84–92 (p. 90).
28. Abington Library comments sheet dated 22 January 1999.
29. Sue Botterill, interviewed by Siobhán Hyland, 15 March 2024.
30. Sue Botterill, interviewed by Siobhán Hyland, 15 March 2024.
31. David Summers, 'Abington Library in Northampton Reopens to the Public after Being Saved by the Community', *Northampton Chronicle and Echo*, 23 April 2021, ww.northamptonchron.co.uk/heritage-and-retro/heritage/abington-library-in-northampton-reopens-to-the-public-after-being-saved-by-the-community-3211603 (accessed 16 July 2024).
32. Sue Botterill, interviewed by Siobhán Hyland, 15 March 2024.
33. Sue Botterill, interviewed by Siobhán Hyland, 15 March 2024.
34. Sue Botterill, email to Siobhán Hyland, 26 January 2024.
35. Co-operatives UK, 'Friends of Abington Library' (2024), www.uk.coop/directory/friends-abington-library (accessed 23 July 2024).
36. Abington Library, 'Events' (2024), https://abingtonlibrarycbs.net/events (accessed 22 July 2024).

37. Sue Botterill, interviewed by Siobhán Hyland, 15 March 2024.
38. Natasha Howard, 'Arts Day: A Creative Intervention for NHS Staff Wellbeing', *Library and Information Research* 43.127 (2020), 2.
39. Sue Botterill, email to Siobhán Hyland, 26 January 2024.
40. Nina Long, 'Twinning of Hospital Libraries: International Resource Sharing', *Bulletin of the Medical Library Association* 74.4 (1986), 374–5 (p. 374).
41. Sue Botterill, email to Siobhán Hyland, 26 January 2024.
42. Sue Botterill, email to Siobhán Hyland, 26 January 2024.
43. Sarah Summers and Steven Buchanan, 'Public Libraries as Cultural Hubs in Disadvantaged Communities: Developing and Fostering Cultural Competencies and Connections', *Library Quarterly (Chicago)* 88.3 (2018), 286–302 (p. 290), https://doi.org/10.1086/697707.
44. Summers and Buchanan, 'Public Libraries', 293.
45. Sue Botterill, email to Siobhán Hyland, 26 January 2024.
46. Colectiva Sembrar and Marina Sitrin (eds), *Pandemic Solidarity: Mutual Aid during the Covid-19 Crisis* (Pluto Press, 2020), 171.

10

Well-being in mental health nurses' working lives and its impact on nursing shortages: Insights from the early years of the National Health Service

Claire Chatterton

The Covid-19 pandemic and its aftermath drew attention to the working lives and conditions of nurses. Subsequent industrial unrest and rising concern about a shortage of nurses signifies that among many nursing staff in the UK, there is considerable discontent and low morale. Much of the attention has been on nurses described as working on the 'frontline', in intensive care and on Covid wards and in general hospital settings. Alongside them, though, are nursing staff working throughout the National Health Service (NHS) and private sector, and this discontent is widespread, with many nurses stating that their working lives negatively impact their feelings of well-being.[1] This chapter will focus on mental health nurses, who arguably receive less attention than their general nursing colleagues, both in the contemporary press and from historians,[2] and the first twenty years of the NHS, 1948–68.

When the NHS was being planned, the shortage of nurses across all specialities was so severe that Aneurin Bevan, the minister of health, described it as approaching 'a national disaster'.[3] Questions were raised in Parliament,[4] and although the situation was to subsequently improve in general nursing, it continued to be an issue in what was then known as mental and mental deficiency nursing (the former now being termed mental health nursing and the latter, learning disability nursing). The period under discussion, 1948–68, is noteworthy for being the time when concerns over shortages in mental health nursing were at its height.[5] It was also the period in which mental health services, still largely provided in former asylums, had been brought into the new NHS. Although they had seen a change in nomenclature following the 1930 Mental Treatment Act, from asylums to mental hospitals, this change in terminology, together with the inception of voluntary status for some patients, had had only limited impact.[6] Charles Webster has described mental nursing as 'the single, most intractable nursing problem of the early NHS'.[7] Shortages of mental nurses (as they were then known) were to remain prominent on the political agenda throughout the 1950s and the 1960s, and Hansard reveals that there were a series of parliamentary debates on this topic during the 1950s.[8]

This shortage of mental health nursing staff was the result of two issues, difficulties in recruitment but also problems with retention (or wastage or attrition, as it was then more commonly termed). This was particularly marked in relation to student nurses, where recruitment was challenging and wastage rates were very high, with up to 80 per cent of entrants failing to complete training.[9] Figures from the General Nursing Council (GNC) for England and Wales show a steady decline in the numbers entering mental nurse training from 3,204 (1,412 women and 1,792 men) in 1948 to just 1,594 (604 women and 990 men) in 1954.[10] Throughout the 1950s and 1960s, concerted attempts were made to improve recruitment including advertising campaigns and exhibitions, recruitment from overseas, educational reform and 'dilution' to change the skill mix within mental health nursing with enhanced use of nursing assistants and, later, enrolled nurses.[11] This period saw some significant changes in the treatment of the mentally ill – for example, the introduction of the concept of social therapy into psychiatry,[12] the 'opening of the doors'[13] and the introduction of new medications.[14] Some writers have, however, argued that in some areas of mental health provision, little changed in this period and that these changes only had limited impact on the working lives of nurses or their patients.[15] Many explanations were given for this mental health nursing shortage by politicians, civil servants, senior nurses, psychiatrists, union leaders and administrators, and these will be explored alongside the views of mental health nurses themselves. In-depth analysis of primary sources reveals a wider variety of interrelated reasons that were given to explain why it was difficult to both recruit and retain mental health nurses in this period. The files of the Ministry of Labour and National Service and the Ministry of Health, together with those of the GNC (all in the National Archives), are a rich source of data together with archival material from the Royal College of Psychiatrists, the Royal College of Nursing and trade union records in the Modern Records Centre at the University of Warwick. Oral history interviews can also give an insight into the views of those who worked in mental health nursing in this period.

Notions of well-being will also be explored in relation to these discussions. Patrician and others have argued that in relation to a consideration of nurses' well-being, 'discernment of wellbeing depends on a personal perception, is subjective and multifaceted, and will vary from person to person, depending on many variables, including context, as well as developmental progression of the person'.[16] It will however also refer to two often utilized concepts in discussions of well-being. The first is that of 'hedonic well-being', which can be encapsulated as having a pleasurable life; thus hedonism means pursuing pleasure to achieve happiness. The other term, 'eudaimonic well-being', refers to well-being which originates from virtuous and purposeful living; so eudaimonism can be seen as pursuing meaning to achieve happiness long term.[17] Current debates about the shortage of mental health nurses can therefore be examined in the light of the events of the past, and it will be argued that well-being has been a constant concern and underpins this debate, albeit not always expressed using that term.

As previously noted, much of the mental health provision in the new NHS from 1948 continued to be in large institutions, which were rooted in their own culture and practices. Many of these were isolated both geographically and culturally, and this was one of the most common reasons that were given for shortages in mental nursing.[18] In 1945, the report of the Subcommittee on Mental Nursing and the Nursing of the Mentally Defective, appointed by the Athlone Interdepartmental Committee on Nursing Services, noted, 'there is a peculiar "isolation" in Mental Hospital life which may deter those who have had only a short experience of it'.[19] Built mostly in the Victorian and Edwardian era, asylums had been deliberately constructed away from towns and cities.[20] On a practical level, it was difficult for staff who did not live on site to get to work. In 1947, Dr Armstrong, the medical superintendent of Littlemore Hospital, bemoaned, 'the handicaps of a location three miles from Oxford on a badly-served bus route', which he argued had a severe impact on his attempts to recruit more staff.[21] However, in addition to the need to get to work for those who lived out, for those who lived in there was the need to be able to get away on their days off. In a 1945 proposed 'Reconstruction Scheme for Mental Nursing', it was noted that both transport and recreational facilities 'need considerable improvement. It is particularly important that mental nurses get right away from their work when they are off duty',[22] arguably an important boost to many nurses' hedonic well-being.

However, the isolation of the large mental hospitals was psychological, as well as geographical. For some nurses, this had a positive impact on their well-being; for example, it is common for nursing staff to recall that they felt that they were part of a large family. This sense of community was a strong theme in the oral history interviews conducted by Nolan, who found that 'most of the men interviewed agreed that it had been the camaraderie amongst the staff which had kept them in nursing'.[23] This was echoed in Chatterton's oral history interviews; one female nurse stated, 'It was hard work, people were nice that you worked with, so you had that kind of sense of family, sense of camaraderie, which I don't think exists now … There was lots of support.'[24] A male nurse interviewed in the same study recalled, 'I liked the friendly and the family atmosphere of psychiatry.'[25] This theme was also a recurrent one in Gittins's study of Severalls Hospital near Colchester. She interviewed over sixty people including past and present staff and patients and noted, 'I was surprised by how many hospital staff used the analogy of the family.'[26]

Mental health nursing often literally ran in families too. It was not uncommon for several generations of one family to work in a mental hospital. One retired nurse said she had been attracted to mental health nursing because 'both my grandmothers had worked in a mental hospital, and I had visited them. I visited when one of my grandmothers was like an assistant matron on night duty and when I went to visit, I got a very good welcome by the patients because I was my grandmother's little granddaughter'.[27] Another interviewee said, 'I needed a job and my parents worked there … and so I got a job as a nursing assistant. And when I went on the ward that I was first employed in, the Sister there I'd gone to school with and I thought, well she wasn't any cleverer than me, because I thought you had got to be some super brain to be a nurse, or vocational at least, and, you know, I thought well if she can do it, so can I.'[28] In addition to recruitment based on familial experience, close friendships and romances between nurses were not uncommon despite the 'great divide', as Gittins described it, which meant that mental hospitals in this period were usually spatially divided on gender lines into male and female sides, which were strictly segregated.[29]

This also contributed to the feeling of community and hedonic well-being among some nursing staff.

For those without any personal contacts with an institution, becoming a mental health nurse sometimes occurred because they lived in close proximity to a large mental hospital. This was often a very visible source of local labour. For example, one man said, 'There were a lot of people actually in the area, that actually worked at the hospital at the time … and I used to see hundreds of people, sort of, going up on their cycles in those days.'[30] He therefore decided to apply, went on to become a Registered Mental Nurse (RMN) and worked there throughout his career. This was echoed by one of the female interviewees,

> Practically everybody who lived in … was working at … in some capacity, whether it was nursing or in the laundry or in the bakery. There were so many departments that local people were employed and the other thing, of course, which was nice was they had a coach which went all round … stopping just about everywhere, picking people up to get there in time for their shifts.[31]

The rural location of many of the large mental health institutions also meant that many had large grounds and often excellent sporting facilities. One feature of mental nurse recruitment had been that nurses, men in particular, had been recruited on the basis of their ability to participate in the social side of the hospital – for example, being able to play a musical instrument or play sport for a hospital team.[32] One nurse remembered that from his interview, 'Mostly the things that they seemed to be interested in those days was "can you play football"?'[33] In an oral history project at Littlemore Hospital near Oxford, Goddard found that sporting activities were popular among the staff of both sexes. In the 1950s and 1960s the hospital had a mixed hockey team, seven tennis courts, badminton and table tennis facilities and a cricket and football team.[34] Social facilities were also on offer and enjoyed by many of the nursing staff. Peter Nolan recalled that on his first morning at Tooting Bec Hospital in London in 1962, having arrived from Ireland to train as a mental nurse, 'I was besieged by enthusiasts inviting me to join the union, the staff social club, the athletics club, the hospital choir and the drama club.'[35] Mental hospitals used their social and sporting activities as a means of recruitment, as brochures of the period illustrate.[36] For many mental nurses, these facilities were to prove a great enhancer of their hedonic well-being.

Conversely, the culture of the large institution could be forbidding and unwelcoming to the newcomer. In his seminal study of asylums, Goffman identified the negative effects that working and living in 'total institutions' could have.[37] As well as being geographically and psychologically isolated, most psychiatric hospitals were also showing their age by the time they were incorporated into the NHS in 1948. This was frequently commented on at the time. For example, as Griffiths and others noted, 'Most mental hospitals are antiquated, inconvenient and hopelessly inadequate.'[38] This was to have serious implications for both patients and staff's well-being and impact on recruitment and retention.

In addition to their age, the mental hospitals were also very overcrowded. The Second World War had exacerbated this situation, and by 1952, nearly all regions reported overcrowding. For example, the Leeds and Manchester Regional Hospital Boards (RHB) had seven hospitals between them with more than two thousand beds in each, even though 1,000 was meant to be the maximum desirable. Of the 140 mental hospitals, 67 had over a thousand beds. In some areas, no new beds had been created since 1948 despite a rapid increase in voluntary admissions and older people, and a vicious circle was created as 'endemic staff shortages were exacerbating the problem of overcrowding and long waiting lists'.[39] A 1952 review prompted by the RHB chairmen stated, 'What we need is more money, more buildings and more steel and more staff – none of which seems very likely.'[40] In 1953, the *Nursing Times* published an expose of the conditions at Menston Mental Hospital, near Leeds, where they reported that one ward was accommodating 103 patients but had only five toilets. Mattresses were laid on the floor between beds to accommodate extra patients.[41]

Some commentators remarked on the noxious miasma that could greet a newcomer. One participant in Goddard's study remembered:

> The first thing that hit you when you walked into a mental hospital was the smell. It was said that it was a combination of paraldehyde, which is a drug, sedative, which was given to patients and had a very strong smell, and then paraffin, they used paraffin wax to polish the floors, and then urine from the incontinent patients and it was the smell that really hit you when you walked on the ward.[42]

Not only were the conditions grim, the overcrowding and low staffing levels meant that large wards were sometimes left with only one nurse on duty. In 1945 a speaker, at the twenty-second meeting of the National Advisory Committee for the Recruitment and Distribution of Nurses and Midwives, pointed to the 'loneliness and responsibility of ward duty' for the nurse in this situation.[43] At the following meeting, one medical superintendent, Dr Boyd, said that such was the shortage of nurses in his hospital that 'it was necessary to move patients from one ward to another to enable nurses to go off duty'.[44] By 1949 a report stated, 'Some wards have been left without nursing staff at all, in the charge of a reliable patient.'[45] The situation did not improve during the 1950s. In 1955 Whittingham Hospital, Lancashire, were unable to hold their annual Christmas pantomime in the ballroom due to their lack of nursing staff, something which would have impacted staff and patient morale and well-being.[46]

Mental nursing was hard work, both physically and mentally. The Wood Report had noted that 26 per cent of nurses' time was spent on domestic duties.[47] This was noted with concern by Griffiths and others in 1945:

> There is usually no domestic staff for these wards, and it is not uncommon for the nurses to do all the domestic work that patients are unable to do. This has so often been stressed that we will not labour it, but some jobs which nurses do are not so commonly spoken of, such as hauling large bales of laundry without trucks or baskets, emptying pig-swill etc. The male staff are in an even worse case. They do farming, gardening and work of the crudest types, with squads of patients.[48]

Ten years later, Dr Bickford, a consultant psychiatrist, stated that he had seen nurses working as cobblers and porters. One he said regularly milked the cows and others cut the grass. He even knew of one nurse who would stand in at the sewerage plant when the normal worker was away.[49]

As well as the heavy burden of domestic work, mental health nursing work could also be challenging for new recruits. The Athlone Subcommittee noted that

> some of the nursing work in the mental hospitals comes as a shock and a surprise, with the result that they abandon the attempt to become Mental Nurses. As one of the witnesses said, a girl of 18 or 19 who has never before done any nursing work cannot be expected to attend to a doubly incontinent patient during their first few weeks in the hospital. Moreover, the responsibility thrown on the young student nurse in a Mental Hospital is, in many ways, heavier than in a General Hospital.[50]

McBrien argued that advertisements for mental nursing were misleading, 'The opportunities for promotion and advancement are mentioned with gay abandon but little mention is made about the demands, both physical and mental, which are inherent in a career mainly concerned with social interaction and human behaviour.'[51] Dr Noel Harris, speaking at the first northwest regional conference on mental nursing in 1954, argued, 'It was easy for a young nurse starting her training to be hurt or be frightened by a patient showing aggression or saying unkind things, before she came to realise they were symptomatic.'[52] Violence towards nurses was also picked up as an issue by Mrs Reisner, from the Ministry of Labour and National Service, who wrote in a memo in 1945, 'I am told that a nurse … went to Rampton and complained because the Medical Officer does not believe in giving sedatives to those difficult criminal lunatics, and the nurses are frequently hurt, and consequently will not stay.'[53]

Nurses' well-being could thus be affected by the physical demands of the job together with the constant threat of violence, but the work could also be emotionally distressing. An anonymous report by a mental nurse in the Royal College of Nursing's archives talked of the 'heartbreak of mental nursing. No results. There is no certain and final hope that years of work expended by the nurses on the patients will ever lead to complete recovery from the suffering, far worse than anything physical, they endure.'[54] However, the minister for health in 1952 painted a very different picture of the new treatments and approaches being utilized in the mental hospitals which he said meant that 'like the general nurse, the mental nurse has the satisfaction of seeing a large proportion of patients cured of their ailments and returned to happy and useful lives.'[55] Oral history accounts from those who remained in mental nursing in this period provide a more nuanced picture, with one nurse reflecting, 'I did enjoy actually working with the patients and fellow staff. It did prove its rewards as well as its disappointments because obviously some patients you never did cure as such, but you do see some results and improvements. So I had that satisfaction. I enjoyed that.'[56] For them, mental nursing was ultimately a satisfying job and provides an example of eudaimonic well-being.

An issue that negatively impacted some nursing staff was corruption and ill-treatment of patients, which Nolan found were important themes in his oral history interviews. He found that among the staff that had begun in the 1960s, 'all the nurses interviewed remembered instances of theft, mostly perpetuated by senior nursing staff who had access to patients' property and money'. He argued that 'common dishonesty simply became part of the folklore of the hospital'.[57] Chatterton also found this, with one interviewee saying, 'Well, I had to really go to town on some of the nurses who were really exploiting the patients. This was not in the acute wards, more the chronic wards ... that was the thing that I disliked most of all.'[58]

Several writers speak of shift work as a deterrent to recruitment and retention. In a 1952 letter, W. A. Higgs (the secretary of the Management Committee of Whittingham Hospital, Lancashire) talked of 'the disadvantages of longer hours, night duty, lack of opportunity to attend dances and entertainments in the evening, and weekend duties which are not part of the conditions of service in the factories, shops and offices of the neighbouring towns'.[59] A memo from Mrs Reisner of the Ministry of Labour and National Service, following a visit to Chartham Mental Hospital in Kent in January 1945, said, 'The "long days" worked in my opinion are iniquitous. The nurses are called at 5.45 am, on duty at 6.30am ... going off duty finally at 7.30pm.'[60] As well as the disadvantages of shift work, attention was also drawn to the difficulties that arose from nurses not being told their shifts well in advance, and the hours of work were also often described as long. The Athlone Subcommittee found that the average working week for mental health nurses varied between institutions and could be between forty-eight and sixty hours a week.[61]

Strict discipline had been a feature of all nurses' lives. As Carpenter notes, 'nursing is, of course, an occupation noted for its authoritarian management',[62] and this had been highlighted as an issue in the interwar years by the Lancet Commission in 1932.[63] Mental health nurses' working lives had also been conducted within a comprehensive and custodial legal framework where a breach of discipline could lead to instant dismissal. As Carpenter notes, 'When staff joined the asylum payroll they were typically issued with a long list of rules and asked to sign "obligation forms". Infringement of any of them could lead to instant dismissal. Even if they wished to marry, they had to first get the medical superintendent's permission.'[64] Living in and long working hours allowed medical superintendents 'almost absolute power' over their nursing staff.[65] Jones notes that even after the Second World War the position of the medical superintendent was still one of great prestige and authority. Whereas, in general nursing, matrons were the chief source of discipline, in mental nursing, power could reside with the medical superintendent, the matron and the chief male nurse.[66]

The issue of discipline was also commented on by the Athlone Subcommittee[67] and in the 'Staffing the Hospitals' report in 1945,[68] and both recognized that although discipline while on duty was important for the efficient running of hospitals this 'should not extend to the nurse when off duty' who should 'be permitted as far as is possible, the personal liberty of a private individual'.[69] The Athlone Subcommittee also found evidence of 'restrictions placed on the use of recreation rooms, decoration of bedrooms and similar matters'. As they said, 'They may be small things in themselves, but they are undoubtedly irksome to staff and lead to discontent and friction.'[70] Similarly, the 'Staffing the Hospitals' report stated, 'In their *off-duty hours* nurses should have the same scope for the unrestricted use of their leisure as any other member of the community. For example, there should be no restrictions on smoking in their own quarters, the wearing of mufti, or on visits by friends of either sex.'[71] However, in 1954 a report by the Royal Medico-Psychological Association still spoke of one of the greatest difficulties to be overcome in improving recruitment as being 'an old fashioned and rigid attitude of mind' (which could be from the matron, medical superintendent or the hospital management committee). Sometimes, they argued, 'brusque and unfair treatment' could lead to nurses resigning, a factor which was not officially cited by those who left, but hidden among some of the more 'conventional causes'.[72]

However, for some new recruits to mental health nursing, the discipline and hierarchy proved attractive. One nurse described the hospital where he had worked as 'very structured, very hierarchical … everybody knew their place … it seemed, kind of, cosy, secure'.[73] McCrae and Nolan pointed out that mental health nursing had always proved attractive to ex-soldiers, and this was noticeable following the Second World War.[74] These staff were 'easily identified by the sharp creases in their trousers, their highly polished shoes, grooming and tendency to stand to attention when being spoken to'.[75] This was partly because it was an occupation that was open to men. It also had much in common with a military organization; in that it offered uniforms, accommodation, rulebooks, routine and a clear hierarchy and arguably improved these ex-service personnel's eudemonic well-being. Nolan also found that some female staff valued the order and routine provided by mental hospital work in their role as nurses, which engendered feelings of safety and security.[76]

The 1932 Lancet Commission had highlighted that the lack of, and quality of, accommodation for nurses was an issue which impacted both recruitment and retention.[77] At a meeting of the National Advisory Committee for the Recruitment and Distribution of Nurses and Midwives in January 1945, discussion took place as to whether nurses were still expected to sleep in rooms adjacent to the ward (where they could be called on in the night to assist the night nurses) as had been the norm in the past.[78] Thus, Griffiths and others in their reconstruction scheme for mental nursing argued that improved accommodation was a vital ingredient in improving better recruitment and retention[79] (and improving nurses' hedonic well-being). However, this did not always materialize, and in 1956, Dr Brookes, medical superintendent at Shelton Hospital near Shrewsbury, spoke of the difficulties his hospital faced in recruitment. This was exacerbated, he said, because of the inadequate residential accommodation for nurses, meaning that he could only recruit from the local area.[80]

Ignorance and stigma regarding mental illness was also felt to be another important factor contributing to difficulties in nurse recruitment, with concurrent low status for those who worked in this field. In 1945 the Athlone Subcommittee noted that 'the fact that mental nurses have so far not been held in the same esteem as men and women in other branches of nursing reflects on the public attitude towards mental disease and those who suffer from it'.[81] This has led to some commentators describing mental health nurses as the 'Cinderellas' of nursing.[82] Those who worked with the mentally ill were affected by stigma, as were their patients. According to the Royal College of Nursing, 'In the 1940s, mental health nursing was seen – even by those who did it for a living – as an embarrassment. Nurses would tell friends outside the hospital that their work there was with patients who had physical diseases, rather than confess that they nursed those suffering from a mental illness.'[83] Writers frequently referred to the prejudice and lack of understanding that surrounded mental illness at this time. Speaking in 1952, Mr Harry Crookshank, the minister for health, suggested, 'One of the main reasons for the staff shortage was the public's ignorance of the conditions in which mental patients are now treated. Not only was the public ignorant about mental illness, but they were also unaware of the new treatments and approaches being utilised in the mental hospitals and were basing their ideas on outdated concepts and images.'[84] One retired nurse, when asked what she had found difficult about being a mental health nurse, said that it was 'not so much what I was doing, but what other people used to say. It was working in the "loony bin", so it was the lowest of the low … I don't think a lot of people understood it well enough'.[85]

In addition to the impact of stigma on mental health nurses, commentators also argued that mental nurses lacked power and status within the mental hospital system itself. At an individual hospital level, head male nurses and matrons were rarely consulted by, or were members of, committees and at governmental level their voices were rarely heard.[86] For example, no nurses were commissioners on the Board of Control, even though it inspected and advised on nursing matters and on the running of mental hospitals. In addition to powerlessness, poor working relations were also sometimes cited as a factor in nurse wastage. The Socialist Medical Association noted in 1945, 'The idea of nurses and midwives as handmaids of the medical profession … rather than as professional colleagues giving mutual assistance, is out of date.'[87] Therefore, the lowly position of mental nurses in the mental health sector itself could be seen as barrier to recruitment and retention and a negative impact on morale and well-being.

The low status of mental health nurses was reflected in both their conditions of service and their pay. National pay scales had been introduced for nurses, as a result of the Rushcliffe Committee,[88] which led to the setting up of the Whitley Council in 1948. Despite this, pay for mental nurses was often highlighted as being inadequate.[89] Firstly, this impacted hospitals' ability to recruit applicants of 'good education and personality'[90] which could be interpreted as a desire to recruit from a higher social class than had hitherto been the case,[91] but low pay also led to wastage, particularly among student nurses. This was evidenced in 1948 when COHSE (the main trade union for mental nurses in this period) fought a vociferous campaign on behalf of student nurses and used budgets supplied by them which showed 'that many were surviving on the edge of subsistence'.[92] This was particularly acute for married men. Although this campaign did prove successful in negotiating some increases, wages remained low. For example, at Warley hospital in Essex in 1955, the matron reported that one male student nurse had left, because he could earn more money delivering cars for Ford.[93] In the following year Dr Masefield, medical superintendent at St Francis Hospital, Sussex, said that seven male nurses, including two students, had recently resigned from his staff. This had been reported in the local newspaper, the *Sussex Daily News*, and the reason given for their departure was their inability to financially support their families.[94]

As Webster pointed out, 'The combination of inferior pay and unattractive conditions of work placed mental nursing in an extremely weak position in a market where employment opportunities were expanding.'[95] Nursing faced competition from teaching and clerical work, which made less physical and emotional demands on their staff and provided more attractive working conditions.[96] In a 1952 report by J. D. I. Waugh (Technical Nursing Officer) on his visit to Roundway Hospital, Wiltshire, he noted the competition the hospital faced 'there are plenty of well paid, accessible jobs in Industry etc in Devizes area. Brewery, Bottle factory, Bacon Factory, Engineering, and a large barracks with NAAFI canteens etc'. In addition, Roundway had to compete for labour with other local hospitals, which were less geographically isolated.[97]

For some nurses though, the pay was a positive reason to stay in mental health nursing. One woman noted,

> Partly it was money, actually, and convenience. It was being near the hospital and, not laziness exactly, but it was the easiest thing to do that would make a reasonable amount of money and easy to get to, where other things would have meant going into areas I wasn't familiar with, trying to get into some other type of thing. And also my son, like a lot of night staff we worked nights, quite a lot of us, because our children were small and your husband would be looking after the child and you didn't have to worry about child care then. And you made a lot more money on nights as well and theoretically could sleep in the day, when they were at school.[98]

One way in which staff could increase pay was to apply for promotion but a lack of opportunities led to much resentment and also contributed to nurses leaving. A particular bone of contention was the fact that dual qualifications (that is general training in addition to mental nurse training) were necessary, in order to apply for senior posts in mental nursing. As Mr Ely (Mental Nursing Officer, Ministry of Health) said at a conference for tutors in mental hospitals in 1954, 'so long as the mental nursing qualification did not by itself render the holder eligible for promotion to the higher posts in the mental hospitals, it was liable to be regarded as having lower professional and career value'. It might seem to the potential student nurse like saying: 'We will train you to become a mental nurse, but the qualification will not enable you to rise to the position of matron or her deputy'.[99] These comments were not however heeded. To make things worse, a 1952 University of Liverpool survey found that male staff could not get access to general training.[100] The interviewers found that there was much bitterness among the male staff about their lack of promotion: 'It was widely held that the colour of a man's eyes was of greater importance than his experience'.[101] In his oral history interviews, Nolan also found that lack of promotion and poor career prospects was an issue among male staff and his interviewees spoke of waiting to fill 'dead man's shoes'.[102] In a 1955 letter J. T. Waite, COHSE's general secretary, argued that male staff nurses could wait ten, fifteen or even twenty years for a vacancy for a higher grade.[103]

It is also important to note that mental health nursing was seen through different lenses. For some, nursing was seen as a profession and vocation, for others it was an occupation or job. To relate this to the concept of well-being, for some nurses it engendered eudaimonic well-being, for others it was more related to hedonism. In 1942, the medical superintendent at the City of Norwich Mental Hospital, Dr F. H. Healey, bemoaned the recruitment situation there saying, 'A number of probationers are sent from the Labour Exchange … [they] … find the work more difficult than they imagined. To do any kind of nursing, one needs to feel the call to do it, and be inspired. To do mental nursing successfully one must be doubly inspired and altruistic.'[104] A 1953 letter to the Nurses and Midwives Council at the Ministry of Health echoed this. The secretary of the Management Committee of Whittingham Hospital, Lancashire, wrote, 'We can see no immediate solution, because girls do not take up mental nursing from a sense of vocation, as they do general nursing, and it is only in times of unemployment amongst young girls that the mental nursing services are able to recruit.'[105]

Russell found that while some nurses said they wanted to help people, others stated they needed a job and some money. He cites one who said, 'I began to run short of money and thought – well I had better find a job. So I was walking past the (hospital) gate and it was just as easy as this. I thought why not go and get a job there … it was not by intention or design, it was by luck.'[106] One retired nurse told Chatterton, 'I just enjoyed it, I enjoyed people and, it wasn't any altruistic things really, it was just fun to work there … I'm not going to go into saying things like, you felt you were doing good and all the rest of it, that's just a load of old rubbish really.'[107] Another male nurse echoed this, 'What kept me in the job was the fact that I wasn't qualified for anything else to start with. One doesn't want to downgrade to stacking shelves in Tesco's or something. The pension scheme of course.'[108]

As noted earlier, the highest drop-out rates in this period were among mental health nurses in training and there were several issues that contributed to this. Recruitment of students was challenging and led to a situation where 'the priority was quantity rather than quality' and 'understaffed hospitals continued to accept almost everyone that applied: as always ideals were trumped by reality'.[109] There was no educational test prior to training, or a minimum educational standard required for entrants to mental nursing in this period. Students complained that the content of their training felt irrelevant.[110] The training provided under the auspices of the GNC for mental nursing followed the 'one portal' system of training which meant that all nurses, regardless of their speciality, were expected to undertake the same preliminary examination at the end of their first year, which focussed on the needs of the physically ill. Miss O'Reilly, principal tutor at Bexley Hospital, decried this: 'The present preliminary state examination syllabus ignored the fact that the student nurse was in a mental hospital, where she needed reasonable intelligence and education, sympathy and sociability.' The first year, she argued, should 'cater for the young student eager to look after people and not particularly interested in dry, dead bones'.[111] An attempt was made to rectify this with the introduction of an experimental syllabus by the GNC in 1957 (formally adopted in 1965) which concentrated on the knowledge base deemed to be desirable for the mental nurse,[112] but this was not universally popular, with one commentator deeming it to be 'somewhat irrelevant, wrongly focussed and largely fictitious'.[113]

Not only was the GNC seen as being too closely aligned to the needs of general nursing but the standards of the GNC were also felt to be too exacting. A 1954 report by the Association of Hospital Management Committees stated that the reports they received offered an 'almost unanimous opinion that the present academic standards required by the General Nursing Council are above what is necessary for the majority of mental nurses and beyond the ambitions and attainments of many who are interested and willing to work'.[114] A rival training scheme for mental nurses, under the auspices of the professional body for psychiatrists, the Royal Medico-Psychological Association had attracted many more entrants until it ended in 1951.[115] Training was also hampered by a shortage of tutors, with a survey in 1954 finding that there were only seventeen qualified tutors teaching in mental hospitals in England and Wales at that time and two of those were trained in general nursing only (SRNs).[116]

As well as a training which was perceived to be irrelevant and exacting, some argued that it was also perfunctory. The 1924 Departmental Committee on Nursing in County and Borough Mental Hospitals had advocated the concept of a preliminary training school (PTS) for new entrants to mental nursing, arguing that it was important that they be given some initial tuition before starting on the wards: 'The sudden introduction of a novice into a ward should be avoided' they said.[117] Even after the establishment of PTSs in some mental hospitals, some commentators still argued that the training given was inadequate and relied too heavily on 'on the job' training. According to McBrien, 'The training facility (if it can be called that) provided in most hospitals acts as a lure for the recruitment of unsuspecting candidates, and as soon as the PTS is over the student is thrown in at the deep end and from then on he or she is a student in name only.'[118]

Nursing students were also often expected to attend lectures during their time off,[119] a negative impact on well-being. Many commentators expressed the belief that students themselves often had an ambivalent, or even indifferent, approach to their training. For example, in 1949 Griffith commented, 'Most students I spoke to were not taking training seriously, but only something to do until they married, their attention being strongly on the latter objective and the means to that end.' In addition, she found 'an almost universal phobia about taking exams'.[120] Perhaps the biggest issue for student nurses was the dissonance some of them felt between the positive images in recruitment brochures and advertising campaigns and the reality of their working lives. Reflecting on his own training in the 1960s, Nolan noted,

> The senior personnel who spoke to us in our first days seemed unaware of the discrepancies between rhetoric and practice, discrepancies that had persisted for decades. They exaggerated the standing of the hospital, the excellence of its medical and nursing staff and the range of facilities available to patients, or did they truly believe what they were telling us? Contradictions abounded.[121]

Times of great change and upheaval characterized the mental health services as they entered the 1960s. These included the 1959 Mental Health Act and new approaches to treatment, both physical and social. The 1960s were to see the mental hospitals coming under ideological attack from writers such as Goffman[122] and Szasz[123] and the rise of the anti-psychiatry movement, which questioned the very basis on which the hospitals functioned.[124] Government policy, most famously heralded by the 'Water Tower' speech given by Enoch Powell in 1961 and the Hospital Plan which followed, was to lead to the eventual closure of the large mental hospitals and their replacement by smaller units, based at district general hospitals, and care in the community.[125] For some nurses, this time of change proved to be both exciting and interesting:

> You were coming into a time when Dr … was there and he was interested in therapeutic communities and ran some parts of the hospital as a therapeutic community and some of the wards were actually like the old asylums. So it was quite an interesting time when you went from one to the other, when you would be told off for putting the wrong knickers on an elderly lady who was wet and you were just a handmaiden, to being consulted on an admission ward by the Consultant Psychiatrist about what treatment you felt the patient should have in a ward meeting. So, perhaps, I don't know if I would have stayed if it all had been the old thing, but it was quite interesting that, sort of contrast, between the old and the new.[126]

For others change was unsettling and difficult, impacting on their hedonic and eudaimonic well-being, and many mourned the loss of stability and community as the move to community care accelerated.[127]

As this discussion has shown, well-being was an issue that impacted significantly on the lives of mental health nurses in the first twenty years of the NHS, both in the hedonic and eudaimonic sense of the term. It has been demonstrated that this contributed significantly to the shortage of mental health nurses in this period. A myriad of interrelated reasons for this shortage have been discussed, which included the isolation of the mental hospitals, low status, stigma and pay, the conditions and nature of the work, discipline, accommodation, problems with training and lack of promotion. In addition, competition from within the broader labour market has also been considered. Beliefs about the nature of mental nursing, that is, whether it was a vocation, profession or job, have also been shown to have contributed. Overall, mental health nursing could be seen as unattractive as an occupation which impacted negatively on individuals' well-being. Conversely, some nurses found fulfilment in their careers and social relationships at work, which enhanced their sense of well-being. Oral history interviews augmented archival primary sources and have added nuance to the narrative. As Nolan states,

> Hearing the voices of nurses from the past, who occupied the lower echelons of mental health services, not only enhances our understanding of the present but also adds to the historiography of mental health nursing. It further emphasizes that there is no one definitive history of mental health care, instead there are many. It is by engaging with the past that we can assess what changes have occurred over time and whether problems have been truly addressed or simply ignored or reformulated.[128]

Notes

1. Jane Ball, Sydney Anstee, Keith Couper, Jill Maben, Holly Blake, Janet E. Anderson, Daniel Kelly, Ruth Harris and Anna Conolly, 'The Impact of Covid-19 on Nurses (ICON) Survey: Nurses' Accounts of What Would Have Helped to Improve Their Working Lives', *Journal of Advanced Nursing* 79.1 (2022), 343–57.

2. Peter Nolan, 'Mental Health Nursing in the 1960s Remembered', *Journal of Psychiatric and Mental Health Nursing* 28 (2021), 462–8.
3. [Anon.], 'The Minister's Speech to Medical Officers of Health', *The Lancet*, 29 September 1945, 412–13.
4. Hansard, *Parliamentary Debates*, House of Commons, fifth series (1949).
5. Mick Carpenter, *Working for Health* (Lawrence and Wishart, 1988).
6. Kathleen Jones, *Asylums and After. A Revised History of the Mental Health Services from the Early Eighteenth Century to the 1990s* (Athlone Press, 1993).
7. Charles Webster, *The Health Services since the War. Volume One: Problems of Health Care* (HMSO, 1988), 4.
8. For example, Hansard, *Parliamentary Debates*, House of Commons, fifth series (1950) 112–13; Hansard, *Parliamentary Debates*, House of Commons, fifth series (1953–4), 2034–6; Hansard, *Parliamentary Debates*, House of Commons, fifth series (1954–5), 167–8.
9. Rosemary White, *The Effects of the National Health Service on the Nursing Profession* (King Edward's Hospital Fund, 1985).
10. Modern Records Centre, Warwick, MSS/229/6/3/11.
11. Claire Chatterton, 'The Weakest Link in the Chain of Nursing? Recruitment and Retention in Mental Health Nursing in England, 1948–68', in Anne Borsay and Pamela Dale (eds), *Mental Health Nursing: The Working Lives of Paid Carers in the Nineteenth and Twentieth Centuries* (Manchester University Press, 2015), 169–89.
12. David Clark, *Social Therapy in Psychiatry* (Churchill Livingstone, 1974).
13. Liam Clarke, 'The Opening of the Doors in British Mental Hospitals in the 1950s', *History of Psychiatry* 4 (1993), 527–51.
14. John Adams, 'Challenge and Change in a Cinderella Service: A History of Fulbourn Hospital, Cambridgeshire, 1953–1995' (unpublished doctoral thesis, Open University, 2009).
15. For example, John Hopton, 'A Blast from the Past?' *Nursing Times* 93.73 (1997), 36–7.
16. Patricia A. Patrician, Deb Bakerjian, Rebecca Billings, Teri Chenot, Vallire Hooper, Carol S. Johnson and Sharon Sables-Baus, 'Nurse Well-Being: A Concept Analysis', *Nursing Outlook* 70.4 (2022), 639–50 (p. 640).
17. Patrician et al., 'Nurse Well-Being'.
18. Peter Nolan, *A History of Mental Health Nursing* (Chapman and Hall, 1993).
19. Ministry of Health and Ministry of Education, *Report of Sub-committee on Mental Nursing and the Nursing of the Mentally Defective* (His Majesty's Stationery Office, 1945), 14 (hereinafter the 'Athlone Report').
20. Jones, *Asylums and After*.
21. Oxfordshire Health Archives, *Littlemore Hospital Annual Report, 1947*.
22. Olive Griffiths, Norman Reid and Margaret Scott, 'Reconstruction Scheme for Mental Nursing', *Nursing Mirror*, 27 October 1945, 46–7.
23. Nolan, *A History of Mental Health Nursing*, 108.
24. Chatterton, 'The Weakest Link in the Chain of Nursing?', 119.
25. Chatterton, 'The Weakest Link in the Chain of Nursing?', 119.
26. Diana Gittins, *Madness in Its Place: Narratives of Severalls Hospital, 1913–1997* (Routledge, 1998), 24.
27. Chatterton, 'The Weakest Link in the Chain of Nursing?', 109.
28. Chatterton, 'The Weakest Link in the Chain of Nursing?', 109–10.
29. Gittins, *Madness in Its Place*, 98.
30. Chatterton, 'The Weakest Link in the Chain of Nursing?', 110.

31. Chatterton, 'The Weakest Link in the Chain of Nursing?', 110.
32. Nolan, *A History of Mental Health Nursing*.
33. Chatterton, 'The Weakest Link in the Chain of Nursing?', 114.
34. Jocelyn Goddard, *Mixed Feelings: Littlemore Hospital – An Oral History Project*, (Oxfordshire County Council, 1996).
35. Nolan, 'Mental Health Nursing in the 1960s Remembered', 463.
36. Such as Winwick Hospital near Warrington, Chester Record Office, NHW3/4972/33.
37. Erving Goffman, *Asylums* (Penguin, 1961).
38. Griffiths et al., 'Reconstruction Scheme for Mental Nursing', 46.
39. Webster, *The Health Services since the War*, 329.
40. National Archives, London (NA), MH90/55.
41. [Anon.], 'Friends of Menston Hospital', *Nursing Times*, November 28, 1953, 1215–16.
42. Goddard, *Mixed Feelings*, 15.
43. NA, LAB8/954.
44. NA, LAB8/954.
45. NA, DT5/382.
46. [Anon.], *Whittingham Hospital. One Hundred Years. 1873–1973* (Mather Bros, 1973), 39.
47. Ministry of Health for Scotland and Ministry of Labour and National Service, *Report of the Working Party on the Recruitment and Training of Nurses (Majority Report)* (His Majesty's Stationery Office, 1947; hereinafter 'The Wood Report').
48. Griffiths et al., 'Reconstruction Scheme for Mental Nursing', 46.
49. J. Bickford, 'The Forgotten Patient', *The Lancet*, 29 October 1955, 917–19.
50. [Anon.], 'The Athlone Report', *Health Services Journal*, February 1946, 3–6 (p. 3).
51. M. McBrien, 'What Is Wrong with Psychiatric Nursing?', *Nursing Mirror*, 10 May 1968, 31–3 (p. 31).
52. [Anon.], 'Royal College of Nursing First Regional Conference on Mental Nursing', *Nursing Times*, 26 November 1954, 1304–6 (p. 1305).
53. NA, LAB8/954.
54. Royal College of Nursing Archives, Edinburgh, RCN/5/1/M/9.
55. [Anon.], 'Nursing Shortage Impedes Mental Health Services', *British Journal of Nursing*, March 1952, 26.
56. Chatterton, 'The Weakest Link in the Chain of Nursing?', 119.
57. Nolan, A History of Mental Health Nursing, 133.
58. Chatterton, 'The Weakest Link in the Chain of Nursing?', 122.
59. NA, MH55/2098.
60. NA, LAB8/954.
61. 'Athlone Report'.
62. Mick Carpenter, *They Still Go Marching On* (C.O.H.S.E, 1985), 12.
63. *The Lancet Commission on Nursing* (The Lancet, 1932).
64. Carpenter, *They Still Go Marching On*, 15.
65. Carpenter, *They Still Go Marching On*, 12.
66. Jones, *Asylums and After*.
67. 'Athlone Report'.
68. Ministry of Health for Scotland and Ministry of Labour and National Service, *Staffing the Hospitals: An Urgent National Need* (HMSO, 1945).
69. 'Athlone Report', 43.
70. 'Athlone Report', 43.

71. Ministry of Health for Scotland and Ministry of Labour and National Service, *Staffing the Hospitals*, 13.
72. NA, DT5/ 383.
73. Chatterton, 'The Weakest Link in the Chain of Nursing?', 123.
74. Niall McCrae and Peter Nolan, *The Story of Nursing in British Mental Hospitals. Echoes from the Corridors* (Routledge, 2016).
75. Nolan, *A History of Mental Health Nursing*, 465.
76. Nolan, *A History of Mental Health Nursing*.
77. Anne Marie Rafferty, *The Politics of Nursing Knowledge* (Routledge, 1996).
78. NA, LAB8/954.
79. Griffiths et al., 'Reconstruction Scheme for Mental Nursing', 46–7.
80. [Anon.], 'Notes and News', *The Lancet*, 7 January 1956, 9.
81. [Anon.], 'The Minister's Speech to Medical Officers of Health', *The Lancet*, 29 September 1945, 412–13.
82. For example, McCrae and Nolan, *The Story of Nursing in British Mental Hospitals*, 144.
83. [Anon.], *50 Years of NHS Nursing* (Royal College of Nursing, 1998), 9.
84. *British Journal of Nursing*, 1952, 26.
85. Chatterton, 'The Weakest Link in the Chain of Nursing?', 114.
86. Griffiths et al., 'Reconstruction Scheme for Mental Nursing'.
87. Socialist Medical Association, *Nursing in the Post-War World* (Socialist Medical Association, 1945).
88. *Report of the Mental Nurses Sub-committee*, Parliamentary Papers, Cmd. 6542, iv (1944) (hereinafter 'Rushcliffe Report').
89. Carpenter, *Working for Health*.
90. Griffiths et al., 'Reconstruction Scheme for Mental Nursing', 47.
91. Claire Chatterton, 'Training Mental Health Nurses in the United Kingdom: A Historical Overview. Part Two: 1948 Onwards', *Bulletin of the UK Association for the History of Nursing* 4 (2015), 5–14.
92. Carpenter, *They Still Go Marching On*, 39.
93. NA, MH55/2587.
94. *The Lancet*, 1956.
95. Webster, *The Health Services since the War*, 337.
96. Elizabeth Scott, 'The Influence of the Staff of the Ministry of Health on Policies for Nursing. 1919–1968' (unpublished doctoral thesis, London School of Economics and Political Science, 1994).
97. NA, LAB8/62.
98. Chatterton, 'The Weakest Link in the Chain of Nursing?', 118–19.
99. [Anon.], 'Training in Mental Nursing and Preparation for Positions of Responsibility', *Nursing Times*, 26 November 1954, 1320–1 (p. 1320).
100. Liverpool Regional Health Board, *The Work and Status of Mental Nurse* (Department of Social Sciences at the University of Liverpool, 1955).
101. Liverpool Regional Health Board, *The Work and Status of Mental Nurse*, 25.
102. Nolan, A History of Mental Health Nursing, 110.
103. Modern Records Centre, Warwick, MS229/6/C/CO/3/3.
104. Norfolk Records Office, HH1/6.
105. NA, MH55/2098.
106. David Russell, 'An Oral History Project in Mental Health Nursing', *Journal of Advanced Nursing* 26 (1997), 489–95 (p. 491).

107. Chatterton, 'The Weakest Link in the Chain of Nursing?', 115.
108. Chatterton, 'The Weakest Link in the Chain of Nursing?', 115.
109. McCrae and Nolan, The Story of Nursing in British Mental Hospitals, 125, 160.
110. Chatterton, 'The Weakest Link in the Chain of Nursing?'
111. *Nursing Times*, 1954, 1306.
112. Chatterton, 'The Weakest Link in the Chain of Nursing?'
113. McBrien, 'What Is Wrong with Psychiatric Nursing?', 320.
114. NA, MH55/2585.
115. Claire Chatterton, 'Caught in the Middle? Mental Nurse Training in England 1919–1951', *Journal of Psychiatric and Mental Health Nursing* 11 (2004), 30–5.
116. NA, MH55/2098.
117. Cited in 'Athlone Report', 29.
118. McBrien, 'What Is Wrong with Psychiatric Nursing?', 31.
119. NA, LAB8/954.
120. NA, DT5/382.
121. Nolan, 'Mental Health Nursing in the 1960s Remembered', 466–7.
122. Goffman, *Asylums*.
123. Thomas Szasz, *The Myth of Mental Illness* (Harper, 1962).
124. Hopton, 'A Blast from the Past?'
125. Anne Rogers and David Pilgrim, *Mental Health Policy in Britain*, 2nd ed. (Palgrave, 2001).
126. Chatterton, 'Caught in the Middle?', 118.
127. Gittins, *Madness in Its Place*.
128. Nolan, 'Mental Health Nursing in the 1960s Remembered', 473.

11

'Caring archives': Well-being challenges in an archive of extremism – Lessons and questions from a decade of the Searchlight Archive

Siobhán Hyland and Daniel Jones

In mid-2013 the Searchlight Archive opened for users, having been deposited with the University of Northampton by *Searchlight* magazine.[1] Based initially on this one collection, the archive remains a leading collection of material on the post-war British and international far right as well as anti-fascist movements. As well as a valuable resource for researchers based at the University, the Searchlight Archive is used by academic researchers from across the globe, by journalists and by community researchers within public engagement and in student teaching. Given the nature and content of the archive, with far-right material designed to offend and encourage hatred or worse towards historically marginalized group, how to share the material responsibly is increasingly under consideration. Consideration around the challenges related to, and resulting from, the well-being of all those who the archive impacts upon – our staff, researchers, students and the wider community – is critical to the archiving of the material.

This examination is placed within an emerging interest in the well-being aspects of archives. In particular, there has been a focus on the role archives can play in recognizing and preserving a more diverse cultural record and allowing vulnerable or historically disempowered groups to improve their own well-being through having their history recognized, recorded and celebrated.[2] Much of this is focused outwards, on how archives can contribute to the well-being of community partners and can be seen in some ways as a response to earlier movements typified by Caswell, who queried whether traditional institutions and archives were appropriate handlers of these collections. This response, as Evans et al. and Thorpe advocate, is to adapt archival processes and practice to enable better engagement with those outside of the archive and to better include their needs.

A focus on the issue of well-being within the archive itself, especially of its staff, is something less focused upon. Where it has been considered, focus is often – quite understandably – on the impact of the precarity and damage done to the heritage sector by cuts and funding difficulties. In particular, as Baker and Cantillon highlight in their exploration of the Australian sector, this has been felt by community heritage groups who are often volunteer-run, presenting challenges to institutional well-being.[3] Even in their explorations, however, Baker and Cantillon did identify work within the archives and museum sector as having positive benefits towards well-being through a sense of contribution to education and other engagement activities.[4] The question of emotional risk to well-being through the simple act of archival and archival research activity, as well as a call to action, has emerged more recently through work exploring the activity that took place during the Covid-19 pandemic. Bannell and Sexton – though focused on rapid response collecting (that is, the rapid documenting or archiving of an immediate crisis or other unfolding event) – explored the emotive potentiality of the archival work and the ways in which the psychological impact of this work was felt by staff members.[5] It is worth highlighting the conclusions of Bannell and Sexton, in which they call for a greater understanding and preparation for the traumatic load experienced in documenting emotional events and material moving forwards. It is into this wider debate, and a quest for a holistic understanding of the many strands (both internally and externally focused) of well-being within archives, that the work undertaken within the Searchlight Archive is considered within this chapter. In particular, the challenges that are presented by the archive and its material to well-being of both internal and external stakeholders.

The Searchlight Archive: The background

The Searchlight Archive itself is hosted within the University of Northampton's Faculty of Arts, Science and Technology (FAST), within the Department of Culture. Its main collection is the archive built up by *Searchlight* magazine about the far right, consisting of publications, reports, pamphlets and many other items. It also contains some internal material from *Searchlight* as well as material from other anti-fascist, left-wing or moderate groups. *Searchlight* was founded in 1964, emerging from the intelligence section of Jewish anti-fascist organization 62 Group. As well as its own magazine, it helped launch numerous similar organizations, including involvement with the Anti-Nazi League, Expo in Sweden and its own Hope not Hate campaign movement. Therefore, the archive could be categorized as a community archive as it preserves an anti-fascist community record which tells their history.[6] It also fulfils Bastian and Flinn's definition, being an archive that engages with a history that has often been lived beyond what is considered mainstream.[7] Further, by making use of decades of work by numerous anti-fascists within Searchlight, the archive documents these activist experiences and so can also take on aspects of activism.[8]

In terms of impact of the material, it must be considered that the items within the archive may hold a great deal of significance for the communities it impacts – anti-fascists, communities within Britain and even the far right. Accordingly, this must be treated seriously by archive staff, and as Wright suggests, the impact work on the archive can have must be taken into account within archive processes.[9] However, this community nature to the archive has often required a reframing of the archival process, as Caswell et al. suggest, seeking ways to accommodate community-based priorities.[10] Also of note is that this is a community-based archive within a wider institution, and as

Ziegler observes, institutions often have tended towards the 'top down approach' and this structure can have implications for archive management and operations.[11]

The communities that may be impacted by the work of the archive has expanded, along with the range of users who come into contact with the material. This has come about through the continued active curation of the archive. Consisting of now around 1,500 archive boxes of material, the archive has also become the home for several other collections, including collections related to Panorama and World in Action investigations into subjects like police corruption, regional anti-fascist and anti-racist activism collections, local oral histories involving experiences of racism and a collection of anti-fascist oral histories. It has also established a regular flow of undergraduate and postgraduate researchers (PGRs) from within the university and is established in contributing to teaching in various disciplines at the university.

In over ten years of operation the Searchlight Archive has matured into a resource that supports researchers and engages the public and represents a leading collection of its type. However, when it was established there was little guidance available for setting up an archive so focused on extreme material, especially within a Higher Education context. Therefore, the archive has had to develop processes and systems to balance the competing needs of maximizing access and accessibility of the material, alongside a duty of care to its users and staff. As Eastwood discusses, this is a key part of the archivist role, and the way in which material is communicated is of upmost importance in terms of preservation and dissemination.[12] However, with the material that the Searchlight Archive holds, the challenge is to ensure the content is accessible, especially to a diverse range of students.[13] This chapter will demonstrate the ways in which researchers in the Searchlight Archive have balanced the need for access to extremist material, with supporting the students so that they do not come to harm. In terms of themes and definitions, the material is concerned with ethnonationalism, opposition to democracy, authoritarianism, racism, xenophobia and conspiracism.[14] This archive is actively contesting the historical record that the extreme and far right put forward, which, as Dittmar and Entin suggest, shifts the burden of education to the user.[15] However, the archivist recognizes that as 'heirs' to the collection, they are also student and teacher, custodian and knowledge producer at the same time – and thus must take a holistic approach rather than one constrained fully by established practice.[16] There is an assumption that the user knows beforehand what they are searching for, however that is an assumption which experience has challenged.[17] Therefore, contextualization can be a useful tool in supporting the user with navigating the catalogue and preparing the user to analyse the materials.[18]

Before the Covid-19 pandemic the archive welcomed around 500 visits to the archive, with a further 150 visits occurring since reopening after pandemic lockdowns. These visitors have ranged from across the UK, as well as international visitors from countries like Norway, Australia, Canada and the United States. The archive also engages the public through talks and increasingly through public events such as contributions to public exhibitions. Archives in general have to, as Forde and Rhys-Lewis discuss, balance the need within archive policy to promote access to collections with the needs of the material itself in terms of preservation.[19] The growth of the Searchlight Archive has spurred work on the safeguarding and well-being practices for these reasons, so that such policies can seek to actively contribute to maintaining that balance and provide for the fullest access possible with the needs of the archive in mind. All of these activities raise questions and considerations around well-being in many ways. How does the archive do all these things, how does it engage with the positive side of revealing these histories, while also being ethical and mindful of the well-being impacts of the material and its surrounding culture?

Archive staff: The impact of solo archiving

As McFarland observes, solo archivists face numerous challenges in their work.[20] These include management of all aspects of an archive, often within wider institutions where the archive functions are not primary to – or well understood by – the organization. In looking at the similar field of libraries, St. Clair and Williamson commented on how the nature of the service and its success is often based around the personality of the librarian, or in this case the archivist – especially when such a service is operated by a solo archivist.[21] Well-being can have a significant impact on solo run archives, not just impacting on service provision but on the wider direction and nature of the archive. Furthermore, as the archivist takes on, as McFarland notes, the management of all aspects of the archive, so it is up to the archivist to put in place procedures and policies to consciously care for their own well-being and those of their paraprofessional or temporary staff. While this can seem self-indulgent, ultimately it is the user who benefits from this. What do such procedures look like in the Searchlight Archive?

The Searchlight Archive exists within a solo archivist context, with the archive being primarily operated by one member of staff, Dr Daniel Jones, though it does occasionally bring in research assistants to assist with project tasks, such as accession or pedagogical research. It does have further academic support, in the form of its academic liaison Prof. Paul Jackson, but essentially day-to-day running is through a solo archivist. This has some impact upon practice within the archive, to keep both the material and the archivist safe and secure. Originally the archive was co-located with the University archive, and so some of these practices emerged post-2018 where solo working was increasingly common. Equally some aspects of staff safety and well-being have been present since the opening of the archive. Broadly these cover working provisions, access controls, contact with extreme groups and emotional impact.

Access to the archive room itself is controlled. The archive is located in a building with access controls and a staffed reception. the archivist makes use of a solo working application operated by the University of Northampton – this allows for an alarm to be sounded in case of problems. In terms of worker well-being, this both reassures the archive staff that if someone malicious did gain entry they could summon help as well as allowing for consideration of the health and safety risks associated with solo archiving. With heavy boxes, as well as floor-to-ceiling rolling shelves, the risks of a box falling from height into the archivist or a crushing injury from the racks is very real and being able to alert security and first aid staff is important.

The archive also operates an access control system, to ensure that only genuine researchers – rather than potentially dangerous or confrontational visitors – are permitted to access the archive. Although, as Eric Ketelaar noted, there is no natural right to access any particular archive, without provision of access where appropriate there is little purpose to an archive. The collection and preservation of material that is never to be seen lacks purpose and will rarely fulfil institutional goals.[22] Therefore there must be a balance struck between the obligation of the archive to protect staff's well-being and the wider need to facilitate access. In the Searchlight Archive we use an access form, which asks for the reasons for a visit. If the user is from an institution such as a university, this can be a relatively cursory check – though confirmation is sought from a student's supervisors that they are a proper researcher. This operates both as a check that they are operating in a monitored fashion under some ethical framework, but also confirms that they have institutional support for their own well-being given the contents of the collection.

The risk, of course, is that such an approach privileges institutional users and disempowers community researchers and activists. This is why the archive considers the access control alongside its other precautions in balancing risk. This can be seen in the archive's track record on access – only one user has ever been fully refused access, with two other users facing some minor restrictions on access or activity. Its success can also be taken from the lack of incidents in the decade of opening. However, the archive can never be complacent – again, solo archiving comes into play here. Users are often alone with the archivist and up to one other user, meaning a bad faith actor can pose a serious concern to safety and well-being.

These controls serve to limit physical interaction with the far right, perceived as the main source of risk to physical safety but also to mental well-being. The archive operates a policy of not collecting material directly from the far right. This is part of a more general policy of non-engagement and non-interaction with the far right more broadly. For example, while the archive will aid people in finding copyright holders for permission, this is not done for far-right groups – it is for the user to make those contacts themselves if they wish. This has not always prevented all contact from the far right, though often this is minor or incidental contact.

The far-right website *Stormfront*, for example, has discussed the archive on at least one occasion, and various mass mailings have been sent to the archive's email inbox as well as to the archivist. There have also been more direct contacts and responses and for the archive has procedures to help handle this challenge to well-being. These contacts are recorded, with copies printed out for an archive box kept on material sent to the archive, and then addresses forwarded on to institutional tech support for blocking at the firewall. However, social media still represents a way that the archive – and the staff – are exposed to contact, and the nature of social media allows for 'swarming', with many accounts following an initial attack to either add their own comments or bulk register for outreach events.

Though there are countermeasures in place to stop these online contacts, the blocking of email mentioned above or through the withdrawal from social media engagement for a time, these have an impact beyond just the loss of outreach impact. There is an anxiety among the archive staff that surrounds not only such contacts but the potential contacts. The organizations and cultures in the far right often promote individual violence, for example. This inability to fully isolate from far-right contact, and the need for exposure to be balanced between these risks and the benefit of outreach, places the archive in the position of being reactive rather than proactive. This reactive positioning carries with it negative implications for well-being. Conversely, the positive impacts of proactivity have been widely explored in relation to employee well-being, proactivity allowing staff to feel more in control and to better upskill to handle a crisis.[23]

The nature of the material in extreme archives like the Searchlight Archive can be upsetting and can also impact on the well-being of staff – it was created to inspire hatred and hostility between people and drive some to action. The material ranges from the controversial through to material that ran afoul of the Race Relations Acts – offensive to the point of illegality. It is not just textual material, but also visual items as well – images of brutal killings, or even genocide, recast into justification for the views of the far right. The essential processes of archive work, of accession, cataloguing, preservation and presentation – all require the staff to look at this material throughout most days in the archive, and this can have an impact upon the sense of normality. It can also lead to emotional responses to events in the wider world that seem to replicate or have surface similarity to narratives within the archive. It is for this reason that building time for decompression is important – and here solo archivist is perhaps a benefit. With a solo archivist having to take on management as well as archival functions, there will be days where archival material is not examined and tasks that can be done which allow for that decompression space.

Archive users: Caring for guests

One of the simplest things that the Searchlight Archive does in terms of supporting users is to provide an expert archivist to be present at all their visits and they receive a small note about the nature of the content as well as a caution if material they are accessing is particularly extreme. The archive also seeks to make sure that users are comfortable. They are advised to bring warm clothes due to the archive reading room also being the storeroom – and so, it is hoped, be calm when seeking to approach emotionally challenging material. There are also warnings given around the legal risks associated with this material – most notably against keeping any material taken as digital images on storage devices after research has been completed. Much of the material does breach the law around hate speech and extremism, and it is hard to construct a public interest defence around material that is not under active research – this is most applicable to students, who in most cases will not go on to further study in this area.

Questions surrounding the way that the material is used also extend to considering which materials should even be made available to them. It should first be noted that the Searchlight Archive has operated on a model of maximum access where possible and reasonable. It was for this reason it adopted practices recognized within archival practice as 'More Product Less Process', or MPLP. Conceptualized by Greene and Meissner, this approach prioritizes making material available by assessing which archival information is crucial before material can be added to the catalogue – making it available sooner than if full processing were performed before any material were shared.[24] When it comes to extreme material, however, this maximal approach should always be balanced against well-being and the law.

If the archive received material that was openly terroristic to the point of being practical manuals that could be used for terrorism, or material that would otherwise breach the law, then that material cannot be shared. A more mundane example of this are membership lists of far-right groups, which contain names, addresses and other personal information. Under GDPR practices, where it cannot be confirmed that all data in the box is now no longer covered – such as by user death – then the boxes must be sealed under a one-hundred-year rule.

The access control process mentioned earlier gives an indication of which users are not attached to institutional support and guidance, and any framing of material is given much more proactively to those users. This is due to institutional researchers having that guidance available through supervisors, ethics boards and often more support. In addition, for all users the archive often recommends that new users consider just visiting for a single day at first so that users can assess what is in the archive and how it is laid out. This also helps users have a gentler introduction to such extreme material if it is their first visit, but also allows users to understand their own reaction to that material, which can be emotional. It is important when handling users that the archive considers they may identify with groups that the material seeks to attack. Following such visits, some users have moderated their later contact – only coming for half days or taking longer breaks, managing their own experience.

Outreach: Sharing responsibly

It is important that archives such as the Searchlight Archive that can be considered community archives engaged in outreach practices. This can present additional challenges, but also opportunities, when it is considered how community archives in particular hold overlapping interests for the archivists, researchers, the collection itself and the public.[25] There are various other considerations to be taken into account when engaging with a community archive which holds extreme or radical material.[26] It is important for the well-being of staff that this outreach is conducted satisfactorily and takes into consideration the state and limitations of the archive – in terms of space, staffing and cataloguing. Care needs to be taken when engaging with partially catalogued collections, outreach where not all material is in order or prepared to the same level of confidentiality commensurate with public access.[27] It is possible to create interest in areas of the archive which are not yet prepared and so create additional stress for the archive staff in preparing these areas; frustration and upset for users who cannot easily access this material; and potential harm to subjects of the archive through improper sharing of the collection. Part of this are simply procedural steps, such as through standard practice of signing out items for loan or exhibit, but the practice extends much deeper than this.

The archive has taken various approaches to its engagement with the public to again balance the need to inform with the real damage that radicalizing material can cause on the well-being and mental health of those exposed to it. Part of this practice also considers the impact that material can have when shared the potential it has to be reshared without the permission or knowledge of the archive. Images could be used in presentations, where they are accompanied by analysis from researchers. Material contextualized in this way serves to denature the radicalizing intent of the content. Therefore, when sharing this material outside of the archive, especially with a broad public audience, care must be taken to do so in a format that doesn't allow for the academic or other contextualizing analysis to be disconnected from the material. If the contextualizing material were removed and the material returned to its original state, then it could once again be used to promote hatred, violence or other harmful narratives. Retaining this connection between content and contextualizing information is relatively straightforward with outreach done face to face, where material might be presented in a computer presentation or via poster where it cannot be physically separated or even decontextualized in a photograph, but online outreach can be more complex

The prevention of any attempt to remove the contextualizing material can be achieved through technical methods, such as embedding images and text together into a single image file that cannot therefore be disentangled by another user. To reduce their utility, images shared are also downscaled by the archive team from the high-quality scans within the archive to a level that is sufficient for the outreach purpose but usually not of a quality sufficient for reprinting purposes. Finally, material outside of the pertinent item can be cropped away, or where that is not possible – for example where an image and a headline are being used – other material that is extraneous can be redacted. In these ways the archive seeks to reduce the potential for its material to become harmful to the public well-being while still maintaining outreach which is believed to have a public good.

Part of that public good is to engage the public with community histories that are not often as prominent in existing national discourses around history, in particular the stories of non-white or other diverse communities in Britain. This outreach work, it is hoped, will seek to curate interest in academic history among these communities. This is especially important for history as a subject, which as Eastwood notes is a feeder subject for the Galleries, Libraries, Archives and Museums (GLAM) sector – with Eastwood pointing out that those who work within archives in will be often be those who engaged with them in their degree.[28] The GLAM sector has, however, remained a predominantly white field.[29] This has an impact on the collection policies and activities of these GLAM organizations and for future engagement of historically marginalized communities with history. Therefore, engaging in outreach using radical collections has, as Landes argues, an important ongoing role in enabling people to overcome the barriers normally in place to accessing this material and becoming engaged with the subjects.[30]

Use in teaching: Framing and vocabulary

It is well established that primary sources are an important and engaging part of education – and there has been an increasing recognition of their value throughout the education system.[31] Through several funded projects, the Searchlight Archive has sought to test the degree to which its material could contribute to student engagement with subjects within history and in wider subjects. As these projects have advanced, they have also raised some questions about practice and well-being – and allowed for further consideration of the best approach that teaching staff should take when exposing their students to radical material in order to maximize benefits while minimizing any harm. In essence, the best way to be considerate of the balance between a student's educational well-being and their physical and emotional well-being.

All three successful projects were run under the auspices of the University of Northampton's Institute for Learning and Teaching (ILT) and their funded schemes. The first of these was a bid in 2016, entitled 'Blended Learning Solutions to Using Archive Material in Teaching', which enabled researchers to produce digital packs of material on specific themes from the archive, using virtual learning environment (VLE) to make these and contextualizing briefing videos available.[32] Physical boxes of archival material (either archival duplicates or reproductions where duplicates were not available) were also available for use in the classroom in multiple subject areas, thereby using an active blended learning option to give students best access to materials. This method was chosen as research shows that this fosters critical thinking and problem-solving skills, all core to primary source driven learning.[33] It also drew upon existing practice within the archive sector, namely the use of collection handling boxes (referred to within the Searchlight Archive as teaching boxes).[34]

In centring the archive as part of the classroom experience, it was important to think about and create course description that allowed for students to prepare for the use of this archival material to be used in class.[35] This pilot study then surveyed the data from 200 students' responses after using the archive to determine whether the use of this material had enhanced their learning. Over 94 per cent of students responding stated that they agreed or strongly agreed that the use of such material deepened their engagement with their subject, with a similar percentage also wanting the material to be used more widely in their education.[36] The rationale behind the use of surveys was to evaluate knowledge transfer from the archive into the student's course and beyond.[37] The project also created a VLE site for teaching staff to easily integrate the material into their modules, recognizing, as Fox and MacKeogh did, that staff well-being around workload, including the impacts that has on motivation and attitude, meant that such a process had to be as accessible as possible. In essence that the archive had to take on some of that processing burden.[38]

A second funded project, with a slightly altered team, the following year further explored different scenarios in which the material might be useful for educational purposes, this was focused on the creation of a critical analysis Massive Open Online Course (MOOC) that could be used to help address key skills within A-level students transitioning to higher education.[39] This again was funded by the ILT and focused entirely on online engagement with material. Part of this project brought together various community, NGO and teaching professionals to discuss the practice of teaching extreme or radical topics. These two pieces of research provided valuable insights into the student experience, but also revealed legitimate concern about how to safeguard students' well-being when using material from an extremist collection. The conference also showed the archive that there was a community interest in engaging with these materials.

This led to the third funded project, which focused on answering those questions raised – namely how to use the material to engage with historically marginalized communities and our own students in a responsible way.[40] There was also a particular interest on whether the use of such material could aim to tackle, in part, the BAME awarding gap within Higher Education by helping students from more diverse backgrounds feel represented within the material of their course. This project sought to understand best practice in this area through desk research of existing studies carried out by Dr Hyland, to consult with students and the community through focus groups and to bring together practitioners in this area to discuss the different ways this is practiced in other archives. Unfortunately, Covid-19 interrupted the focus group format, but the project still emerged with two key findings and a comprehensive best practice guide.

One of the key needs when engaging with students using the material was that of framing. Material had to be contextualized both in its historical sense – the group that produced it and the society at the time that they did – but also in a linguistic sense. There is a need to use appropriate and clear language in both how such sessions are set up and also providing students with the right language to be able to discuss the items. The session itself, to reduce harm to emotional well-being, should be signalled well in advance, and it should be made clear to students that at times people may choose the wrong words or stumble over these complex and quite emotional subjects, and that a respectful patient atmosphere should be in place. Another is to help them understand the terms being used – both the common language meaning and the particular coded and slang terms used within the material. One approach to this is to provide a small dictionary for the session, or to talk through definitions with students – such as how to describe different parts of the LGBT+ community. By so doing students can feel confident in engagement, prepare themselves for this engagement and do their part in managing their own well-being. A note of caution should however be given, that excessive warnings on the upsetting nature of the material can lead to unintended upset as students – having prepared themselves – may not feel that upset and feel they may somehow be at fault for that. As in many other parts of the chapter, a balance – based on the teacher's experience of the class and of wider teaching – must come into play.

The other important factor is that when presenting the material in an educational or outreach setting, the community that the material impacts or targets should ideally be involved. This might be through including community groups in training events, but also through seeking to form advisory meetings on topics such as selection and representation of material. In this way history can be seen to be done with a community rather than compounding the harm of the original material by taking their agency away and having history instead done to them.

Researchers: Building a community of support

To be fully caring as an archive, all parts of well-being for the student or researcher need to safeguarded.[41] This is because the emotional labour of working through difficult or problematic topics, although valuable, can cause distress.[42] Moncur argues that institutional practices and opportunities for support are ways in which to safeguard researchers when working through sensitive or emotion making materials.[43] These responsibilities of the archive are also particularly important when one considers the key role that archives within Higher Education Institutions have in embedding a research culture.[44] Taking a central role within that research culture for the attached researchers means that the archive and its staff have to consider these issues and attempt to act as a vehicle for best practice.

One of the first considerations with regards to researchers is the normalizing effect that constant exposure to extreme material can have. This can both lead to inappropriate use of the material, as the extreme nature is not recognized, but also a potential blindness to the struggles of others with that material. Special care must be given in this to PGRs connected to a radical or extreme archive or collection, especially when considering that PGRs often exist in a hybrid space between student and staff. This space can compound disadvantages present within both relationships to the institution. However, this special care and attention paid to PGRs can stimulate further good practice, as has occurred at the Searchlight Archive.

As Wisker et al. observed, PGRs suffer from isolation even from those at the same institution. Their practice-based research encourages involving PGRs as collaborators within research to help combat part of this isolation and the creation of support networks through web meeting systems.[45] While Wisker et al. envisage much of this being overseen by research supervisors, there are questions on to what extent supervisors are necessarily trained to provide this support, especially when dealing with extreme material. Equally supervisors are not necessarily present within the archive or other research space – and additional support or training therefore would need to be considered by the Higher Education Institution.

The shared communities that Wisker et al. propose are nevertheless interesting, providing as they do a space for PGRs to work through and talk about problematic material they encounter and provide peer support. As Lave and Wenger identified, these PGR communities of practice allow for the community to bring in new members and incrementally introduce them into the work and community.[46] This provides a possible construct for generating a self-sustaining PGR support network for institutionally linked archives and collections, which by their nature will often generate a regular feed of PGR students. Not just a community of practice, but one of peer support.

The need for archives to take an active role in fostering these communities of support, given the extreme and upsetting material, is further emphasized by reports such as Moss et al. which suggest up to 70 per cent of PGRs are suffering mild to severe psychological distress.[47] As this report suggests that this distress peaks at the start of the academic year it can be argued that these peer support models might have some significant impact, due to the induction function suggested by Lave and Wenger. There are also suggestions from Liang et al. that these issues have worsened in the Covid-19 pandemic, further compounding isolation.[48]

During the UK lockdown in 2020 the wider History PGR group at the University of Northampton initiated a PGR peer support group to deal with student support and concerns. The success of this community helped contribute to practice within the Searchlight Archive. There was already long-standing practice around inclusion of PGRs as collaborators on projects, and most recently with the Searchlight Archive Research Group bringing in and foregrounding PGR involvement as part of their work. Building on the success of PGR peer to peer support, the Searchlight Archive Research Group meetings now offer dedicated time for researchers to share concerns or issues they have encountered in their research in a supportive and non-judgemental space. While the extent to which these efforts are successful, and the additional impact that the extreme material causes are speculative, the underlying pedagogy suggests this is a low-cost option that archives and associated researchers should try.

The Searchlight Archive has also taken a position that it should share the experience of its work to help support researchers at other institutions where possible. The archivist has presented training on ethical engagement in this research at other institutions within the UK higher education sector, and presentations have been given by the archivist and researchers at related events and conferences. This has included being open and honest about the processes it has undertaken and where these have failed and where they have been successful. In doing so, the archive hopes to encourage and support a proactive approach to researcher well-being at other institutions. While the archive has also supported community groups engaging with this work, how the archive can support well-being within non-institutional researchers is an ongoing question. The Searchlight Archive Research Group peer support meetings have been offered to external researchers, but work continues on other approaches.

Considering the subjects of our research and the future

Earlier the chapter touched on how outreach increasingly, especially after Covid-19, has at least partially transitioned to the online space. This raises new questions, some of which are already under consideration in the archive field, on how to consider well-being when technologies enable archives to be more virtual in their design and implementation.[49] Online spaces are different from the carefully curated yet safe space of the archive, so how that can be navigated is a question to be considered going forward and one which is still being developed. The intensification of digital communication may mean ethical issues and well-being concerns for the student or researcher.[50] It may also mean that researchers are able to view conflict, networks and relationship building in way not possible within the archive boxes.[51] Also, actions that are performative pieces of social media, such as lies, shares and comments, which amplify the far-right message, again, are not present within traditional archives.[52] This means that archives, especially those within Higher Education Institutions, need to develop new systems and methods to archiving internet content – especially social media content – if historians and other academics are going to be able to study present-day radical movements. Such collections at present are operated without institutional support or not at all, and not necessarily collected with a mind to enabling academic research. This is especially an issue for the social media presence of radical movements, whose accounts, and their associated material, often face bans due to their actions. Considering all of this, it is important to recognize that the capacity to disseminate material through digital means has grown incredibly, and that therefore raises issues for the archivist in terms of ownership, access, censorship and exclusion.[53]

The other issue that must be commented on in terms of well-being are those who are subjects of the archive. The Searchlight Archive contains a great deal of personal information of people who were affiliated or accused of affiliating with various parts of the far right. Data protection laws cover the release of most of this, though consideration must be given by researchers to issues where releasing information might put people at risk – the outing of gay men within homophobic elements of the far right, material that might allow for identification of moles or other figures are examples of these risks. However, what is often not considered is the impact on relatives of the subjects and their well-being.

People have emotional connections to and emotional constructs of relatives – the beloved grandad, the loving husband and so on. When exploring extreme and often secretive groups, the exposing of someone's membership within that might well be unknown to relatives and that revelation could radically alter or shatter that perception. While researchers may well be justified in revealing that information, and it may be important for the historical record, some consideration must be given to whether that revelation and identification is necessary and proportionate. Where someone is a fringe member who simply receives a magazine once a month, but engages in no other activity, it is necessary to name them? Is there evidence of someone's engagement beyond being a name on a list, which could occur because they were simply curious or even were engaging in anti-fascist intelligence gathering? These are questions that must be asked each time, even when the answer may often be to proceed – it is about where that potential harm to well-being of others may occur, the archivist and researcher is certain that it is proportionate and justified.

While these issues come into particular prominence while handling extremist material, due to the scale of the embarrassment or upset it can cause, these questions of the relatives of subjects have a place within wider research ethics practice at any institution. In particular there is active debate within the medical research field on how to handle disclosures of research outcomes to relatives on whom it might impact, especially where the initial subject is deceased.[54] Accordingly this is a subject where wide discussion with the research community would benefit the practice of safeguarding well-being in extreme politics, and where it can seek to draw upon that existing wider practice both within history and other subjects.

Conclusion

This chapter has laid out the ways in which well-being has been considered in the work of the Searchlight Archive and why such approaches have been taken. It has also discussed some of the positives that working with this material can bring, for users of the archive as an archival service as well as through outreach and student teaching. The benefits of using such material have been made clear, despite the risks to well-being but it must also be acknowledged that the ways in which the material is engaged with places a burden on archivists, users, archive procedures and practice.

In particular, while the archivist may feel their responsibility is first to the collection, there is an ethical duty on the archivist to ensure best practice around well-being is proactively followed rather than view themselves as passive custodians. Archivists need to act like teachers, in that they support those using the archive material and think about their emotional well-being.[55] It is also the responsibility of the archivist to help foster those cultures of research, both at their institution and to inform practice beyond their own institution – as this chapter hopes to have done. However, there is a risk of overemphasizing the risk to researchers, which can stifle or inhibit researcher autonomy.[56] That is just one of the many balances for which archivists must find an equilibrium, and which can only come through the experience of continued work in this area. Therefore, there is a balance to be struck between the needs of those who encounter the archive, the benefits that engagement with the archive can bring and also standard archival practices and procedures that aim to perfectly preserve and curate the collections. It is only through actively considering the well-being of those involved that those balances can be struck in an informed manner that both mitigates the negatives and accentuates these benefits.

Notes

1. This essay makes use of information gathered during three projects, funded by the University of Northampton's Institute for Learning and Teaching. The authors wish to express their thanks to the Institute for Learning and Teaching for their support and also express their thanks and acknowledge their co-investigators on these projects: Prof. Paul Jackson, Dr Rachel Moss and William Mann. For information or data related to these projects, please contact the project lead Dr Daniel Jones. For information on the Searchlight Archive, please see www.northampton.ac.uk/about-us/services-and-facilities/the-searchlight-archives/, or its online catalogue can be found as part of the University of Northampton Catalogue at https://northampton.epexio.com/.
2. For examples of this, please see Michelle Caswell, 'Seeing Yourself in History: Community Archives and the Fight against Symbolic Annihilation', *Public Historian* 36.4 (2014), 26–37; Joanne Evans, Jacqueline Wilson, Sue McKemmish, Antonina Lewis, David McGinniss, Gregory Rolan and Siobhan Altham, 'Transformative Justice: Transdisciplinary Collaborations for Archival Autonomy', *Archives and Records* 42.1 (2021), 3–24; Kirsten Thorpe, 'Returning Love to Ancestors Captured in the Archives: Indigenous Wellbeing, Sovereignty and Archival Sovereignty', *Archival Science* 24.2 (2024), 125–42.
3. SarahBaker and Zelmarie Cantillon, 'Safeguarding Australia's Community Heritage Sector: A Consideration of the Institutional Wellbeing of Volunteer-Managed Galleries, Libraries, Archives, Museums and Historical Societies', *Australian Historical Studies* 51.1 (2020), 70–87, https://doi.org/10.1080/1031461X.2019.1659836.
4. Baker and Cantillon, 'Safeguarding Australia's Community Heritage Sector', 72–3; Sarah Baker and Zelmarie Cantillon, 'DIY Heritage Institutions as Third Places: Caring, Community and Wellbeing among Volunteers at the Australian Jazz Museum', *Leisure Sciences* 44.2 (2018), 221–39.

5. Kay Bannell and Anna Sexton, 'Affect and Rapid Response Collecting: Exploring the Significance of Emotion in UK Archives' Covid-19 Collecting Projects', *Archives and Records* 45.2 (2024), 153–75.
6. Baker and Cantillon, 'Safeguarding Australia's Community Heritage Sector', 72.
7. Jeannette A. Bastian and Andrew Flinn, *Community Archives, Community Spaces: Heritage, Memory and Identity* (Facet, 2020), x.
8. Marika Cifor, Michelle Caswell, Alda Allina Migoni and Noah Geraci, 'What We Do Crosses over to Activism: The Politics and Practice of Community Archives', *Public Historian* 40.2 (2018), 70, https://doi.org/10.1525/tph.2018.40.2.69.
9. SteveWright, 'The Nature of "Document Work", and Its Implications for Radical Community Archives and Their Holdings', *Journal of Community Informatics* 15 (2019), 54, https://doi.org/10.15353/joci.v15i.3427.
10. Michelle Caswell, Alda Allina Migoni, Noah Geraci and Marika Cifor, '"To Be Able to Imagine Otherwise": Community Archives and the Importance of Representation', *Archives and Records* 38.1 (2017), 7, https://doi.org/10.1080/23257962.2016.1260445.
11. Scott Ziegler, 'Let's Use What Works: The Radical Archives of Philadelphia and Traditional Archival Literature', in Melissa Morrone (ed.), *Informed Agitation: Library and Information Skills in Social Justice Movements and Beyond* (Library Juice Press, 2014), 107.
12. TerryEastwood, 'A Personal Reflection on the Development of Archival Education', *Education for Information* 33.2 (2017), 80, https://doi.org/10.3233/EFI-170990.
13. Mark Newman, *Vital Witnesses: Using Primary Sources in History and Social Studies* (Rowman and Littlefield, 2014), and Kirk Ankeney, Merrell Frankel and Rebecca Whisney, 'A Story Well Told: Primary Sources and History Education', *Social Studies Review* 43.2 (2004), 12.
14. HilmarMjelde, 'Welcoming Bad Times: Covid-19 Frames on Norway's Far Right', *Patterns of Prejudice* 55.5 (2021), 482, https://doi.org/10.1080/0031322X.2021.1993579.
15. Linda Dittmar and Joseph Entin, 'Introduction: Archives and Radical Education', *Radical Teacher* 105 (2016), 4, https://doi.org/10.5195/rt.2016.317.
16. Kailah R. Carden, Sabina E. Vaught, Arturo Muñoz, Vanessa Pinto, Cecilia Vaught and Maya Zeigler, 'A Critical Archival Pedagogy: The Lesbian Herstory Archives and a Course in Radical Lesbian Thought', *Radical Teacher* 105 (2016), 26, https://doi.org/10.5195/rt.2016.275.
17. Isto Huvila, 'Participatory Archive: Towards Decentralised Curation, Radical User Orientation, and Broader Contextualisation of Records Management', *Archival Science* 8.1 (2008), 16, https://doi.org/10.1007/s10502-008-9071-0.
18. Huvila, 'Participatory Archive', 30.
19. HelenForde and Jonathan Rhys-Lewis, 'Exhibiting Archives', in *Preserving Archives* (Facet, 2013), 160.
20. Colleen McFarland, 'Rethinking the Business of Small Archives', *Archival Issues* 31.2 (2007), 137–49.
21. St. Guy Clair and Joan Williamson, *Managing the New One-Person Library* (Bowker Saur, 1992), 4. In this case solo archivist refers to an acknowledged trend within archive services of a single professional or paraprofessional managing all aspects of an archive rather than the traditional team-based archive that might have input from several professionals into policies, cataloguing and other processes.
22. Arnoud Glaudemans, Rienk Jonker and Frans Smit, 'Beyond the Traditional Boundaries of Archival Theory. An Interview with Eric Ketelaar', in Frans Smit,

Arnoud Glaudemans and Rienk Jonker (eds), *Archives in Liquid Times* (Stichting Archiefpublicaties, 2017), 304.
23. Shunhong Ji, Zhuijun Chen and Frencesco Cangiano, 'Proactivity and Well-Being: Initiating Changes to Fuel Life Energy', in Kelly Z. Peng and Chia-Huei Wu (eds), *Emotion and Proactivity at Work* (Bristol University Press, 2021), 268–9.
24. Mark A. Greene and Dennis Meissner, 'More Product, Less Process: Revamping Traditional Archival Processing', *American Archivist* 68.2 (Fall–Winter 2005), 208–63.
25. Simon Popple, Andrew Prescott and Daniel H. Mutibwa, 'Community Archives and the Creation of Living Knowledge', in Simon Popple, Andrew Prescott and Daniel H. Mutibwa (eds), *Communities, Archives and New Collaborative Practices* (Policy Press, 2020), 7, https://doi.org/10.56687/9781447341932.
26. Mary Stevens, Andrew Flinn and Elizabeth Shepherd, 'New Frameworks for Community Engagement in the Archive Sector: From Handing over to Handing On', *International Journal of Heritage Studies* 16.1–2 (2010), 60, https://doi.org/10.1080/13527250903441770.
27. Susan Pever, 'Success as a Lone Arranger: Setting Priorities and Getting the Job Done', *Journal of Archival Organization* 3.2 (2005), 58.
28. Eastwood, 'A Personal Reflection on the Development of Archival Education', 75–8.
29. IanBeilin, 'The Academic Research Library's White Past and Present', in Gina Schlesselman-Tarango (ed.), *Topographies of Whiteness: Mapping Whiteness in Library and Information Science* (Library Juice Press, 2017), 80.
30. Jordan Landes, 'Introduction: Radical Collections and Radical Voices', in Jordan Landes and Richard Espley (eds), *Radical Collections: Re-examining the Roots of Collections, Practices and Information Professions* (University of London, 2018), 6–8.
31. MarkNewman, *Vital Witnesses: Using Primary Sources in History and Social Studies* (Rowman and Littlefield, 2014), 1–7; Mark Donnelly and Claire Norton, *Doing History* (Routledge, 2011), 65–82; and Kirk Ankeney, Merrell Frankel and Rebecca Whisney, 'A Story Well Told: Primary Sources and History Education', *Social Studies Review* 43.2 (2004), 12–14.
32. Daniel Jones, Paul Jackson and William Mann, 'Blended Learning Solutions to Using Archive Material in Teaching' (2017), funded by the Institute for Learning and Teaching Innovation Funding 2016/17, University of Northampton. Data available from the project lead via Searchlight Archive, University of Northampton, Northampton.
33. Yildizay Ayyildiz and Leman Tarhan, 'Development of the Self-Directed Learning Skills Scale', *International Journal of Lifelong Education* 34.6 (2015), 670, https://doi.org/10.1080/02601370.2015.1091393.
34. Mary Aris, 'Resources for Teacher-Designed Units: Some General Guidelines', in Ron Brooks, Mary Aris and Irene Perry (eds), *The Effective Teaching of History* (Routledge, 2013), 120–2.
35. Carden et al., 'A Critical Archival Pedagogy', 24.
36. Data derives from thirty-three completed responses from *c.*200 students surveyed across three disciplines. Data available from the project lead.
37. NidaDenson, Thomas Loveday and Helen Dalton, 'Student Evaluation of Courses: What Predicts Satisfaction?', *Higher Education Research and Development* 29.4 (2010), 340, https://doi.org/10.1080/07294360903394466.
38. KayMacKeogh and Seamus Fox, 'Strategies for Embedding e-Learning in Traditional Universities: Drivers and Barriers', *Electronic Journal of e-Learning* 7.2 (2009), 150–1.

39. Daniel Jones, Siobhán Hyland and Paul Jackson, 'Engaging Students with Skills Development through Blended Learning' (2018), funded by the Institute for Learning and Teaching Learning Enhancement and Innovation Bids 2017–18, University of Northampton. Data available from the project lead via Searchlight Archive, University of Northampton, Northampton.
40. Daniel Jones, Siobhán Hyland, Paul Jackson and Rachel Moss, 'The Impact of Teaching BAME and Other Targeted Groups Using Radical Collections' (2020), funded by the Institute for Learning and Teaching Learning Enhancement and Innovation Bids 2019–20, University of Northampton. For information on the best practice guide, please contact project lead via the Searchlight Archive, University of Northampton, Northampton.
41. Pat Sikes and Mel Hall, 'Too Close for Comfort? Ethical Considerations around Safeguarding the Emotional and Mental Wellbeing of Researchers Using Auto/Biographical Approaches to Investigate "Sensitive" Topics', *International Journal of Research & Method in Education* 43.2 (2020), 163–4, https://doi.org/10.1080/1743727X.2019.1636025.
42. Wendy Moncur, 'The Emotional Wellbeing of Researchers: Considerations for Practice', *Proceedings of the SIGCHI Conference on Human Factors in Computing Systems* (2013), 1883–4, https://doi.org/10.1145/2470654.2466248.
43. Moncur, 'The Emotional Wellbeing of Researchers', 1888.
44. Mary Ellis, 'Establish a Research Culture for Archive Administration in the UK', *Education for Information* 23.1–2 (2005), 91–101.
45. Gina Wisker, Gillian Robinson and Miri Shacham, 'Postgraduate Research Success: Communities of Practice Involving Cohorts, Guardian Supervisors and Online Communities', *Innovations in Education and Teaching International* 18.21 (2007), 11542.
46. Jean Lave and Etienne Wenger, 'Legitimate Peripheral Participation in Communities of Practice', in Robert McCormack and Carrie Paechter (eds), *Learning and Knowledge* (Paul Chapman, 1999), 21–36.
47. R. A. Moss, P. Gorczynski, W. Sims-Schouten, K. Heard-Laureote and J. Creaton, 'Mental Health and Wellbeing of Postgraduate Researchers: Exploring the Relationships between Mental Health Literacy, Help-Seeking Behaviour, Psychological Distress and Wellbeing', *Higher Education Research and Development* 41.4 (2022), 1168–83.
48. Zhengyan Liang, Derong Kang, Minqiang Zhang, Yuanlin Xia and Qing Zeng, 'The Impact of the Covid-19 Pandemic on Chinese Postgraduate Students' Mental Health', *International Journal of Environmental Research and Public Health* 18.21 (2021), 11542.
49. Dorian Peters, 'Wellbeing Supportive Design: Research-Based Guidelines for Supporting Psychological Wellbeing in User Experience', *International Journal of Human-Computer Interaction* 39.14 (2023), 2965, https://doi.org/10.1080/10447318.2022.2089812.
50. Alan Finlayson, Annie Kelly, Rob Topinka and Ben Little, 'Digital Culture Wars: Understanding the Far Right's Online Powerbase', *Soundings* 81 (2022), 43–4, https://doi.org/10.3898/SOUN:81.03.2022.
51. Ana-Maria Bliuc, John M. Betts, Nicholas Faulkner, Matteo Vergani, rui Jie Chow, Muhammad Iqbal and David Best, 'The Effects of Local Socio-Political Events on Group Cohesion in Online Far-Right Communities', *PloS One* 15.3 (2020), 4, https://doi.org/10.1371/journal.pone.0230302.

52. Larissa Doroshenko and Fangjing Tu, ‘Like, Share, Comment, and Repeat: Far-Right Messages, Emotions, and Amplification in Social Media’, *Journal of Information Technology & Politics* 20.3 (2023), 286–8, https://doi.org/10.1080/19331681.2022.2097358.
53. Dittmar and Entin, ‘Introduction: Archives and Radical Education’, 2.
54. For examples, please see Yvonne Bombard, Kenneth Offit and Mark Robson, ‘Risks to Relatives in Genomic Research: A Duty to Warn?’, *American Journal of Bioethics* 12.10 (2012), 12–14; Ben Chan, Flavio M. Facio, Haley Eidem, Sarah Chandros Hull, Leslie G. Biesecker and Benjamin E. Berkman, ‘Genomic Inheritances: Disclosing Individual Research Results from Whole-Exome Sequencing to Deceased Participants’ Relatives’, *American Journal of Bioethics* 12.10 (2014), 1–8.
55. LeighBurrows, ‘“I Feel Proud We Are Moving Forward”: Safeguarding Mindfulness for Vulnerable Student and Teacher Wellbeing in a Community College’, *Journal of Adult Protection* 19.1 (2017), 39, https://doi.org/10.1108/JAP-08-2016-0015.
56. Jeremy Dixon, *Adult Safeguarding Observed: How Social Workers Assess and Manage Risk and Uncertainty* (Policy Press, 2023), 83.

12

Can heritage places change visitor subjective well-being?

Amy Luck and Faye Sayer

This chapter outlines a robust evaluation framework utilized within a research context, designed to investigate the impact of various heritage places on the subjective well-being of visitors. It offers an overview of research that delves into the intricacies of visitor experiences at diverse heritage locations across England. This research aimed to untangle how the distinctive attributes of each place contribute to impact subjective well-being while identifying specific aspects of visitor well-being that are positively or negatively influenced by visits to particular heritage places. Consequently, this study provides valuable insights and mechanisms for tailoring visitor engagement strategies to maximize positive outcomes and alleviate potential negative effects associated with different heritage places. Additionally, it contributes to the development of policies and practices aimed at enhancing well-being through heritage experiences. This chapter underscores the significance of heritage places as pivotal contributors to the shaping of policies and practices related to well-being. By illuminating the diverse impacts of heritage visits, this study emphasizes the potential of these places to play a central role in promoting individual well-being and advancing broader societal goals related to well-being.

Defining well-being

Well-being has been associated with both physical and mental health; the World Health Organization states that 'health is a state of complex physical, mental and social wellbeing, and not merely the absence of disease or infirmity'.[1] Well-being is also linked to quality of life, prosperity, and sustainable thriving communities, and with liberal concepts such as freedom, liberty, and rights.[2] Positive well-being requires creating and supporting conditions in which attributes and feelings such as contentment, enjoyment, self-confidence, good relationships, engagement in the world, resilience, a sense of ownership, and people's enthusiasm to do things can thrive, and human capabilities can flourish.[3] As a result, an individual's well-being can be affected by external conditions and experiences, which impact how individuals feel and function in society; such experiences might include visiting a heritage place such as a museum or historic site.[4]

This research measured well-being based on a capabilities approach, grounded in determining what attributes and virtues were required for people to flourish and improve their quality of life.[5] The concept of measuring well-being through a capabilities approach provided the foundations for the New Economic Foundation's (NEF) National Accounts of Wellbeing Framework (NAWF) of social and personal well-being indicators and subcomponents, and the Five Ways to Wellbeing.[6] Through the capabilities-based approach, this research measured subjective well-being by considering what people were capable of and felt able to do (for example, to engage or create and maintain supportive relationships).

The National Accounts of Wellbeing Framework, produced following investigation of the experiences of over 40,000 people in over twenty countries, concluded that personal well-being consisted of five indicators: emotional well-being (experiencing positive feelings and the absence of negative feelings); satisfying life; vitality; resilience and self-esteem (including optimism); positive functioning (including autonomy, competence, engagement, meaning and purpose). It concluded that social well-being was made up of two indicators: supportive relationships, and trust and belonging.[7] NEF suggested that there were five actions an individual could take to maintain or improve their well-being, known as the 'Five Ways to Wellbeing': to connect, be active, take notice, keep learning, and to give. The NEF framework has been promoted by the UK's National Health Service and mental health charities.[8] Engaging with the historic and heritage environments and its traditions has been recognized as a mechanism to support well-being, specifically via the Five Ways to Wellbeing and National Accounts of Wellbeing Framework indicators.[9]

Heritage places and well-being

Research investigating public engagement with heritage places, spaces and landscapes has provided evidence of their ability to improve an individual's subjective well-being. Researchers at University College London (UCL) produced foundational quantitative evidence of tangible impact of heritage on user well-being and mental health; their research found that there was a measurable change in hospital patients' subjective well-being after museum object handling sessions.[10] Subsequent research has also predominantly focused on specific user groups; which included day visitors, volunteers or participants involved with specific heritage-based courses or interventions, including those linked to social prescribing or arts on prescription programmes, and demonstrated that physical and digital engagement with heritage places positively affected participants' well-being, specifically via encouraging personal learning, establishing social networks, supporting creativity, improving skills, and fostering self-expression.[11] For example, the Imperial War Museum North and Manchester Museum's Inspiring Futures Project (a volunteering, training and placement program designed to achieve improvement, consistency, and quality in volunteering practice) produced prolonged enhanced physical, emotional, and mental well-being.[12] Likewise, Sofaers et al.'s research indicated that visiting heritage places in the UK supported physical and psychological capabilities including social connections, ontological security, and trust.[13] The UK's Department for Culture Media and Sport's 'Taking Part' survey indicated that in-person engagement with historical sites had higher rates of life satisfaction than involvement in sports, while the National Trust's study using fMRI brain scans compared the impact of historical places and objects, and concluded that 'significant places more likely contain greater emotional importance than objects'.[14] Research has identified that people's experiences and interactions with historic buildings, landscapes, and tangible material remains improved personal and social well-being, supporting meaning and placemaking by evoking feelings, emotions, and self-reflection that contributed to people's sense of security, belonging, identity, and self-esteem, and by forming connections between people and places, enabling individuals to develop relationships that support belonging and identity creation and/or affirmation.[15]

Heritage organizations in the UK have become key proponents of the benefits of heritage places to well-being and have produced open-access well-being-related resources. Examples include the Horniman Museum and Gardens 'Wellbeing Wander' curated museum and garden trail which is intended to nurture well-being, National Museum Scotland's Wellbeing Audio Trail, St Fagans National Museum of History's Self-Guided Mindful Walk, Leicester Museums and Galleries Museum Challenges and Memory Trails, and East Riding Museum's Mindful Art Guides.[16] Such organizations have been significant contributors to Social Prescribing (SP) and Arts on Prescription (AoP) initiatives in the UK. SP and AoP involve individuals being referred (often as a result of stress, anxiety, depression, or low mood) by healthcare professionals and organizations such as community support groups and charities to community-based creative arts and heritage-based courses.[17] Holburne Museum's Pathways to Wellbeing Programme, for example, has provided a safe space for individuals with mental health diagnoses to explore their creativity, connect with others, learn, and be inspired by art and heritage, and the University of Edinburgh Museums Prescribe Culture Programme 6 has facilitated heritage and nature-based small group workshops.[18] Such interventions, resources and projects aim to improve the mental health of participants, support the treatment of mild to moderate mental health conditions, and support positive well-being. These SP and AoP-based heritage initiatives have provided a growing body of evidence as to the effectiveness of creative heritage-based practice in supporting participant well-being and mental health.[19]

Research into heritage places' ability to impact individuals has increasingly linked findings to the NEF's Five Ways to Wellbeing, and to personal and social well-being competencies identified by the National Accounts of Wellbeing Framework.[20] Engagement with heritage places, both through visits and specific courses, has been associated with NEF capabilities keep learning, be active, connect, and take notice; together with indicators of personal well-being (emotional well-being, positive functioning, and vitality) and social well-being (belonging).[21] Despite the growing body of research relating to the impact of heritage on participant or visitor well-being, the comparative efficacy and positive and negative effects of diverse heritage places on specific well-being indicators has yet to be comprehensively and systematically assessed.[22] This research will begin to address this absence of empirical data.

Methodology

Research detailed in this chapter measured and compared the impact of visiting a variety of managed heritage places (Table 12.1) using standardized quantitative public healthcare accredited measures, including the Positive And Negative Affect Schedule (PANAS) and Modified Wellbeing Scale (MWS), which were adapted for use within a heritage context, and qualitative visitor commentary and feedback. The mixed method evaluative approach utilized in this study was grounded in humanistic and value-based theories of well-being, in which heritage places have the potential to have unique impacts on personal and social well-being.[23] This positivist and pragmatic approach, grounded in social and health science-based measurements that collected social value data, enabled the investigation and comparison of the impact of heritage places on individuals' subjective well-being. Engagement was considered an ethnographic process, and users' experiences were perceived as impacting their lives, including personal and social well-being indicators outlined in the National Accounts of Wellbeing Framework. A before and after (pre/post) approach was used to measure change in visitor well-being; surveys containing qualitative questions, the PANAS, MWS and optional demographic questions (resident location via postcodes, age, gender, ethnicity, and if they identified as having a disability) were provided to participants at the start and at the end of their visit to one of nine managed heritage places. This methodology increased the probability that the intervention (in this case, visiting a heritage place) was the cause of any changes to a participant's well-being, as it decreased the possibility that extraneous variables impacted results, ensured contextual applicable 'place-based' data was collected, and minimized the risk of results being limited by specific quantitative or qualitative methodological limitations.

Table 12.1 Heritage places included in this research

Heritage place	Short form	Ticket price	Location	Setting	Management	Index of multiple deprivation
Imperial War Museum Duxford	IWM	£22.70	Duxford	Rural	National Museum Group	26570
Chatsworth House	CH	£24	Bakewell	Rural	Independent	31173
Lyme Park	LP	£14.30	Disley	Rural	National Trust	23395
Audley End House	AE	£20.90	Audley End	Rural	English Heritage	32811
Merchant Adventurers' Hall	MAH	£6.50	York	Urban	Independent	20366
Delapré Abbey	DA	£8.00	Northampton	Urban	Independent	12306
Priory Gardens	PG	Free	Dunstable	Urban	Council	14341
Elizabeth Gaskell's House	EGH	£5.50	Manchester	Urban	Independent	11725
Dulwich Picture Gallery	DPG	£16.50	Dulwich	Urban	Independent	25346

Table 12.2 PANAS survey used in this study

Please tick to indicate how much you agree with these statements at the present moment:					
I feel ...	**Not at all**	**A little**	**Moderately**	**Quite a bit**	**Extremely**
Attentive					
Distressed					
Interested					
Alert					
Jittery					
Excited					
Guilty					
Afraid					
Enthusiastic					
Irritable					
Strong					
Ashamed					
Inspired					
Scared					
Hostile					
Active					
Nervous					
Proud					
Upset					
Determined					

Qualitative methods incorporated free-comment space with direct open-ended questions to provide space for participants to consider their own indicators for improved well-being. Qualitative data enabled the investigation of specific impacts on well-being and helped determine context and specific reasons for improved or reduced well-being. Quantitative pilot-tested public health methodological frameworks of well-being and mental health assessments, such as the Modified Wellbeing Survey (MWS) and the Positive and Negative Affect Schedule (PANAS), were utilized to assess the impact of visiting heritage places and to help understand the similarities and differences between the well-being impact of visiting each place.[24]

The PANAS survey (Table 12.2), developed by Watson, Clark and Tellegen, measured well-being by listing ten words relating to positive emotions (such as enthusiastic, strong, and inspired) and ten words relating to negative emotions (distressed, irritable, and ashamed, for instance).[25] Participants selected how much they felt these words applied to them on a numbered five-point Likert scale (from 1 – 'not at all' to 5 – 'extremely'). PANAS was designed to facilitate repeated use in a longitudinal or pre/post study; the researcher can insert different time periods from the 'present moment' to 'past year' into the survey. This research asked participants how they felt PANAS measures (such as 'attentive') applied to them 'at the present moment'. Repeated PANAS scales can demonstrate change over the period between the completion of surveys.

Table 12.3 MWS survey used in this study

Please tick to indicate how much you agree with these statements at the present moment:					
I feel ...	**Not at all**	**A little**	**Moderately**	**Quite a bit**	**Extremely**
Interested in the world around me					
Connected to the people around me					
Happy with my life					
Satisfied with my life					
I have the opportunity to learn new things					
A sense of accomplishment					
Optimistic about my future					
I have freedom of choice					
I can overcome challenges					
Connected to the local environment					
My life is worthwhile					
I belong to a neighbourhood					
Physically active					
People support each other					
I can trust people					

Sayer developed the Modified Wellbeing Scale (MWS) from a modified version of a Visual Analog Scale (VAS) produced by Thomson, Ander, Menon, Lanceley and Chatterjee.[26] The MWS measures subjective well-being and happiness, drawing on elements from the VAS, the General Health Questionnaire (GHQ), four UK Office for National Statistics (ONS) well-being questions (based on the New Economic Foundation's Five Ways to Wellbeing) and the Warwick Edinburgh Mental Wellbeing Scale.[27] The MWS (Table 12.3) lists a series of fifteen phrases related to capabilities that impact personal and social well-being and participants were asked to select how they felt these phrases related to them at the present moment on a five-point Likert scale.

The selection of heritage places was based on a heterogeneity sampling strategy. The places selected for this research varied widely and covered a broad range of topics, time periods, types of interpretation, management styles, locations, sizes, operating hours, and socio-economic demographics (Table 12.1).[28] These variances enabled investigation of place-specific aspects which could impact visitor well-being.

Convenience sampling was used to locate participants. Individuals who attended one of the nine pre-selected heritage places were approached at the start of their visit and invited to take part. Participants were asked to complete a 'before' survey at the start of their visit and provided with an 'after' survey at the exit. Participants were invited to ask questions about the research (in person or via email) before taking part. 'Before' surveys requested participant email addresses, and those who had not completed the 'after' surveys were contacted and reminded to complete them via an online survey if they had not done so at the end of their visit. Participants were automatically removed if they did not complete both surveys, as change could not be measured without both the before and after scores.

The research was approved by Manchester Metropolitan University on project numbers 23858 and 1367. All participants were given participant information sheets and were required to complete a consent form, to enable the use of anonymized data for research purposes. Participants were required to be over eighteen years old and attend one of the nine heritage places, but no other selection or exclusion measures were applied. All heritage places involved in this research consented to and facilitated data collection.

To determine the differential impact of each heritage place, statistical analysis was conducted on quantitative datasets and results were compared. Percentage differences between the mean before and after results were calculated and compared.[29] Statistical hypothesis testing was used to determine significant changes to individual well-being after visiting each heritage place, via two-tailed non-parametric related sample tests.[30] When the test returned a *p*-value below 0.05 (5 per cent) results were deemed statistically significant, demonstrating real change to well-being after visiting the heritage place, with 95 per cent confidence. When the *p*-value returned was below 0.01 (1 per cent) results were determined to be highly significant.[31] Statistical significance confirmed that changes after engagement were not due to chance and ensured change after visiting could be attributed to visiting the heritage place. Statistically significant results from each heritage place were compared to assess which place had the broadest impact on well-being, and to determine similarities and differences between measures and indicators which were impacted by each heritage place. Thematic analysis based on the National Accounts of Wellbeing Framework personal and social well-being indicators was used to ascertain recurring themes in qualitative data from each heritage place, and the findings of both qualitative and quantitative data from each place were then combined to determine evidence-based conclusions regarding the overall well-being impact of each heritage place.

Results

Between October 2021 and March 2022, 729 participants attending one of the nine heritage places completed both 'before' and 'after' surveys. Participants who provided demographic data were largely female (68 per cent), did not identify as having a disability (92 per cent), were White British (84 per cent) and over half (52 per cent) were over the age of fifty. While this research sought to determine change to well-being and therefore sought to minimize sample demographics underlying well-being characteristics impacting results, sample demographics may have influenced findings. The UK's ONS established that adults who were not disabled reported higher than average levels of happiness, life satisfaction and feeling that the things done in life are worthwhile and those who identified as White reported higher than average levels of life satisfaction and worthwhile in their 2023 personal well-being survey.[32] However, the ONS found there were no statistically significant differences in the proportion of low levels of happiness, life satisfaction and feeling that the things done

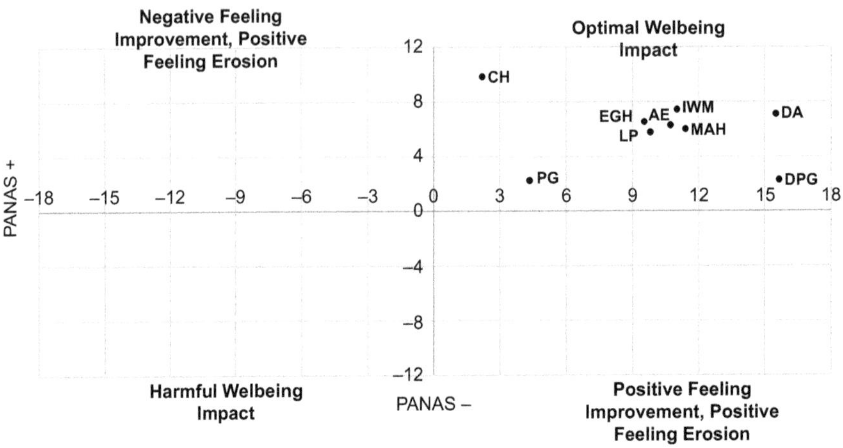

Figure 12.1 PANAS mean average percentage change.

in life are worthwhile between men and women.[33] ONS findings on age were more complex: while a greater proportion of adults aged 50–54 and 55–59 years reported low levels of life satisfaction and low levels of happiness than average and the highest proportion reporting low levels of feeling things done in life are worthwhile were those aged 85–89 years, when averaging findings from respondents 50–90+, those aged 50–90+ on average reported higher than average levels of happiness, life satisfaction and feeling that the things done in life are worthwhile.[34] As such, the potentially largely female sample (not all participants shared demographic data) was unlikely to have influenced the findings of this study. Still, the potential proportion of older, White and non-disabled adults may have caused well-being beginning scores to be higher than the average UK population and impact the generalizability of results.

PANAS mean average percentage change results indicated that visits to all the heritage places included in this study positively affected visitor's 'emotional well-being', by improving their 'positive emotions' and reducing 'negative emotions' (Figure 12.1). Mean average scores indicated Delapré Abbey had the most impact on 'emotional well-being', with an overall change of 22.61 per cent ('positive emotions' improved by 15.52 per cent and 'negative emotions' reduced by 7.09 per cent). While still improving 'emotional well-being', Priory Gardens had the least overall impact on 'emotional well-being' of all the heritage places, with an overall change of 6.64 per cent ('positive emotions' improved by 4.38 per cent and 'negative emotions' reduced by 2.26 per cent).

Chatsworth House had the least impact on improving 'positive emotions' (2.21 per cent) but most on reducing 'negative emotions' (–9.85 per cent) while Dulwich Picture Gallery had the least impact on reducing 'negative emotions' (–2.25 per cent) but the most impact on improving 'positive emotions' (15.66 per cent). The remaining five heritage places (Elizabeth Gaskell's House, Audley End, Imperial War Museum Duxford, Lyme Park, and Merchant Adventurers' Hall) produced similar patterns in visitor experience (with overall change ranging between 15.57 per cent and 18.43 per

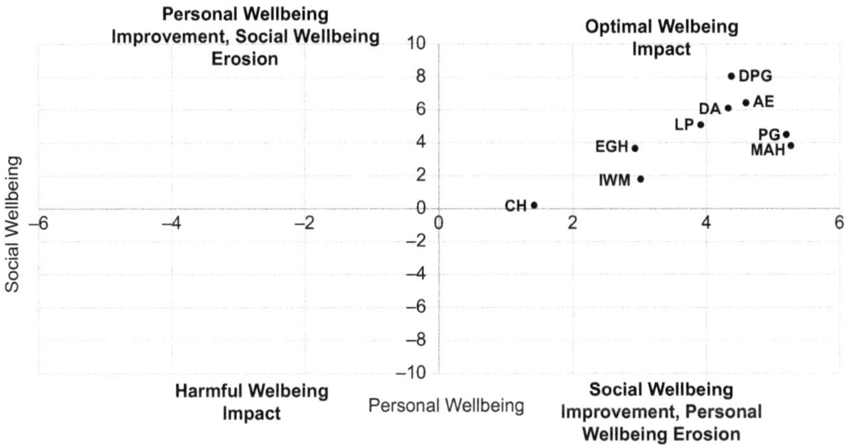

Figure 12.2 MWS mean average percentage change.

cent), the clustering of results indicating a similar impact despite the considerable differences between these places (Figure 12.1).

The categorization of MWS measures mean average scores, based on measures linked to NAWF social and personal well-being indicators, enabled a comparison of the impact on visitors' personal and social well-being experienced at each heritage place (Figure 12.2). MWS mean average percentage change results indicated that all heritage places included in this study improved visitors' personal well-being and social well-being. Mean average scores indicated that Dulwich Picture Gallery had the most overall change to personal and social well-being indicators (12.42 per cent). While still improving personal and social well-being, Chatsworth House had the least overall impact of all the heritage places (1.61 per cent). Merchant Adventurers' Hall had the highest impact on visitors' social well-being (5.26 per cent), and Dulwich Picture Gallery had the greatest impact on personal well-being (8.05 per cent). Chatsworth House had the least impact on both visitors' personal (0.19 per cent) and social well-being (1.42 per cent). Imperial War Museum Duxford also resulted in low levels of personal well-being change in comparison to other places. Heritage places Audley End, Delapré Abbey, Lyme Park, Priory Gardens and Merchant Adventurers' Hall provided evidence of similar experiences in overarching changes to social and personal well-being changes (overall change ranging between 11.02 and 8.97 per cent).

Statistical analysis indicated that visiting these heritage places had a wide-ranging impact on NAWF personal and social well-being indicators and subcomponents. Visiting any of the heritage places within this study resulted in statistically significant improvement in personal well-being in at least one subcomponent. Visiting Lyme Park resulted in the highest number of personal well-being subcomponents undergoing statistically significant change, with all subcomponents improved except 'self-esteem' and 'positive functioning' subcomponent 'competent', followed by Audley End, Merchant Adventurer's Hall, and Dulwich Picture Gallery (Table 12.4). Visiting Chatsworth House resulted in the least number of NAWF personal well-being

Table 12.4 Statistically significant subcomponents (S = significant)

Headline indicator	Indicator	Subcomponent	AE	EGH	LP	MAH	CH	IWM	PG	DPG	DA
Personal well-being	Emotional well-being	Positive emotions			S					S	
		Negative emotions	S	S	S	S	S	S			
	Satisfying life		S	S	S	S	Reduced S	S	S	S	S
	Vitality		S		S	S					
	Resilience and self-esteem	Self-esteem						S			
		Resilience	S		S				S	S	
		Optimism		S	S	S		S		S	S
	Positive functioning	Engaged	S	S	S	S		S	S	S	S
		Competent	S			S			S	S	S
		Autonomy	S		S						
		Meaning and purpose	S	S	S	S				S	
Total personal well-being subcomponents improved			8	5	9	7	1	5	4	7	4
Social well-being	Supportive relationships		S		S	S			S		
	Trust and belonging			S	S	S					S
Total social well-being subcomponents improved			1	1	2	2	0	0	1	0	1
Total subcomponents improved			9	6	11	9	1	5	5	7	5

subcomponents undergoing statistically significant improvements, with only emotional well-being subcomponent 'negative emotions' improved. Chatsworth House was the only place which resulted in a statistically significant reduction in personal well-being: 'satisfying life' (MWS measure I feel my life is worthwhile) reduced after visiting.

Statistically significant changes demonstrated that visiting all the heritage places (except Chatsworth House), improved 'life satisfaction' and 'engagement'. The only place where 'self-esteem' was improved as a result of visiting was the Imperial War Museum Duxford. In relation to social well-being indicators, statistically significant changes demonstrated that 'supportive relationships' were improved by visiting Audley End, Lyme Park, Merchant Adventurers' Hall, and Dunstable Priory Gardens, while 'trust and belonging' were improved by visiting Elizabeth Gaskell's House, Lyme Park, Merchant Adventurers' Hall and Delapré Abbey. All places except Imperial War Museum Duxford, Dulwich Picture Gallery and Chatsworth House significantly improved visitors' social well-being and supported visitors to connect to people and places.

Table 12.5 Subcomponents which were supported by qualitative data (S = supported by qualitative data)

Headline indicator	Indicator	Subcomponent	AE	EGH	LP	MAH	CH	IWM	PG	DPG	DA
Personal well-being	Emotional well-being	Positive emotions	S	S	S	S	S	S	S	S	S
		Negative emotions	S	S	S	S					S
	Satisfying life		S	S							
	Vitality		S	S	S	S	S	S	S		
	Resilience and self-esteem	Self-esteem	S		S	S		S	S		S
		Resilience	S	S	S		S				
		Optimism	S	S	S	S			S		S
	Positive functioning	Engaged	S	S	S	S	S	S	S	S	S
		Competent		S	S						
		Autonomy		S	S		S	S		S	
		Meaning and purpose	S		S	S	S	S	S	S	S
Total personal well-being indicators supported			9	9	10	7	6	6	6	4	6
Social well-being	Supportive relationships		S	S	S	S	S	S	S	S	S
	Trust and belonging		S	S	S	S	S	S	S		S
Total social well being indicators supported			2	2	2	2	2	2	2	1	2
Total social and personal			11	11	12	9	8	8	8	5	8

Visitor commentary indicated all heritage places supported visitors' personal well-being (Table 12.5). Commentary from visitors to Lyme Park demonstrated impact on the greatest number of subcomponents and qualitatively had the most impact on visitors' well-being (Table 12.5), followed by Audley End and Elizabeth Gaskell's House. Dulwich Picture Gallery had the most limited impact, with the fewest number of impacted subcomponents.

Visitor commentary indicated 'positive functioning' was improved as visitors felt more 'engaged' at all places, and reported that their life had more 'meaning and purpose' at all places except Elizabeth Gaskell's House. 'Autonomy' was improved at Elizabeth Gaskell's House, Lyme Park, Chatsworth House, Imperial War Museum Duxford, and Dulwich Picture Gallery. Lyme Park and Elizabeth Gaskell's House supported visitors to feel they were more 'competent'. Commentary indicated all heritage places improved 'emotional well-being' by increasing visitors' 'positive emotions', and 'negative emotions' were reduced at Delapré Abbey, Audley End, Elizabeth Gaskell's House, and Merchant Adventurers' Hall. 'Vitality' was improved at all places except Dulwich Picture Gallery and Delapré Abbey, but only Audley End and Elizabeth Gaskell's House supported visitors to comment on improvements to 'satisfying life'. The personal well-being indicator 'resilience and self-esteem' was impacted at every place, except for Dulwich Picture Gallery, but different places impacted different subcomponents (Table 12.5). Visitors to all heritage places commented that their social well-being had been improved by their experiences at heritage places, including 'supportive relationships', and except for Dulwich Picture Gallery, all heritage places impacted 'trust and belonging'.

Statistically significant results and qualitative data viewed together demonstrated that Lyme Park had the broadest impact on visitor well-being: visiting Lyme Park supported the greatest number of subcomponents (ten), followed by Audley End (seven) and Merchant Adventurers' Hall (six; Table 12.6). Contrastingly, results showed that visiting Chatsworth House did not both quantitatively and qualitatively support any subcomponents. Improved personal well-being was most comprehensively supported by both sets of data from Lyme Park which supported the greatest number of subcomponents (eight), followed by Audley End (six) and Merchant Adventurers' Hall (five). Improvements to visitors' 'positive functioning' subcomponent 'engaged' were supported by both quantitative and qualitative data from all places except Chatsworth House, while subcomponent 'competent' was not supported by both sets of data for any places. Improved social well-being was most comprehensively supported by both sets of data from Lyme Park, which was the sole heritage place where both sets of data supported both indicators.

While overall mean average scores for the PANAS and MWS were positive, visiting Priory Gardens and Chatsworth House had slight negative impacts on mean average scores for specific measures (e.g., individual PANAS words or MWS statements), although only one reduction was statistically significant to visitor well-being. Negative impacts from visiting Chatsworth House were linked to personal well-being, and the subcomponents of 'positive functioning' ('autonomy', 'meaning and purpose', and 'engagement') and emotional well-being (positive and negative emotions), while Priory Gardens' negative impacts to personal well-being were linked to subcomponents of 'self-esteem and resilience' and 'emotional well-being'. At Chatsworth House, these quantitative reductions were explained by qualitative data as the result of jarring experiences, ostentatious displays of wealth and privilege, and lack of diverse narratives or interpretations, while at Priory Gardens this was associated with limited interpretations.

Comparison of visitor quantitative and qualitative data from heritage places revealed variation and patterns between places, and specific impacts on visitors' subjective well-being indicators based on the nature of visitor experiences and type of places (historic estates, archaeological sites, museums, art galleries, historic buildings), and types of experiences (indoor/outdoor). Combined results suggest that heritage places from within a broad historical period (medieval to Victorian) which provide historical narratives focused on a specific period and have internal (houses or buildings) and external places (grounds and gardens) to explore, for example, Audley End, Lyme

Table 12.6 Triangulated data

Headline indicator	Indicator	Subcomponent	AE	EGH	LP	MAH	CH	IWM	PG	DPG	DA
Personal well-being	Emotional well-being	Positive Emotions	Qual	Qual	Both	Both	Qual	Both	Qual	Both	Qual
		Negative Emotions	Both	Both	Both	Both	Quant	Quant			Qual
	Satisfying life		Both	Both	Quant	Quant		Quant	Quant	Quant	Quant
	vitality		Both	Qual	Both	Qual	Qual	Qual	Qual		
	Resilience and self-esteem	Self-esteem	Qual		Qual	Qual		Both	Qual		Qual
		Resilience	Both	Qual	Both	Quant	Qual		Quant	Quant	
		Optimism	Qual	Both	Both	Both		Quant	Qual	Quant	Both
	Positive functioning	Engaged	Both	Both	Both	Both	Qual	Both	Both	Both	Both
		Competent	Quant	Qual	Qual				Quant	Quant	Quant
		Autonomy	Quant	Qual	Both	Quant	Qual	Qual		Qual	
		Meaning and purpose	Both	Quant	Both	Both	Qual	Qual	Qual	Both	Qual
Total personal well-being indicators changed by both sets of data			6	4	8	5	0	3	1	3	2
Social well-being	Supportive relationships		Both	Qual	Both	Both	Qual	Qual	Both	Qual	Qual
	Trust and belonging		Qual	Both	Both	Qual	Qual	Qual	Qual		Both
Total social well-being indicators changed by both sets of data			1	1	2	1	0	0	1		1
Total social and personal			7	5	10	6	0	3	2	3	3

Park, Elizabeth Gaskell House and Merchant Adventurers' Hall, had the most optimal impact on visitor well-being, impacting the highest number of well-being indicators. Historic physical spaces (buildings) with clear and varied interpretative elements both internally and externally were most successful in positively changing visitors' well-being. Places which were predominantly focused on displaying historic material (e.g., objects – Imperial War Museum Duxford; art – Chatsworth House and Dulwich Picture Gallery) were solely outside (Priory Gardens), or did not provide comprehensive or diverse narratives or interpretations (Chatsworth House, Priory Gardens) did improve some aspects of well-being, but not as broadly as sites which met the above criteria.

This study indicated potential mechanisms/actions by which heritage places in England positively affected well-being, including interpretative strategies that supported identity creation and a sense of belonging. For example, places which told stories linked to national identity, such as the First and Second World Wars at Imperial War Museum Duxford, were the only heritage places linked to quantitative and qualitative improvements to feelings of pride, therefore increasing visitors' 'self-esteem'. This research also demonstrated a mechanism through which heritage places can improve social well-being, including through displayed collections; art galleries (Dulwich Picture Gallery), heritage sites that focus on displaying art (Chatsworth House), and large museum-based heritage places (Imperial War Museum Duxford), did not result in statistically significant changes to measures relating to social well-being.

This study highlighted that geographical setting (rural/urban and north/south of England) did not impact the effectiveness of heritage places in improving well-being; the four places which had the most comprehensive impact on well-being were rural and urban places which were located from Cambridgeshire to Yorkshire. However, there were some similarities noticeable: both urban sites were smaller, museum-based historic buildings with outside spaces, while both rural sites were larger historic houses and gardens. There was no correlation between management type (independent/national) and entry prices and well-being impact; the place which was the most expensive to visit (Chatsworth House) had the least comprehensive impact on visitor well-being, followed by the place which was free to visit (Priory Gardens; Figure 12.3). Socio-economic demographics of the local area did not, in this study, affect visitor well-being; the heritage place with the least comprehensive impact (Chatsworth House) was located in the least deprived 10 per cent of areas nationally while the place with the most comprehensive impact (Lyme Park) was located in the least deprived 30 per cent of areas nationally (Figure 12.4).[35]

Participant demographics

Participants who provided demographic data were largely female (68 per cent), did not identify as having a disability (92 per cent), were white British (84 per cent) and over half (52 per cent) were over the age of fifty. While this research sought to determine change to well-being and therefore sought to minimize sample demographics underlying well-being characteristics impacting results, sample demographics may have influenced findings. The UK's ONS established that adults who were not disabled

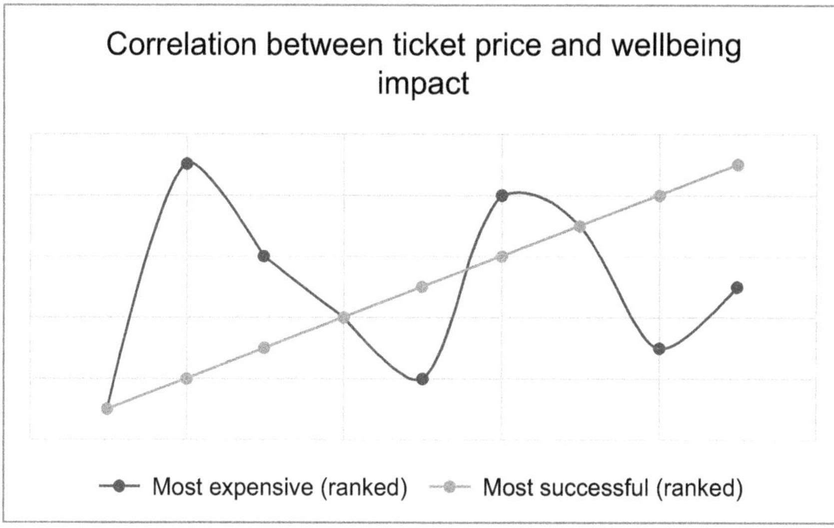

Figure 12.3 Graph depicting the correlation between ticket price and well-being impact.

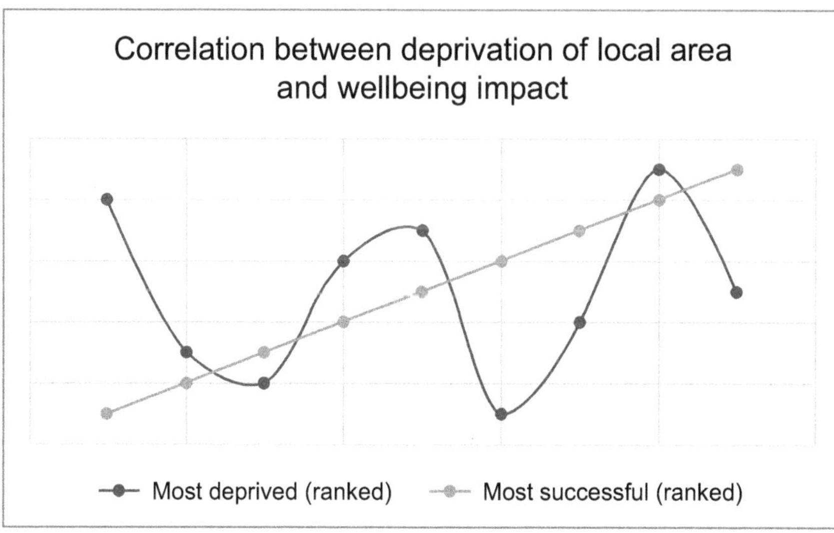

Figure 12.4 Graph depicting the correlation between deprivation of local area and well-being impact.

reported higher than average levels of happiness, life satisfaction and feeling that the things done in life are worthwhile and those who identified as White reported higher than average levels of life satisfaction and worthwhile in their 2023 personal well-being survey.[36] However, the ONS found there were no statistically significant differences in the proportion of low levels of happiness, life satisfaction and feeling that the things done in life are worthwhile between men and women.[37] ONS findings on age were more complex: while a greater proportion of adults aged 50–54 and 55–59 years reported low levels of life satisfaction and low levels of happiness than average and the highest proportion reporting low levels of feeling things done in life are worthwhile were those aged 85–89 years, when averaging findings from respondents 50–90+, those aged 50–90+ on average reported higher than average levels of happiness, life satisfaction and feeling that the things done in life are worthwhile.[38] As such, the potentially largely female sample (not all participants shared demographic data) was unlikely to have influenced the findings of this study. Still, the potential proportion of older, White and non-disabled adults may have caused well-being beginning scores to be higher than the average UK population and impact the generalizability of results.

Conclusions

Heritage places had a significant impact on visitors' subjective personal well-being and social well-being. Comparative analysis indicated that irrespective of location, socio-economic demographics of the local area, management type, entry price, or historical period, as detailed above, had a positive effect on subjective well-being: most predominantly on visitors feeling 'engaged', followed by feeling that their visit provided 'meaning and purpose' and facilitated 'supportive relationships'. However, participant demographics may have impacted these findings, particularly qualitatively. This study indicated that there were subtle differences between different heritage places on the well-being indicators affected, which included variation between benefits to social and personal well-being, including those linked to 'positive functioning', 'vitality', 'self-esteem and resilience'. These measurable differences can be attributed to interpretative strategies and place characteristics, for example, historic buildings and gardens located in rural areas and smaller historic house museums located in urban areas had the greatest measurable and significant impact on visitors' subjective well-being across all indicators. Visitor commentary suggested that visiting heritage places resulted in the greatest positive impact on visitors' qualitative perceptions of their subjective 'emotional well-being'. All heritage places assessed within this research supported visitors in relation to NEF Five Ways to Wellbeing and have provided preliminary evidence that heritage places can provide experiences that encourage visitors to take notice of the world around them and each other, to connect with people and places, and to learn.[39]

Notes

1. World Health Organisation, *Constitution of the World Health Organization* (World Health Organisation, 1946).
2. Cathy Baldwin, Penny Vincent, Jamie Anderson and Patrick Rawstorne, 'Measuring Well-Being: Trial of the Neighbourhood Thriving Scale for Social Well-Being among Pro-social Individuals', *International Journal of Community Well-Being* 3.3 (2020),

361–90; Tyler J. VanderWeele, 'Measures of Community Well-Being: A Template', *International Journal of Community Well-Being* 2.3 (2019), 253–75; S. M. Skevington and J. R. Böhnke, 'How Is Subjective Well-Being Related to Quality of Life? Do We Need Two Concepts and Both Measures?', *Social Science & Medicine* 206 (2018), 22–30; Ed Diener and Eunkook Suh, 'Measuring Quality of Life: Economic, Social, and Subjective Indicators', *Social Indicators Research* 40.1–2 (1997), 189–216; E. Diener, W. Ng, J. Harter and R. Arora, 'Wealth and Happiness across the World: Material Prosperity Predicts Life Evaluation, Whereas Psychosocial Prosperity Predicts Positive Feeling', *Journal of Personality and Social Psychology* 99 (2010), 52–61; Amartya Sen, 'Capability and Wellbeing', in Martha Nussbaum and Amartya Sen (eds), *The Quality of Life* (Oxford University Press, 1993), 30–53.

3. Marie J. C. Forgeard, Eranda Jayawickreme, Margaret L. Kern and Martin E. P. Seligman, 'Doing the Right Thing: Measuring Well-Being for Public Policy', *International Journal of Wellbeing* 1.1 (2011); Saamah Abdallah, Hanna Wheatley and Annie Quick, *Drivers of Wellbeing Inequality* (What Works Welbeing, 2017); Sarah Reily, Claire Nolon and Linda Monckton, *Wellbeing and the Historic Environment* (Historic Environment, 2018); Anneyce Knight and Allan McNaught, *Understanding Wellbeing: An Introduction for Students and Practitioners of Health and Social Care* (Lantern, 2011); Karen Scott, *Measuring Wellbeing: Towards Sustainability* (Routledge, 2012); Jody Aked, Nic Marks, Corrina Cordon and Sam Thompson, *Five Ways to Wellbeing. A Report Presented to the Foresight Project on Communicating the Evidence Base for Improving People's Well-Being* (New Economics Foundation, 2008); Ian Bache and Karen Scott, 'Wellbeing in Politics and Policy', in Ian Bache and Karen Scott (eds), *The Politics of Wellbeing: Theory, Policy and Practice* (Palgrave Macmillan, 2018), 1–24.
4. Abdallah et al., *Drivers of Wellbeing Inequality.*
5. Sen, *Capability and Wellbeing*; Scott, *Measuring Wellbeing*; Amartya Sen, 'Equality of What?', in Sterling McMurrin (ed.), *Tanner Lectures on Human Values* (Cambridge University Press, 1980); Martha Nussbaum, 'Wellbeing, Contracts and Capabilities', in Leonore Manderson (ed.), *Rethinking Wellbeing* (API Network, 2005), 27–44.
6. Aked et al., *Five Ways to Wellbeing*; Juliet Michaelson, Saamah Abdallah, Nicola Steuer, Sam Thompson and Nic Marks, 'National Accounts of Well-Being: Bringing Real Wealth onto the Balance Sheet', *New Economic Foundation* (2009), https://neweconomics.org/uploads/files/2027fb05fed1554aea_uim6vd4c5.pdf (accessed 5 January 2021); Carol Ryff, 'Happiness Is Everything, or Is It? Exploration of the Meaning of Psychological Well-Being', *Journal of Personality and Social Psychology* 57 (1989), 1069–81.
7. Michaelson et al., 'National Accounts of Well-Being'.
8. National Health Service, '5 Steps to Mental Wellbeing', www.nhs.uk/conditions/stress-anxiety-depression/improve-mental-wellbeing/ (accessed 1 April 2020); Mind, '5 Ways to Wellbeing', www.mind.org.uk/workplace/mental-health-at-work/taking-care-of-yourself/five-ways-to-wellbeing/ (accessed 1 May 2023).
9. Claire Smith, Vincent Copley Senior, Kylie Lower, Ania Kotaba and Gary Jackson, 'Using Archaeology to Strengthen Indigenous Social, Economic and Economic Wellbeing', in Paul Everill and Karen Burnell (eds), *Archaeology, Heritage and Wellbeing: Authentic, Powerful and Therapeutic Engagement with the Past* (Routledge, 2022), 119–44.
10. Linda Thomson, Eric Ander, Usha Menon, Anne Lancely and Helen Chatterjee, 'Quantitative Evidence for Wellbeing Benefits from a Heritage-in-Health Intervention with Hospital Patients', *International Journal of Art Therapy* 17.2 (2012), 63–79;

Linda Thomson and Helen Chatterjee, 'Assessing Well-Being Outcomes for Arts and Heritage Activities: Development of a Museum Well-Being Measures Toolkit', *Journal of Applied Arts & Health* 5 (2014), 29–50.

11. Eirini Gallou, David Uzzell and Joanna Sofaer, 'Perceived Place Qualities, Restorative Effects and Self-Reported Wellbeing Benefits of Visits to Heritage Sites: Empirical Evidence from a Visitor Survey in England', *Wellbeing, Space and Society* 3 (2022), 100106; Faye Sayer, 'Can Digging Make You Happy? Archaeological Excavations, Happiness and Heritage', *Arts & Health* 7.3 (2015), 247–60; Tim Darvill, 'Monuments for Life: Building Human Henge at Stonehenge and Avebury', in Tim Darvill, Kerry Barrass, Laura Drysdale, Vanessa Heaslip and Yvette Staelens (eds), *Historic Landscapes and Mental Well-Being* (Archaeopress, 2019), 65–84; Paul Everill, Richard Bennett and Karen Burnell, 'Dig In: An Evaluation of the Role of Archaeological Fieldwork for the Improved Wellbeing of Military Veterans', *Antiquity*, 94.373 (2020), 212–27; A. Pennington, R. Jones, A.-M. Bagnall, J. South and R. Corcoran, *Heritage and Wellbeing: The Impact of Historic Places and Assets on Community Wellbeing – A Scoping Review* (What Works Centre for Wellbeing, 2019); Timothy Darvill and Kerry Barrass, *Historic Landscapes and Mental Well-Being* (Archaeopress, 2019); Thomson and Chatterjee, *Assessing Well-Being Outcomes for Arts and Heritage Activities*; Christina Smiraglia, 'Museum Programming and Mood: Participant Responses to an Object-Based Reminiscence Outreach Program in Retirement Communities', *Arts & Health* 7.3 (2015), 187–201; Michelle Kindleysides and Emma Biglands, '"Thinking Outside the Box, and Making It Too": Piloting an Occupational Therapy Group at an Open-Air Museum', *Arts & Health* 7.3 (2015), 271–8; Thomson et al., 'Quantitative Evidence for Wellbeing Benefits'; 'About', *Happier Museum Project*, http://happymuseumproject.org/about/ (accessed 12 December 2019); Helen Chatterjee and Paul Camic, 'The Health and Well-Being Potential of Museums and Art Galleries', *Arts and Health* 7.3 (2015), 183–6; L. J. Thomson, B. Lockyer, P. M. Camic and H. J. Chatterjee, 'Effects of a Museum-Based Social Prescription Intervention on Quantitative Measures of Psychological Wellbeing in Older Adults', *Perspectives in Public Health* 138.1 (2018), 28–38; Laura Phillips, 'Reminiscence: Recent Work at the British Museum', in Helen Chatterjee (ed.), *Touch in Museums: Policy and Practice in Object Handling* (Berg, 2008), 199–204; Sonia Rasbery and Jocelyn Goddard, *Mental Health and Heritage Working in Partnership: 4 Linked Projects in Surrey* (Renaissance Southwest, 2011); Paul Belford, 'Archaeology, Community and Identity in a New English Town', *Historic Environment* 2.1 (2011), 46–67; Mary Ryan, 'Pathways to Wellbeing Evaluation 2016–19' (2019); Mary Ryan, 'Pathways to Wellbeing Evaluation 2019–22' (2022); David Cutler, *Creatively Minded at the Museum: Creative and Mental Health Activity in Museums* (Baring Foundation, 2022).
12. Danielle Garcia and Andrea Winn, *Inspiring Futures: Volunteering for Wellbeing. Final Report 2013–2016. Social Return on Investment* (Manchester Museum, Imperial War Museum North, 2017).
13. Gallou et al., *Perceived Place Qualities, Restorative Effects and Self-Reported Wellbeing Benefits of Visits to Heritage Sites.*
14. Pennington et al., *Heritage and Wellbeing*; Gallou et al., *Perceived Place Qualities, Restorative Effects and Self-Reported Wellbeing Benefits of Visits to Heritage Sites*; Daniel Fujiwara, Thomas Corwall and Paul Dolan, *Heritage and Wellbeing* (English Heritage, 2014); Historic England, *A Strategy for Wellbeing and Heritage 2022–2025* (Historic England, 2022), https://historicengland.org.uk/content/docs/about/strat

egy-wellbeing-heritage-2022-25/; Department for Culture Media and Sport, 'Taking Part 2015/16 Quarter 4 Statistical Release' (July 2016), www.gov.uk/government/statistics/taking-part-201516-quarter-4-statistical-release; National Trust, *Places That Make Us: Research Report* (National Trust, 2018), www.nationaltrust.org.uk/who-we-are/research/why-do-places-mean-so-much0.

15. Francesca Benetti, Katharina Möller and Francesco Ripanti, 'Working with Communities: Public Participation from the Archaeologists' Perspective', *Journal of Community Archaeology & Heritage* 9.4 (2022), 287–303; Briony Clifton, 'People and Making Places', in Tim Darvill, Kerry Barrass, Laura Drysdale, Vanessa Heaslip and Yvette Staelens (eds), *Historic Landscapes and Mental Well-Being* (Archaeopress, 2019), 144–52; Darvill, *Monuments for Life*; Claire Nolan, 'The Prehistoric Landscape as Transitional Space', in Tim Darvill, Kerry Barrass, Laura Drysdale, Vanessa Heaslip and Yvette Staelens (eds), *Historic Landscapes and Mental Well-Being* (Archaeopress, 2019), 163–78; Allison Williams, 'Introduction: The Continuing Maturation of the Therapeutic Landscape Concept', in Allison Williams (ed.), *Therapeutic Landscapes* (Ashgate, 2007), 1–12; Wilbert Gesler, 'Therapeutic Landscapes: An Evolving Theme', *Health and Place* 11 (2005), 295–7.
16. Horniman Museum & Gardens, 'Wellbeing Wander', www.horniman.ac.uk/plan-your-visit/around-the-horniman/wellbeing-wander/ (accessed 25 November 2023); Leicester Museums & Galleries, 'Wellbeing Resources', www.leicestermuseums.org/learning-engagement/health-wellbeing/wellbeing-resources/ (accessed 13 January 2024); National Museums Scotland, 'Wellbeing Audio Trail', www.nms.ac.uk/national-museum-of-scotland/things-to-see-and-do/museum-trails/wellbeing-trail/ (accessed 13 January 2024); Amgueddfa Cymru, 'St Fagans Self-Guided Mindful Walk', https://museum.wales/blog/2117/St-Fagans-Self-guided-Mindful-Walk (accessed 13 January 2024); East Riding Museums, 'Health and Wellbeing', www.eastridingmuseums.co.uk/get-involved/health-and-wellbeing/ (accessed 13 January 2024).
17. Nicola J. Holt, 'Tracking Momentary Experience in the Evaluation of Arts-on-Prescription Services: Using Mood Changes during Art Workshops to Predict Global Wellbeing Change', *Perspectives in Public Health* 140.5 (2020), 270–6; G. Clayton and S. Potter, 'Arts on Prescription: A Creative and Cost Effective Approach to Improve Mental Health', in T. Stickley and S. Clift (eds), *Arts, Health and Wellbeing: A Theoretical Enquiry for Practice* (Cambridge University Press, 2017), 160–81.
18. Darvill and Barrass, 'Historic Landscapes and Mental Well-Being'; S. Desmarais, L. Bedford and H. J. Chatterjee, *Museums as Spaces for Wellbeing: A Second Report from the National Alliance for Museums, Health and Wellbeing* (ACE, 2018); Cutler, *Creatively Minded at the Museum*; Faye Sayer, 'Understanding Well-Being: A Mechanism for Measuring the Impact of Heritage Practice on Well-Being', in Angela M. Labrador and Neil Asher Silberman (eds), *The Oxford Handbook of Public Heritage Theory and Practice* (Oxford University Press, 2018), 387–404; Darvill, *Monuments for Life*; Ryan, 'Pathways to Wellbeing Evaluation 2016–19'; Ryan, 'Pathways to Wellbeing Evaluation 2019–22'; Horniman Museum & Gardens, 'Wellbeing Wander'; University of Edinburgh Museums, 'Programme 6', www.ed.ac.uk/information-services/library-museum-gallery/heritage-collections/in-the-community/prescribe-culture/programme-6-edinburgh (accessed 13 January 2024).
19. Cutler, *Creatively Minded at the Museum*; Linda J. Thomson, Erica E. Ander, Usha Menon, Anne Lanceley and Helen J. Chatterjee, 'Evaluating the Therapeutic Effects of Museum Object Handling with Hospital Patients: A Review and Initial Trial of Well-Being Measures', *Journal of Applied Arts & Health* 2.1 (2011), 37–56; Linda J.

Thomson, Erica E. Ander, Usha Menon, Anne Lanceley and Helen J. Chatterjee, 'Enhancing Cancer Patient Well-Being with a Nonpharmacological, Heritage-Focused Intervention', *Journal of Pain and Symptom Management* 44.5 (2012), 731–40; Thomson et al., 'Quantitative Evidence for Wellbeing Benefits'; Erica Ander, Linda Thomson, Guy Noble, Anne Lanceley, Usha Menon and Helen Chatterjee, 'Heritage, Health and Well-Being: Assessing the Impact of a Heritage Focused Intervention on Health and Well-Being', *International Journal of Heritage Studies* 19.3 (2013), 229–42; Thomson et al., 'Effects of a Museum-Based Social Prescription Intervention'.

20. Sayer, *Can Digging Make You Happy?*; Gallou et al., *Perceived Place Qualities, Restorative Effects and Self-Reported Wellbeing Benefits of Visits to Heritage Sites*; Andres Siegfried Dobat, Torben Trier Christiansen, Mads Dengsø Jessen, Mogens Bo Henriksen, Peter Jensen, Stine Vestergaard Laursen, Rikke Ruhe, Mads Kähler Holst and Freddy Arntsen, 'The Dime Project: Background, Status and Future Perspectives of a User Driven Recording Scheme for Metal Detector Finds as an Example of Participatory Heritage', *Danish Journal of Archaeology* 8 (2019), 1–15.
21. Linda Monkton, 'Wellbeing and the Historic Environment: A Strategic Approach', in Paul Everill and Karen Burnell (eds), *Archaeology, Heritage and Wellbeing: Authentic, Powerful and Therapeutic Engagement with the Past* (Routledge, 2022), 239–60.
22. What Works Centre for Wellbeing, 'Heritage and Wellbeing', https://whatworkswellbeing.org/resources/heritage-and-wellbeing-2 (accessed 11 September 2020).
23. Aked et al., *Five Ways to Wellbeing*; Michaelson et al., 'National Accounts of Well-Being'; Elsa Sereke Tesfazghi, J. A. Martinez and J. J. Verplanke, 'Variability of Quality of Life at Small Scales: Addis Ababa, Kirkos Sub-City', *Social Indicators Research* 98.1 (2010), 73–88; Guido Veronese, Alessandro Pepe, Jamal Dagdouke, Loredana Addimando and Shaher Yagi, 'Measuring Well-Being in Israel and Palestine: The Subjective Well-Being Assessment Scale', *Psychological Reports* 120.6 (2017), 1160–77.
24. Sayer, *Can Digging Make You Happy?*; Sayer, *Understanding Well-Being.*
25. David Watson, Lee Anna Clark and Auke Tellegen, 'Development and Validation of Brief Measures of Positive and Negative Affect: The Panas Scales', *Journal of Personality and Social Psychology* 54.6 (1988), 1063–70.
26. Sayer, *Understanding Well-Being.*
27. D. P. Goldberg and V. F. Hillier, 'A Scaled Version of the General Health Questionnaire', *Psychological Medicine* 9.1 (1979), 139–45; Office for National Statistics, 'Surveys Using Our Four Personal Well-Being Questions', www.ons.gov.uk/peoplepopulationandcommunity/wellbeing/methodologies/surveysusingthe4officefornationalstatisticspersonalwellbeingquestions (accessed 18 March 2020); Warwick Medical School, 'About Wemwbs', https://warwick.ac.uk/fac/sci/med/research/platform/wemwbs/about/ (accessed 7 February 2020); Aked et al., *Five Ways to Wellbeing.*
28. Patricia Leavy, *Research Design: Quantitative, Qualitative, Mixed Methods, Arts-Based, and Community-Based Participatory Research Approaches* (Guilford, 2017).
29. For all datasets, percentage differences between mean results (the percentage difference between before and after mean scores of PANAS words such as 'excited', for example) were calculated. Percentage difference changes among scores from each heritage place were then compared to assess the amount of impact participants experienced after visiting that place.
30. Either Wilcoxon signed rank test or the paired-sample sign test was utilized. In all tests, the null hypothesis assumed that the median of differences between (measured pre-test) and (measured post-test) equalled 0.

31. Robert A. Donnelly, Jr. and Fatma Abdel-Raouf, *Statistics* (Alpha, 2016). The two-tailed test was applied to test for change to an individual's well-being. The greater number of positive or negative differences observed determined the direction of change. If there were more negative matched pairs than positive, for example, the direction of change was determined to be negative. If a negative measure such as 'scared' had a negative direction of change (i.e., reduced), well-being was deemed to have improved.
32. Office for National Statistics, 'Personal Well-Being in the UK: April 2022 to March 2023', www.ons.gov.uk/peoplepopulationandcommunity/wellbeing/bulletins/measuringnationalwellbeing/april2022tomarch2023 (accessed 17 December 2024).
33. Office for National Statistics, 'Personal Well-Being in the UK'.
34. Office for National Statistics, 'Personal Well-Being in the UK'.
35. The socio-economic demographics of areas were measured by the UK government in the English Indices of Deprivation 2019. The overall Index of Multiple Deprivation 2019 describes each area by combining information from all seven domains: income deprivation, employment deprivation, health deprivation and disability, education skills and training deprivation, barriers to housing and services, living environment deprivation, and crime. Scores were located based on heritage place postcode via Ministry of Housing Communities & Local Government, 'English Indices of Deprivation 2019', http://imd-by-postcode.opendatacommunities.org/imd/2019 (accessed 27 April 2020).
36. Office for National Statistics, 'Personal Well-Being in the UK'.
37. Office for National Statistics, 'Personal Well-Being in the UK'.
38. Office for National Statistics, 'Personal Well-Being in the UK'.
39. Aked et al., *Five Ways to Wellbeing*.

13

'Art power': Creative workshops and social justice in the museum

Tamsin Greaves

Art Power is the name of a socially engaged project which took place at Mansfield Museum in the East Midlands of the UK between April 2022 and April 2024. It was funded by the Esmée Fairbairn Foundation, and forty-four women with lived experience of trauma have been involved in the programme which delivered 165 workshops. The project has since gained further funding and is continuing. I have the roles of community project coordinator at the museum and postgraduate researcher at Nottingham Trent University whose research explores whether creative workshops in museum spaces can improve the well-being of vulnerable participants. As such, I am positioned as a caring practitioner embedded in the delivery of the project with a research eye on the process. The chapter is written as the data generation phase is completed and two years of practice come to an end; it will foreground the participants' involvement in the recent exhibition 'Windrush: It Runs through Us' at Mansfield Museum.[1] It uses this case study to demonstrate how participants' engagement gradually develops as relationships build and trust is fostered. The case study offers a useful way to understand the benefits and challenges of a vulnerable group with shared experience. The chapter will firstly introduce the project's aims and its establishment, then interrogate the ideas of social justice and people care in the museum and finally explore the Windrush case study to frame the benefits and challenges which this careful but risky work has exposed. Its aim is to pause and reflect on the outcomes of this work as the second iteration of the project is planned and the qualitative data is analysed.

Well-being

The term well-being is defined as 'feeling good and functioning well' by the 2008 National Economic Foundation (NEF) report and the ONS uses 'how we are doing' as individuals. Measuring national well-being began in 2010 to look beyond GDP with the aim of developing a trusted set of national statistics to help understand and monitor well-being.[2] Well-being is a measure of how an individual feels within themselves and the website whatworkswellbeing.org offers 'the different things that make up our well-being: the quality of our health, work, relationships; how happy, anxious or satisfied we feel; how confident, purposeful, or connected our lives are', and the World Health Organization constitution defines health as 'physical, mental and social well-being, not merely the absence of disease or infirmity'.[3] The NEF report provides evidence for the five ways to well-being which have been adopted by the NHS and museums, they are 'connect', 'be active', 'keep learning', 'give' and 'take notice'. Well-being is now included in National Heritage Lottery Fund grant applications: museums must explain how, 'people will have greater well-being' as an impact of funding.

Art Power

The aims of the Art Power project are to develop self-confidence and social connections and to redefine a relationship to place for vulnerable women, particularly those living with the aftermath of domestic and sexual abuse. Art Power's participants are often not feeling good or functioning well as characterized above, and the project attempts to assist them towards a state of well-being. A sense of belonging is a fundamental human need and one that is often eroded in abusive relationships where isolation is a feature. Mansfield is a town of 110,000 people in the East Midlands, about half an hour north of Nottingham. It started out as a market town and has a beautiful square of soft yellow limestone. Mansfield has an industrial background, there used to be cotton mills, coal mining, metal tin manufacture, textiles and shoe production, but now there are significant levels of deprivation. Coming out of the pandemic, Mansfield District Council noticed an increase in calls for domestic abuse support and the cultural services manager, Sian Booth, successfully made the case for funding from the Esmée Fairbairn Foundation.

Following a period of relationship building with local services, which included making contact, sharing our aims and delivering some taster workshops in their premises, the Art Power project began to receive referrals from local service providers. These include Nottinghamshire Independent Domestic Abuse Service (NIDAS), Nottinghamshire Sexual Violence Support Service (NSVSS), Women's Aid, the Department of Work and Pensions (DWP) and social prescribers. However, it is one thing to collect a list of names and phone numbers, it is quite another to encourage women who are survivors of domestic and sexual abuse or other trauma to come to a new place, meet strangers and take part in an unknown creative well-being workshop. Often, they are managing complex intersectional challenges, such as mental ill health, administrative hurdles to benefits and income, the criminal justice system and power imbalances within the family court and divorce proceedings, child maintenance bureaucracy, housing challenges, anti-social behaviour issues, neighbour disputes, stalking and harassment, loneliness, poverty and unemployment among others. The impacts of domestic abuse, whether violent or coercive control, are long term, insidious and impact holistically on well-being. Women who are surviving such attacks on their selfhood are likely to have symptoms of post-traumatic stress disorder, are likely to demonstrate hyper-alert behaviours, to be socially anxious and lacking in confidence and self-worth. They may have been isolated and divided from families and friendships therefore, creating new social groups post-trauma can be challenging. These are the obstacles which the Art Power project was envisioned to mitigate, to try to improve the prospects and well-being of participants. The support services who refer women to the project offer crisis support and sometimes talking therapies and support groups. The museum project was established to continue the journey of recovery, to offer a longer term creative and social opportunity for participants to rediscover the confidence and social connections to take the next steps in rebuilding lives with positive futures.

To enable the participants to access the project, as many barriers as possible are removed: the project is cost free, the art materials, travel, childcare and refreshments are all taken care of, this enables the women to come for themselves, with no outgoings. Five groups were set up, each meeting every two to three weeks and including four to eight participants. The museum's collection of social history which includes ceramics, paintings, jewellery and taxidermy is used to inspire creative activity, curiosity and ultimately a stronger sense of place and identity. The participants are welcomed into the museum's store, where they often discover objects and artefacts which ground them in a sense of belonging and ownership. A range of freelance artists bring skills such as printing, felt making, collage and stitch, and an art therapist contributes her expertise. It has been a process of experimenting, of trial and error, seeing what works, and it is the collection, the creative activity, and the social connections which are regularly cited by the participants as the crux of the success of the project, as measured in their long-term commitment and the building of a supportive community.

Ethical approval was granted in April 2022 for the generation of data via the use of semi-structured interviews and peer-to-peer conversations. The participants gave informed consent for their dialogue to be recorded, and pseudonyms are used rather than numbered participants as it is more human and less distant. The quotations included in this chapter are taken from these conversations, for example:

> And yeah, just doing this, coming to the museum and doing whatever you choose for us to do. It takes me back to a happier time and a happy place and I forget my personal issues and I just do what I like doing and enjoying myself, yeah. (Annie)[4]
>
> I think the felt making was great. I know you can really get into it. It's like you're massaging it away and things and then you've got to roll it. And it was fun and really relaxing. And nerve wracking, but not to the same degree as some of the other things, yeah, but it was just like, right, OK, focus on what's being said. Get stuck, just ask. And I don't feel awkward asking here. (Sally)[5]
>
> I have tendencies I think sometimes, to just be quite insular and don't really interact and actually, here, I don't have to feel like I've got to be like that. (Ginny)[6]

People care in the museum

The chapter posits the museum as a site of people care in a post-pandemic world with its focus on well-being. Accepting that the museum is now a site for social care has come about in part because of its unique set of attributes, namely its space, collection and staff – as well as what it aims not to be, including authoritarian or judgemental. Woodham et al. in an illuminating article consider the ethics of care in the National Slag Collection.[7] Slag is a biproduct of the iron manufacture process and the collection belongs to the Ironbridge Gorge Museum Trust in Shropshire. The article considers this 'unloved' collection through the lens of care. They claim that it is reasonable to consider the museum as a site of care and that care in the museum goes beyond the collection and includes nurturing connections between people.[8] The Art Power project builds on work done in this field by many practitioners who are creatively caring for participants living with a range of challenges in museums and other sites all over the UK and further afield. Two recent examples are the Crannog pottery project in Scotland,[9] which worked with participants with experience of domestic abuse, and the Image through Time project in Doncaster, which partnered with the NHS and engaged with participants living with eating disorders.

The Art Power workshops propose the hypothesis that a local, small-town museum such as Mansfield can provide an entry point to a potentially beneficent experience. Can creative workshops in the museum enable marginalized women to enjoy artmaking and develop new social connections? There are many elements to consider when establishing such a scheme, not least that the demographic of women who are surviving domestic and sexual abuse is likely to throw up curveballs which require solid planning and quick reflexes. Unsurprisingly, a participant's first visit can be very challenging, as Jenny describes: 'Well, I was very nervous about coming 'cause to me, going new places and being places I don't know before … I can't do it no matter what. I could have got to the bus station – but I couldn't have walked out of the bus station so.'[10]

Coming to a new place, meeting new people, possibly feeling exposed in your artistic capacity: Will I be good enough? What will I be expected to do? Who will be there? All these considerations may be obstacles to participation. Although many strategies have been reviewed to enable and empower women to come, this is often the hardest element. To mitigate some of these obstacles, Monday workshops mean that the public are not at the museum, which is helpful, particularly for women who are afraid of meeting a perpetrator who is still at large, for example. For some participants an orientation visit is useful, giving time and space to meet the facilitator so that at least one face is known. Mansfield Museum is a complicated space having originally been built in 1905 and added to in the 1960s and 1980s. The workshops can take place in several different rooms and spaces, and it is helpful to let participants know where we will be meeting. Women who are living with (C)PTSD tend to dislike surprises, so making sure they know who will be there, where we will be and what we will be doing, all serve to mitigate hyper-alert states.

It is impossible to guess the triggers which might lead to retraumatizing a participant. WhatsApp groups have been set up to facilitate communication, originally between the museum and the participants but, increasingly, as a communication tool intragroup. A focus on belonging which is designed into the groups' structure is bearing fruit, the philosophy is based on 'trying things out and modifying to ensure meaningful inclusion'.[11] The participants bring their own expertise and knowledge to the museum, and several have delivered workshops to their Art Power groups. This skill sharing is a powerful tool, and participants have developed confidence and garnered positive feedback from their peers. As assurance in their abilities has increased, higher stakes contributions have developed, for example two participants sold their craft items at the museum's Christmas Fair. This involved them displaying their work and engaging with visitors and was both challenging and empowering.

Alongside the practical art workshops, the project organizes trips to local art galleries, museums and heritage sites. These safe space[12] events are popular, with several participants saying that these are their only social outings. The events primarily offer a day out, visits to inspirational sites, the chance to engage with artworks, a social activity and always include a visit to the café; they offer the participants social time for themselves without cost. During a visit to Nottingham Castle one of the participants dissolved into tears at the café table, saying, 'I just can't believe something so nice is happening to me.' Many of the participants have caring responsibilities, which mean that time to focus on their own needs and desires is rare:

> I think I've most enjoyed just having the space with other people and listening to them and their enthusiasm, we've had some day trips out and I found that to be absolutely amazing. I love that time I saw a Lowry, an original Lowry, and I literally had to drag myself away and she said 'no, go back and have another look if you want to', and I don't feel rushed, I could take my time and that's what surprised me, that every time I get home I feel more energised. (Ginny)[13]

The space has become a trusted environment, and as the staff and participants become mutually familiar, staff are able to signpost and reveal opportunities and embed cultural participation. For example, a participant attending a holiday activity with her children was offered free seats at a family performance staged in the museum, and the project funds our participants' children to attend pay-to-access workshops and subsidizes places for summer drama camps and dance workshops.

Magic happens. To explain, here is a description of what can happen when a group of participants are in the museum space together. They are engaged and engrossed in an art activity in a time and space which is exclusive to them. They are exploring a new technique; it might be clay, felt, enamelling, and they are focused, concentrating on making it turn out how they imagine it. The task is challenging but achievable, and they are talking to each other: one is describing her daughter's situation, how her partner is threatening to leave with their child and how he has control of her money, how he wants her to work and earn money but also be at home keeping house. The other women listen and empathize with noises and joining in, recognizing from their own experience, adding details and making suggestions. Another participant describes her burlesque dance routine, telling how it allows her to reclaim her sense of self and she demonstrates some moves amidst screams of laughter and giggles. The women have created a supportive safe space for conversation, disclosure and fun; the magic is happening. The art workshop is the vehicle, it provides a powerful reason to claim the space, connecting with artworks and objects in their town museum, their history, their place. It is time out of time, with the focus on the process as much as the outcome.

The shared life and work experience of group members is used to the benefit of participants, for example, a participant's son was struggling to fit in at a large primary school in part due to his SEND[14] status, another participant was able to give insider advice through experience gained in her role as special needs adviser. Subsequently, the mother was empowered to manage his move to a smaller school with a proactive special needs department where her child is now flourishing. Other opportunities are practical, such as access to a foodbank[15] and clothes swap-shop. Being part of a local authority means signposting and connecting with council services such as the domestic abuse team and housing are available, and we have relationships with services which can expedite seeking advice for our participants. Following an exhibition about the history of chocolate, a participant with Caribbean heritage shared her skills and knowledge of the traditional method of making a chocolate drink from a raw cacao pod. Another participant who is a metal detectorist shared her finds with the curator at the archaeology museum which we visited. These contacts are meaningful and empowering.

Social justice

Social justice work in the museum lies in a sweet spot at the intersection of art practice, art therapy and social work, and its analysis draws on literature from a range of contexts. Social justice is defined by the 2012 UK government report as follows: 'Social Justice is about making society function better – providing the support and tools to help turn lives around [and] it must be about changing and improving lives.'[16] The manifesto of the museum's association for learning and engagement states, 'Museums have a responsibility to work with their communities to overcome the challenges of poverty and exclusion and to achieve equality of outcomes'; in addition 'social justice means museums working with their communities to enhance health and well-being, create better places to live and work, and provide opportunities for debate and reflection'.[17] The museum's curator, Jodie Henshaw, describes Mansfield Museum as a community centre with a collection, and this is an accurate description. The museum has evolved into a porous public space with multiple entry points, including doorways for visitors, volunteers, work experience, associate artists and groups hosted at the museum including Better by Change (work opportunities for people with disabilities), an under-five group, a reminiscence café, Young Curators, Make a Start (a social group for people suffering from isolation) and Growing Bolder (a craft group). The Art Power participants have come through some extremely uncomfortable, difficult and traumatic experiences, nevertheless, they have formed a joyous and supportive community which demonstrates the potential for such a project to care for participants who suffer multiple disadvantage in the personal politics of the UK in 2024. The participants referred to the Art Power project by various support services tend to live on the bumpy side of the uneven playing field of life. Most are survivors of domestic or sexual abuse, all have faced multiple challenges. A simply stated goal of the project is to ensure that however the participants feel as they arrive at the museum, they feel better when they leave. In the words of another participant:

> And you've kind of isolated yourself a little bit and you feel sometimes like you're the only person who's gone through something rubbish. It's really good when you meet other people. Like I say, we don't always discuss what we've gone through, but it's obviously a common thing. And everyone's so lovely. I think it's important to like, rebuild different connections and yeah it does that. (Jenny)[18]

A feature of trauma-informed services is that people are prioritized above systems in a responsive and flexible culture of care, and the following case study at the museum provides a framework to consider this.[19]

Benefits and challenges: 'Windrush: It Runs through Us'

Mansfield Museum co-curated a Windrush exhibition designed as part of the interrogation of Mansfield's colonial past. The participants of the Art Power project became engaged with, and in some cases involved with, this piece of work. The exhibition ran from February to November 2023 and is the first outcome of an ongoing project to collect oral histories from local people of the Windrush generation and their descendants. One such local Windrush pioneer was Samuel Case, a coal miner and the first Black man elected as a deacon by a 120-strong congregation at Mansfield's Baptist Church. The Art Power participants also delved into the background of a full-length oil portrait in its collection, of Laetitia Hollins, painted by an unknown artist. Laetitia was the wife of William Hollins, whose family ran the mill at Pleasley which produced Viyella, the first branded fabric, from 1890. During a visit to the Harley Gallery in Welbeck, UK, the Art Power group saw a 2020 relief print by the British Nigerian artist, Yinka Shonibare. His work *Mayflower, All Flowers* shows an image of the Mayflower ship. It is a potent symbol of colonial expansion illustrating the departure of the ship to the New World in 1620. Shonibare's Mayflower has sails made from multicoloured batik fabric which was produced by Dutch colonists and sold to the colonies in West Africa. As a symbol of African identity, the fabric's history is a metaphor of changing cultural identity over time. In the Mansfield portrait, which is the largest in the museum's collection, the mill owner's wife, Laetitia Hollins, is depicted wearing a black Victorian dress, interpreted as mourning the death of her husband. For the exhibition, a new version of it was created, replacing panels of the dress and elements of the face, with Dutch wax prints. The two portraits, old and new, were displayed adjacently, suggesting opportunities for discussion around colonization and gender for the Art Power groups, as well as the wider audience.

A mural illustrating the arrival of the HMT Windrush at Tilbury docks in 1948 was painted on the gallery wall. The image by Joelle Avelino was borrowed from Dame Floella Benjamin's book *The Place for Me: Stories about the Windrush Generation*, and some Art Power participants joined in the painting. The team completed a wall-to-floor mural in time for the exhibition's opening. Another participant, an expert crochet-crafter made various elements for the exhibition including a crocheted fedora hat, a suitcase and passport. She gained a sense of empowerment and belonging from her work being included in the exhibition: 'Yeah, but like, you know the Windrush things, yes, I know I was a bit not on time with getting everything ready but it's an honour. To have these things or be asked to do these things, and appreciated that's a biggie, you know?' (Sally)[20]

The first Mansfield Carnival also grew out of the work on the exhibition and the Art Power project became involved. The organic nature of deepening engagement becomes naturally occurring as the museum space is shared with the participants. As they have developed confidence and trust in the staff and purpose of the museum, they have become empowered to offer ideas and opinions. Following discussions during workshops around the Windrush exhibition, the participants suggested that an Art Power troupe could be possible. Together a workshop was planned to create carnival headdresses. Some women were happy to show their faces and others wore masks with their head pieces to protect their anonymity. In June 2023 twenty women and children paraded through the centre of Mansfield as part of their own Art Power troupe. To see women who had been hesitant attendees of their first workshops at the museum, sporting Art Power t shirts and wearing their handmade headgear was moving and compelling:

> I really enjoyed it, the carnival. Yeah, I came to that and made the feather headdresses. And that was with a bigger group as well.
>
> I found it really fun because I was allowed to bring my daughter. It's like, oh, and I thought it would be a really good experience for her and also … when I'm with her, I tend to make out everything is all great and wonderful. 'Oh, this is really great.' We're going to do this even though I'm feeling really nervous because I don't want her to pick up on my anxiety. And she was a bit nervous that day.
>
> But obviously we knew Ange anyway because she came along. It was just really fun experience being part of the carnival and it's like I said to her, you know, this opportunity might not come again and it's nice to do things that are different and make memories. And we've got some really nice pictures that we've taken of both of us. (Jenny)[21]

Some of these artworks have been accessioned into Mansfield Museum's collection, endowing the artists with a sense of belonging and pride. Social connections have also developed independently of the workshops and some friendships are blossoming, for instance two participants always leave together and have an explore of Mansfield's charity shops and a coffee together before going home, and one introduced another to a single friend and the pair have begun a relationship; participants help each other out with childcare and these social relationships are a direct result of the workshops. Making friends in a context where both have some shared experience appears to be empowering and helps trust to develop.

> It's made me feel that I have got that creative outlet that I've got likeminded people to share with and actually it's a really safe space. (Ginny)[22]
>
> That's one of the things I've loved about this group, actually, that you feel like you've got that lovely, warm environment, so yeah. (Samantha)[23]

The WhatsApp group provides a safe space for connection beyond the workshops: a participant in a custody dispute asked for help, and others in the group who have experience of family courts and non-molestation orders contributed advice.

Judith Herman emphasizes the danger of retraumatizing in a group situation if the risks are not mitigated and Catherine Cartwright's study of trauma-informed practice makes the point, 'The lack of understanding about trauma by practitioners working with people affected by trauma risks compounding their effects.'[24] The Art Power group sits within Herman's model of the three stages of recovery from trauma: safety, remembrance and mourning and reconnection. These stages are not necessarily distinct and there is much overlap, but the third stage of reconnection is where a museum group can enable the creation of interpersonal relationships. The Art Power group is not a therapy group, but it can be therapeutic and a permissive leadership style is aimed for, Herman's description of a third stage interpersonal group matches the experience of the Art Power group, 'interpersonal groups are typically open-ended, with a stable, slowly evolving membership … and are relatively unstructured … they offer the possibility of rejoining a wider world and forming connections with a broader range of people'.[25] This analysis is borne out by Jenny's comments:

> It's just a nice group of people and I think sometimes people who've gone through some not very nice stuff, are often some of the nicest people, they've had the worst things happened to them. So I think we've all got that kind of respect for each other's feelings as well, which I think is nice in this group as well, you know, and we all give each other time to talk if we're saying something, yeah. (Jenny)[26]

The membership of the Mansfield group has stabilized during the twenty-month period to a committed cohort of twenty-five participants shared over five groups. A total of eighty women have had some connection, fifty-five have attended at least one session, and thirty-five have attended at least two sessions.

Social justice through shared experiences

During the two years of the Art Power project there have been many positive outcomes, artistically and socially, but also real challenges. As the relationships between participants and museum staff have developed, often the connections with the referring services have diminished and sometimes disappeared. This may signal a positive step as the participant continues her recovery but also means the museum has become the primary source of support when difficulties arise. Emotional upsets caused by impossible-to-predict triggers, safeguarding reports, disclosures of abuse, a participant sectioned under the mental health act, a move out of refuge into a new home, support for a participant to give a police statement, and respite accommodation for a family in flight – are all instances of real scenarios. All have presented the framework of the Art Power project with new challenges. The structure, services and support of Mansfield District Council are instrumental in meeting such challenges, but the emotion work is considerable. The surrounding framework of the district council has provided expertise and facilitated information gathering, signposting and advice. As trust is built, emotional responses increase, as a safe space for sharing is created and museum staff become trusted friends: these outcomes were unforeseen at the establishment of the project but have developed with the depth of engagement. Working together with agencies such as Women's Aid, the council's housing department, social prescribers and the Department of Work and Pensions (DWP), it is possible to provide a helping hand in rebuilding lives. NIDAS[27] was an early referring partner of the project and supplied initial domestic abuse awareness training to the museum team. Since then, Mansfield District Council has gained DAHA[28] accreditation, which involved training for all council employees and signposting across the council. The museum's relationship with the DWP has expanded and connections have been made with the J9 Domestic Abuse Initiative, which trains professionals and members of the community to recognize domestic abuse and respond to survivors.[29]

The museum space is not the NHS with its system of clear clinical patient/health worker boundaries. In the museum, the staff are facilitators, carers, friends, and the relationships don't end at 5 p.m. or at the weekend. The boundaries have to be worked out, negotiated in each case, and it is difficult sometimes to know if boundaries are even relevant. A strong team who can take the time to consider, discuss and advise is crucial to the success of social justice work in the museum. It is a very human-centred way of working which creates a circle of care encompassing participants, facilitators, freelancers and museum staff. There are clear connections with concepts used in a social work context, particularly around boundaries. It is comforting to know that social work also interrogates the idea of boundaries, with their subjectivity and awareness of cultural contexts. An open, relational understanding of where boundaries might lie, as described by O'Leary et al., requires sensitive, context-specific responses which include care and concern.[30] Rather than static barriers, decisions are negotiated in the interpersonal space, relationally, between participants and staff.

The emotion work engendered by caring in the museum is substantial and should not be underestimated when considering the delivery of social justice initiatives. All involved are engaged in the work of recovery and support: the participants themselves, the facilitators and the wider museum staff. The position of Mansfield Museum as part of the cultural services provided by Mansfield District Council (MDC) means access can be provided to all the services, which again and again have improved outcomes for the participants and kept the whole team safe. For example, a participant arrived in a distressed state, unable to join the workshop because she had just received upsetting news. She had received the results of her application to the Domestic Violence Disclosure Scheme (DVDS), also known as Clare's Law, which allows someone to apply for relevant information from their partner's past history if there is a concern of abuse or risk to the applicant. The results were given in confidence but had clearly revealed disturbing news regarding the background of the perpetrator. Through listening, acknowledging and discussing and by an intervention of kindness by another group member, the participant concerned came into the workshop and left an hour later with an open, smiling face, better able to tackle the rest of her day. Later she posted a message to the group: 'There is a real strength in weaknesses. And you know from all the wounds and obstacles we have all had to face, the scars are something to be thankful for in the end because without them you wouldn't realize how beautiful you all are' (Paula).[31]

Every member of the MDC workforce has received domestic abuse awareness training. The input of artists and practitioners who share their skills to demonstrate techniques and develop ideas and solutions are a crucial element of the project. The pace of a workshop can be fast or slow in response to the mood of the room: sometimes conversation is prioritized, sometimes there is an energy to complete a task, but the visiting artists who are the most successful just 'get it'. It is important to ensure that time is taken to consider the experience of the freelance artists and art therapist who are valued collaborators. The freelance artists who play a pivotal role in delivering workshops yet whose emotional labour can be overlooked as they arrive, deliver and depart. The well-being of the freelance artists is integral to this model of museum care: these experts are peripatetic museum visitors, and opportunities to gather their feedback, as well as to support their well-being, are important to build into the project's structure. The museum staff includes mental health first aiders as well as 24/7 online mental health support. Staff facilitating the project have access to supervision, which is an important element of a healthy project working with marginalized communities. It provides an important space to offload and reflect with a professional.

Conclusions

Mansfield Museum is a site of people care, so far, the evidence for the well-being benefits of creative workshops in the museum is demonstrating concrete results such as continued engagement of more than two years. Notable increases in confidence and autonomy have led to outcomes such as one participant volunteering with a mental health support group, another now independently travelling to the museum and one leading a church craft group. The necessity for the work is clear. Many interventions such as talking therapies offered by the NHS and the third sector are short term, usually lasting only a few weeks, and the relief of being part of a long-term engagement is very apparent in this group. At the project's start, many participants were encouraged by the relatively long duration (two years), extended funding has since been secured and the participants feel valued as a result.

Looking ahead to the next iteration of the project, the focus will be on a sustainable agenda, driven by the participants' interests. One suggestion which has come from the group is a request for targeted workshops with the purpose of discussing the trauma that brought them to the project. Although this does happen in an ad hoc fashion, there is a desire in some to create a space for a more overt opportunity. The expertise of the art therapist will be important here to ensure the well-being of all. An exhibition 'Red Flags' is being planned to explore the warning signs of abusive relationships, and we have become custodians of a Victorian greenhouse in a park next door to the museum and have grown vegetables and held well-being workshops in the fresh air. We are also beginning to incorporate some dance and movement sessions to ensure the five ways to well-being are all being exploited to further develop the well-being of participants and staff. Our ultimate goal is to secure core funding for this social museology.

Notes

1. Mansfield District Council, 'Windrush Pioneers Celebrated in Mansfield Museum', 15 February 2023, www.mansfield.gov.uk/news/article/12637/windrush-pioneers-celebrated-in-mansfield-museum-exhibition.

2. Office for National Statistics, *Measuring National Well-being: Quality of Life in the UK* (ONS Report, 2018), www.ons.gov.uk/peoplepopulationandcommunity/wellbeing/articles/measuringnationalwellbeing/qualityoflifeintheuk2018.
3. World Health Organization, 'Health and Well- Being', www.who.int/Data/Gho/Data/Major-Themes/Health-and-Well-Being (accessed 11 January 2024).
4. Participant 9 semi-structured interview, 2 October 2023.
5. Participant 1 semi-structured interview, 6 September 2023.
6. Participant 8 semi-structured interview, 24 August 2023.
7. Anna Woodham, Alison Hess, Rhianedd Smith, *Exploring Emotion, Care, and Enthusiasm in 'Unloved' Museum Collections*, 1st ed. (Arc Humanities Press, 2020).
8. Woodham et al., *Exploring Emotion, Care, and Enthusiasm.*
9. Crannog Centre, 'Launch of the Pottery Project', 2023, https://crannog.co.uk/blog/category/projects-blogs (accessed 28 November 2023).
10. Participant 5 semi-structured interview, 18 September 2023.
11. Susie Wise, *Design for Belonging* (Ten Speed Press, 2022).
12. The term safe space refers to places 'intended to be free of bias, conflict, criticism, or potentially threatening actions, ideas, or conversations'; safe space has its origins in LGBT culture but now includes any place where a marginalized minority can be together to share experiences.
13. Participant 8 peer-to-peer conversation, 14 September 2022.
14. SEND stands for Special Educational Needs and Disabilities, an acronym used in schools.
15. Information about local food banks and food clubs is available on a notice board where the group meets.
16. Iain Duncan Smith, *Social Justice: Transforming Lives* (Department of Work and Pensions, 2012).
17. David Anderson, Dhikshana Pering and Sharon Heal, 'A Manifesto for Museum Learning and Engagement', *Museums Association*, www.museumsassociation.org/campaigns/learning-and-engagement/manifesto (accessed 27 November 2023).
18. Participant 3 semi-structured interview, 18 September 2023.
19. Jo Wilton and Alec Williams, 'Engaging with Complexity', *Centre for Mental Health*, www.centreformentalhealth.org.uk/publications/engaging-complexity (accessed 5 January 2024).
20. Participant 1 semi-structured interview, 6 September 2023.
21. Participant 6 semi-structured interview, 18 September 2023.
22. Participant 8 peer-to-peer conversation, 14 September 2022.
23. Participant 11 peer-to-peer conversation, 11 August 2022.
24. Catherine Cartwright, 'Careful Museums Conference', Nottingham Trent University, 29 June 2023.
25. Judith Lewis Herman, *Trauma and Recovery: The Aftermath of Violence – From Domestic Abuse to Political Terror* (Basic Books, 2022), 343.
26. Participant 6 semi-structured interview, 18 September 2023.
27. Nottinghamshire Independent Domestic Abuse Service.
28. Domestic Abuse Housing Alliance.

29. Janet Dalrymple, 'J9 Initiative', www.saferplaces.co.uk/about/meet-the-team (accessed 27 November 2023).
30. Ming-Sum Tsui, Gillian Ruch and Patrick O'Leary, 'The Boundaries of the Social Work Relationship Revisited: Towards a Connected, Inclusive and Dynamic Conceptualisation', *British Journal of Social Work* 43.1 (2013).
31. Participant 7 WhatsApp message, 25 November 2023.

> Leisure is also a medium through which other rights and related benefits set out in the Universal Declaration of Human Rights and associated covenants can be exercised, including: the physical, mental, emotional and social development of the child through play; support for family life; personal expression and development; sustaining of the cultural life of the community; and promotion of physical and mental health and well-being through sport, physical activity and cultural engagement. Conversely, denial of time for beneficial leisure activity can have serious consequences for the well-being of individuals and societies.

Underpinning the rights to leisure in this provision is the claim for individual and societal well-being. This obligation to achieve these rights is specifically assigned to national governments as detailed in Article 7 with a specific commitment to ensure the inclusion of access for all to leisure highlighted in subsection (f):

> Recognizing that governments at all levels are not the only providers of facilities and services for leisure and that they face many challenges and competing demands for resources, they nevertheless have particular responsibilities to:
>
>> ensure that all members of the community, regardless of age, gender, sexual orientation, ethnicity, religion, ability or income, have access to beneficial leisure facilities and services.[13]

Despite these covenants of Human Rights, stark disparities persist in the level of participation in outdoor leisure and tourism by ethnic minority and marginalized communities across the developed countries of Europe and the United States.[14]

Several theories have been postulated to explain the lower levels of participation of ethnically diverse communities in outdoor leisure and tourism. Historically, the lower economic and social status of Black and Asian communities was deemed to be the key reason for their limited participation in the UK.[15] This thinking was conceptualized in marginalization theory that contended that the low participation in leisure of ethnic minoritized groups was attributable to their relative lower incomes and financial wealth. It was further argued that this lack of resources shaped their perception of leisure and travel that resulted in distinct differences and preferences for leisure activities from the white majority population.[16]

As ethnic minorities have been predominantly resident in urban areas the conventional view was that they were not accustomed to or appreciative of the countryside. Their limited presence in rural settings was therefore deemed to be consequent to their inherent alienation from these landscapes where they were likely to be uncomfortable, lacking in the social competencies to benefit from the outdoors and ignorant on how to preserve its natural patrimony. This presumption of the cultural deficit regarding rural mores was factored into the sentiment that non-whites in the countryside were transgressors simply by their visibility and behaviour. According to Askins,[17] the white community had the privilege of being visible in rural settings which conformed with social norms which was essentially opposed to ethnic difference which was deemed a signifier of deviant behaviour. Askins explains this notion of the visible community that defined the countryside as an essentially white space:

> Thus the stereotype of visible community absence from the countryside shifts to a new stereotype, which describes non-whites as behaving differently from a white 'norm': only visiting national parks in large extended family groups, not wearing 'appropriate' (read 'normal') clothing for walking, and so on. This production recoups visible communities, again, as essentially 'other', through contrasting the behaviours of white and non-white groups.[18]

This construction of the pastoral as essentially white spaces was also extended to the seaside. According to Burdsey,[19] the English seaside has traditionally been represented as a 'white' environment in the popular imagination, and racialized bodies are frequently marked as 'out of place'. He argues that these cultural inflections of English identity were spatially associated with leisure and mass tourism at the seaside:

> Yet, as a source of popular culture, the English seaside has always been an inherently (albeit subtly) racialized environment. Ever since its modern designation as a venue for mass leisure, and the pursuit of liminal experiences and carnivalesque behaviours, the English seaside has been a site for the consumption of Orientalist, neo-colonial and, at times, overtly racist themed amusements and entertainments. Since the post-war era, it has held strong associations with particular forms of white working-class popular culture and middle-class leisure, along with celebrations of 'traditional' Englishness. Indeed, like the countryside, it can be conceptualized as 'a repository of white values, ideologies and lifestyles'.[20]

With the spatial conceptualization of white spaces of leisure in British cultural lifestyles and praxis, the absence of Black and Asian Britons in these settings was explained by a discourse of difference. This meant that these communities were considered to have different patterns of leisure and travel behaviour that were distinctly related to their culture and religious beliefs that determined their lack of inclination for varied outdoor leisure activities such as rambling or sea-bathing on the coast. Furthermore, this acceptance of the cultural deficit model of the Black and British Asians justified the claim that as a market segment they did not generate sufficient effective demand, to justify their targeted marketing or even their representation along white people in leisure and travel media advertisements and campaigns.

However, a seminal study of the travel preferences of British Asian in Bradford, England by Mary S. Klemm found that the travel behaviour of this community was not significantly different from the white community as they all did not wish to travel only to their ancestral home countries.[21] Her findings indicated that Asians expressed similar motivation for outdoor leisure and recreational experiences as white residents in Bradford. They also expressed their desire to engage in traditional mass tourism holidays and would participate more if they were presented in 'culturally appropriate ways and the promotional methods at the local level were designed to reach their community'. The underlying claims of the marginality thesis have been undermined by evidence that shows that despite the narrowing of the income gap, racial disparities in leisure and participation endure. Notably, even as Back and Asian communities' spending on travel has surpassed that of the white population, they are still not acknowledged as a viable market by leisure and tourism service providers and marketers in the UK.[22]

The marginalization thesis and other ethno-cultural theories therefore implicate race and some ethnic cultural practices as the main factors that determine differences in leisure and tourism preferences. From this vantage point, lower levels of participation were viewed as an inherent and intrinsic cultural practice, rather than attributable to external, structural factors that were intentionally exclusionary and racist.[23] Since the late twentieth century, the application of race conscious theories has gained prominence with research that indicates that the construction of the pastoral, outdoor and leisured spaces primarily as white spaces have been the main drivers of lower participation levels. Critical race theory which is one of the more popular variants has been applied in a range of studies to deepen understanding of how racism accounts for the systemic differences in leisure and travel preferences across diverse ethnic groups.[24]

Generally, the study of leisure and tourism has mainly reflected the views and experiences of the 'promoters of tourism or tourists themselves, particularly of Europeans travelling in the empire and Europeans travelling within Europe' that have obscured the lives of non-white, colonialized subjects that were always present.[25] However, there has been a noticeable turn among some researchers to reclaim the presence and visibility of people of colour in the historical narratives of Britain, by recording and valuing the experiences of ethnic minoritized communities in social and economic development. The influential work of Imtiaz Habib on *Black Lives in the English Archives* has convincingly contested the notion of the hidden, secret and invisible population of Black people in early English society. Habib uncovered in his archival research the practice of what he refers to as 'ontological anonymity' that either rendered Black people as human fetishes or obscured them from sight as having 'nothing in themselves'.[26] Fowler has also challenged this notion of the invisibility of Black and Asian communities in the history and experiences of the pastoral countryside and rural life.[27] Her central thesis argues that the story of empire must include their contribution to the reimagining of the pastoral in their literary writings, photography and horticultural work in plants and gardens from the nascent period of colonization to the present day. Fowler's research reinscribes tropes of the British landscape through the imagination of the Black and Asian British writers which undermines the traditional erasure of people of colour in the historiography of the English countryside.

By tracing the historical roots of the exclusion of ethnic minorities from the countryside, leisured spaces and domestic tourism, the case has been presented of the structured barriers that may account for their lower levels of participation in these activities. This study therefore examines how far these systemic barriers continue to be perceived as hindrances among people of colour in the UK. There have been shifts in the socio-economic status of the Black and Asian communities with rising income and educational levels among second and third generation immigrants that could possibly influence contemporary changes in travel preferences and behaviour. Furthermore, the legal and regulatory environment has raised wider public awareness of racism with the passing of the Equality Act in 2010 which combined various anti-discrimination laws into one to *provide protection from any unlawful treatment (discrimination, harassment, or victimization) for persons with protected characteristics*. These have been named as disability, race including colour, nationality, ethnic or national origin, religion, belief, or sex. With the obligation of employers in both the public and private sectors to make provisions of reasonable adjustments and to mainstream equality in their operations, the focus has been on addressing systemic inequalities. Nevertheless, the dismantling of racial barriers to access and participation in leisure and tourism seem to be intractable as evidenced in data indicating the gaps compared with those of the white population in the UK.

Well-being and ethnic minority travel

The promise of well-being and a healthier life as motivation to travel was promoted by the tourism pioneer Thomas Cook in selling his packaged tours to the Victorian middle classes in the UK.[28] This was aligned to his temperance values that campaigned against alcohol consumption while extolling the virtues of travel as a force for moral and educational upliftment as well as physical and mental rejuvenation. Seaside visits to 'take the waters'; hiking in the Peak District and other greenspaces were activities that both the elite and working class engaged in for rest and recreation. Particularly for the growing numbers of urban factory workers, Thomas Cook tours provided the opportunity to escape the pollution and drudgery of industrial cities and for them to see and enjoy more salubrious landscapes and the great outdoors.[29] This rise of mass tourism fuelled by the desire for escape, to renew and recreate from the debilitating effects of the harsh industrial working life were the dominant push factors driving the white majority population in the UK and which continues to define the consumer behaviour of the modern tourist.

With the post-war years there was the influx of Asian and West Indian immigrants to the UK to join the workforce and to supply the shortfall of labour needed to rebuild the infrastructure and economy of the country. As ethnic minoritized communities who were invited and recruited to work in the UK, the notion of taking time out for recreation and well-being seemed improbable as they were predominantly employed in low paying jobs which denied them the financial means to even go on one-day excursions in the UK. The stereotypes associated with Asians was that as a cultural group they were for the most part motivated to work as many hours possible in a twenty-four-hour day. For the West Indians and those from the African subcontinent, holidays and vacations were only earned after years of penny-pinching saving to take a trip back home to their countries of origin to see family and friends. This widespread view that ethnic minorities in the UK didn't really share the same desires for escape and well-being in going on domestic or international holidays as the white population is recounted in this passage below on the history of the tour company Thomas Cook:

> The holiday is a concept of comparatively recent origin and for a variety of reasons has been artificially promoted quite apart from social acquisitiveness generated by emulation of other people's pleasure. This is surely proved by the attitude of the several million immigrations from Asia and the West Indies who have been quite bewildered by this annual migration of British people to the sea and to the

> Continent. Days off they can understand and feast days like Diwali but the notion of leaving home for a week or a fortnight once a year unless it is to visit distant relatives is a very difficult notion to adopt. The West Indian even if he is attracted to the idea, cannot contemplate the expense since his saving are often dedicated to his triennial trip home to Jamaica, Guyana or Barbados. The Asian cannot afford the time.

This assumption of the travel motivations of immigrants mainly from the British colonies in post war Britain may account for the lack of representation of ethnic minoritized communities in domestic UK tourism marketing and the paucity of sustained research on their travel behaviour that persists to this day. Arguably the perceptions that well-being was not a primary travel motivation of ethnic minoritized immigrants became institutionalized in leisure, tourism and hospitality organizations that in turn reinforced barriers to their participation as their needs and preferences were not accommodated.

In the United States there has been growing activism challenging stereotypes of a lack of motivation for escape and well-being among Afro-American travellers. Recent studies conducted in the United States, refer to the phenomenon of Black tourism as 'simultaneously an emancipatory and community-building force, an expression of joy and discovery, and a site of contest and resilience against racialized oppression'.[30] The pursuit of well-being as a key motivation for Black leisure travel was also highlighted in a study of the sentiments expressed by Afro-American travellers on the social media platform Instagram. Based on the findings of their study, the authors concluded:

> Black travel is motivated and influenced in part by the desire to enhance well-being or to flourish – a state of being in which an individual feels positive emotions towards life and is functioning well in the social, physical, emotional, and spiritual, and psychological domains of life.[31]

These indicators of the motivations for well-being and flourishing expressed by ethnic minority travellers in these studies from the United States are clear contradictions of pervasive yet dubious claims of their travel behaviour.

Ethnic minority participation in domestic tourism and outdoor leisure in the UK

Statistics from VisitBritain, the ethnic minority segment represents 0.1 per cent of the total domestic tourism market in the UK. The latest data on domestic tourism disaggregated by ethnicity, which was conducted in 2018, show that there were 2.8 million overnight holiday trips taken by ethnic minorities in the UK. This compared to nearly 55 million by the White population. Overall, the UK domestic tourism market is dominated by the British white population that represents 88 per cent of all visitors. Moreover, ethnic whites seem to take more trips (e.g. three trips to every one taken by a non-white) and more diverse trips ranging from the countryside and urban locations to the seaside, coastal areas as well as to historic and heritage attractions.[32]

There is a similar level of low participation in the other leisure sectors of outdoor recreation and sports that show a pattern of comparable racial disparities. These sectors intersect with tourism as the backbone of the domestic holiday experience, as the range of activities they offer are pull factors that attract both day trippers and overnight stay visitors to destinations. Many domestic tourists engage in outdoor activities and a range of sporting activities such as golf, cycling and sailing among others as a part of their holiday package. As such, data from surveys and studies conducted by agencies and organizations who steward the natural environment and the national sport governing body are useful sources of information to glean an understanding of the differing levels of ethnic participation in leisure activities that occur on day trips and overnight holidays.

The historic underrepresentation and engagement of ethnic minorities in outdoor recreational leisure activities have been a pressing concern of agencies mandated with stewardship of the natural environment. In March 2005, the Countryside Agency, now Natural England, published the *Diversity Review: Options for Implementation* which represented a focal, comprehensive study on the scope of racial marginalization that was captured from interviews of the lived experiences of ethnic minority groups. The main findings indicated that ethnic minorities were hindered from visiting the countryside due to factors such as the cost of visiting the countryside, transport problems, limited knowledge of the English countryside and a lack of 'cultural habit' of visiting the countryside. Ethnic minorities also reported other barriers such as the fear of discrimination and the lack of culturally appropriate provisions. This list features structural and systemic barriers that require top-down interventions to support widening participation among people of colour. However, barriers such as the lack of 'cultural habit' to visit the countryside and fear of discrimination suggest that these are perceptual issues that have influenced the leisure and travel behaviour and choices of people of colour.

Nonetheless, the report noted that there was keen awareness and appreciation of outdoor leisure in providing extensive benefits for their well-being. Among these were physical health (breathing fresh air and taking light exercise), psychological health and emotional well-being (getting away from the stresses and strains of everyday urban life. They also noted the advantages of the outdoors in helping them to reconnect with nature, finding inner peace, recreating with family or friends, personal identity and social inclusion and civic participation. For immigrants, there was the perception that outdoor leisure would assist them in learning about English society and feeling integrated, respected and empowered as ethnic minorities.

This expression of the positive physical and social cultural gains from outdoor leisure suggests there is an inherent demand for these activities across ethnic minority groups. More importantly, it challenges the assumption of the findings of this report of the lack of the 'cultural habit' of visiting the countryside as an intrinsic or innate characteristic that differentiates ethnic communities from the White population. Notions of a racial/cultural attribute, as a reason for limited participation, reinforces the 'deficit model' approach that posits cultural limitations as the basis for the differences in behaviour or outcomes of ethnic minority groups. The *Glover Landscape Review* that was commissioned by the Department of Environment, Food & Rural Affairs (DEFRA) and published in 2019, identified governance of parks and Areas of Outstanding Natural Beauty (AONB) as a major obstacle to widening participation among ethnic groups.[33] In proposing a management role to redress racial disparities, the report noted that 'Black, Asian and minority ethnic board members are extremely rare' and that there are only 0.8 per cent Black, Asian or other ethnic minorities represented all the boards National Parks and AONBs.

Based on findings of ethnographic research that was conducted for the review, powerful video footage was filmed that evidenced the unfriendliness experienced by people of colour who ventured out into the countryside for recreation, while highlighting their intense desire for more opportunities to experience leisure activities in the outdoors. The response to ethnic minority presence in the countryside seemed to be a novelty for residents as noted in the quote from the Glover report: 'One person told how they got inquisitive looks and comments when in the countryside: "look, an Asian person in the woods". And the team directly experienced this when visiting with black and minority ethnic families, having to stop filming to minimize stares from passers-by.'

According to Glover, evidence of a lack of welcome presents another barrier which he describes as a feature of 'the Club' that is not inclusive of ethnic minorities. Hence the conclusion of the *Glover Landscape Review* is that both the white and ethnic minority groups share the perspective that the countryside is primarily a 'white environment'. Proposal nine of the report directly addresses this issue with the recommendation for the implementation of 'new long-term programmes' to increase the ethnic diversity of visitors starting with the racial diversification of their boards and top management.

The mandate to increase the level of ethnic diverse participation in sport is also echoed by Sport England. Based on the findings of an in-depth report,[34] on comparative levels of participation in sport across ethnic groups, there was a call to action to redress long term inequalities within sport and physical activity. The data shows that across England, people of ethnic backgrounds are less likely to walk or cycle for leisure, or go swimming compared to the national average. However, when compared with the national average, adults from 'Other' ethnic backgrounds are overrepresented in sports such as basketball and boxing. The significance of these findings is that ethnic minorities are less likely to be participating in the main sport activities associated with active lifestyles such as walking for leisure, cycling and swimming that intersect with recreational holidays and short breaks. These are key activities associated with domestic tourism and may be a factor that contributes to the lower participation rates of ethnic minorities.

Role of the cultural industries and heritage sectors

Across a range of agencies established to promote the arts, heritage, cultural industries, there have been several initiatives aimed at widening participation among ethnic groups. The designation of funding for projects that include the values of Equality, Inclusion and Diversity (EDI) as key criteria for grants, has been a stimulus for change. Agencies such as the Arts Council England, Historic England and The Heritage Trust, among others, are sometimes referred to as Arm's Length Bodies (ALB) and, as with outdoor agencies intersect with tourism in the product provision and marketing of tourism. These agencies are taking a lead role in the development of policies and in facilitating the delivery of targeted interventions promoting inclusion of ethnic communities.

Several studies on ethnic minority travellers indicate similarities in motivations and desire to see unfamiliar places and cultures, for rest and relaxation, health and well-being as the white traveller.[35] They also report similar constraints of time, resources and transportation in restricting their desire to go on holiday. There are no apparent major differences in their propensity to travel, in the prioritization of holiday making, going outdoors and on short breaks in their travel choices.[36] This suggests that ethnic minorities encounter more extrinsic and structural barriers than the white population that impede their effective demand for travel.

To gain a deeper insight of the perceptual barriers to outdoor leisure and domestic tourism, this study draws on the findings of research that was conducted in 2022 by this author to fill the gap in information regarding the travel motivations and preferences of local, diverse ethnic groups in the UK. For this study, ten focus group sessions were conducted with fifty-one participants from mixed ethnic groups which sought to determine their perceptual barriers to participation in domestic leisure and tourism activities, as well as to identify enabling factors that will encourage higher levels of engagement. The findings that are discussed below show that while some of the traditional barriers identified in the literature are relevant, yet there are some changes in how they are influencing the travel preferences and behaviour of ethnic minority leisure and tourism consumers.

Marginality, socio-economic status as a barrier

Historically, lower incomes and poorer life chances were identified as the main hindering factors that hindered people of colour from participation in leisure, recreational and tourism experiences. However, trends towards positive socio-economic indicators among ethnic minority communities in the UK, suggest that ethnic minorities increasingly have discretionary income for short breaks and holidays.[37] Most of the participants in the focus groups stated that they had engaged in domestic tourism and would welcome the opportunity to participate more frequently. But the higher cost of holidaying in Britain was viewed as a deterrent particularly as international destinations were perceived as offering better value for money. The travel behaviour of most of the participants showed a pattern of international holiday travel over domestic breaks. This suggests that the discretionary spending of ethnic minorities for short breaks and travel was mainly for overseas trips rather than for domestic tourism. This view was expressed by the male participant below:

> Well, price to be honest is one of the things that is one of the main factors, especially in the UK, because I believe it's a very expensive country. I mean, if

> I want to go and spend a few days in let's say in Cornwall, it would cost me much more than going to Spain and spend the whole week; flight tickets and everything. So the price is always an issue. (Black Caribbean male participant 1)[38]

However, for this female Afro-Caribbean participant, the higher cost of a British holiday was not a major factor in the making the travel decision:

> When I think about the cost of going on holidays, if it's somewhere where I want to go, I will pay. Like for example. I mean, I've been to the Lake District at Christmas time and that's not cheap. You pay a bit more, but it was so lovely and the people there was so welcoming. It was a mixed group, and it was gorgeous. (Black Afro-Caribbean female participant 2)[39]

The quote below summarizes the views of most of the participants, that although cost was a major factor in choosing the holiday, even more significant, was the overall experience on offer along with the assurance that there would be a warm welcome at the destination:

> I think cost as well as much as I have a bucket list and I want to go everywhere. I want to go to Scotland, Ireland and I do think in the back of my mind about where am I going to go. Am I going to be well-received? The more touristy it is the better because then you don't think about it. And I think when you go abroad you go to an airport, it's international, everybody's got that buzz. No one's looking at each other. They're going. it's a different buzz, but if you do go into areas that are unknown in this country and we know the issues with this country, they're ongoing. We've seen it happen even with the Brexit thing all over again. I do second guess to make sure whom I'm traveling with, and I want to be able to be comfortable and relaxed and I have to think about that. So I think definitely about the cost of things but to a lesser extent. (Black Afro-Caribbean female participant 1)[40]

These findings indicate that marginality was not necessarily a major barrier for not choosing to engage specifically in domestic tourism. While affordability or costs were important in the decision-making, this was more in relation to the consideration of value for money rather than not going on a holiday at all. For some consumers travelling overseas represented a better option than the UK where prices were higher and there was the perceived risk of not being warmly welcomed.

The barrier of accessibility: Poor transport infrastructure

Predominantly, the high costs and poor connectivity provided by public transportation, mainly the trains were named as barriers to taking more domestic shorts breaks and overnight stays. Some participants stated that they preferred taking public transportation and did not always wish to drive to the destination:

> Because sometimes you can see some great places, but they're not necessarily always accessible by public transport together. You know you've got to go through hurdles to get there. If you've got a car and you're comfortable to drive a car for a long period, then it's accessible. (Afro-Caribbean female participant 4)[41]

> I don't want to be driving, you know, for hours and hours and hours you know. I want to be able to get there in good time. I want to feel like I'm going on holiday and it's not a mission to get there. (Asian female participant 1)[42]

> I generally don't drive or haven't I think for more than say 3 hours. Yeah that would be my biggest obstacle really. (Afro-Caribbean female participant 4)[43]

Apart from the limitations of public transportation, there was the length of time it takes to get to a preferred destination locations in the UK:

> So for me the most, the biggest turnoff is the travel time. Yeah, and it's just nothing more than geography. I think the shape of the island of Britain, you know everything is quite 'longitude' from top to bottom, and it takes forever to get anywhere. For that reason, it's just a big turnoff to go on short breaks here. It's 8 hours on a flight to Barbados and the same time to get to some places in Britain. If there was door to door service to go somewhere, for example, if I'm going to Cornwall and I'll get picked up at the door, my service starts straight away. This gets us into the party mode to start all the way until dropping me right back to my door. That would be perfect. (African Caribbean male participant 5)[44]

These challenges in the provision of public transportation that hinder accessibility to destinations in the UK, is a wider structural problem that will require government intervention to resolve. Local Destination Marketing Organizations may play a key role in highlighting the benefits to the visitor economy of improvement in train connections between urban city centres where the ethnic minority communities are concentrated and regional destinations. It is important that they take the lead in lobbying for cheaper costs for public transportation across Britain, that could increase the overall level of participation in domestic tourism.

Winter weather barrier

There were some participants who never considered and who would never readily go on a domestic holiday due to the cold and uncertainty of wintry weather. This was particularly the case in the winter months that for them were not traditionally associated with a holiday or short break except perhaps for an occasional celebratory event. This view is captured below:

> I don't go anywhere in the winter, only for my partner's birthday on the 11th of January. There are a lot of offers at that time, but we only stay one night because

> it is just too cold and we can't do anything. We're just stuck in a hotel. Because if it is cold then you know what other things are there to attract you? Or you know in terms of entertainment and enjoyment, what are they doing to actually make it so fun? Could you feel really comfortable that you're going to have a good time regardless if the weather is really bad, because we know this is what usually happens. (Asian female participant 2)[45]

But there were those participants who didn't mind going out in the winter months:

> I have to say cold is not always that bad. I quite like it sometimes. (Afro-Caribbean male participant)[46]

> I don't mind going on cold holidays. I'd go, but it's just the rest of the family that would whinge. (Asian male participant 2)[47]

Nevertheless, some younger participants expressed their desire to engage in winter sports as novel experiences to pursue. According to Wenona Barnieh, co-founder of Mount Noir, a London-based winter sport travel company targeting ethnic minorities, the lack of familiarity with winter sports has been a major barrier to wider participation:

> I'll talk from my own sort of personal experience. I think it's a matter of knowing about it, if you've not heard much about a particular destination, or a particular sport, you probably not go. Many people will be more inclined to just go out of their comfort zone to knowing about it. So that's where our company comes in and making sure that people know that black people do go skiing. If you know, something that you can do, it is in your remit. And of course, if there are some people who do have the economic problems, because skiing isn't cheap. But there are ways to get around it, and there are ways to sort of make sure you get that opportunity, as such sometimes again going back to lack of visibility.[48]

While participants expressed some resistance to outdoor winter leisure experiences, this view was not universal with some indication of willingness by younger people to explore the novelty of winter sport. With the support of travel specialists catering to the ethnic minority consumers in equipping them with the knowledge and the means to learn winter sports such as skiing and snowboarding there is the possibility of increasing the numbers willing to engage in outdoor leisure and tourism during the winter months.

Racism: The foremost barrier

The dearth of information on the travel behaviour of ethnic minorities in the UK both in the grey literature and the wider academic literature may be viewed as another barrier in addressing the challenges of increasing access and participation. Limited information on this market segment may be reinforcing assumptions that the ethnic market is not economically viable to warrant targeted tourism marketing investment. While ethnic minorities comprise a relatively large percentage of the lower income class categories, this does explain why there is still the underrepresentation of targeted marketing to middle-class and wealthier domestic tourists of colour who have high disposable incomes.[49]

Additionally, the lack of visible presence of people of colour at popular attractions and mass tourist market destinations seem to affirm stereotypical assumptions that they are less motivated to travel. Ethnic minorities have often been viewed as not having the required social capital or knowledge of countryside codes, mores and the 'habitus' to meaningfully appreciate and navigate various outdoor landscapes. Furthermore, it is widely held that ethnic, diasporic groups in white majority countries usually prefer to return to their ancestral home countries for holidays. This is supported by the availability of more competitive prices for overseas holidays at these destinations, with the promise of more gracious welcome and higher levels of service quality, with due attention to their dietary and lifestyle preferences. However, the findings of this research point to the predominant fear of racism in the leisured landscape in the UK as a deterrent in choosing domestic holiday experiences. Both industry and academic research have been unequivocal in reporting empirical evidence of the systemic reality of racism as a major barrier to ethnic travellers. This is primarily the case for those who live in white majority destinations.[50]

In the United States, studies on the travel behaviour of Black Americans have shown that the legacy of slavery and racial segregation still haunts the spatial landscape.[51] A study conducted in the United States in 2017 found four salient themes influencing the travel behaviour of Afro-Americans.[52] These were (1) racial discrimination during travel, (2) fear of racism, (3) storytelling and safety instructions: social reproduction of the fear of racism and (4) race-related travel choices. While the legacy of slavery is different in the UK, there is the historical context of longstanding racism restricting the spatial movement of ethnic peoples in both urban and rural spaces that persists even today. Consequently, there is a mirroring of the travel behaviour of African Americans in the UK that extends to all ethnic minority groups. This is particularly the case in rural spaces that are dominated by a 'prevailing ideology that views rural England as a predominantly 'white landscape' and excludes minority ethnic groups from rural imagery.[53]

In the UK, instances of race crimes are much higher in rural areas than urban settings, even with extensive underreporting of such incidents.[54] Therefore, the sense of personal risk is heightened in rural environments where racial boundaries exist between the host community and visitors. In a study of tourism experiences and travel encounters of ethnic minority citizens living in member-states of the European Union in 2006, Stephenson found that their risk perceptions were aligned to the need for safety and security in pursuing the leisure and tourism experience.[55]

Accounts of the lived experiences of racism in tourism in the UK

The myth of the countryside as a 'white space' is still pervasive.[56] This belief stems from historic social constructions of rural areas as the patrimony of the white British population. Consequently, there is a legacy of non-representation and exclusion that is a major hindrance to widening participation. According to Maxwell Ayamba who pioneered the Black Men Walking CIC, people of colour have not been traditionally encouraged to go out and explore the natural countryside:

> You find out that the environmental sector is more like a Green Insiders club which has historically led to the perception that the natural world belongs to white people, these perceptions and narratives continue. It's a gatekeeping philosophy that perpetuates white supremacy. Then obviously people of colour don't see those spaces as belonging and wouldn't want to go there. They want to go abroad where they can feel comfortable. You know, they feel they are respected and treated with dignity and respect and can enjoy their time. Why should they take their money and go to holidays in Britain here where they are treated like second class citizens, even though they are British? These are some of the problems or the barriers that really impact on tourism for minority groups.[57]

The comments of the participants in the focus groups of their lived experiences going outdoors to the countryside, the seaside and generally holidaying in Britain expose an overwhelming sense of racism as a risk across all ethnic minority communities. Some of the accounts of racism while travelling the UK were harrowing, yet these memories capture the basis for their reservations in choosing domestic holidays and illustrate the reasons for low repeat visits to destinations where these encounters occurred. The following accounts are some examples of racist encounters from participants:

> Myself and my partner when we went camping in Wales and the first thing that happened is my partner was pulled over by the police who said that he was speeding. And he said that he wasn't and there was a big debate and he said look, you know I've got this satnav built into my car. It tells me the speed limit. It automatically slows down. And you know they didn't want to listen to him at all anyway, so he got fined for that and then when we got to the campsite, the people who owned the campsite were fine and so were a lot of the people who were also staying there with their families. But we were very mindful of the Saint George's cross flags that people clearly put up around their tent to almost, and, you know, I'm not saying that that means that they are particularly racially biased or anything, but whenever I see that flag, I do. (Afro-Caribbean female participant)[58]
>
> A friend of mine was visiting in Hampshire, so and I went the few girlfriends to spend the weekend, and we again we were the only blacks in the village. And in that they I had an awful experience while we're at the pub, and a group of white people were sitting across in another table in the beer garden. And they were talking and laughing. And then they came to me because I had my hair in an Afro. And it was quite a large Afro. Then I got the question, oohh, can I touch your hair? Can I take a picture with you? I wasn't frightened but you know, because I suppose I expected it, but I was just annoyed. So, for me I wouldn't automatically go to certain places. I have to be with people who are I'd say maybe brave enough or kind of just don't care and feel they have as much of a right to be in those spaces, because sometimes I do feel I don't want to start a fight. I just want some peace and quiet.[59]

The racist encounters in hospitality and service settings were even more uncomfortable as there was the expectation of courtesy and parity of treatment. As seen in this story below, even at popular tourist seaside resorts, there was still no escape from such negative racialized encounters:

> Just for an example we just went to Bournemouth, so we went to go on this boat and this guy the way he was kind of looking at the floor, wasn't a lot of eye contact. There was no smile on his face and the way he was so sharp, he was like he didn't want us on the boat. But in the back of my mind, thinking we are not getting on that boat, I'm going to have to make an excuse now not to get on the boat. We're not going to let them ruin it for us. So it's just this kind of the tone, the tension, the look, there's no smiling face, there's no welcoming. It's like we don't want to, but I won't call you the 'N' word but it's almost like you're not welcome here and I thought well. (Afro-Caribbean female participant)[60]

The extension of the everyday trauma of racism into the leisure and holiday experience in Britain, means that more time is spent in gathering pre-trip information, with the travel decision being highly involved with a search for safer, secure spaces for vacations. This young male Afro-Caribbean participant explains the reasons for his pre-purchase travel behaviour:

> You know I know growing up, the school that I used to go to it was in an area that was predominantly kind of represented by the National Front. So you have to, you know, going into school and coming away from the school you had to be thinking who you were traveling with and what times. So, I think that there are places that that exist in the UK. You're thinking well if I do go there, you know what is, what is it going to be like? Are there any people that look like me or culturally represent me? Are they going to be there as well? It's not something that I would say that bothers me and would stop me from going anywhere. You know, I go to a lot of places for walking and traveling in the UK. But I think there is some aspects of it that we have to think about that when we travel. (Afro-Caribbean male participant)[61]

But for most middle-aged participants, group travel was preferred particularly with people of their own ethnic group as a respite from the everyday racist microaggressions. These group trips created safe spaces to enjoy domestic tourism in the secure environment of the community of shared interests and understandings of their lived experiences. While for participants this safe space was essential for their holiday activities, for others it depended on the type of experience sought for on the trip. As this Chinese participant explained, the companionship of friends from the same ethnic group could make the travel experience more meaningful:

> For me it depends on who's available, but at the same time, if I feel I need more from it, if I want to have a more relaxed experience, a knowing experience, then I will contact my Chinese friend. (Chinese female participant)[62]

Overall, there are a range of factors that seem to pose barriers to participation differently across the ethnic groups. But generally there is clear evidence of the desire for well-being and flourishing is dominant push factor. This is clearly expressed by this statement below from a female Afro-Caribbean participant:

> So I'm trying to think. I think honestly, a lot of people when they think about going on holiday or travelling, the big part of it, is the feeling of relaxing or like release. And I think a lot of people are looking for sunshine which doesn't happen here. And when you pile all these kind of cons against the UK, so it's not going to be sunny, it's potentially going to be expensive. And you might be discriminated against, or you might stick out like a sore thumb. It just seems better traveling to places like Spain or whatever. Those kinds of lads abroad holidays are so cheap. And you do get the sunshine, and you do get the food because also food is quite expensive in the UK, like in terms of like that nice food, that people like to have that fresh food.[63]

From this quote, there is the expression of the desire for escape from the everyday and the choice of destinations is determined by the attributes of sunshine and healthy food. This points to the desire for the holiday experiences that that offer the prospect of enhancing health and well-being.

Yet there was evidence of differing attitudes to travel between younger people who were born in the UK compared with their parents who were first generation immigrants. In her study of the Pakistani community in Bradford, Klemm observed that younger people saw trips to the homeland as 'duty visits and important for the family'.[64] However, they expressed a desire for other vacation experiences such short breaks, visits to attractions like Disneyland and even beach holidays which that was regarded as 'attractive or acceptable' among some of the younger respondents. Ethnic minority young people seem to be demonstrating confidence in their British identity while embracing their religious and cultural values. This is an empowering factor in their confidence in confronting racism and the related restrictions on their movement and participation in a wider range of leisure and tourism experience. It is apparent that increasingly, the younger ethnic population in the UK are mobilizing themselves in different demographic collectives under the banner of their ethnic identity and are challenging traditional 'white spaces' of leisure and tourism.

This middle-aged Afro-Caribbean female who was born in England observed that travel habits and preferences have been changing, with the younger generation being less anxious about racism and more willing to take domestic holidays:

> I'm not sure what it is. I think perhaps it's that comfort thing, I remember when I was growing up. I mean, you know. I remember it always used to be seen that White people went on holiday and black people stayed at home. It was really quite a strange thing and when we used to break up from school, there's six weeks holiday. We didn't necessarily go away and what used to happen is members within the family would be going back to say the Caribbean and that that was the big thing. But you never really went on holiday. You went on trips, the occasional day

> trips, but you never really went on holiday. That was a white person thing. The generation now don't really care that they're everywhere, but I think, especially with the older generation, they're perhaps still that little bit of uncomfortableness feeling. (Afro-Caribbean female participant)[65]

The changing attitudes to the perception of exclusion in leisure and tourism are further manifested in the formation of Black and Muslim collectives in the UK aimed at providing group support for minority communities to overcome the barriers to access the outdoor countryside. These groups have gained national prominence in the aftermath of the murder of George Floyd on 25 May 2020. With the ferment of social unrest and protests, there was some mobilization in creating safe spaces for groups of hikers to venture to the Peak District and other areas of outstanding natural beauty. Black Girls Hike, which was formed in 2019 by Rhiane Fatinikun gained extensive media attention and on social media sites when an episode of BBC's Countryfile featured the group that led to subsequent complaints to the corporation. Although the BBC did not detail the nature of the complaints, the following response was issued:

> For a variety of reasons, as the presenter explained, it has been the case that historically some groups have felt less able than others to take part in outdoor activities such as hiking or mountain walking, so any initiative which seeks to redress that balance is to be welcomed.[66]

For Fatinikun, the purpose of Black Girls Hike goes beyond creating safe spaces for outdoor leisure and tourism experiences, but to also encourage and inspire Black women to engage in more active lifestyles to improve their overall health and mental well-being. In these safe spaces, groups such as the pioneering Black Men Walking, Black Girls Hike and Muslim Walkers have been free to share their stories of racism, to be understood and affirmed in their racial identity, while reaping the benefits of gaining the skills to navigate the outdoors and leading more active, healthier lifestyles.

A clear thread that runs through the various reports and studies of the barriers to participation in leisure and tourism, chronicled in the lived experiences of ethnic minorities, is a strong sentiment of their desire and aspiration to take part in outdoor leisure and domestic tourism. None of the research covered in this study reported any overt expressions of animus or inherent disassociation from the British leisured landscape. Instead, the emergence of the outdoor collectives of hikers and walkers attests to their longing to share in the enjoyment of these spaces and to enhance their health and well-being. These collectives are expressions of their intentionality to actively overcome these barriers with communal action and mobilization. In many respects, this bottom-up activism resembles the organized activities of the savings clubs and unions by the working classes during the Industrial Revolution which revisionist studies contend have been pivotal to the development of leisured lifestyles in the British countryside and seaside. But it is somewhat ironic that in achieving universal rights to leisure in the seaside and countryside, these rural settings were then imagined as white only spaces that erected barriers against minority ethnic peoples from enjoying these privileges of leisure and tourism. While scholarly research continues in understanding the reasons for this exclusionary framing of leisured spaces, there is some ground to support the assertion that racism in leisure and tourism 'coalesce(s) around the practice of defining a particular aesthetic and kind of person as "in place" in a particular locale'.[67]

Conclusion

The trope of the summer holiday as popularized in Cliff Richard's hit song in the 1960s as an opportunity to make dreams come true is still appealing decades later. Despite some reservations of the dangers and the risk of the unsustainability of increasing tourist hordes and 'over-tourism' that advocate for policies to curb untrammelled growth in the numbers of pleasure seekers; yet the appetite for leisure and mass tourism seems irrepressible. Rival discourses on the social construction of leisured spaces contend between preservation and conservation that implies limiting mass leisure tourism, and arguments countering that such views are romantic, elitist and restrictive of the rights of the working middle classes. But while mass tourism has been rendered as a triumph of labour in asserting access to green and pleasant landscapes and the therapeutic blue seaside, this leisure and travel imaginary did not necessarily extend to non-white British residents. The democratization of leisure and tourism has arguably been colour-blind in the production of leisured spaces and praxis.[68]

As discussed in this chapter, the ontological anonymity of Black and Asian Britons has been justified by attributing their absence to socio-economic barriers and the cultural deficit of ethnic minority groups. These arguments have been deployed to account for their low participation and differing travel preferences, of which the latter, has been deemed inimical to the patrimony of the British landscape. These essentialist theories of the travel behaviour of ethnic minority groups have been debunked in both academic research and industry reports that have revealed desire, longing and pent-up demand by people of colour resident in the UK to share in the delights of the outdoor countryside as well as inland waterways and beaches. This sentiment for wider access and participation in leisure and tourism has been primarily driven by second and third generation Black and Asian Britons as well as higher income earning, minority ethnic professional immigrants residing in the UK. Their growing activism has been buttressed by public discourses on equality, diversity and inclusion (EDI) that is fuelling contestations on normative mores and values of the coastal beaches and the countryside for white only bodies in white landscapes. Even more contentious has been the representation of Blacks and Asians in British colonial history and heritage at National Trust properties that have been criticized as a deviant form of revisionism that attacks British identity. It is indeed a paradox, that the quest for inclusiveness in leisured spaces is generating such divisive contestations and angst around experiences promoting well-being, pleasure, escape and fun. The unsettling and disruption of entrenched beliefs of the 'everybody' who has a summer holiday and the 'we' who are represented and included in these leisured spaces, perhaps in retrospect, will be reckoned as the rites of passage in the aspirational journey towards more equitable social transformation and justice.

Notes

1. Jim Butcher, 'Constructing Mass Tourism', *International Journal of Cultural Studies* 23.6 (2020), 898–915.
2. Susan Barton, *Working-Class Organisations and Popular Tourism, 1840–1970* (Manchester University, 2006).
3. Mike Huggins, 'Working-Class Organisations and Popular Tourism, 1840–1970', *English Historical Review* 121.492 (2006), 957–8.
4. Susan Barton, 'Working-Class Organisations and Popular Tourism, 1840–1970', https://networks.h-net.org/node/15531/reviews/15590/zuelow-barton-working-class-organisations-and-popular-tourism-1840-1970 (accessed 4 April 2024).
5. Ramblers, 'Expand the Freedom to Roam', www.ramblers.org.uk/what-we-care-about/expand-freedom-roam (accessed 4 April 2024).
6. E. P. Thompson, *The Making of the English Working Class*, Penguin Modern Classics (Penguin Books, 2013).
7. Huggins, 'Working-Class Organisations and Popular Tourism, 1840–1970'.
8. Christos Efstathiou, 'E. P. Thompson's Concept of Class Formation and Its Political Implications: Echoes of Popular Front Radicalism in the Making of the English Working Class', *Contemporary British History* 28.4 (2014), 404–21.
9. Yi Chien Jade Ho and David Chang, 'To Whom Does This Place Belong? Whiteness and Diversity in Outdoor Recreation and Education', *Annals of Leisure Research* (2021); The Countryside Agency, 'What about Us? Diversity Review Evidence – Part One Challenging Perceptions: Under-Represented Visitor Needs', https://publications.naturalengland.org.uk/publication/63060 (accessed 4 April 2024).
10. Corinne Fowler, *Green Unpleasant Land: Creative Responses to Rural England's Colonial Connections* (Peepal Tree Press, 2020), 50.
11. John Urry, *The Tourist Gaze: Leisure and Travel in Contemporary Societies* (Sage, 1990).
12. Atara Sivan and A. J. Veal, 'Leisure and Human Rights: The World Leisure Organization Charter for Leisure: Past, Present and Future', *World Leisure Journal* 63.2 (2021), 133–40.
13. World Leisure Organization, 'Charter for Leisure', December 2018, www.worldleisure.org/wlo2019/wp-content/uploads/2019/06/WLO_Charter_for_Leisure_FOR_COMMENT_DECEMBER_2018.pdf (accessed 4 April 2024).
14. Sandro Sandro Carnicelli and Ricardo Uvinha, 'Leisure, Inequalities, and the Global South', *Leisure Studies* (2023), 1–10, https://doi.org/10.1080/02614367.2023.2168032.
15. Daniel Burdsey, '"The Foreignness Is Still Quite Visible in This Town": Multiculture, Marginality and Prejudice at the English Seaside', *Patterns of Prejudice* 47.2 (2013), 95–116.
16. Marcus L. Stephenson and Howard L. Hughes, 'Racialised Boundaries in Tourism and Travel: A Case Study of the UK Black Caribbean Community', *Leisure Studies* 24.2 (2005), 137–60.
17. Kye Askins, 'Multicultural Country/Side? Visible Communities' Perceptions and Use of English National Parks', *University of Durham*, http://etheses.dur.ac.uk/3169/ (accessed 4 April 2024).
18. Kye Askins, 'Multicultural Country/Side'?, 56.
19. Burdsey, 'The Foreignness Is Still Quite Visible in This Town'.
20. Burdsey, 'The Foreignness Is Still Quite Visible in This Town', 102.

21. Mary S. Klemm, 'Tourism and Ethnic Minorities in Bradford: The Invisible Segment', *Journal of Travel Research* 41.1 (2002), 85–91.
22. Mary S. Klemm and Sarah J. Kelsey, 'Ethnic Groups and the British Travel Industry: Servicing a Minority?', *Service Industries Journal* 24.4 (2004), 115–28
23. Perry L. Carter, 'Coloured Places and Pigmented Holidays: Racialized Leisure Travel', *Tourism Geographies* 10.3 (2008), 265–84; Neil Chakraborti and Jon Garland, *Rural Racism* (Routledge, 2013).
24. Steven F. Philipp, 'Race and Tourism Choice. A Legacy of Discrimination?', *Annals of Tourism Research* 21.3 (1994), 479–88; Dominic Davies, 'Green Unpleasant Land: Creative Responses to Rural England's Colonial Connections: By Corinne Fowler', *Journal of Postcolonial Writing* 58.2 (2022), 286–7; Stefanie Benjamin and Alana K. Dillette, 'Black Travel Movement: Systemic Racism Informing Tourism', *Annals of Tourism Research* 88 (2021), 103169.
25. Jenny Chio, Tiffany Gill, Vernadette Vicuna Gonzalez, Stephen L. Harp, Kate Mcdonald and Adam T. Rosenbaum, 'Discussion: Tourism and Race', *Journal of Tourism History* 12.2 (2020), 173–97 (p. 120).
26. Imtiaz Habib, *Black Lives in the English Archives, 1500–1677 – Imprints of the Invisible* (Routledge, 2020), 73.
27. Fowler, *Green Unpleasant Land.*
28. T. S. Newmeyer, 'Moral Renovation and Intellectual Exaltation: Thomas Cook's Tourism as Practical Education', *Journal of Tourism and Cultural Change* 6.1 (2008), 1–16, https://doi.org/10.1080/14766820802140414.
29. S. A. Cohen, G. Prayag and M. Moital, 'Consumer Behaviour in Tourism: Concepts, Influences and Opportunities', *Current Issues in Tourism* 17.10 (2013), 872–909, https://doi.org/10.1080/13683500.2013.850064
30. A. Dillette, S. Benjamin and D. Alderman, 'Traveling to Escape, Resist, and Belong: Centering Black Experiences within Tourism Scholarship', *Tourism Geographies* 26.1 (2024), 1–12, https://doi.org/10.1080/14616688.2024.2305869.
31. Soyoung Park, Christa Thandi Mahlobo and Jerrica Oliver Peets, 'Flourishing through Traveling while Black: Unfiltered Voices of Black Travelers', *Tourism Management* 91 (2022), 104514, https://doi.org/10.1016/j.tourman.2022.104514.
32. VisitBritain, *Regional Spread of Inbound Tourism 2018* (VisitBritain, 2019), 1–42.
33. Julian Glover, *The Landscape Review* (DEFRA, 2019), https://assets.publishing.service.gov.uk/media/5d8a19a3e5274a083d3b78bd/landscapes-review-final-report.pdf (accessed 4 April 2024).
34. Sport England, 'Sport for All? Why Ethnicity and Culture Matters in Sport and Physical Activity', www.sportsthinktank.com/research,126912.html (accessed 4 April 2024).
35. A. N. Kimbu, S. Ramakrishna, Y. R. Kim and P. Saha, *Engaging New Travel Audiences: Understanding the UK BAME Travellers' Decision-Making Process* (University of Surrey in collaboration with Women in Travel CIC, 2021).
36. Klemm and Kelsey, 'Ethnic Groups and the British Travel Industry'.
37. Klemm and Kelsey, 'Ethnic Groups and the British Travel Industry'.
38. This quote is taken from Marcella Daye, *EXPERIENCE: Norfolk Ethic Domestic Tourism Market Report* (April 2022), 26, which was commissioned by Norfolk County Council under the EU Interreg EXPERIENCE European Development Fund. This report is available at: www.tourismexperience.org/downloads/English%20content/Resource%20hub/Marketing%20reports/pp1_b2ctesting_report_en.pdf.
39. Daye, *EXPERIENCE*, 26.

40. Daye, *EXPERIENCE*, 26.
41. Daye, *EXPERIENCE*, 28.
42. Daye, *EXPERIENCE*, 28.
43. Daye, *EXPERIENCE*, 28.
44. Daye, *EXPERIENCE*, 28.
45. Daye, *EXPERIENCE*, 29.
46. Daye, *EXPERIENCE*, 29.
47. Daye, *EXPERIENCE*, 29.
48. Daye, *EXPERIENCE*, 29.
49. Kimbu et al., *Engaging New Travel Audiences*.
50. Chakraborti and Garland, *Rural Racism*.
51. Benjamin and Dillette, 'Black Travel Movement'.
52. Kang Jae Jerry Lee and David Scott, 'Racial Discrimination and African Americans' Travel Behavior: The Utility of Habitus and Vignette Technique', *Journal of Travel Research* 56.3 (2017), 381–92.
53. Ricky Lee Allen, 'Whiteness and Critical Pedagogy', *Educational Philosophy and Theory* 36.2 (2004), 121–36; Neil Chakraborti and Jon Garland, 'England's Green and Pleasant Land? Examining Racist Prejudice in a Rural Context', *Patterns of Prejudice* 38.4 (2004), 383–98.
54. Jon Garland and Neil Chakraborti, 'Recognising and Responding to Victims of Rural Racism', *International Review of Victimology* 13.1 (2006), 49–69.
55. Marcus L. Stephenson, 'Travel and the "Freedom of Movement": Racialised Encounters and Experiences amongst Ethnic Minority Tourists in the EU', *Mobilities* 1.2 (2006), 285–306.
56. Craig Simpson, 'British Countryside Is a "Racist and Colonial" White Space, Wildlife Charities Claim', *Daily Telegraph*, 7 February 2024, www.proquest.com/central/docview/2923156843/citation/67E324EB004249BEPQ/1 (accessed 9 February 2024).
57. Daye, *EXPERIENCE*, 33.
58. Daye, *EXPERIENCE*, 33.
59. Daye, *EXPERIENCE*, 33–4.
60. Daye, *EXPERIENCE*, 34.
61. Daye, *EXPERIENCE*, 34.
62. Daye, *EXPERIENCE*, 35.
63. Daye, *EXPERIENCE*, 35.
64. Klemm, 'Tourism and Ethnic Minorities in Bradford'.
65. Daye, *EXPERIENCE*.
66. 'Countryfile', BBC One, 14 January 2021', https://web.archive.org/web/20210126154555/https://www.bbc.co.uk/contact/complaint/countryfilewalkinggroup (accessed 4 April 2024).
67. Chio et al., 'Discussion: Tourism and Race'.
68. Bedelia Nicola Richards, 'When Class Is Colorblind: A Race-Conscious Model for Cultural Capital Research in Education', *Sociology Compass* 14.7 (2020), e12789.

Index

www.ingramcontent.com/pod-product-compliance
Ingram Content Group UK Ltd.
Pitfield, Milton Keynes, MK11 3LW, UK
UKHW020803290926
15470UKWH00003B/936

9 781350 499843